Cognitive Therapy of Personality Disorders

Cognitive Therapy of Personality Disorders

Aaron T. Beck, M.D.
Center for Cognitive Therapy
University of Pennsylvania

Arthur Freeman, Ed.D.
Cognitive Therapy Institute
University of Medicine and Dentistry of New Jersey

and Associates

The Guilford Press
New York   London

© 1990 The Guilford Press

A Division of Guilford Publications, Inc.

72 Spring Street, New York, NY 10012

Printed in the United States of America

This book is printed on acid-free paper.

Last digit is print number: 9   8   7   6   5   4   3   2

Library of Congress Cataloging-in-Publication Data

Beck, Aaron T.
    Cognitive therapy of personality disorders / Aaron T. Beck, Arthur Freeman, and associates.
      p.   cm.
    Includes bibliographical references (p.).
    ISBN 0-89862-434-7
     1. Personality disorders—Treatment. 2. Cognitive therapy.
  I. Freeman, Arthur M. II. Title.
  RC554.B43   1990
  616.85'8—dc20   90-33575
                                         CIP

Contributing Authors

James Pretzer, Ph.D.   *Cleveland Center for Cognitive Therapy, Cleveland, Ohio*

Denise D. Davis, Ph.D.   *Vanderbilt University, Nashville, Tennessee*

Barbara Fleming, Ph.D.   *Case Western Reserve University and Cleveland Center for Cognitive Therapy, Cleveland, Ohio*

Regina Ottaviani, Ph.D.   *Cognitive Therapy Center, Chevy Chase, Maryland*

Judith Beck, Ph.D.   *Center for Cognitive Therapy, University of Pennsylvania, Philadelphia, Pennsylvania*

Karen M. Simon, Ph.D.   *Center for Cognitive Therapy, University of Pennsylvania, Philadelphia, Pennsylvania*

Christine Padesky, Ph.D.   *Newport Beach Center for Cognitive Therapy, Newport Beach, California*

James Meyer, Ph.D.   *Depression Treatment Center, Denver, Colorado*

Lawrence Trexler, Ph.D.   *Friends Hospital, Philadelphia, Pennsylvania*

Acknowledgments

There are five significant events in the publication of a book. The first is the thrill and excitement of the initial conceptualization and development of the book. During this early stage ideas are offered, developed, modified, discarded, re-evaluated, and reformulated. This volume began, as so much of our work has begun, from clinical necessity coupled with scientific curiosity. The personality-disordered patient was part of the caseload of virtually every therapist at our Center. The idea for this volume grew out of the weekly clinical seminars led by Aaron T. Beck. As the idea developed, the input and clinical insights of our colleagues at the University of Pennsylvania and the various Centers for Cognitive Therapy around the country were sought and must be acknowledged here. Many of them became coauthors and had a significant impact on the direction and content of this volume. Their brilliance and clinical acumen have given this volume a particular sparkle.

The second major event in the birth of a book is the collection and collation of the manuscript. Ideas have now been concretized and set to paper. It is at this point that the shaping process is begun. Lawrence Trexler deserves a tremendous vote of thanks for taking the responsibility for reviewing and polishing the various chapters. He helped to provide continuity and cohesiveness to the project.

The third major point occurs when the draft manuscript is mailed to the publisher. Seymour Weingarten, Editor-in-Chief of The Guilford Press, has been a friend of cognitive therapy for many years. (It was Seymour's wisdom and foresight that led him to publish the now classic *Cognitive Therapy of Depression* over a decade ago.) His support, encouragement, and goading have helped this volume to move toward the finished state. Judith Grauman, Editorial Supervisor, and Marie Sprayberry, our copy editor, worked to make the copy easily readable while staying true to the content and intent of the text. They and the rest of the staff at Guilford brought this volume to completion.

The fourth stage in the development of a book comes with the final editing and typing of the manuscript. Tina Inforzato did yeoman's work throughout the production by typing and retyping various drafts of chapters. It was in the end game, however, where she really shone. She collected errant references, typed in the myriad changes, and produced the copy and computer disks from which this volume was typeset. Karen Madden was the keeper of the successive drafts of the book and deserves thanks for her persistence. Donna Battista helped Arthur Freeman to keep organized despite all of his various projects. Barbara Marinelli, Executive Director of the Center for Cognitive Therapy at the University of Pennsylvania, shouldered a large burden, as always, and allowed for Beck to focus on creating this volume and other scholarly works. Dr. William F. Ranieri, Chair, Department of Psychiatry, University of Medicine and Dentistry of New Jersey, School of Osteopathic Medicine, has been an advocate of cognitive therapy.

The final stage comes with publication. Given all that has come before, this final stage is almost anticlimactic. Our work is now in the hand of you, our colleagues, who we hope will profit from this volume.

Our heartfelt thanks go to Judge Phyllis Beck and Dr. Karen M. Simon. As our partners in life, they have given us support and encouragement for this and so many other ventures.

The ongoing collaboration between the senior authors began as one of student and teacher and has progressed over the last 13 years to one of mutual respect, admiration, affection, and friendship. We have learned much from each other.

Finally, the patients with whom we have worked over the years have allowed us to share the burden they carried. It was their pain and anguish that motivated us to develop the theory and techniques that are called cognitive therapy. They taught us much and we hope that we have helped them to lead fuller, more complete lives.

Aaron T. Beck
Arthur Freeman

Preface

In the decade since Aaron T. Beck and his colleagues published the now classic *Cognitive Therapy of Depression,* cognitive therapy has developed in an almost exponential fashion. From the early work of treating depression, the model has been advanced and applied to the treatment of all of the commonly seen clinical syndromes, including anxiety, panic disorder, and eating disorders. Outcome studies have demonstrated its efficacy in a wide range of clinical disorders. In addition to its application to practically all of the clinical populations, with modifications, cognitive therapy has been applied to all ages (children, adolescents, geriatric patients) and has been utilized in a variety of settings (outpatient, inpatient, couples, groups, and families).

The interest in and development of the clinical work in treating those patients with personality disorders have grown with the clinical sophistication and skill of the cognitive therapists. This volume is the first to focus specifically on this diverse and difficult group.

The work in cognitive therapy has drawn interest from around the world, and centers for cognitive therapy (or cognitive therapy study groups) have been established throughout the United States and in Europe. Based on his survey of clinical and counseling psychologists, Smith (1982) concluded "that cognitive-behavioral options represent one of the strongest, if not *the* strongest theoretical emphasis today" (p. 808). The interest in cognitive approaches among therapists has increased 600% since 1973 (Norcross, Prochaska, & Gallagher, 1989).

The vast majority of the research, conceptual development, and clinical training in cognitive therapy has occurred at the Center for Cognitive Therapy at the University of Pennsylvania or at centers established by those trained at this center. The present work has grown organically from early case discussions and seminars led by Beck over many years. When we decided to write a book that would allow a sharing of the understandings gained from our work, we realized that it would be impossible for one or two people to be expert in treating all of the various disorders. We therefore enlisted a distinguished and talented group of therapists trained at the Center for Cognitive Therapy to coauthor the text, all writing in their specific area of expertise. We rejected the notion of an edited text that offered a series of disparate (or redundant) observations. In the interest of uniformity and consistency in presentation, we decided in favor of a volume that would represent a total collaborative production of all of the contributors.

Different authors took responsibility for different specific topics or disorders. The draft material on each topic was then circulated to stimulate cross-fertilization and facilitate consistency, and was then returned to the original author(s) for revisions and further development. Finally, the entire manuscript was reviewed by one of the authors to insure continuity in style, language, and content. While the book is the product of several authors, all authors take responsibility for the content. The major authors of each of the chapters will, however, be identified below. The integration, final editing, and continuity of the volume are the work of Lawrence Trexler.

We have organized the volume into two sections. The first offers a broad overview of historical, theoretical, and therapeutic aspects. This section is followed by the clinical chapters that detail the individualized treatment of specific personality disorders. The clinical chapters are arranged according to the three clusters described in the revised third edition of the *Diagnostic and Statistical Manual of Mental Disorders* (DSM-III-R; American Psychiatric Association, 1987). Cluster A, those disorders that are described as "odd or eccentric," include the paranoid, schizoid, and schizotypal personality disorders. Cluster B includes the antisocial, borderline, histrionic, and narcissistic personality disorders, which are described as "dramatic, emotional, or erratic." Cluster C includes the "anxious or fearful persons" that fall into the categories of avoidant, dependent, obsessive-compulsive, and passive-aggressive personality disorders.

The material in Part I was developed by Aaron T. Beck, Arthur Freeman, and James Pretzer. In the first chapter, Freeman and Pretzer begin by outlining the cognitive-behavioral approach to the general problems of referral, diagnosis, and treatment of personality-disordered patients. A discussion of the concept of schema formation and its effect on behavior offers the reader an introduction to this vital issue, which will be expanded in later chapters. The chapter then discusses the clinical studies and research done to date on the cognitive-behavioral treatment of personality disorders.

In Chapter 2, Beck offers an explication of how personality processes are formed and serve adaptive functions in the individual's life.

Starting with an evolutionary focus, Beck elaborates on how the schemas (and the idiosyncratic combinations of schemas) contribute to the formation of various disorders. The basic strategies for adaptation are then outlined, along with the basic beliefs/attitudes for each of the personality disorders. The processing of information and the specific types of distortion of the available information are then tied to the schematic characteristics, including the density, activity, and valence of the schemas.

Within each personlity disorder, certain beliefs and strategies predominate and form a characteristic profile. In Chapter 3, Beck further identifies the typical overdeveloped and underdeveloped strategies for each disorder. The strategies may, he posits, be derivative from or compensation for particular developmental experiences. By offering cognitive profiles, including the view of self, view of others, general beliefs, major perceived threat, main strategy for coping, and primary affective responses, he places the disorders in a perspective that allows the application of the broad range of cognitive and behavioral interventions.

In Chapter 4, Beck and Freeman discuss the general principles for the cognitive therapy of personality disorders. The core schemas can be inferred by first looking at the patient's automatic thoughts. Utilizing imagery and reawakening of past traumatic experiences can activate the core schemas. These can then be examined within the therapeutic context. Basic cognitive therapy techniques are outlined, with particular emphasis on the development of case conceptualization. Therapeutic collaboration, role modeling, and the use of homework are also delineated. The therapeutic relationship, important in any therapeutic work, is especially important with personality-disordered patients. Finally, the chapter discusses specific patient-therapist problems, often labeled as "resistance." Examining the various reasons for therapeutic noncompliance, Beck and Freeman identify several categories of difficulty; problems of the patient (e.g., rigidity, fear of change), problems of the therapist (e.g., rigidity, lack of skill), and problems inherent in the therapeutic relationships (e.g., issues of power, secondary gain) are explored.

In Chapter 5, the last chapter in this section, Beck and Freeman detail specific cognitive and behavioral techniques for the treatment of the personality-disordered patient. They outline three conceptual possibilities for schematic change: schematic reconstruction, schematic modification, and schematic reinterpretation. By defining and testing the patient's schemas, the therapist can identify both content and direction for treatment, and can then help the patient work toward modifying dysfunctional schemas and possibly building new schemas that are more functional.

Chapter 6, by James Pretzer, begins the clinical applications section.

In this chapter, he offers an introduction to the problem of the paranoid personality disorder. This little-studied group presents several idiosyncratic problems, not least among them being the high degree of suspiciousness. Pretzer develops a conceptualization that then leads to the therapeutic interventions he illustrates. Using numerous case vignettes, he demonstrates for the reader both the process and progress of the cognitive therapy. He also identifies some of the typical therapist problems encountered in working with paranoid individuals.

Regina Ottaviani describes both the schizoid and schizotypal personality disorders in Chapter 7. The history of the term and diagnosis "schizoid" is detailed through the present DSM-III-R diagnosis. The diagnostic and treatment issues are described, along with the basic beliefs of the schizoid patient. Therapist issues are discussed to help to identify potential roadblocks in the therapy. Ottaviani then goes on to describe the schizotypal patient. Offering a cognitive therapy conceptualization, she also describes the frequent Axis I problems that are associated with the schizotypal disorder.

With Chapter 8, Denise D. Davis introduces the Cluster B disorders with a discussion of the antisocial personality disorder. Given that antisocial patients generally seek treatment at the request (or demand) of others, usually the legal system, they present several unique treatment problems. Davis elaborates on the importance of engaging the patient in treatment, setting limits, and involving the patient in the planning of the homework. She demonstrates the importance of a noncoercive and collaborative alliance. Associated Axis I disorders, such as alcohol or substance abuse, are discussed, with an eye toward helping the clinician be aware and prepared for the potential for suicide—a possibility that is often overlooked in this group of patients.

Pretzer sets out in Chapter 9 to deal with the most common and possibly most problematic disorder in this group, the borderline personality disorder. The diagnosis of borderline disorder has evolved over the years, and in many cases continues to be a wastebasket category where many patients are placed when they fail to fit easily into other categories. The schematic issues that are introduced in the theoretical chapters are discussed at great length by Pretzer. These issues help to clarify the cognitive processes in this syndrome. As the prime "dichotomizer," the borderline patient can impose a strain on the therapist. Here again, the setting of firm limits, a focus on the collaborative nature of the therapeutic endeavor, and an emphasis on the goal-oriented nature of the cognitive therapy approach are underscored.

The histrionic personality disorder is the focus of Chapter 10 by Barbara Fleming. "Hysteria," an early focus of the psychoanalysts, has been around as a diagnostic category for about four thousand years. Fleming takes the reader through the historical ideas to the present day.

She reconceptualizes the disorder in cognitive terms and then sets out a treatment protocol. The special cognitive distortions of the histrionic patient are identified as both diagnostic markers and targets for treatment. Helping such patients to modulate their behavior and alter their strategic approach to life tasks is explicated in great detail.

Denise Davis returns with a discussion of the narcissistic personality in Chapter 11. After a review of the various conceptualizations of "narcissism," Davis applies a social learning perspective to an understanding of the personality disorder. She follows with a cognitive conceptualization as a basis for the treatment. The narcissistic personality disorder often complicates the treatment of associated Axis I disorders. Given that therapy is an "ordinary" pursuit, the patient with a narcissistic personality disorder may leave therapy so as not to be considered ordinary. Using a number of clinical examples, Davis develops and demonstrates the treatment model.

Judith Beck and Christine Padesky collaborate on Chapter 12, which describes cognitive therapy of the avoidant personality disorder. This chapter, beginning the discussion of the Cluster C disorders, points out the themes of self-deprecation, expectation of rejection, and a belief that any unpleasant emotion or encounter is intolerable. The avoidant patient shuns many things, including unpleasant emotions, other people, and experiences. Even the most casual problem is often interpreted as catastrophic and to be avoided. After identifying the typical automatic thoughts and beliefs, the authors describe the schemas that underlie this disorder. The treatment of the anxiety component and need for specific skill training are emphasized in both didactic and case material.

Chapter 13 represents Barbara Fleming's second contribution to the volume. Focusing on the dependent personality disorder, she contrasts the apparent cooperation of the dependent patient with the noncollaborative response typical of many of the other personality disorders. The initial cooperation and improvement are often followed by the frustration (for the therapist) of a maintenance of symptoms. While sometimes able to use their interpersonal strategies in the service of the therapy by complying with homework assignments and engaging in more independent new behaviors, these patients may resist substantive change so as to maintain their dependent relationship with the therapist. A patient's beliefs relative to competence, abandonment, and independence are discussed in conjunction with a number of clinical examples.

Chapter 14 focuses on the obsessive-compulsive personality disorder. Karen M. Simon and James Meyer discuss this most common of the personality disorders. Inasmuch as society places such a premium on efficacy and performance, systems involving emotional control, self-discipline, perseverance, reliability, and politeness are highly prized.

These characteristics, however, are taken to the extreme by the obses-sive-compulsive personality, and what may once have been a con-structive strategy becomes dysfunctional. The patient is rigid, per-fectionistic, dogmatic, ruminative, and indecisive. The cognitive content of the automatic thoughts, beliefs, and strategies of this type of patient are explored. The authors discuss the associated problems of depres-sion, sexual problems, and psychosomatic problems. Simon and Meyers utilize several clinical examples to demonstrate their treatment ap-proach.

In Chapter 15, Regina Ottaviani presents cognitive therapy treat-ment of the passive-aggressive personality disorder. The oppositional and sometimes obstructionist style that often characterizes this clinical group presents major obstacles to treatment. Inasmuch as they tend to avoid confrontation, these patients may passively accept being in ther-apy, but put constant roadblocks in the way of change. Change for these patients often represents a surrender to the therapist, so that the patient's style is best characterized by the phrase "Yes . . . but." Through the use of clinical examples, Ottaviani develops her conceptualization and demonstrates how the cognitive therapy approach is implemented.

Finally, in Chapter 16, Beck and Freeman offer a synthesis and prospects for clinical and research work with the personality-disordered patient.

Contents

*Cognitive Therapy of
Personality Disorders*

Part I
History, Theory, and Research

Chapter 1
Overview of Cognitive Therapy of Personality Disorders

The therapy of patients with various disorders of personality have been discussed in the clinical literature since the beginning of the recorded history of psychotherapy. Freud's classic cases of Anna O (Breuer & Freud, 1893–1895/1955) and the Rat Man (Freud, 1909/1955) can be rediagnosed within current criteria as personality disorders. With the development of the first *Diagnostic and Statistical Manual of Mental Disorders* (DSM-I) of the American Psychiatric Association (APA, 1952) through to the present version of the manual (DSM-III-R; APA, 1987), the definitions and parameters for understanding these serious and chronic states have been gradually expanded and refined. The general literature on the psychotherapeutic treatment of personality disorders has emerged more recently, and is growing quickly. The main theoretical orientation in the present personality disorder literature, or psychotherapeutic literature generally, has been psychoanalytic (Abend, Porder, & Willick, 1983; Chatham, 1985; Goldstein, 1985; Gunderson, 1984; Horowitz, 1977; Kernberg, 1975, 1984; Lion, 1981; Masterson, 1978, 1980, 1985; Reid, 1981; Saul & Warner, 1982; Waldinger & Gunderson, 1987).

The Cognitive-Behavioral Approach to Personality Disorders

More recently, behavioral (Linehan, 1987a,b; Linehan, Armstrong, Allmon, Suarez, & Miller, 1988; Linehan, Armstrong, Suarez, & Allmon, 1988) and cognitive-behavioral therapists (Fleming, 1983, 1985; Fleming & Pretzer, in press; Freeman, 1988a,b; Freeman & Leaf, 1989;

Freeman, Pretzer, Fleming, & Simon, 1990; Pretzer, 1983, 1985, 1988; Pretzer & Fleming, 1989; Young & Swift, 1988) have begun to conceptualize and offer a cognitive-behavioral treatment approach. The volume by Millon (1981) is one of the few in the area of personality disorders to offer a social-behavioral focus. When first introduced, cognitive approaches drew upon the ideas of "ego analysts," derived from the works of Adler, Horney, Sullivan, and Frankl. Though their therapeutic innovations were seen as radical by psychoanalysts, their earliest cognitive therapies were in many ways "insight therapies," in that the therapy used largely introspective techniques designed to change a patient's overt "personality" (Ellis, 1962; Beck, 1967). Building on this early work, Beck (1963, 1976; Beck, Rush, Shaw, & Emery, 1979; Beck & Emery with Greenberg, 1985) and Ellis (1957a,b, 1958) were among the first to include the use a wide range of behavioral treatment techniques in their treatment, including structured *in vivo* homework. They have consistently emphasized the therapeutic impact of the cognitive and behavioral techniques not only on symptom structures, but also on the cognitive "schemas" or controlling beliefs. Cognitive therapists work at the dual levels of the symptom structure (manifest problems) and underlying schema (inferred structures). Most analyses of psychotherapeutic practice have found that patients usually present with basic or "core" problems—problems that are central both for dysfunctional cognitions (e.g., negative self-concept) and for problematic behavior (e.g., dependent behavior) (Frank, 1973). The cognitive therapy model posits the thesis that important cognitive structures are categorically and hierarchically organized. A broad range of a patient's difficulties may be subsumed under one class, and can be influenced by changes in a single schema or a few schemas. This formulation is consistent with the principal contemporary theories of cognitive structure and cognitive development, all of which stress the function of schemas[1] as determinants of rule-guided behavior (Neisser, 1976; Piaget, 1970, 1974, 1976, 1978; Schank & Abelson, 1977). Schemas provide the instructions to guide the focus, direction, and qualities of daily life and special contingencies.

Cognitive therapy theorists share with psychoanalysts the concept that it is usually more productive to identify and modify "core" problems in treating personality disorders. The two schools differ in their views of the nature of this core structure, the difference being that the psychoanalytic school sees these structures as unconscious and not easily

---

[1] In this discussion, the terms schemas, rules, and basic beliefs are used more or less interchangeably. More strictly, "schemas" are the cognitive structures that organize experience and behavior; "beliefs" and "rules" represent the content of the schemas and consequently determine the content of the thinking, affect, and behavior. Phenomena such as automatic thoughts are regarded as the product of the schema (Beck et al., 1979).

available to the patient. The cognitive therapy view holds that the products of this process are largely in the realm of awareness (Ingram & Hollon, 1986) and that with special training, even more may be accessible to consciousness. Dysfunctional feelings and conduct (according to cognitive therapeutic theory) are largely due to the function of certain schemas that tend to produce consistently biased judgments and a concomitant consistent tendency to make cognitive errors in certain types of situations. The basic premise of the cognitive therapy model is that attributional bias, rather than motivational or response bias, is the main source of dysfunctional affect and conduct in adults (Hollon, Kendall, & Lumry, 1986; Mathews & MacLeod, 1986; MacLeod, Mathews, & Tata, 1986; Zwemer & Deffenbacher, 1984). Other work has shown that clinically relevant cognitive patterns are related to psychopathology in children in a way that parallels the cognitive and affective relationship patterns typically found among adults (Beardslee, Bemporad, Keller, & Klerman, 1983; Leitenberg, Yost, & Carroll-Wilson, 1986; Quay, Routh, & Shapiro, 1987; Ward, Friedlander, & Silverman, 1987), and that effective cognitive therapy can follow similar lines in children and adults (DiGiuseppe, 1983, 1986, 1989).

Given the long-term nature of personality-disordered patients' characterological problems, their general avoidance of psychotherapy, their frequent referral through family pressure or legal remand, and their seeming reluctance or inability to change, they are often the most difficult patients in a clinician's caseload. They generally require more work within the session, longer time for therapy, greater strain on the therapist's skills (and patience), and more therapist energy than do most other patients. Given this expenditure, there are often less therapeutic gain, greater difficulty in treatment compliance, and reduced rates of change and satisfaction for both therapist and patient than are experienced with other patients.

These patients typically come for therapy with presenting issues other than personality problems, most often with complaints of depression and anxiety coded on Axis I of DSM-III-R. The reported problems of depression and anxiety may be separate and apart from the Axis II patterns, or derived from and fueled by the Axis II personality disorder. The course of therapy is far more complicated when there is a combination of Axis I and Axis II disorders. The duration of treatment, frequency of treatment sessions, goals and expectations for both therapist and patient, and available techniques and strategies need to be altered in the cognitive therapy of personality disorders. Given the difficulties inherent in working with the personality disorders, it is surprising how much these patients improve with the kind of modified cognitive therapy approaches to be described in this volume.

Personality-disordered patients will often see the difficulties that they encounter in dealing with other people or tasks as external to them, and generally independent of their behavior or input. They often describe being victimized by others or, more globally, by "the system." Such patients often have little idea about how they got to be the way they are, how they contribute to their own problems, or how to change. These patients are often referred by family members or friends who recognize a dysfunctional pattern, or who have reached their personal limit in attempting to cope with these individuals. Still other patients are referred by the judicial system. Individuals in this latter group are often given a choice, for example, to go to prison or go to therapy (Henn, Herjanic, & VanderPearl, 1976; Moore, Zusman, & Root, 1984).

Other patients are very much aware of the self-defeating nature of their personality problems (e.g., overdependence, inhibition, excessive avoidance) but are at a loss as to how they got to be the way they are, or how to change. Still other patients may have insight into the etiology of their personality disorder, but do not have the skills to change.

While the diagnosis of some personality disorders may be based on the history taken in the initial sessions, for other patients the diagnostic indicators may not appear until early in treatment. The clinician may not be aware initially of the characterological nature, chronicity, and severity of the patients' personality problems (Koenigsberg, Kaplan, Gilmore, & Cooper, 1985; Fabrega, Mezzich, Mezzich, & Coffman, 1986; Karno, Hough, Burnam, Escobar, Timbers, Santana, & Boyd, 1986). Often, these are the very patients whose social functioning is worst (Casey, Tryer, & Platt, 1985). Some patients come only for symptomatic treatment for acute problems. When schema-focused treatment for a personality disorder may also be indicated (see Chapters 3, 4, and 5), the patient and therapist do not automatically agree on a problem list or agenda of treatment goals. When Axis II problems are identified at intake, the patient may not be willing to work on the personality disorders, but rather may choose to work on the symptoms for which he or she was referred. It is important to remember that the patient's goals, and not those of others (including the therapist), are the initial focus of treatment. Inasmuch as the patient's schemas are the agent as well as the target of therapeutic change, the therapist may work with the patient to develop the trust to follow the therapist's lead and work on both the symptoms and the schema. Early diagnosis and treatment planning are likely to be more effective (Morrison & Shapiro, 1987).

Certain Axis II patients are silent about their personality problems because of a lack of insight or recognition or because of a recognition and denial. Other personality-disordered patients deny the problems as a reflection of the disorders themselves. The effectiveness of cognitive therapy at any given point in time depends on the degree to which patients' expectations about therapeutic goals are congruent with those of their therapist (Martin, Martin, & Slemon, 1987). Mutual trust and acknowledgment of the patients' requests by the therapist are important, as they are in a medical setting (Like & Zyzanski, 1987). Power struggles over conflicting goals usually impede progress (Foon, 1985). The collaborative nature of goal setting is one of the most important features of cognitive therapy (Beck et al., 1979; Freeman et al., 1990).

In some cases, a patient may be unwilling to change because what the therapist may conceptualize as an Axis II disorder has been functional for the patient across many life situations. The behaviors may have been functional in a work situation, but at a great personal cost to the individual. For example, Mary, a 23-year-old computer programmer, came to therapy because of "tremendous work pressure, inability to enjoy life, a perfectionistic approach to virtually all tasks, and a general isolation from others." She was working very diligently at her job and getting very little satisfaction from the work. She was constantly late in getting her work completed. "He doesn't understand that I work very slowly and carefully. He just wants the work done quickly, and I have my standards of what I consider good enough to submit." She would have to take work home on weekends and stay in the office until 7 or 8 P.M. during the week to get the work done according to her "standards." Her compulsive personality traits had been rewarded in school and at home. Teachers always remarked on her neat, perfect work, which resulted in her receiving many awards at graduation. Without the school focus, work took all of her time, and she was no longer rewarded for her perfectionism. She had little time for friends, leisure activities, or fun (Freeman & Leaf, 1989, pp. 405–406).

Patients with dependent personalities are sometimes ideal for service in the military because they are compliant with orders. A 66-year-old man, diagnosed as having both obsessive-compulsive and avoidant personality disorders, stated, "The best time in my life was in the army. I didn't have to worry about what to wear, what to do, where to go, or what to eat."

Heuristic signs that may point to the possibility of Axis II problems include the following scenarios:

1. A patient or significant other reports, "Oh, he (she) has always done that since he (she) was a little boy (girl)," or the patient may report, "I've always been this way."

2. The patient is not compliant with the therapeutic regimen. While this noncompliance (or "resistance") is common in many problems and for many reasons, ongoing noncompliance should be used as a signal for further exploration of Axis II issues.

3. Therapy seems to have come to a sudden stop, for no apparent reason. The clinician working with these patients can often help the patients to reduce the problems of anxiety or depression, only to be blocked in further therapeutic work by the personality disorder.

4. Patients seem entirely unaware of the effect of their behavior on

others. They report the responses of others, but fail to address any provocation or dysfunctional behavior that they might exhibit.

5. There is a question regarding the motivation of the patient to change. This problem is especially true for those patients who have "been sent" to therapy by family members or the courts. The patient gives lip service to the therapy and to the importance of change, but seems to manage to avoid changing.

6. Patients' personality problems appear to be acceptable and natural for them. For example, a depressed patient without an Axis II diagnosis may say, "I just want to get rid of this depression. I know what it is like to feel good, and I want to feel that way again." The Axis II patient may see the problems as *being* them: "This is how I am," "This is who I am." This does not, in any way, indicate that the patient is comfortable with the personality style and concomitant behaviors. The patient with avoidant personality disorder may very much want to be more actively involved with others, but has thoughts of inherent inferiority. On the other hand, a patient with a narcissistic personality disorder may not recognize any problems except the refusal or reluctance of others to admire and regard him or her highly.

The personality disorder is probably one of the most striking representations of Beck's concept of "schema" (Beck, 1964, 1967; Beck et al., 1979; Freeman, 1987; Freeman et al., 1990). Schemas (specific rules that govern information processing and behavior) can be classified into a variety of useful categories, such as personal, familial, cultural, religious, gender, or occupational schemas. Schemas can be inferred from behavior or assessed through interview and history taking. With the Axis II patient, the schematic work is at the heart of the therapeutic endeavor. The position of particular schemas on the continuum from active (hypervalent or valent) to inactive (dormant or latent), and their position on the continuum from impermeable to changeable, are among the essential dimensions for the therapist to use in conceptualizing the patient's problems and developing a treatment strategy.

Given the chronic nature of the problems and the price paid by these patients in terms of their isolation, dependence on others, or external approbation, one must question why these dysfunctional behaviors are maintained. They may cause difficulty at work, at school, or in personal life. In some cases they are reinforced by society (e.g., the teachers who encourage a child who is "a real worker," "a kid who doesn't fool around," "a kid who hasn't messed around while other kids are messing around," "a kid who really works hard and gets A's"). Often, compelling schemas that a patient will often "know" are erroneous are hard to change. Two factors seem most important: First, as DiGiuseppe (1986) has pointed out, the problem may be partly due to the difficulty people (including scientifically oriented therapists) have in making a "paradigm shift" from a sometimes accurate hypothesis to a less familiar one; second, as Freeman (1987; Freeman & Leaf, 1989) has noted, people often find ways to adjust to and extract short-term benefits from fundamentally biased schemas that restrict or burden their long-term capacity to deal with the challenges of life. With respect to the first problem, DiGiuseppe (1989) recommends therapeutic use of a variety of examples of the error that a particular schema produces, so that its biasing effect can be seen as having an impact on broad areas of a patient's life, and repeated explication of the consequences of an un-biased alternative. Although one would expect that therapy following these recommendations would often be prolonged, the recommended strategies for dealing with this problem are largely under the control of the therapist, and can usually be implemented when indicated. The second problem is not so tractable. When patients adjust their lives to compensate for their anxieties, for example, they have to change their lives and face their anxieties in order to change. The patient mentioned earlier who described the period of his military service as "the best time in my life" reacted that way because "I didn't have to worry about what to wear, what to do, where to go, or what to eat." Given the patient's history and general manner of response, we would not expect the patient to seek or embrace a therapeutic strategy requiring him to practice homework exercises that exposed him to a constant array of new risks (Turner, Beidel, Dancu, & Keys, 1986). Before a patient would adopt an appropriate therapeutic strategy, the therapist would probably have to try to reshape the patient's initial expectations about the goals, time course, and procedures of therapy; help the patient achieve some relatively immediate and practical gains; and develop a trusting and supportive collaborative relationship.

One of the most important treatment considerations in working with personality-disordered patients is to be aware that the therapy will evoke anxiety because the individuals are being asked to go far beyond chang-ing a particular behavior or reframing a perception. They are being asked to give up who they are and how they have defined themselves for many years. While the schematic structure may be uncomfortable, limit-ing, and lonely, to change means that a patient is in new territory, where the land is alien: "I may get hurt, I perceive great threat, and therefore I feel anxious." The recognition of the anxiety generated by changing is crucial to the successful treatment of the personality-disordered patient. The patient must be apprised of the potential for anxiety, so that it does not appear out of the blue as a great shock or surprise. Beck et al. (1985), in discussing the treatment of agoraphobia, state:

> It is crucial that the patient experience anxiety in order to ensure that
> the primitive cognitive levels have been activated (since these levels are

directly connected to the affects). The repeated, direct, on-the-spot
recognition that the danger signals do not lead to catastrophe . . .
enhance[s] the responsivity of the primitive level to more realistic
inputs from above. (p. 129)

One patient responded that "it's good to have that safety and I don't
understand why I should ever give it up." As the therapist starts to help
these patients to allow themselves to be more vulnerable, the patients will
be more anxious. Unless they are able to successfully cope with the
anxiety, they will block or leave therapy. (Space limitations preclude a
detailed discussion of anxiety treatment. See Beck et al., 1985; Freeman
& Simon, 1989.)

Given the importance of the schematic changes, the schemas are
difficult to alter. They are held firmly in place by behavioral, cognitive,
and affective elements. The therapeutic approach must take a tripartite
approach. To take a strictly cognitive approach and try to argue patients
out of their distortions will not work. Having the patients abreact within
the session to fantasies or recollections will not be successful by itself. A
therapeutic program that addresses all three areas is essential. A patient's cognitive distortions serve as signposts that point to the schema.
The style of distorting, and the content, frequency, and consequences of
the distortions, are all important elements.

An unfortunate life history may contribute to the compelling quality
of biased schemas and the development of personality disorders. An
example appears in data reported by Zimmerman, Pfohl, Stangl, and
Coryell (1985). They studied a sample of women who had been hospitalized for acute depressive episodes, coded as DSM-III Axis I disorders.
When they divided their sample into three groups, distinguished by
differential severity on a negative life events scale designed to assess Axis
IV (Severity of Psychosocial Stressors) status, all three groups were
similar on acute symptomatic measures such as the Hamilton Rating
Scale for Depression (Hamilton, 1967) and the Beck Depression Inventory. Despite the apparent similarity in presenting symptoms among
the groups differing in negative life events, the severity of the cases
within each life events frequency group and the difficulty of treatment
for these individuals did differ significantly. Among the 30% of all
patients who attempted suicide during the course of the study, the
attempt rate was four times as high in the high-stress as in the low-stress
group. Personality disorders were evident in 84.2% of the high-stress
group, 48.1% of the moderate-stress group, and only 28.6% of the
low-stress group. The investigators interpreted their finding that frequent negative life events were associated with personality disorder and
case severity as at least partly due to the chronicity of the events and the
patients' response to this chronicity; if unusually frequent negative

events have occurred in someone's life, a pessimistic bias about one's self, world, and future is not unlikely. In contrast, patients who successfully avoid life stressors may live in a relatively secure personal world and may have very low rates of *clinically evident* personality disorders. In a study of psychiatric referrals in a peacetime military hospital, for example, the only striking difference between the patient population and those similarly referred in civilian settings was a very low rate of diagnosable personality disorders (Hales, Polly, Bridenbaugh, & Orman, 1986). The clinical appearance of a personality disorder is not itself a clue to whether or not patients have biased schemas. As the large literature on self-fulfilling prophecies testifies, it is possible to make consistently biased predictions from inaccurate schemas and yet live in such a way, because one restricts risk taking and does not test more accurate alternative schemas, that one will consistently be correct (Jones, 1977).

Clinical Studies and Research

The majority of publications presenting newly developed approaches to conceptualizing and treating personality disorders have been theoretically or clinically based, and research into the effectiveness of cognitive-behavioral treatment of these disorders is in its infancy (see Fleming & Pretzer, in press, and Pretzer & Fleming, 1989, for recent reviews). In particular, there are few well-controlled outcome studies that specifically examine the effectiveness of cognitive-behavioral interventions with individuals who clearly meet diagnostic criteria for personality disorders. Fortunately, there is a growing body of evidence regarding the adequacy of cognitive-behavioral conceptualizations of the personality disorders, as well as the effectiveness of cognitive-behavioral therapy with individuals diagnosed as having personality disorders (see Table 1.1). An examination of this evidence provides grounds for optimism, but also makes it abundantly clear that much more empirical research will be needed to provide a basis for effective treatment of these complex problems.

Clinical Reports of the Effectiveness of Cognitive-Behavioral Interventions

The first publications to explicitly consider the treatment of personality disorders from a cognitive-behavioral perspective were based on the uncontrolled observations of practitioners who encountered clients with personality disorders in the course of their clinical practice. Some of the earliest discussions of the effectiveness (or lack thereof) of cognitive-behavioral treatments with clients diagnosed as having personality dis-

TABLE 1.1

Evidence Regarding the Effectiveness of Cognitive-Behavioral Interventions with Personality Disorders

Personality Disorder	Uncontrolled Clinical Reports	Single-Case Design Studies	Studies of the Effects of Personality Disorders on Treatment Outcome	Controlled Outcome Studies
Antisocial	+	−	+	a
Avoidant	+	+	±	+
Borderline	±	−	+	±
Dependent	+	+	+	
Histrionic	+	−		
Narcissistic	+	+		
Obsessive-compulsive	+	−		
Paranoid	+	+		
Passive-aggressive	+		+	
Schizoid	+			
Schizotypal	+			

Note. +, cognitive-behavioral interventions found to be effective; −, cognitive-behavioral interventions found not to be effective; ±, mixed findings.

[a]Cognitive-behavioral interventions were effective with antisocial personality disorder subjects only when the individuals were depressed at pretest.

orders appeared in discussions of individuals who failed to respond to treatment. For example, in a chapter discussing failures in treating depression by cognitive therapy, Rush and Shaw (1983) reported that individuals with borderline personality disorder accounted for a substantial proportion of negative outcomes in cognitive therapy for depression and suggested that individuals with this disorder could not be successfully treated with cognitive therapy.

However, in that same year, several clinically based papers were presented that reported success in treating a number of personality disorders with cognitive therapy (Fleming, 1983; Pretzer, 1983; Simon, 1983; Young, 1983). A steady flow of clinically based material has appeared in recent years (Fleming, 1985, 1988; Freeman et al., 1990; Linehan, 1987a,b; Mays, 1985; Overholser, 1987; Perry & Flannery, 1982; Pretzer, 1985, 1988; Simon, 1985) and at this point at least limited success has been reported in treating each of the personality disorders. Nevertheless, caution is needed in interpreting clinical reports of success in treating personality disorders. When a clinician reports positive or negative results for the use of particular interventions with a particular patient, it is impossible to determine with any certainty whether the outcome was due to the particular interventions that were used, to nonspecific treatment effects, to idiosyncratic characteristics of that particular patient, to events independent of the treatment, or to spontaneous remission. These limitations are amplified when the report suffers from additional methodological flaws, which, while not inherent in clinical reports, are quite common.

For example, in the one study of the effectiveness of behavioral interventions with histrionic clients that has been reported, Kass, Silvers, and Abrams (1972) describe an inpatient group treatment in which group members reinforced assertion and extinguished dysfunctional, overly emotional responses; the authors assert that this approach was helpful to four out of five group members. Although these results are encouraging, this study suffers from several flaws. First, the diagnoses were based on idiosyncratic diagnostic criteria that did not clearly correspond to DSM-II diagnostic criteria, and no check on the reliability of diagnoses was included. Therefore, it is not clear to what extent the subjects were representative of individuals diagnosed as having histrionic personality disorder. Second, the report of improvement in four of five subjects was based on the authors' subjective evaluation, and no outcome or follow-up data were reported. Thus, it is difficult to evaluate the effectiveness of the treatment or the extent to which the reported changes persisted. Finally, since only one therapist was used, it is difficult to determine whether the results obtained were due to the particular treatment employed or were due to non-treatment-specific factors, such as the emotional support provided by the group or the therapist's charisma and enthusiasm. Clinical reports are interesting and provocative and can be very valuable for generating hypotheses and spurring more rigorous research, but the lack of experimental controls and the many possible factors that can distort the results make it impossible to interpret the results conclusively or to resolve conflicting reports.

Studies Based on Single-Case Designs

Given the limitations on the generalizability of results reported in uncontrolled case reports, there is an obvious need for empirical research on the cognitive-behavioral treatment of personality disorders. However, practical problems make it difficult to conduct the number of studies that would be needed to develop and refine cognitive-behavioral approaches to the personality disorders. In addition to the problems encountered in conducting any treatment outcome study, it can be difficult to assemble a sample of individuals who clearly meet diagnostic criteria for the personality disorder being investigated, and the length of treatment required for many individuals with personality disorders makes an outcome study a major undertaking.

Turkat and his colleagues (e.g., Turkat & Carlson, 1984; Turkat & Levin, 1984; Turkat & Maisto, 1985) have proposed an empirically based approach to understanding and treating personality disorders, which avoids many of the practical problems encountered with controlled outcome studies. Their approach is to use single-case experimental designs to investigate personality disorders. First, conceptualizations of individual clients that are based on thorough assessments are developed. Specific hypotheses are then generated and tested, using the most appropriate available measures, in order to confirm the validity of the conceptualization. After this, a treatment plan is developed on the basis of the conceptualization, and, if the interventions prove to be effective, this is seen as providing additional support for the investigators' formulation of the case. Unsuccessful interventions are seen as raising questions about the validity of the conceptualization and spur a re-evaluation.

The results reported by Turkat and Maisto (1985) are summarized in Table 1.2. The case examples reported by these authors provide empirical evidence that cognitive-behavioral interventions based on individualized conceptualizations can be effective with at least some individuals with personality disorders. Since both behavioral observation and established measures were used to document changes at both posttest and follow-up in some of the cases, these reports provide stronger evidence than can be provided by simple case reports. In several cases, interventions based on an individualized conceptualization of the client's disorder were effective when symptomatic treatment alone had not been effective. For example, Turkat and Carlson (1984) present an interesting case example of a 48-year-old woman who reported anxiety and avoidance behavior following the diagnosis of her daughter as diabetic. When a strictly symptomatic, behavioral treatment was used to decrease the client's anxiety and avoidance, the client's symptoms improved substantially, but returned in full force when the frequency of therapy sessions was decreased. When the case was reconceptualized as anxiety regarding independent decision making, and the treatment was revised to focus on gradual exposure to independent decision making, the treatment proved successful, with significant improvements on self-ratings of anxiety being maintained at an 11-month follow-up. Examples such as this provide support for Turkat's contention that formulation-based interventions are more effective than treatment based on simply matching interventions to symptoms.

The type of single-case design advocated by Turkat as a means of advancing our understanding of personality disorders has substantial advantages over uncontrolled case reports. Insofar as specific hypoth-

TABLE 1.2
Personality Disorder Cases Reported by Turkat and Maisto (1985)

Personality Disorder	N	% of Sample[a]	N with Outcome Reported	Reported Outcome	Type of Outcome Data
Antisocial	2	2.7	2	Subjects not interested in treatment	
Avoidant	4	5.4	1	Gradual improvement over 2 years of treatment	Anecdotal
Borderline	1	1.4	11	Discontinued treatment prematurely	
Compulsive	6	8.1	5	Subjects unwilling to engage in treatment	
Dependent	1	1.4	1	Decreased anxiety, avoidance, and depression; increased independence	Self-ratings on hierarchy items, 1-year follow-up
Histrionic	8	10.8	1	Unable to develop formulation and treatment plan	
Narcissistic	2	2.7	1	Improved mood, impulse control, and compliance, but terminated prematurely	Self-report, observation
Paranoid	8	10.8	1	Improved social skills and tolerance of criticism; decreased defensiveness	Self-report, observation
Passive-aggressive	1	1.4	1	Unable to develop formulation and treatment plan	
Schizoid	2	2.7	2	Unable to develop formulation and treatment plan	
Schizotypal	0	0			
Total	35	47.4	16		

Note. Adapted from "Personality Disorders: Application of the Experimental Method to the Formulation and Modification of Personality Disorders" by I. D. Turkat and S. A. Maisto, 1985, in D. H. Barlow (Ed.), *Clinical Handbook of Psychological Disorders.* New York: Guilford Press. Copyright 1985 by The Guilford Press. Adapted by permission.
[a]The total sample consisted of 74 patients seen in a clinical psychology service housed in a diabetes research and training center.

eses are clearly formulated and are tested using appropriate measures, it is possible to minimize subjective bias in interpreting observations and to test the validity of conceptualizations. However, a major limitation of single-case designs is that it is difficult to determine to what extent the subject in a particular treatment trial is typical of other individuals in the same diagnostic category. A conceptualization or treatment intervention that proves valid in one particular case may or may not be generalizable to other individuals. For example, while Turkat and his colleagues have presented individualized conceptualizations and strategies that were used with particular clients, they are cautious about generalizing these ideas to other individuals with the same diagnoses.

Conceivably, a sufficiently large series of single-case studies that produced similar results could provide a basis for generalizing the findings to other samples. However, conducting a large series of single-case studies would sacrifice many of the practical advantages of this methodology, without gaining the benefits in terms of improved experimental controls and more sophisticated statistical analysis that are possible with controlled outcome studies. It appears that single-case designs are well suited to developing and refining conceptualizations and intervention strategies that are based on clinical experience. Once the conceptualizations and treatment strategies have been refined in this way, studies using more traditional multisubject designs will be needed to test their generalizability.

It should be noted that the overall results obtained by Turkat and his colleagues, shown in Table 1.2, indicate that treatment was ineffective with many personality-disordered clients. The most common difficulties mentioned by the investigators were inability to develop a formulation-based treatment approach, subjects' being unwilling to engage in treatment, and premature termination. Turkat's approach is quite promising, but this research program is in its initial phase with data published from only a limited sample.

Studies of the Effects of Symptomatic Treatment

The behaviors and symptoms characteristic of personality disorders are not unique to these disorders. Behavioral and cognitive-behavioral treatments for problems such as impulsive behavior, poor social skills, and inappropriate expression of anger have received considerable empirical support. This has led some to suggest that the treatment of personality disorders is simply a matter of systematically treating each of the problematic behaviors or symptoms presented by the patient. For example, Stephens and Parks (1981) discuss treating these clients symptom by symptom, without presenting any broader conceptualization of personality disorders and without discussing whether treatment of these symptoms in clients with personality disorders differs from the treatment of these symptoms in other clients.

Often, it has been assumed that interventions that have been found to be effective in treating individuals not diagnosed as having personality disorders will be equally effective in treating similar problems in individuals diagnosed as having such disorders. For example, in reviewing the empirical support for this approach, Stephens and Parks cite evidence of the efficacy of behavioral interventions for the treatment of each of the 10 categories of maladaptive behavior characteristic of individuals with personality disorders. However, the vast majority of the studies cited were conducted either with subjects *not* diagnosed as having personality disorders or with subjects having a variety of diagnoses, including some subjects with personality disorders. Similarly, Pilkonis (1984), in discussing the treatment of avoidant personality disorder, provides a concise summary of the literature on social anxiety and interpersonal avoidance, but fails to note that the studies cited utilized subjects ranging from shy undergraduates to psychotic inpatients, with few subjects clearly meeting diagnostic criteria for avoidant personality disorder.

The reports, cited previously, asserting that behavioral and cognitive-behavioral interventions are less effective with personality-disordered clients (e.g., Mays, 1985; Rush & Shaw, 1983) make it obvious that the finding that a particular symptom or problematic behavior can be treated effectively in a heterogeneous sample of subjects does not necessarily imply that the intervention in question will be equally effective when applied with clients diagnosed as having personality disorders. It is essential that the validity of generalizing findings of research on non-personality-disordered subjects to individuals with personality disorders be investigated empirically.

Evidence regarding this issue has been provided by several studies that have examined the effectiveness of standard behavioral treatment for subjects diagnosed as having personality disorders, as compared to subjects without personality disorders. In testing a cognitive-behavioral treatment for severely bulimic outpatients, Giles, Young, and Young (1985) found that a treatment program combining response prevention, education, and cognitive restructuring was effective for most subjects (22 subjects were treated successfully, 6 dropped out of treatment, and 6 failed to respond to treatment). Of the six subjects who were not treated successfully despite their continuing in treatment throughout the study, four met DSM-III diagnostic criteria for borderline personality disorder. None of the subjects who were successfully treated manifested borderline personality disorder. Similarly, Turner (1987) found that socially phobic patients without concurrent personality disorders improved markedly after a 15-week group treatment and maintained their gains at a 1-year follow-up. However, he found that subjects who met diagnostic criteria for personality disorder diagnoses in addition to their social phobia showed little or no improvement either posttreatment or at the 1-year follow-up.

In a study of the treatment of agoraphobia, Mavissakalian and Hamman (1987) found that 75% of agoraphobic subjects who were rated as being low in personality disorder characteristics responded well to a time-limited behavioral and pharmacological treatment. However, only 25% of subjects who were rated as being high in personality disorder characteristics responded to this treatment. Interestingly, the investigators found that four of the seven subjects who had met diagnostic criteria for a single personality disorder diagnosis before treatment no longer met criteria for such a diagnosis following treatment, while subjects who had been diagnosed as having more than one personality disorder tended to merit either the same diagnoses or different personality disorder diagnoses following treatment. Furthermore, Mavissakalian and Hamman found that all personality disorders were not equally responsive or resistant to treatment. Characteristics associated with borderline, dependent, and passive-aggressive personality disorders were most affected by treatment for agoraphobia, while characteristics associated with histrionic and avoidant personality disorders showed little change.

Chambless and Renneberg (1988) conducted a study similar to that of Mavissakalian and Hamman, studying the impact of personality disorders on treatment outcome with agoraphobic subjects. These investigators found that while an intensive group treatment was more effective than weekly individual therapy overall, subjects with a concurrent diagnosis of avoidant personality disorder did not respond significantly better to the intensive group treatment than to weekly individual treatment in terms of agoraphobic symptoms. Subjects with passive-aggressive personality disorder responded particularly poorly to weekly individual therapy and did better in intensive group therapy.

In each of these outcome studies, the majority of individuals with personality disorder diagnoses responded poorly to well-established behavioral treatments, suggesting that the effectiveness of behavioral interventions with standard samples cannot be assumed to generalize to samples of persons diagnosed as having personality disorders. However, despite these generally poor results, behavioral interventions were effective with at least some personality-disordered individuals. It is particularly interesting to note that when behavioral interventions were effective, broad changes in many aspects of the patients' lives were achieved; the improvement was not confined to the specific problem behaviors that were the focus of treatment.

Controlled Outcome Studies

Thus far, controlled studies of the outcome of cognitive-behavioral treatment of clients diagnosed as having personality disorders have been conducted with only a few of the personality disorders, and none of these studies has been replicated. Therefore, these studies do not provide a basis for drawing firm conclusions. However, the findings published to date are encouraging.

In a study of the treatment of individuals complaining of social anxiety, both short-term social skills training and social skills training combined with cognitive interventions were demonstrated to be effective in increasing the frequency of social interaction and decreasing social anxiety in subjects with avoidant personality disorder (Stravynski, Marks, & Yule, 1982). This study found that the combination of social skills training and cognitive treatment was no more effective than social skills training alone, and the authors interpret this finding as demonstrating the "lack of value" of cognitive interventions. However, it should be noted that all treatments were provided by a single therapist (who was also the principal investigator), and that only one of many possible cognitive interventions (disputation of irrational beliefs) was used. Greenberg and Stravynski (1985) observe that the avoidant client's fear of ridicule appears to contribute to premature termination in many cases, and suggest that it is necessary for social skills training to include training in how to respond to rejection and embarrassment as well as training in socially appropriate behavior. They suggest that interventions that modify relevant aspects of the clients' cognitions might add substantially to the effectiveness of intervention.

Antisocial personality disorder has widely been considered to be unresponsive to outpatient treatment. However, a recent report demonstrates that short-term outpatient cognitive-behavioral therapy can be effective with at least some clients with this disorder. In a study of the treatment of opiate addicts in a methadone maintenance program, Woody, McLellan, Luborsky, and O'Brien (1985) found that subjects who met DSM-III diagnostic criteria for both major depression and antisocial personality disorder responded well to short-term treatment with either Beck's cognitive therapy (Beck et al., 1979) or a supportive-expressive psychotherapy systematized by Luborsky (Luborsky, McLellan, Woody, O'Brien, & Auerbach, 1985). These subjects showed statistically significant improvement on 11 of 22 outcome variables used, including psychiatric symptoms, drug use, employment, and illegal activity. Subjects who met criteria for antisocial personality disorder but not major depression showed little response to treatment, improving on only 3 of 22 variables. This pattern of results was maintained at a 7-month follow-up. Subjects not diagnosed as manifesting antisocial personality disorder responded to treatment better than the sociopaths did; however, sociopaths who were initially depressed did only slightly worse than the nonsociopaths, while the nondepressed sociopaths did much worse. The finding that two quite dissimilar treatment approaches were both effective might suggest that the improvement was due to nonspecific treatment effects. However, the degree to which the therapist adhered to the relevant treatment manual was significantly correlated with degree of improvement both across therapists and within each therapist's caseload (Luborsky et al., 1985). This provides evidence that the improvement was indeed treatment-specific.

Linehan and her colleagues (Linehan, Armstrong, Allmon, Suarez, & Miller, 1988; Linehan, Armstrong, Suarez, & Allmon, 1988) have recently reported the results of an outcome study of dialectical behavior therapy versus "treatment as usual" with a sample of chronically parasuicidal borderline subjects. They found that the patients in the dialectical behavior therapy condition had a significantly lower dropout rate and significantly less self-injurious behavior than subjects receiving "treatment as usual." However, the two groups showed only modest overall improvement in depression or other symptomatology and did not differ significantly in these areas. While these results are modest, it is encouraging to find that 1 year of cognitive-behavioral treatment could produce lasting improvement with a sample of subjects who not only met diagnostic criteria for borderline personality disorder, but also were more disturbed than many persons diagnosed as having this disorder. Linehan et al.'s subjects were chronically parasuicidal, had histories of multiple psychiatric hospitalizations, and were unable to maintain employment due to their psychiatric symptoms. Many individuals who meet diagnostic criteria for borderline personality disorder are generally not parasuicidal, are hospitalized infrequently, and are able to maintain employment.

The evidence that cognitive-behavioral treatment can produce beneficial results with difficult problems such as avoidant personality disorder, antisocial personality disorder, and borderline personality disorder is quite encouraging. However, it is clear that conclusions regarding the efficacy of cognitive-behavioral therapy with specific personality disorders would be premature. In particular, many of the more comprehensive treatment approaches that have been proposed in recent years have not yet been tested empirically, and it is clear that "standard" cognitive-behavioral interventions often prove ineffective with clients diagnosed as having personality disorders.

Conclusions

Given the prevalence of personality disorders and the consensus that behavioral and cognitive-behavioral intervention is greatly complicated in clients with personality disorders, it is clearly important that these disorders be a continued focus of empirical research, theoretical innovation, and clinical experimentation. For the time being, treatment recommendations based on clinical observation and a limited empirical base are the best we can offer to clinicians who must try to work with personality-disordered clients today, rather than waiting for empirically validated treatment protocols to be developed. Fortunately, a number of clinicians report that when cognitive-behavioral interventions are based on individualized conceptualizations of the clients' problems and the interpersonal aspects of therapy receive sufficient attention, many clients with personality disorders can be treated quite effectively.

Chapter 2
Theory of Personality Disorders

This chapter presents an overall theory of personality disorders within the broad context of their origin, development, and function of personality. A major thrust of this exposition is how personality processes are formed and operate in the service of adaptation. Before presenting a synopsis of our theory of personality disorder, we will review our concepts of personality and then relate them to their disorders.

We start the discourse with a speculative explanation of how the prototypes of our personality patterns could be derived from our phylogenetic heritage. Those genetically determined "strategies" that facilitated survival and reproduction would presumably be favored by natural selection. Derivatives of these primitive strategies can be observed in an exaggerated form in the symptom syndromes, such as anxiety disorders and depression, and in personality disorders, such as the dependent personality disorder.

Our discussion then progresses along the continuum from evolutionary-based strategies to a consideration of how information processing, including affective processes, is antecedent to the operation of these strategies. In other words, evaluation of the particular demands of a situation precedes and triggers an adaptive (or maladaptive) strategy. How a situation is evaluated depends in part, at least, on the relevant underlying beliefs. Those beliefs are embedded in more or less stable structures, labeled "schemas," that select and synthesize incoming data. The psychological sequence progresses then from evaluation to affective and motivational arousal, and finally to selection, and implementation of a relevant strategy. We regard the basic structures (schemas) upon which these cognitive, affective, and motivational processes are dependent as the fundamental units of personality.

Personality "traits" identified by adjectives such as "dependent," "withdrawn," "arrogant," or "extraverted" may be conceptualized as the overt expression of these underlying structures. By assigning meanings to events, the cognitive structures start a chain reaction culminating in the kinds of overt behavior (strategies) that are attributed to personality traits. Behavioral patterns that we commonly ascribe to personality traits or dispositions ("honest," "shy," "outgoing"), consequently represent interpersonal strategies developed from the interaction between innate dispositions and environmental influences.

Attributes such as dependency and autonomy, which are conceptualized in motivational theories of personality as basic drives, may be viewed as a function of a conglomerate of basic schemas. In behavioral or functional terms, the attributes may be labeled as "basic strategies." These specific functions may be observed in an exaggerated way in some of the overt behavioral patterns attributed, for example, to the dependent or schizoid personality disorders.

Our presentation then moves on to the topic of activation of the schemas (and modes) and their expression in behavior. Having laid the groundwork for our theory of personality, we go on to review the relation of these structures to psychopathology. The pronounced activation of dysfunctional schemas lies at the core of the so-called Axis I disorders, such as depression. The more idiosyncratic, dysfunctional schemas displace the more reality-oriented, adaptive schemas in functions such as information processing, recall, and prediction. In depression, for example, the mode that is organized around the theme of self-negation becomes dominant; in anxiety disorders, the personal danger mode is hyperactive; in panic disorders, the mode relevant to imminent catastrophe is mobilized.

The typical dysfunctional beliefs and maladaptive strategies expressed in personality disorders make individuals susceptible to life experiences that impinge on their cognitive vulnerability. Thus, the dependent personality disorder is characterized by a sensitivity to loss of love and help; the narcissistic to trauma to self-esteem; the histrionic by failure to manipulate others to provide attention and support. The cognitive vulnerability is based on beliefs that are extreme, rigid, and imperative. We speculate that these dysfunctional beliefs have originated as the result of the interaction between the individual's genetic predisposition and exposure to undesirable influences from other people and specific traumatic events.

The Evolution of Interpersonal Strategies

Our view of personality takes into account the role of our evolutionary history in shaping our patterns of thinking, feeling, and acting. We can better understand personality structures, functions, and processes if we examine attitudes, feelings, and behavior in the light of their possible relation to ethological strategies.

Much of the behavior that we observe in nonhuman animals is generally regarded as "programmed." The underlying processes are programmed and are expressed in overt behavior. The development of these programs frequently depends on the interaction between genetically determined structures and experience. Similar developmental processes may be assumed to occur in humans (Gilbert, 1989). It is reasonable to consider the notion that long-standing cognitive-affective-motivational programs influence our automatic processes: the way we construe events, what we feel, and how we are disposed to act. The programs involved in cognitive processing, affect, arousal, and motivation may have evolved as a result of their ability to sustain life and promote reproduction.

Natural selection presumably brought about some kind of fit between programmed behavior and the demands of the environment. However, our environment has changed more rapidly than have our automatic adaptive strategies—largely as a result of our own modifications of our social milieu. Thus, strategies of predation, competition, and sociability that were useful in the more primitive surroundings do not always fit into the present niche of a highly individualized and technological society, with its own specialized cultural and social organization. A bad fit may be a factor in the development of behavior that we diagnose as a "personality disorder."

Regardless of their survival value in more primitive settings, certain of these evolutionary-derived patterns become problematic in our present culture because they interfere with the individual's personal goals, or conflict with group norms. Thus, highly developed predatory or competitive strategies that might promote survival in primitive conditions may be ill suited to a social milieu, and eventuate in an "antisocial personality disorder." Similarly, a kind of exhibitionistic display that would have attracted helpers and mates in the wild may be excessive or inappropriate in contemporary society. In actuality, however, these patterns are most likely to cause problems if they are inflexible and relatively uncontrolled.

The symptom syndromes—Axis I disorders—can also be conceptualized in terms of evolutionary principles. For example, the fight-flight pattern, while presumably adaptive in archaic emergency situations of physical danger, may form the substrate of either an anxiety disorder or a chronic hostile state. The same response pattern that was activated by the sight of a predator, for example, is also mobilized by threats of psychological traumas such as rejection or devaluation (Beck & Emery with Greenberg, 1985). When this psychophysiological response—perception of danger and arousal of the autonomic nervous system—is triggered by exposure to a broad spectrum of potentially aversive interpersonal situations, the vulnerable individual may manifest a diagnosable anxiety disorder.

Similarly, the variability of the gene pool could account for individual differences in personality. Thus, one individual may be predisposed to freeze in the face of danger, another to attack, a third to avoid any potential sources of danger. These differences in overt behavior, or strategies—any of which may have survival value in certain situations—reflect relatively enduring characteristics that are typical of certain "personality types" (Beck et al., 1985). An exaggeration of these patterns may lead to a personality disorder; for example, the avoidant personality disorder may reflect a strategy of withdrawing from or avoiding any situation involving the possibility of social disapproval.

Why do we apply the term "strategy" to characteristics that have been traditionally labeled "personality traits" or "patterns of behavior"? Strategies in this sense may be regarded as forms of programmed behavior that are designed to serve biological goals. Although the term implies a conscious, rational plan, it is not used in that sense here, but rather as it is employed by ethologists—to denote highly patterned stereotyped behaviors that promote individual survival and reproduction (Gilbert, 1989). These patterns of behavior may be viewed as having an ultimate goal of survival and reproduction: "reproductive efficacy" or "inclusive fitness." These evolutionary strategies were described 200 years ago by Erasmus Darwin (1791; cited in Eisely, 1961), grandfather of Charles Darwin, as expressions of hunger, lust, and security.

Although organisms are not aware of the ultimate goal of these biological strategies, they are conscious of subjective states that reflect their mode of operation: hunger, fear, or sexual arousal, and the rewards and punishments for their fulfillment or nonfulfillment (namely, pleasure or pain). We are prompted to eat to relieve the pangs of hunger, but also to obtain satisfaction. We seek sexual relations in order to reduce sexual tension as well as to gain gratification. We "bond" with other people to relieve loneliness, but also to achieve pleasure of camaraderie and intimacy. In sum, when we experience internal pressure to satisfy certain short-range wishes, such as obtaining pleasure and relieving tension, we may, to some degree at least, be fulfilling long-range evolutionary goals.

In humans, the term "strategy" can be analogously applied to forms of behavior that may be either adaptive or maladaptive, depending on the circumstances. Egocentricity, competitiveness, exhibitionism, and avoidance of unpleasantness may all be adaptive in certain situations but grossly maladaptive in others. Since we can observe only the overt behavior of other people, the question arises as to how our conscious internal states (thoughts, feelings, and wishes) are related to the strategies. If we examine the cognitive and affective patterns, we see a specific relationship between certain beliefs and attitudes on the one hand and behavior on the other.

One way to illustrate this relationship is to examine the exaggerated processes observed in individuals with various personality disorders and to compare specific typical attitudes associated with these disorders with the corresponding strategies. As indicated below in Table 2.1, it is possible to demonstrate a typical attitude associated with each of the traditional personality disorders. It can be seen that the specific strategy representative of a particular disorder would flow logically from this characteristic attitude.

This table, as well as relevant tables in Chapter 3, does not include the borderline and schizotypal personality disorders. These two disorders do not show a typical idiosyncratic set of beliefs and strategies, as do the rest. The borderline disorder, for example, may show a wide variety of typical beliefs and patterns of behavior that are characteristic of the broad range of personality disorders. This disorder is distinguished by characteristics more relevant to "ego deficit" than to a specific content of beliefs. Schizotypal disorder is characterized more precisely by peculiarities in thinking rather than an idiosyncratic content.

The first column in Table 2.1 lists the personality disorder; the second presents the corresponding attitude underlying the overt behavior; and the third column translates the idiosyncratic behavioral pattern of the personality disorder into a strategy. It follows logically that a dependent personality disorder characterized by clinging behavior would stem from a cognitive substrate based in part on the fear of abandonment; avoidant behavior from a fear of being hurt; and passive-

TABLE 2.1
Basic Beliefs and Strategies Associated with Traditional Personality Disorders

Personality Disorder	Basic Beliefs/Attitudes	Strategy (Overt Behavior)
Dependent	I am helpless.	Attachment
Avoidant	I may get hurt.	Avoidance
Passive-aggressive	I could be stepped on.	Resistance
Paranoid	People are potential adversaries.	Wariness
Narcissistic	I am special.	Self-aggrandizement
Histrionic	I need to impress.	Dramatics
Obsessive-compulsive	Errors are bad. I must not err.	Perfectionism
Antisocial	People are there to be taken.	Attack
Schizoid	I need plenty of space.	Isolation

aggressive patterns from a concern about being dominated. The clinical observations from which these formulations are derived will be discussed in subsequent chapters.

We suggest that such strategies may be analyzed in terms of their possible antecedents in our evolutionary past. The dramatic behavior of the histrionic personality, for example, may have its roots in the display rituals of nonhuman animals; the antisocial in predatory behavior; and the dependent in the attachment behavior observed throughout the animal kingdom (cf. Bowlby, 1969). By viewing people's maladaptive behavior in such terms, we can review it more objectively and reduce the tendency to stamp it with pejorative labels such as "neurotic" or "immature."

The concept that human behavior can be viewed productively from an evolutionary perspective was developed fully by McDougall (1921). He elaborated at length on the transformation of "biological instincts" into "sentiments." His writing paved the way for some of the current biosocial theorists such as Buss (1987), Scarr (1987), and Hogan (1987). Buss has discussed the different types of behaviors displayed by humans, such as competitiveness, dominance, and aggression, and traced their similarity to the behaviors of other primates. Particularly, he focuses on the role of sociability in humans and other primates.

Hogan postulates a phylogenetic heritage, according to which biologically programmed mechanisms emerge in developmental sequence. He views culture as providing the opportunity through which genetic patterns may be expressed. He regards the driving force of adult human activity, such as the investment in acceptance, status, power, and influence, as analogous to that observed in primates and other social mammals, as well as in humans. He emphasizes the importance of "fitness" in his evolutionary theory of human development.

Scarr specifically emphasizes the role of genetic endowment in determining personality. She states (1987, p. 62):

> Over development, different genes are turned on and off, creating maturational change in the organization of behavior as well as maturation changes in patterns of physical growth. Genetic differences among individuals are similarly responsible for determining what experiences people do and do not have in their environments.

Interaction between the Genetic and Interpersonal

The processes highlighted in the personality disorders can also be clarified by studies in the field of developmental psychology. Thus, the kind of clinging behavior, shyness, or rebelliousness observed in the growing child may persist through the developmental period (Kagan, 1989). We predict that these patterns persist into late adolescence and adulthood and may find continued expression in certain of the personality disorders, such as the dependent, avoidant, or passive-aggressive types.

Regardless of the ultimate origin of the genetically determined prototypes of human behavior, there is strong evidence that certain types of relatively stable temperaments and behavioral patterns are present at birth (Kagan, 1989). These innate characteristics are best viewed as "tendencies" that can become accentuated or diminished by experience. Furthermore, a continuous, mutually reinforcing cycle can be set up between an individual's innate patterns and patterns of other significant people.

For example, an individual with a large potential for care-eliciting behavior may evoke the care-producing behavior of other people, so that his or her innate patterns are maintained long beyond the period that such behavior is adaptive (Gilbert, 1989). For example, a patient, Sue, whom we will discuss in detail later, was described by her mother as having been more clinging and demanding of attention than her siblings practically from the time of birth. Her mother responded by being especially nurturant and protective. Throughout her developmental period and into adulthood, Sue succeeded in attaching herself to stronger people who would respond to her expressed desires for continuous affection and support. Another aspect was her belief that she was unlovable. She was picked on by older brothers and laid the foundation for a later belief: "I cannot maintain the affection of a man." Because of these beliefs, she tended to avoid situations in which she could be rejected.

Up until now we have been speaking of "innate tendencies" and "behavior" as though those characteristics can account for individual differences. Actually, our theory stipulates that integrated cognitive-affective-motivational programs decide an individual's behavior and differentiate him or her from other people. In older children and in adults, shyness, for example, is a derivative of an infrastructure of attitudes such as "it's risky to stick your neck out," a low threshold for anxiety in interpersonal situations, and a motivation to hang back with new acquaintances or strangers. These beliefs may become fixed as a result of repetition of traumatic experiences that seem to confirm them.

Despite the powerful combination of innate predispositions and environmental influences, some individuals manage to change their behavior and modify the underlying attitudes. Not all shy children grow into shy adults. The influences of key people and purposeful experiences in cultivating more assertive behaviors, for example, may shift a shy person toward greater assertiveness and gregariousness. As we shall see in subsequent chapters in this book, even strongly maladaptive patterns may be modified by focusing therapy on testing these attitudes and forming or strengthening more adaptive attitudes.

Our formulation up until now has addressed, very briefly, the question of how innate endowment can interact with environmental influences to produce quantitative distinctions in characteristic cognitive, affective, and behavior patterns to account for individual differences in personality. Each individual has a unique personality profile, consisting of varying degrees of probability of responding in a particular way to a particular degree to a particular situation.

A person entering into a group including unfamiliar people may think, "I'll look stupid," and will hang back. Another person may respond with the thought, "I can entertain them." A third may think, "They're unfriendly and may try to manipulate me," and will be on guard. When differing responses are characteristic of individuals, they reflect important structural differences represented in their basic beliefs (or schemas). The basic beliefs, respectively, would be: "I am vulnerable because I am inept in new situations," "I am entertaining to all people," and "I am vulnerable because people are unfriendly." Such variations are found in normal, well-adjusted people, and provide a distinctive coloring to their personalities. However, these kinds of beliefs are far more pronounced in the personality disorders; in the example above, they characterize the avoidant, histrionic, and paranoid disorders, respectively. Individuals with personality disorders show the same repetitive behaviors in many more situations than do other people. The typical maladaptive schemas in personality disorders are evoked across many or even most situations, have a compulsive quality, and are less easy to control or modify than are their counterparts in other people. Any situation that has a bearing on the content of their maladaptive schemas will activate those schemas in preference to more adaptive ones. For the most part, these patterns are self-defeating in terms of many of these individuals' important goals. In sum, relative to other people, their dysfunctional attitudes and behaviors are overgeneralized, inflexible, imperative, and resistant to change.

Origin of Dysfunctional Beliefs

Given that the personality patterns (cognition, affect, and motivation) of people with personality disorders deviate from those of other people, the question arises: How do these patterns develop? In order to address this question—although briefly—we need to return to the nature-nurture interaction. Individuals with a particularly strong sensitivity to rejection, abandonment, or thwarting may develop intense fears and beliefs about the catastrophic meaning of such events. A patient, predisposed by nature to overreact to the more commonplace kinds of rejection in childhood, may develop a negative self-image ("I am unlovable"). This image may be reinforced if the rejection is particularly powerful, or occurs at a particularly vulnerable time, or is repeated. With repetition, the belief becomes structuralized.

The patient mentioned earlier, Sue, developed an image of herself as inept and inadequate because she was always criticized by her siblings whenever she made a mistake. In order to protect herself as much as possible from pain and suffering, she tended to avoid situations in which this could occur. Her overgeneralized attitude was "If I allow myself to be vulnerable in any situation, I will get hurt."

Information Processing and Personality

The way people process data about themselves and others is influenced by their beliefs and the other components of their cognitive organization. When there is a disorder of some type—a symptom syndrome (Axis I)[1] or a personality disorder (Axis II)—the orderly utilization of these data becomes systematically biased in a dysfunctional way. This bias in interpretation and the consequent behavior is shaped by dysfunctional beliefs.

Let us return to the example of Sue, who had both dependent and avoidant personality disorders and felt great concern about being rejected. In a typical scenario, she heard noises coming from the next room, where her boyfriend, Tom, was attending to some chores. Her perception of the noise provided the raw data for her interpretation. This perception was embedded in a specific context—her knowledge that Tom was in the next room putting up some pictures. The fusion of the stimulus and the context constituted the basis for information.

Since raw sensory data, such as noises, have limited informational value in themselves, they need to be transformed into some kind of meaningful configuration. This integration into a coherent pattern is the product of structures (schemas) operating on the raw sensory data within the specific context. Sue's instant thought was "Tom is making a lot of noise." In most instances, people might conclude their information processing at this point, with the storing of this inference in short-term memory. But since Sue was rejection-prone, she was disposed to infer important meanings from such situations. Consequently, her information processing continued and she attached a personalized meaning: "Tom is making a lot of noise *because he's angry at me.*"

Such an attribution of causality is produced by a higher order of structuring that attaches significance to events. A component (schema) of this higher-level system would be her belief: "If an intimate of mine is

---

[1]Throughout this volume, we follow the revised third edition of the *Diagnostic and Statistical Manual of Mental Disorders* (American Psychiatric Association, 1987). The conventional syndromes, such as major depressive disorder or generalized anxiety disorder, manifested by strong subjective symptom complexes, are classified as Axis I, and personality disorders as Axis II.

noisy, it means he's angry at me." This type of belief represents a conditional schema ("If . . . then") in contrast to a basic schema ("I am unlovable").

In this case, it was possible that Tom was angry at Sue. However, because Sue's basic belief was very strong, she was apt to make this interpretation whenever an intimate like Tom was noisy, whether or not he actually was angry. Furthermore, prominent in the hierarchy of her beliefs was the formula "If an intimate is angry, he will reject me," and, at a more generalized level, "If people reject me, I will be all alone," and "Being alone will be devastating." Beliefs are organized according to a hierarchy that assigns progressively broader and more complex meanings at successive levels.

This example illustrates a relatively new concept in cognitive psychology—namely, that information processing is influenced by a "feedforward" mechanism (Mahoney, 1980). At the most basic level, Sue had a belief that she was unlovable. This belief was manifested by a disposition to assign a consistent meaning when a relevant event occurred (Beck, 1964, 1967). The belief took a conditional form: "If men reject me, it means I'm unlovable." For the most part, this belief was held in abeyance if she was not exposed to a situation in which personal rejection by a man could occur. This belief (or schema) would supersede other more reasonable beliefs (or schemas) that might be more appropriate, however, when a situation relevant to this belief occurred (Beck, 1967). If there were data that could conceivably indicate that Tom was rejecting her, then her attention became fixed on the notion of her unlovability. She molded information about Tom's behavior in a way to fit this schema, even though other formula might fit the data better—for example, "Loud hammering is a sound of exuberance." Since Sue's rejection schema was hypervalent, it was triggered in preference to other schemas, which seemed to be inhibited by the hypervalent schema.

Of course, Sue's psychological processes continued beyond her con clusion about being rejected. Whenever a schema of personal loss c threat is activated, there is a consequent activation of an "affectiv schema"; such a schema led in Sue's case to intense sadness. A negat interpretation of an event is linked to an affect that is congruent with

Although phenomena such as thoughts, feelings, and wishes may flash only briefly into our consciousness, the underlying structures responsible for these subjective experiences are relatively stable and durable. Furthermore, these structures are not in themselves conscious, although we can, through introspection, identify their content. Nonetheless, through conscious processes such as recognition, evaluation, and testing of their interpretations (basic techniques of cognitive therapy), people can modify the activity of the underlying structures and, in some instances, substantially change them.

Characteristics of Schemas

It would be desirable at this point to review the place of schemas in personality and to describe their characteristics.

The concept of "schema" has a relatively long history in 20th-century psychology. The term, which can be traced to Bartlett (1932, 1958) and Piaget (1926, 1936/1952), has been used to describe those structures that integrate and attach meaning to events. The content of the schemas may deal with personal relationships, such as attitudes toward the self or others, or impersonal categories (e.g., inanimate objects). These objects may be concrete (a chair) or abstract (my country).

Schemas have additional structural qualities, such as breadth (whether they are narrow, discrete, or broad), flexibility or rigidity (their capacity for modification), and density (their relative prominence in the cognitive organization). They also may be described in terms of their valence—the degree to which they are energized at a particular point in time. The level of activation (or valence) may vary from latent to hypervalent. When schemas are latent, they are not participating in information processing; when activated, they channel cognitive processing from the earliest to the final stages. The concept of schemas is similar to the formulation by George Kelly (1955) of "personal constructs."

In the field of psychopathology, the term "schema" has been applied to structures with a highly personalized idiosyncratic content that are activated during disorders such as depression, anxiety, panic attacks, and obsessions, and become prepotent. When hypervalent, these idiosyncratic schemas displace and probably inhibit other schemas that may be more adaptive or more appropriate for a given situation. They consequently introduce a systematic bias into information processing (Beck, 1964, 1967; Beck et al., 1985).

The typical schemas of the personality disorders resemble those that are activated in the symptom syndromes, but they are operative on a more continuous basis in information processing. In dependent personality disorder, the schema "I need help" will be activated whenever a problematic situation arises, whereas in depressed persons it will be prominent only during the depression. In personality disorders, the schemas are part of normal, everyday processing of information.

Personality may be conceptualized as a relatively stable organization composed of systems and modes. Systems of interlocking structures (schemas) are responsible for the sequence extending from the reception of a stimulus to the end point of a behavioral response. The integration of environmental stimuli and the formation of an adaptive response depend on these interlocking systems of specialized structures. Separate but related systems are involved in memory, cognition, affect, motivation, action, and control. The basic processing units, the schemas, are organized according to their functions (and also according to content). Different types of schemas have different functions. For example, the cognitive schemas are concerned with abstraction, interpretation, and recall; the affective schemas are responsible for the generation of feelings; the motivational schemas deal with wishes and desires; the instrumental schemas prepare for action; and the control schemas are involved with self-monitoring and inhibiting or directing actions.

Some subsystems composed of cognitive schemas are concerned with self-evaluation; others are concerned with evaluation of other people. Other such subsystems are designed to store memories, either episodic or semantic, and provide access to them. Still other subsystems function to prepare for forthcoming situations, and provide the basis for expectancies, predictions, and long-range forecasts.

When particular schemas are hypervalent, the threshold for activation of the constituent schemas is low: They are readily triggered by a remote or trivial stimulus. They are also "prepotent"; that is, they readily supersede more appropriate schemas or configurations in processing information (Beck, 1967). In fact, clinical observation suggests that schemas that are more appropriate to the actual stimulus situation are actively inhibited. Thus, in clinical depression, for example, the negative schemas are in ascendancy, resulting in a systematic negative bias in the interpretation and recall of experiences as well as in short-term and long-term predictions, whereas the positive schemas become less accessible. It is easy for depressed patients to see the negative aspects of an event, but difficult to see the positive. They can recall negative events much more readily than positive ones. They weigh the probabilities of undesirable outcomes more heavily than positive outcomes.

When a person goes into a clinical depression (or anxiety disorder), there is a pronounced "cognitive shift." In energy terms, the shift is away from normal cognitive processing to a predominance of processing by the negative schemas that constitute the depressive mode. The terms "cathexis" and "countercathexis" have been used by psychoanalytic writers to describe the deployment of energy to activate unconscious patterns (cathexis) or to inhibit them (countercathexis). Thus, in depression, the depressive mode is cathected; in generalized anxiety disorder, the danger mode is cathected; in panic disorder, the panic mode is cathected (Beck et al., 1985).

The Role of Affect in Personalities

Discussion of cognitive and behavioral patterns may seem to slight the subjective aspects of our emotional life—our feelings of sadness, joy, terror, and anger. We are aware that we are likely to feel sad when we are separated from a loved one or experience a loss of status, to be pleased when we receive expressions of affection or reach a goal, and to be angry when we are unfairly treated. How do these emotional—or affective—experiences fit into the scheme of personality organization? What is their relationship to basic cognitive structures and strategies?

According to our formulation, the affects related to pleasure and pain play a key role in the mobilization and maintenance of the crucial strategies. The survival and reproductive strategies appear to operate in part through their attachment to the pleasure–pain centers. As pointed out previously, activities that are directed toward survival and reproduction lead to pleasure when successfully consummated and to "pain" when thwarted. The appetitive urges related to eating and sex create tension when stimulated and gratification when fulfilled. Other emotional structures producing anxiety and sadness, respectively, reinforce the cognitive signals that alert us to danger or accentuate the perception that we have lost something of value (Beck et al., 1985). Thus, the emotional mechanisms serve to reinforce behaviors directed toward survival and bonding through the expectation and experience of various types of pleasure. At the same time, complementary mechanisms serve to dampen potentially self-defeating or dangerous actions through the arousal of anxiety and dysphoria (Beck et al., 1985). Other automatic mechanisms, those associated with the control system and involved in modulating behavior, will be discussed presently.

From Perception to Behavior

Among the basic components of the personality organization are sequences of different kinds of schemas that operate analogously to an assembly line. For purposes of simplification, these structures may be viewed as operating in a logical linear progression. For example, exposure to a dangerous stimulus activates the relevant "danger schema," which begins to process the information. In sequence, then, the affective, motivational, action, and control schemas are activated. The person interprets the situation as dangerous (cognitive schema), feels anxiety (affective schema), wants to get away (motivational schema), and becomes mobilized to run away (action or instrumental schema). If the person judges that running away is counterproductive, he or she may inhibit this impulse (control schema).

In Axis I disorders, a specific mode becomes hypervalent and leads, for example, to preoccupation with loss, danger, or combat. In the case of depression, a chain reaction is set up: cognitive → affective → motivational → motor. In personally meaningful situations, the interpretation and the affect feed into the "effector loop" or action system. For instance, after her interpreting a rejection, a sad expression would sweep across Sue's face. This process, which occurred automatically, might have served phylogenetically as a form of communication—as a distress signal, for example. Concomitantly, "action schemas" were triggered: Her own particular strategy for dealing with rejection was activated, and she experienced an impulse to go into the next room and ask Tom to reassure her. She was mobilized to act according to her stereotyped strategy. At this point, she might or might not yield to her impulse to run to Tom.

The Internal Control System

We know that people do not give in to every impulse, whether it is to laugh, cry, or hit somebody. Another system—the "control system"—is operative in conjunction with the action system to modulate, modify, or inhibit impulses. This system also is based on beliefs, many or most of which are realistic or adaptive. While the impulses constitute the "wants," these beliefs constitute the "dos" or the "do nots" (Beck, 1976). Examples of such beliefs are "It is wrong to hit somebody weaker or bigger than you." "You should defer to authorities." "You should not cry in public." These beliefs are automatically translated into commands: "Don't hit." "Do what you're told." "Don't cry." The prohibitions thus exercise a counterforce to the expression of the wishes. Sue had specific personal beliefs—here, in particular, "If I ask Tom too much for reassurance, he will get mad at me" (a prediction). Hence, she inhibited her wish to run into the next room and ask him whether he still loved her.

In therapy, it is important to identify those beliefs (e.g., "I'm unlikable") that shape the personal interpretations; those in the instrumental system that initiate action (e.g., "Ask him if he loves me"); and those in the control system that govern anticipations and consequently facilitate or inhibit action (Beck, 1976). The control or regulatory system plays a crucial—and often unrecognized—role in personality disorder, and consequently deserves further elaboration.

The control functions can be divided into those concerned with self-regulation—that is, inner-directed—and those involved with relating to the external, primarily social, environment.

The self-directed regulatory processes of particular relevance to the personality disorders are concerned with the way people communicate with themselves. The internal communications consist of self-monitoring, self-appraisal and self-evaluation, self-warnings, and self-instructions (Beck, 1976). When exaggerated or deficient, these processes become more conspicuous. People who monitor themselves too much tend to be inhibited—we see this in the avoidant personality, as well as in anxiety states—whereas too little inhibition facilitates impulsivity.

Self-appraisals and self-evaluations are important methods by which people can determine whether they are "on course." Whereas self-appraisal may simply represent observations of the self, self-evaluation implies making value judgments about the self: good-bad, worthwhile-worthless, lovable-unlovable. Negative self-evaluations are found overtly in depression, but may operate in a more subtle fashion in most of the personality disorders.

In normal functioning, this system of self-evaluations and self-directions operates more or less automatically. People may not be aware of these self-signals unless they specifically focus their attention on them. These cognitions may then be represented in a particular form labeled as "automatic thoughts" (Beck, 1967). As noted earlier, these automatic thoughts become hypervalent in depression, and they are expressed in notions such as "I am worthless" or "I am undesirable."

The self-evaluations and self-instructions appear to be derived from deeper structures: namely, the self-concepts or self-schemas. In fact, exaggerated negative (or positive) self-concepts may be the factors that move a person from being a "personality type" into having a "personality disorder." For example, the development of a rigid view of the self as helpless may move a person from experiencing normal dependency wishes in childhood to "pathological" dependency in adulthood. Similarly, an emphasis on systems, control, and order may predispose a person to a personality disorder in which the systems become the master instead of the tool—namely, obsessive-compulsive personality disorder.

In the course of maturation, we develop a medley of rules that provide the substrate for our self-evaluations and self-directions. These rules also form the basis for setting standards, expectations, and plans of action for ourselves. Thus, a woman who has a rule with a content such as "I must always do a perfect job" may be continuously evaluating her performance, praising herself for attaining a specific goal, and criticizing herself for falling short of the mark. Since the rule is rigid, she cannot operate according to a practical, more flexible rule, such as "The important thing is to get the job done, even if it isn't perfect." Similarly, people develop rules for interpersonal conduct: The dos and don'ts may lead to marked social inhibition, such as we find in avoidant personalities. These people also will feel anxious at even entertaining thoughts of violating a rule such as "Don't stick your neck out."

Transition to Axis II Disorder. We have already discussed the notion of the "cognitive shift." When people develop an Axis II disorder, they tend to process information selectively and in a dysfunctional way.

Changes in Personality Organization

Beliefs that the patient held prior to developing depression or anxiety become much more plausible and pervasive. Beliefs such as "If you aren't successful, you are worthless," or "A good parent should always satisfy her children's needs," become more absolute and extreme. Moreover, certain aspects of the negative self-image become accentuated and broadened, so that the patient begins to perseverate in the thought "I am worthless," or "I am a failure." Negative thoughts that were transient and less powerful prior to the depression become prepotent and dominate the patient's feelings and behavior (Beck, 1963).

Some of the more specific conditional beliefs become broadened to include a much broader spectrum of situations. The belief or attitude "If I don't have somebody to guide me in new situations, I won't be able to cope" becomes extended to "If somebody strong isn't accessible at all times, I will flounder." As the depression increases, these beliefs may be broadened to "Since I'm helpless, I need somebody to take charge and take care of me." The beliefs, thus, become more absolute and more extreme.

The ease with which these patients accept their dysfunctional beliefs during depression or anxiety disorders suggests that they have temporarily lost the ability to reality-test their dysfunctional interpretations. For example, a depressed patient who gets the idea "I am a despicable human being" seems to lack the capacity to look at this belief, to weigh contradictory evidence, and to reject the belief even though it is unsupported by evidence. The cognitive disability seems to rest on the temporary loss of access to and application of the rational modes of cognition by which we test our conclusions. Cognitive therapy aims explicitly to "re-energize" the reality-testing system. In the interim, the therapist serves as an "auxiliary reality tester" for the patient.

Depressed patients differ also in the way that they automatically process data. Experimental work (Gilson, 1983) indicates that they rapidly and efficiently incorporate negative information about themselves, but are blocked in processing positive information. Dysfunctional thinking becomes more prominent, and it becomes more difficult to apply the corrective, more rational cognitive processes.

As pointed out earlier, the way people utilize data about themselves and others is influenced by their personality organization. When there is a disorder of some type—a clinical (symptom) syndrome (Axis I) or personality disorder (Axis II)—the orderly processing of these data becomes systematically biased in a dysfunctional way. The bias in interpretation and the consequent behavior is shaped by the patients' dysfunctional beliefs and attitudes.

Changes in Cognitive Organization

Many of the basic beliefs that we find in Axis II disorders become apparent when the patient develops generalized anxiety disorder or major depressive disorder. For example, some of the more specific conditional beliefs become broadened to include a much broader spectrum of situations. The belief or attitude "If I don't have somebody to guide me in new situations, I won't be able to cope" becomes extended to "If somebody strong isn't accessible at all times, I will flounder." As the depression increases, these beliefs may be broadened to "Since I'm helpless, I need somebody to take charge and take care of me." The beliefs thus become more absolute and more extreme.

Further, beliefs that the patient held prior to developing depression (or other Axis I disorder) become much more plausible and pervasive: for example, "If you aren't successful, you are worthless," or "A good mother should always satisfy her children's needs." Also, beliefs about the self (the negative self-image) become accentuated and expanded to occupy the entire self-concept (Beck, 1967), so that the patient begins to perseverate in the thought "I am worthless" or "I am a failure." Negative beliefs or thoughts that were transient and less powerful prior to the depression become prepotent and dominate the patient's feelings and behavior.

The Cognitive Shift

The shift in the cognitive functions in the transition from a personality disorder into an anxiety state and then to depression is illustrated by Sue's experience. As far back as Sue could remember, she had questions about her acceptability. When her relationship with Tom was threatened, these sporadic self-doubts became transformed into continuous worry. As she moved into depression, her belief that she might be undesirable shifted to the belief that she *was* undesirable.

Similarly, Sue's attitude about the future shifted from a chronic uncertainty to a continuous apprehension, and ultimately—as she became more depressed—to hopelessness about her future. Further, she tended to catastrophize about the future when anxious, but accepted the catastrophe as though it had already occurred when she became depressed.

When she was not clinically depressed or anxious, Sue was capable of accessing some positive information about herself: She was a "good person," a considerate and loyal friend, and a conscientious worker. As she became anxious, she could credit herself with these positive qualities, but they seemed less relevant—perhaps because they apparently did not insure her a stable relationship with a man. With the onset of her depression, however, she had difficulty in acknowledging or even thinking of her positive assets; even when she was able to acknowledge them, she tended to disqualify them, since they were discordant with her self-image.

We have already noted that patients' dysfunctional beliefs become more extreme and rigid as the affective disorders develop. Prior to this, Sue would only occasionally endorse the belief "I can never be happy without a man." As her anxiety and depression developed, this belief moved to "I will always be unhappy if I don't have a man."

The progression of cognitive dysfunction from the personality disorder to anxiety and then to depression is illustrated by the gradual impairment of reality testing. When in an anxious state, Sue was able to view some of her catastrophic concerns with some objectivity. She could see that the thought "I will always be alone and unhappy if this relationship breaks up" was only a thought. When she became depressed, the idea that she would indeed always be unhappy was no longer simply a possibility; it was, for her, reality—a fact.

In therapy, the long-standing beliefs that form the matrix of the personality disorder are the most difficult to change. The beliefs that are associated only with the affective and anxiety disorders are subject to more rapid amelioration because they are less stable. Thus, it is possible for a person to shift from a depressive mode to a more normal mode with psychotherapy, chemotherapy, or simply with the passage of time. There is a shift in energy—or cathexis—from one mode to the other. When this shift takes place, the features of the "thinking disorder" in depression (systematic negative bias, overgeneralization, personalization) greatly diminish. The "normal" mode of the personality disorder is more stable than the depressive or anxious mode. Since the schemas in the normal mode are denser and more heavily represented in the cognitive organization, they are less amenable to change. These schemas give the normal personality and the personality disorder their distinctive characteristics. Within each personality disorder, certain beliefs and strategies are predominant and form a characteristic profile. These distinctive features will be discussed in the next chapter.

Chapter 3

Cognitive Profiles

One simple way to approach the personality disorders is to think of them in terms of certain vectors. Following the formulation of Horney (1950), we can view these interpersonal strategies in terms of how personality types relate to and act toward other people, how they use interpersonal space. Individuals may move or place themselves against, toward, away from, above, or under others. The dependent moves *toward* and often *below* (submissive, subservient). Another "type" *stays still* and may obstruct others: the passive-aggressive. The narcissists position themselves *above* others. The compulsive may move *above* in the interest of control. The schizoid moves *away*, and the avoidant moves closer and then *backs off*. The histrionic personalities use the space to *draw others* toward them.[1] As we shall see, these vectors may be regarded as the visible manifestations of specific interpersonal strategies associated with specific personality disorders.[2]

This simplified sketch presents one way of looking at personality types and personality disorders—in terms of the way individuals position themselves in relation to other people. Insofar as this patterning is regarded as dysfunctional, the diagnosis of personality disorder is deemed to be justified when it leads to (1) problems that produce suffering in the patient (e.g., avoidant personality) or (2) difficulties with other people or with society (e.g., antisocial personality). However, many people with a diagnosed personality disorder do not regard themselves as having such a disorder. Individuals generally regard their personality patterns as undesirable only when they lead to symptoms (e.g., depression or anxiety) or when they seem to interfere with important social or

---

[1] As noted in Chapter 2, the borderline and schizotypal disorders are not included in our differentiation of strategies because these two disorders are not characterized by a specific thought content.

[2] Dr. Yutaka Ono (personal communication, 1988) independently arrived at a similar formulation.

occupational aspirations (as in the case of the dependent, avoidant, or passive-aggressive personalities).

When confronted with situations that interfere with the operation of their idiosyncratic strategy—for example, when a dependent person is separated from or threatened with separation from a significant other, or the obsessive-compulsive is thrown into an unmanageable situation— then the person may develop symptoms of depression or anxiety. Other people with personality disorders may regard their own patterns as perfectly normal and satisfactory for them, but acquire a diagnostic label because their behavior is viewed negatively by other people, as in the case of narcissistic, schizoid, or antisocial personalities.

The observable behaviors (or strategies), however, are only one aspect of the personality disorders. Each disorder is characterized not only by dysfunctional or asocial behavior, but by a composite of beliefs and attitudes, affect, and strategies. It is possible to provide a distinctive profile of each of the disorders based on their typical cognitive, affective, and behavioral features. While this typology is presented in pure form, it should be kept in mind that specific individuals may show features of more than one personality type.

Overdeveloped and Underdeveloped Patterns

Individuals with a personality disorder tend to show certain patterns of behavior that are hypertrophied, or overdeveloped, and other patterns that are underdeveloped. The obsessive-compulsive disorder, for example, may be characterized by an excessive emphasis on control, responsibility, and systematization, and a relative deficiency in spontaneity and playfulness. As illustrated in Table 3.1, the other personality disorders similarly show a heavy weighting of some patterns and a light representation of others. The deficient features are frequently the counterparts of the strong features. It is as though when one interpersonal strategy is overdeveloped, the balancing strategy fails to develop properly. One can speculate that as a child becomes overinvested in a predominant type of behavior, it overshadows and perhaps weakens the development of other adaptive behaviors.

As will be shown in the subsequent chapters on each of the personality disorders, certain overdeveloped strategies may be a derivative from or compensation for a particular type of self-concept, and a response to particular developmental experiences. Also, as indicated in Chapter 2, genetic predisposition may favor the development of a particular type of pattern in preference to other possible patterns. Some children, for example, appear to be oriented toward entertaining, while others appear shy and inhibited from the early stages of development. Thus,

TABLE 3.1
Typical Overdeveloped and Underdeveloped Strategies

Personality Disorder	Overdeveloped	Underdeveloped
Obsessive-compulsive	Control Responsibility Systematization	Spontaneity Playfulness
Dependent	Help seeking Clinging	Self-sufficiency Mobility
Passive-aggressive	Autonomy Resistance Passivity Sabotage	Intimacy Assertiveness Activity Cooperativeness
Paranoid	Vigilance Mistrust Suspiciousness	Serenity Trust Acceptance
Narcissistic	Self-aggrandizement Competitiveness	Sharing Group identification
Antisocial	Combativeness Exploitativeness Predation	Empathy Reciprocity Social sensitivity
Schizoid	Autonomy Isolation	Intimacy Reciprocity
Avoidant	Social vulnerability Avoidance Inhibition	Self-assertion Gregariousness
Histrionic	Exhibitionism Expressiveness Impressionism	Reflectiveness Control Systematization

the narcissistic personality may develop as an individual fights fiercely to overcome a deep sense of unworthiness. The obsessive-compulsive personality may develop in response to chaotic conditions in childhood—as a way of bringing order to a disordered environment. A paranoid personality may be formed in response to early experiences of betrayal or deception; a passive-aggressive personality may develop in response to manipulation by others. The dependent personality often represents a fixation on a close attachment that, for a variety of reasons, may have been reinforced by family members rather than normally attenuated over the developmental period. Similarly, a histrionic personality may be evoked from experiences of being rewarded for successful exhibitionism—for example, entertaining others to get approval and affection.

It should be noted that different pathways may lead to personality disorders. Narcissistic, obsessive-compulsive, paranoid, and even anti-social personality disorder, for example, may develop either as a compensation or a fear (i.e., as a result of a sense of chaos, manipulation, or victimization) as a result of reinforcement of the relevant strategies by significant others; or through both methods.

One cannot overlook the importance of identification with other family members. Some individuals seem to adopt certain dysfunctional patterns of their parents or siblings and build on them as they grow older. In other individuals, personality disorders seem to evolve from the inheritance of a strong predisposition. Thus, recent research by Kagan (1989) indicates that a shyness exhibited early in life tends to persist. It is possible that an innate disposition to shyness could be so reinforced by subsequent experience that, instead of simply being nonassertive, the individual develops into an avoidant personality.

It is useful to analyze the psychological characteristics of individuals with personality disorders in terms of their views of themselves and others, their basic beliefs, their basic strategies, and their main affects. In this way, therapists can obtain specific cognitive-behavioral-emotive profiles that help them to understand each disorder and that facilitate treatment.

Specific Cognitive Profiles

Avoidant Personality Disorder

People diagnosed as having avoidant personality disorder, using the DSM-III-R criteria, have the following key conflict: They would like to be close to others and to live up to their intellectual and vocational potential, but they are afraid of being hurt, rejected, and unsuccessful. Their strategy (in contrast to the dependent) is to back off—or avoid getting involved in the first place.

View of self: They see themselves as socially inept and incompetent in academic or work situations.

View of others: They see others as potentially critical, uninterested, and demeaning.

Beliefs: Not infrequently, persons with this disorder have these *core* beliefs: "I am no good . . . worthless . . . unlovable. I cannot tolerate unpleasant feelings." These beliefs feed into the next (higher) level of *conditional* beliefs: "If people got close to me, they would discover the 'real me' and would reject me—that would be intolerable." Or, "If I undertake something new and don't succeed, it would be devastating."

The next level, which dictates their behavior, consists of *instrumental* or self-instructional beliefs such as "It is best to stay clear of risky involvement," "I should avoid unpleasant situations at all costs," "If I feel or think of something unpleasant, I should try to wipe it out by distracting myself or taking a fix (drink, drug, etc.)."

Threats: The main threats are of being discovered to be a "fraud," being put down, demeaned, or rejected.

Strategy: Their main strategy is to avoid situations in which they could be evaluated. Thus, they tend to hang back on the fringes of social groups and avoid attracting attention to themselves. In work situations, they tend to avoid taking on new responsibilities or seeking advancement because of their fear of failure and of subsequent reprisals from others.

Affect: The main affect is dysphoria, a combination of anxiety and sadness, related to their deficits in obtaining the pleasures they would like to receive from close relationships and the sense of mastery from accomplishment. They experience anxiety, related to their fear of sticking their necks out in social or work situations.

Their low tolerance for dysphoria prevents them from developing methods for overcoming their shyness and asserting themselves more effectively. Since they are introspective and monitor feelings continually, they are acutely sensitive to their feelings of sadness and anxiety. Ironically, despite their hyperawareness of painful feelings, they shy away from identifying unpleasant thoughts—a tendency that fits in with their major strategy and is labeled "cognitive avoidance."

Their low tolerance for unpleasant feelings and their sensitivity to failure and rejection pervade all of their actions. Unlike the dependent person, who handles fear of failure by leaning on others, the avoidant person simply lowers expectations and stays clear of any involvement that incurs a risk of failure or rejection.

Dependent Personality Disorder

Individuals with dependent personality disorder have a picture of themselves as helpless, and therefore try to attach themselves to some stronger figure who will provide the resources for their survival and happiness.

Self-view: They perceive themselves as needy, weak, helpless, and incompetent.

View of others: They see the strong "caretaker" in an idealized way: as nurturant, supportive, and competent. In contrast to the avoidant personality, who stays clear of "entangling relationships" and consequently does not gain social support, the dependent personality can function quite well as long as a strong figure is accessible.

Beliefs: These patients believe that "I need other people—specifically, a strong person—in order to survive." Further, they believe that their happiness depends upon having such a figure available. They believe that they need a steady, uninterrupted flow of support and encouragement. As one dependent patient put it, "I cannot live without a man." Or, "I can never be happy unless I am loved."

In terms of the hierarchy of beliefs, their *core* belief is likely to be "I am completely helpless," or "I am all alone." Their *conditional* beliefs are "I can function only if I have access to somebody competent," "If I am abandoned, I will die," "If I am not loved, I will always be unhappy." The *instrumental* level consists of imperatives such as "Don't offend the caretaker," "Stay close," "Cultivate as intimate a relationship as possible," "Be subservient in order to bind him or her."

Threat: The main threat or trauma is concerned with rejection or abandonment.

Strategy: Their main strategy is to cultivate a dependent relationship. They will frequently do this by subordinating themselves to a "strong" figure and trying to placate or please this person.

Affect: Their main affect is anxiety—the concern over possible disruption of the dependent relationship. They periodically experience heightened anxiety when they perceive that the relationship actually is strained. If the figure they depend on is removed, they may sink into a depression. On the other hand, they experience gratification or euphoria when their dependent wishes are granted.

Passive-Aggressive Personality Disorder

Individuals with passive-aggressive personality disorder have an oppositional style, which belies the fact that they do want to get recognition and support from authority figures. The chief problem is a conflict between their desire to get the benefits conferred by authorities on the one hand, and their desire to maintain their autonomy on the other. Consequently, they try to maintain the relationship by being passive and submissive, but as they sense a loss of autonomy, they subvert the authorities.

Self-view: They may perceive themselves as self-sufficient but vulnerable to encroachment by others. (They are, however, drawn to strong figures and organizations because they crave social approval and support. Hence, they are frequently in a conflict between their desire for attachment and their fear of encroachment.)

View of others: They see others—specifically, the authority figures—as intrusive, demanding, interfering, controlling, and dominating, but at the same time capable of being approving, accepting, and caring.

Beliefs: Their *core* beliefs have to do with notions such as "Being controlled by others is intolerable," or "I have to do things my own way," or "I deserve approval because of all I have done."

Their conflicts are expressed in beliefs such as "I need authority to nurture and support me" versus "I need to protect my identity." (The same kind of conflicts are often expressed by borderline patients.) The *conditional* belief is expressed in terms such as "If I follow the rules, I lose my freedom of action." Their *instrumental* beliefs revolve around postponing action that is expected by an authority, or complying superficially but not substantively.

Threat: The main threat or fears revolve around loss of approval and abridgement of autonomy.

Strategy: Their main strategy is to fortify their autonomy through devious opposition to the authority figures while ostensibly courting the favor of the authorities. They try to evade or circumvent the rules in a spirit of covert defiance. They are often subversive in the sense of not getting work done on time, not attending classes, and so on—ultimately self-defeating behavior. Yet, on the surface, because of their need for approval, they may seem to be compliant and cultivate the good will of the authorities. They often have a very strong passive streak. They tend to follow the line of least resistance; they often avoid competitive situations, and are interested more in solitary pursuits.

Affect: Their main affect is unexpressed anger, which is associated with rebellion against an authority's rules. This affect, which is conscious, alternates with anxiety when they anticipate reprisals and are threatened with cutting off of "supplies."

Obsessive-Compulsive Personality Disorder

The key words for obsessive-compulsives are "control" and "should." These individuals make a virtue of justifying the means to achieve the end to such an extent that the means becomes an end in itself. To them, "orderliness is godliness."

View of self: They see themselves as responsible for themselves and others. They believe they have to depend on themselves to see that things get done. They are accountable to their own perfectionistic conscience. They are driven by the "shoulds." Many of the people with this disorder have a core image of themselves as inept or helpless. The deep concern about being helpless is linked to a fear of being overwhelmed, unable to function. In these cases, their overemphasis on systems is a compensation for their perception of defectiveness and helplessness.

View of others: They perceive others as too casual, often irresponsible, self-indulgent, or incompetent. They liberally apply the "shoulds" to others in an attempt to shore up their own weaknesses.

Beliefs: In the serious obsessive-compulsive disorder, the *core* beliefs are "I could be overwhelmed," "I am basically disorganized or disoriented," "I need order, systems, and rules in order to survive." Their *conditional* beliefs are "If I don't have systems, everything will fall apart," "Any flaw or defect in performance will produce a landslide," "If I or others don't perform at the highest standards, we will fail," "If I fail in this, I am a failure as a person."

Their *instrumental* beliefs are imperative: "I must be in control," "I must do virtually anything just right," "I know what's best," "You have to do it my way," "Details are crucial," "People *should* do better and try harder," "I have to push myself (and others) all the time," "People should be criticized in order to prevent future mistakes." Frequent automatic thoughts tinged with criticalness are "Why can't they do it right?" or "Why do I always slip up?"

Threats: The main threats are flaws, mistakes, disorganization, or imperfections. They tend to "catastrophize" that "things will get out of control" or that they "won't be able to get things done."

Strategy: Their strategy revolves around a system of rules, standards, and "shoulds." In applying rules they evaluate and score other people's performance as well as their own. In order to reach their goals, they try to exert maximum control over their own behavior and that of others involved in carrying out their goals. They attempt to assert control over their own behavior by "shoulds" and self-reproaches, and over other people's behavior through being overly directing, or disapproving and punishing. This instrumental behavior may amount to coercion and slave driving.

Affect: Because of their perfectionistic standards, these individuals are particularly prone to regrets, disappointment, and chastisement of themselves and others. The affective response to their anticipation of substandard performance is anxiety. When serious "failure" does occur, they may become depressed.

Paranoid Personality Disorder

The key word for paranoid personality disorder is "mistrust." It is conceivable that, under certain circumstances, wariness, looking for hidden motives, or not trusting others may be adaptive—even life-saving—but the paranoid personality adopts this stance in most or all situations, including the most benign.

View of self: The paranoid personalities see themselves as righteous and mistreated by others.

View of others: They see other people essentially as devious, deceptive, treacherous, and covertly manipulative. They believe that other people want to interfere with them, put them down, discriminate against them—but all in a hidden or secret way under the guise of innocence. Paranoids may think that others form secret coalitions against them.

Beliefs: The *core* beliefs consist of notions such as "I am vulnerable to other people," "Other people cannot be trusted," "Their motives are suspect," "They are deceptive," "They're out to undermine me or depreciate me." The *conditional* beliefs are "If I am not careful, people will manipulate, abuse, or take advantage of me," "If people act friendly, they are trying to use me," "If people seem distant, it proves they are unfriendly." The *instrumental* (or self-instructional) beliefs are "Be on guard," "Don't trust anybody," "Look for hidden motives," "Don't get taken in."

Threats: The main fears are concerned with being secretly manipulated, controlled, demeaned, or discriminated against.

Strategies: With this notion that other people are against them, the paranoid personalities are driven to be hypervigilant and always on guard. They are wary, suspicious, and looking all the time for cues that will betray the "hidden motives" of their "adversaries." At times, they may confront these "adversaries" with allegations about being wronged, and consequently provoke the kind of hostility that they believed already existed.

Affects: The main affect is anger over the presumed abuse. Some paranoid personalities, however, may additionally experience constant anxiety over the perceived threats. This painful anxiety is often the prod for their seeking therapy.

Antisocial Personality Disorder

The antisocial personalities may assume a variety of forms: the expression of antisocial behavior may vary considerably (see DSM-III-R; APA, 1987) from conniving, manipulating, and exploiting to direct attack.

View of self: In general, these personalities view themselves as loners, autonomous, and strong. Some of them see themselves as having been abused and mistreated by society, and therefore justify victimizing others because they believe that they have been victimized. Others may simply cast themselves in the predatory role in a "dog-eat-dog" world in which breaking the rules of society is normal and even desirable.

View of others: They see other people as either exploitative and thus deserving of being exploited in retaliation, or as weak and vulnerable and thus deserving of being preyed upon.

Beliefs: The *core* beliefs are "I need to look out for myself," "I need to be the aggressor or I will be the victim." The antisocial personality also believes that "Other people are patsies or wimps," or "Others are exploitative, and therefore I'm entitled to exploit them back." This person believes that he or she is entitled to break rules—rules are arbitrary and designed to protect the "haves" against the "have nots." This view is in contrast to that of people with narcissistic personalities, who believe that they are such special, unique individuals that they are above the rules—a prerogative that they believe everybody should easily recognize and respect.

The *conditional* belief is "If I don't push others around (or manipulate, exploit, or attack them), I will never get what I deserve." The *instrumental* or imperative beliefs are "Get the other guy before he gets you," "It's your turn now," "Take it, you deserve it."

Strategy: The main strategies fall into two classes. The overt antisocial personality will openly attack, rob, and defraud others. The more subtle type—the "con artist"—seeks to inveigle others and, through shrewd, subtle manipulations, to exploit or defraud them.

Affect: When a particular affect is present, it is essentially anger—over the injustice that other people have possessions that they (the antisocial personalities) deserve.

Narcissistic Personality Disorder

The key word for narcissists is "self-aggrandizement."

View of self: The narcissistic personalities view themselves as special and unique—almost as princes or princesses. They believe that they have a special status that places them above the mass of ordinary people. They consider themselves superior and entitled to special favors and favorable treatment; they are above the rules that govern other people.

View of others: While they may regard other people as inferior, they do not do this in the same sense as do the antisocial personalities. They simply see themselves as prestigious and as elevated above the average person; they see others as their vassals or constituents. They seek admiration from others primarily to document their own grandiosity and preserve their superior status.

Beliefs: The *core* narcissistic beliefs are as follows: "Since I am special, I deserve special dispensations, privileges, and prerogatives," "I'm superior to others and they should acknowledge this," "I'm above the rules."

The *conditional* beliefs are "If others don't recognize my special status, they should be punished," "If I am to maintain my superior status, I should expect others' subservience." The *instrumental* belief is "Strive at all times to insist upon or demonstrate your superiority."

Strategy: Their main strategies consist of doing whatever they can to reinforce their superior status and to expand their personal domain.

Thus, they may seek glory, wealth, position, power, and prestige as a way of continuously reinforcing their "superior" image. They tend to be highly competitive with others who claim an equally high status. They also will resort to manipulative strategies in order to gain their ends.

Since they are above the rules that govern ordinary humankind, "anything and everything goes" for them. Unlike the antisocial personality, they do not have a cynical view of the rules of human conduct; they simply consider themselves exempt from them. They do regard themselves as part of society, but at the very top stratum.

Affect: Their main affect is anger when other people do not accord them the admiration or respect that they believe they are entitled to, or otherwise thwart them in some way. They are prone to becoming depressed, however, if their strategies are foiled. For example, psychotherapists have treated several "inside traders" on Wall Street who became depressed after their manipulations were discovered and they were publicly disgraced. They believed that by tumbling from their high position, they had lost everything.

Histrionic Personality Disorder

The key word for histrionic personalities is "expressiveness," which embodies the tendency to emotionalize or romanticize all situations and to try to impress and captivate others.

View of self: They view themselves as glamorous, impressive, and deserving of attention.

View of others: They view others favorably as long as they can elicit their attention, amusement, and affection. They try to form strong alliances with others, but with the proviso that they be at the center of the group and that others play the role of attentive audience. In contrast to narcissistic personalities, they are very much involved in their minute-to-minute interactions with other people, and their self-esteem depends on their receiving continuous expressions of appreciation.

Beliefs: The person with a histrionic disorder often has *core* beliefs such as "I am basically unattractive," or "I need other people to admire me in order to be happy." Among the compensatory beliefs are "I am very lovable, entertaining, and interesting," "I am entitled to admiration," "People are there to admire me and do my bidding," "They have no right to deny me my just deserts."

Conditional beliefs include the following: "Unless I captivate people, I am nothing," "If I can't entertain people, they will abandon me," "If people don't respond, they are rotten," "If I can't captivate people, I am helpless."

Histrionic people tend to be global and impressionistic in their thinking, a factor that is reflected in their *instrumental* belief, "I can go by my feelings." If the obsessive-compulsives are guided by rationally or intellectually derived systems, the histrionics are guided primarily by feelings. Histrionics who feel angry may use this as sufficient justification for punishing another person. If they feel affection, they consider it a justification for pouring on affection (even though they may switch over to another type of expression a few minutes later). If they feel sad, this is sufficient rationale for them to cry. They tend to dramatize their ways of communicating their sense of frustration or despair, as in the "histrionic suicide attempt." These general patterns are reflected in imperatives such as "Express your feelings," "Be entertaining," "Show people that they have hurt you."

Strategies: They use dramatics and demonstrativeness to bind people to them. When they don't get their own way, however, they believe they are being treated unfairly, and they try to coerce compliance or get even by having temper tantrums. Their tolerance for frustration is low, and they may resort to crying, assaultive behavior, and suicidal gestures to get their way or to "punish" the offender. Their suicidal attempts may be serious and potentially fatal, even though they are impulsive.

Affect: The most prominent affect is gaiety, often mixed with mirth and other high spirits when they are successfully engaging other people. They generally experience an undercurrent of anxiety, however, that reflects their fear of rejection. When thwarted, their affect can change rapidly to anger or sadness.

Schizoid Personality Disorder

The key word in schizoid personality disorder is "isolation." These persons are the embodiment of the autonomous personality. They are willing to sacrifice intimacy in order to preserve their detachment and autonomy.

View of self: They see themselves as self-sufficient and as loners. They prize mobility, independence, and solitary pursuits. They would rather make decisions by themselves and carry out solo activities than be involved in a group.

View of others: They see other people as intrusive. They view closeness as opening opportunities for other people to fence them in.

Beliefs: Their *core* beliefs consist of notions such as "I am basically alone," "Close relationships with other people are unrewarding and messy," "I can do things better if I'm not encumbered by other people" "Close relationships are undesirable because they interfere with my freedom of action."

The *conditional* beliefs are "If I get too close to people, they will get their hooks into me," "I can't be happy unless I have complete mobility." The *instrumental* beliefs are "Don't get too close," "Keep your distance," "Don't get involved."

Strategy: Their main interpersonal strategy is to keep their distance from other people, insofar as this is feasible. They may get together with others for specific reasons, such as vocational activities or sex, but otherwise prefer to distance themselves. They are readily threatened by any actions that represent encroachment.

Affect: As long as schizoids keep their distance, they may experience a low level of sadness. If they are forced into a close encounter, they may become very anxious. In contrast to histrionic personalities, they are not inclined to show their feelings either verbally or through facial expressions, and consequently they convey the impression that they do not have strong feelings.

Thinking Styles

The personality disorders may also be characterized by their cognitive styles, which may be a reflection of the patients' behavioral strategies. These cognitive styles deal with the *manner* in which people process information, as opposed to the specific *content* of the processing. Several of the personality types have such distinctive cognitive styles that it is worthwhile to describe them.

People with histrionic personality disorder use the strategy of "display" to attract people and satisfy their own desires for support and closeness. When the strategy of impressing or entertaining people is unsuccessful, they show an open display of "dramatics" (weeping, rage, etc.) to punish the offenders and coerce them to comply. The processing of information shows the same global, impressionist quality. These individuals "miss the trees for the forest." They make stereotyped, broad, global interpretations of a situation at the expense of crucial details. They are likely to respond to their gestalt of the situation, based on inadequate information.

People with histrionic disorder are also prone to attach a pattern to a situation even though it doesn't fit. For example, if other people seem unresponsive to their entertaining, they judge the situation in its entirety—"They are rejecting me"—rather than seeing the specifics that might account for other people's behavior. Thus, they are oblivious to the fact that the other people may be fatigued, bored, or preoccupied with other things. This impressionistic quality is also evident in the way they put a gloss on every experience: Events are romanticized into high drama or grand tragedy. Finally, since they are more attuned to the subjective rather than the objective measuring of events, they tend to use their feelings as the ultimate guide as to their interpretation. Thus, if they feel bad in an encounter with another person, this means the other person is bad. If they feel euphoric, then the other person is wonderful.

People with obsessive-compulsive personality, in marked contrast to histrionics, "miss the forest for the trees." These persons focus so much on details that they miss the overall pattern; for example, a person with this disorder may decide on the basis of a few flaws in another person's performance that the other person has failed, even though the flaws may have simply represented some variations in an overall successful performance. Further, in contrast to histrionics, people with obsessive-compulsive personality disorder tend to minimize subjective experiences. Thus, they deprive themselves of some of the richness of life and of access to feelings as a source of information that enhances the significance of important events.

The thinking style of people with avoidant personality disorder differs from that of the above-described individuals. Just as they tend to avoid situations that will make them feel bad, they also employ a mechanism of "internal avoidance." As soon as they start to have an unpleasant feeling, they try to damp it down by diverting their attention to something else or by taking a quick fix, such as having a drink. They also avoid thoughts that might produce unpleasant feelings.

The cognitive styles of the other personality disorders are not as sharply delineated as those of the disorders just described.

Summary of Characteristics

Table 3.2 lists the characteristics of nine personality disorders. The first two columns list the view of the self and view of others; the next column gives the specific beliefs; and the last column lists the specific strategies. It can be seen from this table how the view of self and others and the beliefs lead into the specific strategy. Although the strategy, or behavior, provides the basis for making the diagnosis of personality disorder, it is important for a full understanding of the nature of the disorder to clarify the self-concept, concept of others, and beliefs. These cognitive components are involved in information processing and, when activated, trigger the relevant strategy.

An avoidant person, Jill, for example, *viewed herself* as socially inept and was vulnerable, therefore, to depreciation and rejection. Her *view of others* as critical and demeaning complemented this sense of vulnerability. Her *belief* that rejection was terrible added enormous valence to her sensitivity and tended to blow up the significance of any anticipated rejection or actual rejection. In fact, this particular belief tended to screen out positive feedback. Her anticipation of rejection made her feel

TABLE 3.2
Profile of Characteristics of Personality Disorders

Personality Disorder	View of Self	View of Others	Main Beliefs	Main Strategy
Avoidant	Vulnerable to depreciation, rejection Socially inept Incompetent	Critical Demeaning Superior	It's terrible to be rejected, put down If people *know* the real me, they will reject me Can't tolerate unpleasant feelings	Avoid evaluative situations Avoid unpleasant feelings or thoughts
Dependent	Needy Weak Helpless Incompetent	(Idealized) Nurturant Supportive Competent	Need people to survive, be happy Need for steady flow of support, encouragement	Cultivate dependent relationships
Passive-aggressive	Self-sufficient Vulnerable to control, interference	Intrusive Demanding Interfering Controlling Dominating	Others interfere with my freedom of action Control by others is intolerable Have to do things my own way	Passive resistance Surface submissiveness Evade, circumvent rules
Obsessive-compulsive	Responsible Accountable Fastidious Competent	Irresponsible Casual Incompetent Self-indulgent	I know what's best Details are crucial People *should* do better, try harder	Appy rules Perfectionism Evaluate, control "Shoulds," criticize, punish

Paranoid	Righteous Innocent, noble Vulnerable	Interfering Malicious Discriminatory Abusive motives	Motives are suspect Be on guard Don't trust	Wary Look for hidden motives Accuse Counterattack
Antisocial	A loner Autonomous Strong	Vulnerable Exploitative	Entitled to *break* rules Others are patsies, wimps Others are exploitative	Attack, rob Deceive, manipulate
Narcisstic	Special, unique Deserve special rules; superior Above the rules	Inferior Admirers	Since I'm special, I *deserve* special rules I'm above the rules I'm better than others	Use others Transcend rules Manipulative Competitive
Histrionic	Glamorous Impressive	Seducible Receptive Admirers	People are there to serve or admire me They have no right to deny me my just deserts I can go by my feeling	Use dramatics, charm; temper tantrums, crying; suicide gestures
Schizoid	Self-sufficient Loner	Intrusive	Others are unrewarding Relationships are messy, undesir- able	Stay away

chronically anxious around people, and her magnification of any signs of nonacceptance made her feel bad.

Two other beliefs contributed to her hanging back from involvements: namely, that if she got close to people, they would recognize her as inferior and inadequate; and that she could not tolerate unpleasant feelings, which led her to try to avoid their arousal. Hence, as a result of the pressure of her various beliefs and attitudes, she was propelled toward the only strategy that would accommodate her serious concerns—namely, to avoid any situations in which she could be evaluated. In addition, because of her low tolerance for unpleasant feelings or thoughts, she chronically turned off any thoughts that could evoke unpleasant feelings. In therapy she had difficulty in making decisions, identifying negative automatic thoughts, or examining her basic beliefs, because these would lead to such feelings. The basic flow is illustrated in Figure 3.1.

A similar flow chart can be constructed for each of the other personality disorders. The chart should incorporate the distinctive beliefs and the resultant behavior patterns. The person with dependent personality disorder, for example, differs from one with avoidant personality in that the former tends to idolize other potentially nurturant persons and believes that they will help and support him or her. Thus, he or she is drawn to people. The passive-aggressive wants approval but cannot tolerate any semblance of control, so he tends to thwart others' expectations of him or her, and thus defeats himself or herself. The obsessive-compulsive idealizes order and systems and is driven to control others (as well as himself or herself). The paranoid is extremely vigilant

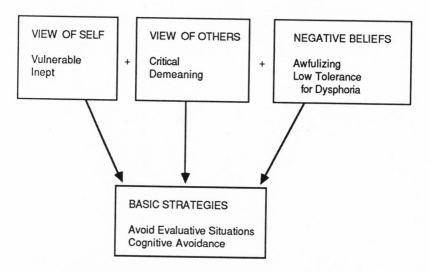

FIGURE 3.1   Relation of views and beliefs to basic strategies.

of other people because of a basic mistrust and suspiciousness, and is inclined to accuse them (either overtly or mentally) of discrimination. The antisocial personality asserts that he or she is entitled to manipulate or abuse others, because of a belief that he or she has been wronged or that others are wimps, or that we live in a "dog-eat-dog" society. The narcissist sees himself or herself as above ordinary mortals and seeks glory through any methods that can safely be used. Histrionic individuals try to draw others to them by being entertaining, but also through temper tantrums and dramatics to coerce closeness when their charm is ineffective. The schizoid, with the belief that relationships are unrewarding, keeps his or her distance from other people.

The understanding of the typical beliefs and strategies of each personality disorder provides a road map for therapists. They should keep in mind, however, that most individuals with a specific personality disorder will manifest attitudes and behaviors that overlap other disorders. Consequently, it is important for therapists to expose these variations in order to make a complete evaluation.

Chapter 4
General Principles of Cognitive Therapy

Most patients who have recovered from their depression, for example, no longer blame themselves for every mishap that occurs, stop making negative predictions about the future, and are less prone to think that they are inferior or inadequate. Some patients, however, continue to show these characteristics and acknowledge that they have "always" thought this way. Nonetheless, they are no longer clinically depressed.

The patients return to their premorbid cognitive mode after the Axis I disorder subsides. The Axis II mode differs from the Axis I mode in a variety of ways. The frequency and intensity of dysfunctional automatic thoughts observed during the acute disorder level off when the patients return to their regular level of cognitive functioning. Although the patients may readily identify and test their dysfunctional automatic thoughts during their "normal neurotic period," these exaggerated or distorted interpretations and the associated disruptive affect continue to occur in specific situations. A highly intelligent and competent woman, for example, would automatically have the thought "I can't do it" whenever she was offered a position requiring a higher level of intellectual functioning.

The most plausible explanation for the difference between Axis I and the personality disorders is that the extreme faulty beliefs and interpretations characteristic of the symptomatic disorders are relatively plastic—and, indeed, become more moderate as the depression subsides even without any therapeutic intervention. However, the more persistent dysfunctional beliefs of the personality disorder are "structuralized"; that is, they are built into the "normal" cognitive organization. Hence, considerably more time and effort are required to produce the kind of structural change necessary to change a personality disorder then to change the dysfunctional thinking of, say, the affective disorders.

The therapist generally uses "standard" cognitive therapy techniques to relieve acute Axis I episodes (American Psychiatric Association, 1987) such as depression (Beck, Rush, Shaw, & Emery, 1979) or generalized anxiety disorder (GAD; Beck & Emery with Greenberg, 1985). This approach is effective in dealing with the dysfunctional automatic thoughts and helps to produce the cognitive shift from the depressive (or GAD) mode of processing back to the "normal" mode. The testing of automatic thoughts and beliefs during the depressive or anxious episode is good practice for dealing with these cognitive processes during the relatively quiescent period. The patients observed during this period have been described in earlier psychiatric and colloquial terminology as "neurotic." The characteristics of the "neurotic personality" have generally been described in terms of labels such as "immature" or "childish": emotional lability, exaggerated responses to rejection or failure, unrealistically low or high concept of self, and—above all—intense egocentricity.

The dysfunctional beliefs are still operative because they form the substrate for patients' orientation to reality. Since people rely on their beliefs to interpret events and to guide them in selecting methods to cope with these events, they cannot relinquish these beliefs until they have incorporated new adaptive beliefs and strategies to take their place. When patients return to their premorbid level of functioning, they rely once again on the strategies they customarily use. The underlying beliefs are generally less dysfunctional in this phase than during the depression or GAD, but they are less amenable to further modification than during the acute phase.

Both patient and therapist need to acknowledge that these hardcore residual beliefs (schemas) are deeply ingrained and do not yield readily to the techniques used in the standard antidepressant or antianxiety treatment. Even when patients are convinced that their basic beliefs are dysfunctional or even irrational, they cannot make them disappear simply by questioning them or "wishing" them away.

A long, sometimes tedious process is necessary to effect change in these patients' character structure. The "characterological phase" of treatment tends to be prolonged and much less punctuated by dramatic spurts of improvement.

Conceptualization of the Case

Specific conceptualization of each case is crucial to provide a framework for understanding the patient's maladaptive behavior and modifying dysfunctional attitudes. Consequently, the therapist should formulate the case early, preferably during the evaluation process. Of course, as new data are collected, the therapist modifies the formulation accordingly. Some hypotheses are confirmed, others are modified or dropped, and still others are entered into the formulation.

Sharing this conceptualization with the patient can help the data-gathering process; it provides a guide to the patient as to what experiences to focus on, and what interpretations and underlying beliefs to identify. Patient and therapist can then test fresh material for "fit" into the preliminary formulation. As new data are collected, the therapist reformulates the case on the basis of these new data.

Drawing diagrams for patients can show them how to fit subsequent experiences into this overall formulation. It often helps for the patients to take the diagrams home with them. Some therapists use a blackboard or flip cards to demonstrate to the patients how their misconstruction of reality is derived from their beliefs. The dependent personality who tells the therapist "I need help" when confronting a new challenge, for example, needs to see the connection between this notion and the core belief "I am not capable of doing anything without help" or "I am helpless." Since the beliefs are so entrenched, they do not yield to the kind of everyday disconfirmations that generally lead to modification or elimination of less rigid beliefs. Repeated, systematic disconfirmations through devising and carrying out "behavioral experiments" can eventually erode these dysfunctional beliefs and lay the groundwork for more adaptive attitudes, such as "I can carry out a wide range of tasks without help."

Table 4.1 presents a structural formulation of the problems of a couple who had somewhat similar sets of beliefs, but who differed in

TABLE 4.1
Cognitive Processing from Core Schemas: An Example

	Beverly's Beliefs	Gary's Beliefs
Should	Gary should help when I ask.	Beverly should show more respect.
Must	I must control others' behavior.	I must control others' behavior.
Special conditional belief	If Gary doesn't help, I won't be able to function.	If I give them a chance, people will dump on me.
Fear	I will be abandoned.	I will be dumped on.
Core schema	I am a helpless baby.	I am a wimp.

crucial ways. The presenting problems of this couple have been presented in detail elsewhere (Beck, 1988). In brief, Gary, who had a narcissistic personality disorder, had periodic violent outbursts against Beverly, whom he accused of needling him all the time for not attending to specific chores. Gary believed the only way he could control Beverly, who had a dependent personality disorder, was to strike out at her, force her to "shut up." Beverly, on the other hand, believed that she had to control his continuous defaulting on his role as husband and father by "reminding" him in a reproachful way of his derelictions. She believed that this was the only way she could carry out her responsibility as housewife and mother. Beneath this was her firm belief that she could not function at all unless she had somebody to lean on.

Gary had been brought up in a household in which "might makes right." His father and older brother had intimidated him into believing he was a "wimp." He compensated for this image of himself by adopting their interpersonal strategy: In essence, the best way to control other people's inclination to dominate or demean one is to intimidate them—if necessary, through threat of force. The initial formulation, which was borne out by subsequent conjoint and individual interviews, was as follows. Gary's core schema was "I am a wimp." This concept of himself threatened to surface whenever he regarded himself as vulnerable to being demeaned. To protect himself, he consolidated the belief "I have to control other people" that was inherent in his father's behavior. Later, we will return to the methods used to deal with these beliefs. In essence, the therapist was able to trace his behavior to these beliefs.

Beverly similarly believed that "I need to control Gary." Her imperative was derived from a fear of being incapable of performing her duties without help. Her core schema was "I am a helpless child." Note that Gary's behavior ("not helping") was processed by her core schema ("Without help from somebody, I am helpless"), which led to a limp feeling. Beverly reacted to this debilitating feeling by blaming Gary and becoming enraged.

Through imagery and reliving past experiences of helplessness, the therapist was able to activate the core schema and help Beverly to recognize that her profound involvement in getting Gary to help out was derived from her image of herself as a helpless child. Consequently, her nonadaptive "nagging" was an attempt to stave off her profound sense of helplessness. The interaction of Gary and Beverly demonstrates how partners' personality structures can aggravate each other's problems, and illustrates the importance of viewing personality problems as they are expressed in a particular context, such as a marital situation.

Identification of Schemas

The therapist should use the data that he or she is collecting to extract patients' self-concept and the rules and formulas that they live by. Often, the therapist has to determine the patients' self-concept from its manifestations in their descriptions across a variety of situations.

For example, say a patient makes statements such as the following: "I made a fool of myself when I gave the conductor the wrong change," "I don't know how I got through college or even through law school. I always seem to be fouling up," and "I don't think that I can describe situations properly to you." The therapist can pick up a thread that suggests that at a basic level the patient perceives himself or herself as inadequate or defective. The therapist also makes a quick judgment as to whether there is any validity to the patient's self-description. Of course, when the patient is depressed, this broad global generalization (core belief) comes out full-blown so that after the patient has described a problematic situation, he or she concludes with a remark such as "This shows how worthless, inadequate, and unlikable I am."

The therapist can elicit the *conditional* assumptions through statements that specify the conditions under which the negative self-concept will express itself. For example, if the person has thoughts such as "Bob or Linda doesn't like me any more" under circumstances where another individual shows less than the usual friendly response, the therapist can derive the underlying formula, such as "If other people do not show a strong expression of affection or interest, it means they don't care for me." Of course, for some people under some circumstances, there may be truth in this formula, and they may require special attention to deficiencies in social skills or abrasive interpersonal style. Individuals with personality problems, however, tend to apply the formula arbitrarily, willy-nilly, in an all-or-nothing fashion across all relevant situations, even when there are alternative explanations or compelling evidence that is contradictory to this belief.

Similarly, the therapist tries to elicit the patient's views of other people. Certain statements of a paranoid personality, for example, may indicate that the basic schema is that other people are devious, manipulative, prejudiced, and the like. This schema would be manifested in statements such as "The doctor smiled at me. I know it's a phony professional smile that he uses with everybody because he is anxious to have a lot of patients," or "The clerk counted my change very slowly because he doesn't trust me," or "My wife is acting extra nice to me tonight. I wonder what she wants to get out of me." Such patients often reach these conclusions without any evidence to support them or when there is strong contradictory evidence.

When such persons are in an acute paranoid state, then the global thoughts run through their minds, such as "He's trying to put something over on me" or "They are all out to get me." The core schemas are "People can't be trusted" and "Everybody has devious motives." A consequent pattern of arbitrary conclusions reflects a cognitive bias and is said to be "schema-driven."

Specification of Underlying Goals

People generally have broad goals that are very important to them but that may not be completely in their awareness. The therapist has the job of translating the patient's stated aspirations and ambitions into the underlying goal. A patient, for instance, may say, "When I got to the party, I felt bad because only a few people came up to say hello to me," or "I had a great time because a lot of people crowded around me and wanted to know how my trip went." From a wide range of descriptions across a number of diverse situations, the therapist can infer that the underlying goal is something like "It is very important for me to be liked by everybody." Goals are derived from the core schema; in this case it would be phrased, "If I'm not liked, I'm worthless."

Another patient, for example, stated that he felt bad because he did not get a perfect grade on an exam. He also felt a little put out when he was unable to recall the name of a particular scientist during a conversation with a friend. In addition, he became so excited that he had a sleepless night after being told that he was going to get a full scholarship into graduate school. His goal, which he did not articulate until he was questioned about his experiences, was "to be famous." Associated with this goal was this conditional assumption: "If I do not become famous, then my whole life will be wasted."

Other kinds of goals may be inferred in much the same way. Take an individual who rejects any offer of help, insists on having complete freedom to move around, and is reluctant to become involved in any type of "relationship." Once the therapist extracts the common theme, "I need to have space," he or she can test this striving by observing the patient's reaction in therapy and in other situations. If the patient, for example, tends to seek physical distance during the interview, terminates the interview promptly, and expresses the desire to work on his or her problems alone, these are indicators of an underlying goal for autonomy. The conditional assumption may well be "If I get too dependent on anybody or too intimate, then I can no longer be free." Associated with this notion is the belief that "I am helpless unless I have complete freedom of action."

After the therapist has all of the data and has extracted the core assumptions, conditional beliefs, and goals, he or she can then formulate the case according to the cognitive model (cf. the formulation of Gary and Beverly's case above).

Emphasis on the Therapist-Patient Relationship

Collaboration

One of the cardinal principles of cognitive therapy is instilling a sense of collaboration and trust in the patient. The building of the relationship is probably more important in the chronic personality disorder than in the acute symptomatic phase. In the period of acute distress (usually depression and/or anxiety), the patient can usually be motivated to try out the therapist's suggestions and is rewarded by the fairly prompt reduction of suffering. In the chronic personality disorder, the changes take place much more slowly and the payoff is much less perceptible. Hence, therapist and patient have considerable work to do on the long-term project of personality change.

Patients frequently need to be motivated to do homework assignments. The patients' motivation often declines after the acute episode has subsided, since the unpleasant feelings (anxiety, sadness, anger) that acted as a spur to action subside. Further, the personality disorder itself frequently interferes with carrying out assignments. The avoidant personality may think, "Writing down my thoughts is too painful"; the narcissistic, "I'm too good for this sort of thing"; the paranoid, "My notes can be used against me" or "The therapist is trying to manipulate me." The therapist should regard these forms of "resistance" as "grist for the mill" and should subject them to the same kind of analysis as that is used for other forms of material or data.

Guided Discovery

Part of the artistry of cognitive therapy consists of conveying a sense of adventure—in unraveling and ferreting out the origins of patients' beliefs, exploring the meanings of traumatic events, and tapping into the rich imagery. Otherwise, therapy can decline into a repetitive process that becomes increasingly tedious in time. In fact, varying the way hypotheses are presented, using different phrases and words, and illustrating points with metaphors and anecdotes all help to make the relationship into a human educational experience. A certain lightness and judicious use of humor can also add spice to the experience.

In the chronic phase, the therapist spends more time with patients on unraveling the *meaning* of experiences, in order to determine the patients' specific sensitivities and vulnerabilities and to ascertain why they overreact to specific situations. As indicated in Chapter 3, the meanings are determined to a large extent by the underlying beliefs ("If somebody criticizes me, it means that person doesn't like me"). To determine the meaning, the therapist may have to proceed gradually through a number of steps.

Use of "Transference" Reactions

The therapist should allow negative reactions to him or her to arise, but should not deliberately provoke them. He or she should be vigilant for signs of anger, disappointment, and frustration experienced by the patient in the therapeutic relationship.

These reactions to the therapist open windows into the patient's private world. If not explored, moreover, the distorted interpretations will persist and may interfere with collaboration. If brought out into the open, they often provide rich material for understanding the meanings and beliefs behind the patient's idiosyncratic or repetitious reactions.

The therapist should look for tell-tale signs of a "transference" cognition. These are the same signs that suggest the presence of any automatic thoughts during the session. For instance, there may be a sudden change in the patient's nonverbal behavior—pauses in the middle of a train of statements, sudden change in expression, clenching fists, slumping posture. Or the patient may abruptly switch to a new topic, stammer, block, and so on. One of the more revealing signs is a shift in the patient's gaze, especially if he or she has had a thought but prefers not to reveal it. When questioned, the patient may say, "It's not important. It's nothing." The therapist should press the patient nonetheless— it might be important. Some patients may have automatic thoughts throughout the interview, and it is not practical to report more than a few. However, they can keep track of the automatic thoughts and record them on paper.

In dealing with personality disorders, the therapist needs to be especially careful to be nonjudgmental. In fact, the very terms that we use to describe these disorders (narcissistic, compulsive, dependent, etc.) carry a pejorative taint. Once the therapist has made the diagnosis, it is much better to avoid labels and think in terms of beliefs, sensitivities, meanings, and so forth. Needless to say, it is valuable for the therapist to be sympathetic with the patient. By trying to put himself or herself in the patient's shoes—perhaps imagining himself or herself with the same set of sensitivities, sense of helplessness, and vulnerability—the therapist can better understand the patient. At the same time, the therapist has to be on guard not to become so involved with the patient's problems objectivity is lost.

Building the Therapeutic Relationship

With most personality-disordered patients, a closer, warmer therapeutic relationship is necessary than in an acute (Axis I) disorder such as anxiety or depression. In the acute disorder, the therapist usually takes on the role of an authority who knows the necessary procedures to help the patient release the painful symptoms. In return, the patient often feels warmth and gratitude toward the expert helper, first in anticipation of being relieved of acute distress and then in recognition of the rapid improvement in the clinical state.

During the more chronic phase, the role of the therapist subtly shifts. A large portion of the therapy time is devoted to becoming familiar with the patient's total life—children, spouse, job. Such involvement by the therapist, provided it is kept within reasonable bounds, casts him or her in the role of friend and advisor. In fact, much of the therapist's role consists of drawing on his or her own life experiences and wisdom to propose possible solutions to problems, as well as to educate the patient regarding the nature of intimate relationships. This process of re-education is particularly important in treating patients with borderline personality disorder, whose own personality deficits may have prevented them from acquiring and consolidating many of the basic skills of self-control and stable relations with others.

In the course of time, the therapist becomes a role model for the patient—somebody the patient can emulate in showing consideration, tact, sensitivity, and understanding toward his or her own circle of intimates and friends. Many patients have remarked how they have incorporated their therapists' characteristics (e.g., being cool and relaxed under stress, not overreacting to disappointment, thinking before talking or acting). On rare occasions, patients may go too far and incorporate their therapists' entire personae, but this experience may be dealt with cognitively. For example, the therapist may want to explore why the patient may want to discard his or her own identity.

Problems in Collaboration

Difficulties in therapeutic collaboration are not the exclusive province of the personality-disordered patient. "Resistance," "noncompliance," "lack of compliance," or "negative transference" are descriptors that have been used to denote problems in the therapeutic relationship, lack of progress in therapy, slowed therapeutic progress, or premature termination of therapy. The Axis II patient, by virtue of the chronicity and nature of the disorder, may be more prone to be noncollaborative or noncompliant than the Axis I patient.

Patient noncollaboration with the therapeutic regimen has been termed by analytic writers "resistance," with the implication that the patient, for either conscious or unconscious reasons, chooses to maintain the status quo. Jones (1948/1967) saw the resistance phenomenon as "instinctive" and expected in therapy. Given the historical use of the term, and the implications of the phenomenon, we have chosen to use the term "noncollaboration" as opposed to the more familiar terminology. A number of recent behaviorally oriented volumes have addressed this important issue (Ellis, 1985; Harris & Watkins, 1987; Shelton & Levy, 1981; Wachtel, 1982).

As discussed earlier, the schemas regarding change, view of self, and view of others can be extreme and highly exaggerated. This exaggerated view may then become manifest in a number of ways. The noncollaboration may be manifested directly (e.g., tardiness or missing of appointments), or more subtly through omissions in the material reported in the sessions. The most common themes involve distrust of the therapist, personal shame, grievances against others (either persons or institutions), deprecation of self or others, or fear of rejection. There are, however, many reasons for noncompliance other than the patient's not wanting to change, or a pitched battle's taking place between the patient's intrapsychic structures. They can appear in any combination or permutation, and the relative strength of any noncompliant action may change with the patient's life circumstances, with progress in therapy, with changes in the therapeutic relationship, with the therapist's skill in resolving the noncompliance, and so forth.

We can identify the following reasons for therapeutic noncompliance. The ability to conceptualize the various causes can then serve to mitigate the therapeutic noncollaboration.

1. *The patient may lack the skill to be collaborative.* Not every patient has developed the skills to perform particular behaviors effectively. For many patients, their difficulty in complying with the therapeutic regimen may parallel their problems in performing particular actions in their lives. Both areas of difficulty stem from or are based on inadequately developed skills. While their skills may be adequate for "getting by" in certain areas, their skills may not be adequate for more complex tasks. Teachers have often labeled certain children "street smart," indicating a native cunning and ability, but those same children may be severely deficient in academic skills. For many of our Axis II patients, the reverse is true: They may have mastered intellectual or

academic skills, but lack practical or life skills. Given that a patient may never have developed skills, or may not have developed them to the level necessary for adequate functioning, the therapist may need to teach particular skills to help the patient move along in therapy and thereby in life.

Clinical example: Alan was a 39-year-old lawyer, diagnosed as having avoidant personality disorder. He entered therapy during his divorce because of his thinking that he could never find another woman, he would always be hurt, and therefore life was not worth living. He saw the goals of getting over his hurt and developing a social life as unrealistic for him. "It's not me," he would repeat over and over. A homework assignment over several sessions involved his calling a woman whose number was given to him by a colleague. During the eighth session, the therapist questioned Alan as to why the call was so difficult to make. Alan replied that he had virtually no experience in calling women for dates. The therapist asked Alan to role-play the phone call to the woman and discovered that Alan had no idea of what to say to her. After practicing several different approaches, Alan attempted the call in the office and was successful in setting a date for a drink after work.

His limited experience, combined with his characterological avoidance, made it difficult for Alan to comply with the homework. If the therapist had not discovered this, Alan might never have complied, and could then possibly have used that failure as further evidence for his hopelessness about ever having a mate again.

2. *The therapist may lack the skill to develop collaboration.* As we recognize the individual differences in our patients, we must also acknowledge that there are differences in therapists' skills. Because of limited experience with a particular patient problem (e.g., depression), a particular population (e.g., the elderly), or the level of severity of a problem (e.g., severely disturbed), a therapist may not have the skill to work with a particular patient. The therapist working within the context of an agency or hospital may be able to call in colleagues for consultation or to seek supervision on a particular case/problem. In some situations, however, consultative services may not be available. If the therapist's skills are not adequately developed to cope effectively with a problem, transfer to another therapist is the ethical requirement. If, however, another therapist is not available, it is incumbent upon therapists to constantly develop, enhance, and upgrade their skills through additional training. Postgraduate courses, continuing education programs, seminars, workshops, or institutes should be part of the professional growth of therapists, no matter what their training.

Clinical example: Maureen B was a postdoctoral psychology fellow. She was referred a case of an 18-year-old female student, identified as having obsessive-compulsive personality disorder, with a presenting problem of psychogenic urinary retention. This situation was not only unhealthy and painful but socially problematic, because the student lived in a university dormitory, which required that she share toilet facilities. Given the therapist's lack of experience with this problem, it was quickly brought to supervision. The supervisor also had limited experience in treating this problem. A number of local references contacted had no experience with female urinary retention. Calls were made to colleagues around the country to collect as much data as possible on treatment of the disorder. In addition, Dr. B spent time at the library searching for literature on treatment.

Given the unusual nature of the problem, the therapist needed to develop strategies and interventions so that she and her supervisor could work effectively with the patient. The therapist, utilizing her research into female anatomy, exercise, and muscle control, found the solution in a women's physical workout book: the Kegel exercises. The patient was taught the exercises in the session, and was able to gain greater control over her bladder. The behavioral therapy was done concurrently with the cognitive work of identifying and responding to the dysfunctional thoughts about urinating in a public toilet. This led in turn to the work of modifying the schema related to cleanliness, goodness, and perfectionism.

3. *Environmental stressors may preclude changing or reinforce dysfunctional behavior.* There may be circumstances or individuals in the patient's environment that serve to maintain the dysfunctional schema and the resultant dysfunctional behaviors. The schemas of significant others may work actively against the patient's making the changes that the patient has identified as important or that the therapist may believe to be important. With or without malice or intent, the significant others may work toward maintaining the patient's dysfunctional and self-destructive behavior. Patients may get the message "Do not change" either overtly or covertly. Overtly, the patient may be assaulted for going to therapy, assailed for talking of "private family matters with a stranger," or teased or stigmatized for being a "psycho" and needing to "get your head shrunk." Covertly, the message may be sent by the withdrawal of significant others while the patient is in therapy.

Clinical example: Al was a 30-year-old single male who lived at home with his parents. He was a college graduate presently employed as a customer service representative for a large corporation. Even though he made ample money to support himself, his parents continued to press for his living at home. Their genuine concern was that if he lived on his own, he would not take care of himself and would begin to eat and gain weight. He would then go up to his previous weight of 290 pounds. Although he presently weighed 225 pounds, was in therapy, and was committed to losing weight, their concern was obvious, both overtly and covertly. Their concern frightened him. He had thoughts of not pleasing them, of being bad, and of disappointing them and other family members. These thoughts kept him from living on his own. He stayed at home to allay their concern, to remain dependent and continue to be their little boy, and to cope with his own fears of a loss of control.

4. *Patients' ideas and beliefs regarding their potential failure in therapy may contribute to noncollaboration.* "Classical" cognitive therapy focuses on helping patients to examine their cognitions vis-a-vis failing in therapy and being able to make changes in thought or behavior. Examining the cognitions and schemas and learning to respond in an adaptive manner to these negative and self-deprecatory thoughts are, after all, major goals of the therapy work. Changes need to be seen as dimensional rather than as all-or-nothing. Through the use of graded task assignments, small sequential steps, evaluation of responses and reactions to the attempted changes, stress and anxiety inoculation, and therapeutic support, the patient may be more likely to attempt to make changes.

Clinical example: Mitch, a 20-year-old college junior, was diagnosed as having an avoidant personality disorder. His social and dating experience was very limited. After observing other men and women in his dorm date over a period of 2 years, he moved into an apartment off campus so that he would not have to see the active social life of his dormmates. When he entered therapy, he had intellectually accepted that he should be using his college years as a way of establishing social contacts, but recognized his lack of skill, anxiety, and reluctance. His ideas about therapy were similar to his ideas about dating. In both situations, he saw himself as opening up to the new experience, wanting to invest himself in the experience, being rejected because of his lack of skill and competence, and then suffering even more from the failure. His automatic thoughts about therapy (and dating) were as follows: "I'm better off not opening myself up to failure and ridicule. In fact, I'm better off dead. No one would even miss me. Anything I do is doomed to failure, even this therapy."

5. *Patients' ideas and beliefs regarding effects of the patients' changing on others may preclude compliance.* Another set of obstructive cognitions involves the patient having catastrophic ideas relative to the effect of his or her attempting to change on significant others. The patient often catastrophizes the effects of his or her changing on others: "If I change, something terrible will happen." The therapist needs to work with the patient to decatastrophize the potential, or to examine whether there are still advantages to changing despite the potentially negative sequelae.

Clinical example: Marta, a 42-year-old woman diagnosed as having dependent personality disorder, was employed as a secretary and lived with her mother. Marta was the youngest of three children. Both of her siblings were married, but Marta had never been married and had always lived with her mother. Her mother, by Marta's description, was tyrannical. She constantly demanded Marta's attention and services. Though quite healthy, she was constantly going to doctors at Marta's expense. The medical expenses represented a substantial drain on Marta's finances. When Marta would refuse to pay for the doctor's appointments any longer, her mother would launch into a diatribe about what a bad daughter Marta was and how Marta would be the cause of the mother's loss of health and then death. Marta would then be alone.

While Marta voiced in therapy her goal of someday being able to move out and live a life of her own, she nevertheless was reluctant to do so, in part because of her thoughts about her mother's health, ability to cope, and imminent death. If she were at home, Marta thought she would extend her mother's life. She thought that her changing and becoming less dependent and possibly moving would, in effect, kill her mother—an idea reinforced by the mother.

6. *Patients' fears regarding changing and the "new" self may contribute to noncompliance.* By definition, changing means altering ideas, beliefs, or behaviors. Axis II patients may perceive such alterations as inimical to their survival. While this may seem paradoxical, in that their thinking makes them anxious, depressed, suicidal, or generally dysfunctional, these patients fear change as an unknown. They often choose the familiarity of their discomfort to the discomfort of the uncertainty of a new mode of thinking or behavior.

Clinical example: Mary had been chronically depressed and suicidal for 3 years. She had been diagnosed as having histrionic personality disorder. She had been hospitalized four times for suicidal ideation, though she had never made an attempt. Her ideas about suicide were very dramatic. When confronted by her therapist with her style of thinking, she would state, "This is how I am. I've never been different." While she realized that her suicidal thinking was painful not only to herself but to significant others, she had great difficulty changing her perspective because of her maintenance of her position that "This is me."

7. *The patient's and therapist's dysfunctional beliefs may be harmoniously blended.* A therapist's blind spot may be fatal, in that the therapist and patient may share a particular dysfunctional idea (e.g., "Things are hopeless"). This sharing of belief, based on congruent underlying schemas, can result in the therapist's "buying into" the patient's hopeless ideas and beliefs.

Clinical example: Dr. M's therapy work was very careful and precise. She was prone to become obsessive when stressed and anxious, and her general belief was that when she was stressed, extreme care and effort would help to reduce the stress. Her extra carefulness and work were major factors in her graduating from a major university with a 4.0 grade point average. In presenting a patient for the first time in supervision, she described the patient as "perfectionistic, obsessive, and internally demanding." In supervision, Dr. M reported that her goals for this patient would be "to help him get rid of all the perfectionism that makes him feel so hopeless." Rather than working to modify the patient's perfectionism, she saw the total removal of the perfectionism as the therapeutic goal. In response to her supervisor's comment that such a goal might in fact reinforce the patient's problems, Dr. M tried to develop a case to support the need for perfectionistic striving always to do one's best.

8. *Poor socialization to the model may be a factor in noncompliance.* Patients who do not understand what is expected of them in the therapy will, of necessity, have difficulty complying with the therapeutic regimen. It is essential that the therapist spend as much time as necessary early in the therapy to educate the patient in the basics of the cognitive therapy model, including the terminology, therapeutic constructs, and specific skill. Further, the therapist needs to elicit feedback to assess the level of understanding of the model throughout the therapy work. The patient's ability to listen and understand may be impaired by hopelessness, impulsivity, selective abstraction, or personalizing. The therapist cannot assume that having read any or all of the books about cognitive therapy guarantees adequate socialization to therapy in general, or to cognitive therapy in particular. There may, in addition, be proactive interference because of patients' involvement in previous therapy; that is, they may continue to use the old strategies and approaches in the current therapy.

Clinical example: Ed was a 42-year-old physician referred for cognitive therapy subsequent to his analyst's dying. He had been in psychoanalysis for 15 years to deal with his chronic depression and periodic suicidal thinking. He had been seen three times a week for most of that time. After his analyst died, he tried to continue his analysis with another analyst for several months, but terminated by mutual consent and started cognitive therapy to deal specifically with his depression. Ed would come into each session and begin to speak immediately. Although the therapist tried to keep the session focused, utilizing agenda setting, Ed would free-associate, discussing dreams, fantasies, and everything that came to mind. Constant redirection and a scheduling of 10 to 15 minutes of free association at the beginning of the session helped to keep the rest of the session directed and focused.

9. *A patient may experience secondary gain from maintaining the dysfunctional pattern.* There may be situations where the patient may have great difficulty in initiating or affecting change because of the gain that accrues from continuing dysfunctional thinking and/or behavior. Family members may treat the patient with "kid gloves," not put any pressure

on the patient, avoid confrontation, and generally allow the patient to do whatever he or she wishes so as to decrease acting-out potential. Secondary gain may be obtained from family, friends, employers, or other individuals with whom the patient has interaction. This includes the interaction between the patient and the therapist. Such a patient needs to look at the "primary loss" that goes into achieving his or her secondary gain.

Clinical example: Sid was a 38-year-old, unemployed carpenter, diagnosed as having both passive-aggressive personality disorder and dependent personality disorder. He had not worked regularly in 5 years. His time was spent at home, watching television. His wife worked full-time and he collected disability. He reported that when he exerted himself in any way, he was concerned about having a heart attack or stroke. Even though he had never had either problem or, indeed, any major illness, his wife and two children were so concerned about his health that they never asked him to do anything at home. If pressed to find work, Sid would consider killing himself rather than expose himself to the excruciating pain of the anxiety. A local community mental health center had been giving him letters that allowed him not to be pressured into working. Sid's day involved getting up at 11:00 A.M., reading the newspaper until noon, and then watching television. When his children came home from school, he would take a nap and get up in time for dinner. After dinner he would watch television or listen to records or tapes until it was time for bed. It was very difficult to try to have him give up his early "retirement."

10. *Poor timing of interventions may be a factor in noncompliance.* Interventions that are untimely or rushed can have the effect of the patient's failing to see the importance or relevance of the therapeutic work, and thereby appearing to be noncompliant. If the therapist, because of his or her anxiety, tries to push or rush the Axis II patient, the result may be the loss of collaboration, the missing of sessions, a misunderstanding of the therapeutic issues, or a premature termination of therapy.

Clinical example: Marie, a predoctoral intern, was learning to conduct cognitive therapy. As a result of her anxiety and internal pressure to succeed, she tended to attempt to interpret schemas without gathering enough data to support her interpretations or interventions. As a result, patients often responded by telling her that she was not understanding them, which further increased her anxiety and often caused her to make more grandiose leaps of interpretation and mistiming.

11. *Patients may lack motivation.* Many patients are sent to therapy against their will. Significant others may have threatened them to seek therapy or else suffer some great consequence. Other patients may have been referred against their will by the courts. Or, in yet other cases, Axis

II patients may, as part of the clinical picture, lack motivation for most things or see their problems as external to them. The therapy work in such cases must focus initially on building a relationship and motivation for therapy.

Clinical example: Sam was a 59-year-old jeweler who had been severely depressed and suicidal for several years because of his failing business. His perception was that his business difficulty was not his fault, but had to do with the jewelers in large malls undercutting his prices. He saw no way to regain the lost income, customers, and status that he had once had, and refused to "waste" money on ads in newspapers. Although he went to work daily, he allowed the store to become piled up with boxes of what he described as "junk" and sought no new business. He approached therapy in the same way. He did not want to come to therapy, saw no benefit in coming to therapy, and agreed to come only to quiet his wife and daughter.

12. *Patients' rigidity may foil compliance.* The very problem that brings patients to therapy may be the major contributor to the noncompliance. With patients who are obsessive-compulsive or paranoid, among others, the rigidity may preclude compliance. Such patients may, in fact, question the therapist's motives or goals. More frequently, they find themselves unable to break out of the rigid position that they see themselves as having to maintain to stay relatively safe.

Clinical example: Elena, a 28-year-old nurse diagnosed as having paranoid personality disorder, saw the therapy (and the therapist) as extensions of her mother's need to control her. By maintaining her right to do whatever she wanted, including killing herself, she saw herself as being able to overcome her mother's power. The therapist had to take great care not to feed the distortion, as it might have meant Elena's making an attempt to die.

13. *The patient may have poor impulse control.* For patients with poor impulse control, the constraints of weekly sessions, a structured therapeutic approach, a set time for the session, or the time limit of the therapeutic hour may create anxiety. The schemas of "doing what one wants, when one wants" may fly in the face of the therapy. These patients often require the therapist to do what we term "brushfire therapy"—that is, constantly working at putting out the small brushfires and dealing with the crisis of the moment, rather than working on more general problem solution.

Clinical example: Therapy with Alice was always interesting. At 23 years of age, she was in constant motion. She met criteria for borderline personality disorder. Her crises were related to her frequent job changes, frequent changes in friends and love relationships, and frequent changes in therapists. Within the session, she was quite labile, and any attempts to focus her either in the sessions or in her life were met with the familiar refrain, "It's just not me." Her missing of sessions, lateness for sessions, and inability to pay the fee because of her impulsive purchases and the expenses coupled with losing her job—all these served to sabotage the therapy work and the therapeutic goal of reducing her impulsivity.

14. *The goals of therapy may be unrealistic.* This issue can come either from the patient or from the therapist. Goals that are unrealistically high or unrealistically low may serve to establish a very negative set in the therapy. If the patient wants to be a totally new person—that is,. exactly opposite to the way he or she has been for the past 40 years—the therapist may have to help the patient set more realistic and graded goals. Change is possible, but setting out the goal of total change may set the patient up for failure. Similarly, if the therapist has unrealistically high goals for the patient, failure may be the result.

Clinical example: Nick, aged 52, came for therapy because of his depression and isolation. He stated in the first session that he wanted to change his whole life. He had never been married, had not dated until he was 31, and had only dated a few times in his life. He saw the world as passing him by. He saw himself as aging and being alone in his old age. He reported watching television shows about families and crying. His goal was to start dating immediately and be married within the year, as he wasn't getting any younger. This unrealistic goal would likely have set up a failure situation and sabotaged the therapy.

15. *The goals of therapy may be unstated.* There are times when the goals of therapy may appear implicit in the initial presentation of the problem list. For example, implicit in "marital discord" may be relationship skill deficits, communication deficits, sexual skills deficits, depression, or many other problems. The goals of therapy need to be made explicit in the establishment of the problem list. This list can, of course, be modified as the therapy progresses. Without baseline information about what the targets of therapy are, it becomes difficult to assess the progress of the therapy.

Clinical example: Maryann, aged 51, entered therapy for anxiety. It was clear after several sessions that the anxiety was part of a clinical picture that included obsessive-compulsive personality disorder. The therapist, working on helping Maryann to be more flexible, found that she became more agitated as the sessions progressed. At the sixth session, she announced that she was leaving therapy because of her increased anxiety: "I thought that therapy was supposed to help, not make me worse." The therapist had assumed that Maryann would be willing to change her rigid personality pattern without ever discussing that pattern as a focus of the therapy.

16. *The goals of therapy may be vague and amorphous.* Patients typically present with vague statements about "getting my act together," "getting

my head on straight," "dealing with my depression/anxiety," or "improving the communication in our relationship." The therapist must work to restate these goals as workable, operationally defined goals.

Clinical example: Seth, aged 19, was referred by his resident dormitory counselor because of his constant fighting. Seth had seen a counselor at the college counseling center and worked on "anger" and "problems in my background." After eight sessions, the counselor terminated the counseling with the note that Seth now had sufficient insight to allow change. The present referral was based on the insight's not eventuating in behavioral change. This time the goals of the therapy were made clear and specific, with specific criteria for change, a graded task approach to relating to dormmates, and a discrete focus on his impulse control.

17. *There may have been no agreement between therapist and patient relative to the treatment goals.* Given that the goals of therapy are explicit and operationally defined, the patient and therapist need to work on agreeing on the therapeutic goals. Developing a treatment plan and having the patient read and sign the plan are parts of the informed consent procedure for treatment that is required in many mental health settings today. Stating the goals for a set period of time (e.g., for 3 months), discussing the rationale for the goals, accepting patient input, negotiating changes, and getting and giving feedback are intrinsic to the cognitive therapy model.

18. *The patient or therapist may be frustrated because of a lack of progress in therapy.* Given the long-term nature of Axis II problems, their generalized effect throughout the patient's life, and the long-term nature of the therapy, either the patient, the therapist, or both can become frustrated. In either case, the result may be negative reactions to further therapy, thoughts about failure (either therapist's or patient's failure), and anger toward the source of the frustration (either therapist or patient).

Clinical example #1: Alicia, a psychologist under supervision, was "thoroughly frustrated" by Lara, a patient with borderline personality disorder: "She doesn't change; she just stays angry, usually at me. I really dread the day when she is scheduled to come in, and am happy when she has to cancel." Having been quite successful in her work as a cognitive therapist working with more typical, uncomplicated depression, Alicia was not used to patients' taking so long in treatment or being oppositional: "I've read about borderlines, heard about them, but never thought that I would have this kind of trouble." The focus of supervision was on helping Alicia deal with her dysfunctional thoughts and expectations regarding therapy, the treatment of complex and difficult cases, and countertransference.

Clinical example #2: Marla had originally come to therapy to relieve her depression. The depression was superimposed on an obsessive-compulsive personality disorder. She chose cognitive therapy after reading of its short-term nature and demonstrated effectiveness, as described in several mass media publications. After 25 sessions she demanded to know why she wasn't "cured" yet. The therapist had neglected to differentiate the symptom versus schema focus of the therapy.

19. *Issues involving the patient's perception of lowered status and self-esteem may be factors in noncompliance.* For many people, becoming "patients" implies that there is something very wrong with them. They are unable to deal with their lives, or to cope with stressors that they may at one time may have effectively dealt with. In addition, they may be stigmatized by others as "psychos," "sick," or "crazy."

Clinical example: Roy, aged 60, a successful businessman, was referred by his family physician because of his depression. His first statement in therapy was this: "I don't want to be here. Coming here has actually made me more depressed. I've never had to ask for help before, and I don't know how to now. I sneak out of the house to come here. I never want you to call me at the office or at my home. No one can know that I come here."

The therapist must be aware of the myriad reasons for a patient's lack of collaboration or noncompliance with the therapeutic regimen. These include lack of patient skill; lack of therapist skill; environmental stressors that preclude compliance; patient cognitions regarding failure in therapy; patient cognitions regarding the effects on both self and others of the patient's changing; distorted congruence of patient and therapist; poor socialization to the model; secondary gain; poor timing of interventions; patient's lack of motivation; rigidity or poor impulse control; the goals of therapy being unstated, vague, or unrealistic; patient or therapist frustration; and issues revolving around the patient's lowered self-esteem.

It is essential to plan strategies and techniques that effectively deal with the relevant issues, and that move the therapy along within the collaborative framework. Given the complexity of the personality disorder itself, combined with the acute Axis I problems that spark the referral for therapy, many problems can interfere with the therapeutic collaboration. Our focus in this chapter has been to help the therapist to develop a conceptual framework for applying the general principles of cognitive therapy to the treatment of the patient with personality disorder. Armed with the theoretical and practical skills of case conceptualization, the therapist can develop treatment strategies and specific treatment interventions.

For experienced cognitive therapists the chapters in Part I will serve as an essential review of the basic cognitive model and allow them to move on to the more difficult work of treating Axis II patients. For the therapist for whom the cognitive therapy model is new, these beginning chapters will serve as an introduction. We consider it essential that therapists master the conceptual model of cognitive therapy and follow the general and specific treatment guidelines. Working to encourage collaboration will limit therapeutic noncompliance, resulting in a stronger working alliance.

Chapter 5
Specialized Techniques

The planning and application of specific strategies and techniques need to take into account not only the specific pathology of the patients, but also their unique methods for integrating and utilizing information about themselves. Different patients learn in different ways. Furthermore, methods that are successful at a particular time with a given patient may be ineffective at another time. Therapists must use their best judgment in designing treatment plans and selecting the most useful techniques from the wide variety available, or improvising new ones. A certain amount of trial and error may be necessary. At times, introspection may be most successful; at other times, ventilation or skills training may be what is called for.

The most effective application of techniques depends not only on a clear conceptualization of the case (see Chapter 4) and the formation of a friendly working relationship, but also on the artistry of the therapist. The *art of therapy* involves the judicious use of humor, anecdotes, metaphors, and self-disclosure of the therapist's experiences, as well as the standard cognitive and behavioral techniques. Skillful therapists know when to draw out sensitive material, draw back when necessary, and confront avoidances. They can heat up a monotonous rendition or cool off an overly heated flow. They vary their words, style, and mode of expression.

Flexibility within a given session is important: The therapist may vary his or her approach from active listening, to focusing and probing, to modeling new behavioral styles. It is expected that therapists reading this volume will have mastered the basic principles of cognitive-behavioral psychotherapy. Many of these have been covered in volumes such as that by Beck, Rush, Shaw, and Emery (1979). We have arbitrarily divided techniques into those that are primarily "cognitive" and those that are "behavioral." We need to keep in mind that no techniques are purely either cognitive or behavioral. Further, cognitive strategies can produce behavioral change, and behavioral methods generally instigate some cognitive restructuring.

Among the most effective tools in treating personality disorders are the so-called *experiential techniques,* such as reliving childhood events and imagery. Such dramatic techniques seem to open up the sluices for new learning—or unlearning. A rule of thumb is that cognitive change depends on a certain level of affective experience (Beck, 1987).

Cognitive and behavioral techniques play complementary roles in the treatment of personality disorders. The main thrust is to develop new schemas and to modify old ones. Ultimately, of course, the cognitive techniques probably account for most of the change that occurs (Deffenbacher, Storey, Stark, Hogg, & Brandon, 1987). The cognitive work, like the behavioral, requires more precision and persistence than usual when patients have personality disorders. Since specific cognitive schemas of these patients continue to be dysfunctional, even after more adaptive behaviors have been developed, a larger variety and longer duration of cognitive reworking are typically required.

Cognitive Strategies and Techniques

Below is a list of cognitive techniques from which therapists can draw in treating Axis II disorders. Since several methods have been described elsewhere in the treatment of depression (Beck et al., 1979), they will not be discussed in detail here. We will, however, expand on specific techniques for Axis II problems. This list is representative and by no means exhaustive.

Some of the cognitive techniques that are helpful in dealing with personality disorders include (1) guided discovery, which enables the patient to recognize stereotyped dysfunctional patterns of interpretation; (2) searches for idiosyncratic meaning, since these patients often interpret their experiences in unusual or extreme ways; (3) labeling of inaccurate inferences or distortions, in order to make the patient aware of bias or unreasonableness of particular automatic patterns of thought; (4) collaborative empiricism—working with the patient to test the validity of the patient's beliefs, interpretations, and expectations; (5) examining explanations for other people's behavior; (6) scaling—translating extreme interpretations into dimensional terms to counteract typical dichotomous thinking; (7) reattribution—reassigning responsibility for actions and outcomes; (8) deliberate exaggeration—taking an idea to its extreme, which places a situation in high relief and facilitates reevaluation of a dysfunctional conclusion; (9) examining the advantages and disadvantages of maintaining or changing beliefs or behaviors, and clarifying primary and secondary gains; (10) decatastrophizing—

enabling the patient to recognize and counter the tendency to think exclusively in terms of the worst possible outcome of a situation.

The "Cognitive Probes"

The same techniques used in eliciting and evaluating automatic thoughts during depression or generalized anxiety disorder (Beck et al., 1979; Beck & Emery with Greenberg, 1985) are useful when dealing with personality problems. Specifically, the therapist and patient identify incidents that illuminate the personality problems, and focus on the cognitive underpinnings of these incidents. Let us say that an avoidant patient, Lois, becomes upset when the other workers at her place of work appear to ignore her. The first cognitive probe should attempt to recover her automatic thoughts (Beck, 1967). If the patient is well trained at identifying automatic thoughts, she might say, for example, "I thought 'They don't like me.' "

If the patient fails to recover the automatic thought, she might then be encouraged to *imagine* the experience "as though it is happening right now." As the experience is brought to life, as it were, she is likely to experience the automatic thoughts just as she would in the actual situation. Of course, she would have many opportunities in future encounters to ascertain the automatic thoughts as they occur without priming. If a patient can anticipate a particular "traumatic" experience, it is useful for her to prepare herself in advance by starting to tune in to her train of thought prior to entering the aversive situation ("I wonder whether Linda will snub me at lunch today"). Our patient, Lois, thus is primed to catch the relevant thought of rejection. Noting that Linda seems to be aloof, she can pick up the negative thoughts: "She doesn't like me." "There is something wrong with me." Of course, automatic thoughts are not necessarily dysfunctional or unrealistic and, as we shall see, need to be tested.

Of most importance is the ultimate meaning of the event. For example, Lois could shrug off Linda's seeming rejection with the thought, "So what? I don't like her either," or "She's not one of my friends." However, when the patient has a specific vulnerability to rejection, a chain reaction is started—that may culminate in a prolonged feeling of sadness.

Sometimes the patient is able to discern the chain reaction through introspection. Often, through skillful questioning, therapist can arrive at the salient starting point (core schema). He or she can also use this exercise as a way of demonstrating the particular fallacy or flaw in the patient's process of making inferences and drawing conclusions. Take the following interchange between the therapist and Lois, who has become very upset because Linda, her friend, has been absorbed in conversation with a fellow worker at lunch:

THERAPIST: What thought went through your mind at lunch?
LOIS: Linda is ignoring me. [Selective focus, personalization]
THERAPIST: What did that mean?
LOIS: I can't get along with people. [Self-attribution, overgeneralization]
THERAPIST: What does that mean?
LOIS: I will never have any friends. [Absolute prediction]
THERAPIST: What does it mean "not to have friends"?
LOIS: I am all alone. [Core schema]
THERAPIST: What does it mean to be *all alone?*
LOIS: That I will always be unhappy. *(Starts to cry)*

Since the patient starts to cry, the therapist stops the line of questioning because he believes he has come to the bedrock, the core schema ("I will always be unhappy"). The arousal of a strong feeling suggests not only that a core schema has been exposed, but also that the dysfunctional thinking is more accessible to modification. This type of questioning, attempting to probe for deeper meanings and access to the core schema, has been called the "downward arrow" technique (Burns, 1980; Beck et al., 1985). At a later date, therapist and patient will want to explore further to ascertain if there are other core schemas.

In this particular case, Lois's problem centers around her beliefs: "If people are not responsive to me, it means they don't like me," and "If one person doesn't like me, it means I'm unlikable." When she goes into the cafeteria in the office building in which she works, she is very sensitive to how receptive the other workers are—whether they seem eager to have her sit next to them, whether they include her in the conversation, whether they are responsive to her remarks. Since she has an avoidant personality disorder and tends to avoid entering situations of possible rejection, she is inclined not to sit at a table with people she knows, particularly Linda. One way to deal with this is to confront the issue head on, as illustrated in the following dialogue.

Lois has become upset after sitting down at a table where a group of women have been carrying on an animated conversation. The therapist probes for the meaning of this event.

THERAPIST: Suppose the people don't welcome you with open arms, then what?
LOIS: I don't know. I suppose I would feel they don't like me.
THERAPIST: If they showed they liked you, then what?

Lois: I'm not sure. I really don't have much in common with them. I'm not really interested in the kind of things they are.

THERAPIST: Would you choose to have any of them as your close friends?

Lois: I guess not.

THERAPIST: You really aren't interested in being friendly with any of them. So it's the meaning, the importance you attach to "being liked" or "not liked" rather than the practical importance that throws you. Is that right?

Lois: I guess it is.

Because of her core schemas revolving around the issue of likability, almost every encounter Lois has with other people involves a test of her acceptability, becoming almost a matter of life and death. By exposing the core schema through the downward arrow technique, the therapist is able to bring the underlying meanings of "being ignored" to the surface, and demonstrate that the belief about the necessity of being liked by everyone is dysfunctional.

Once the underlying beliefs are made accessible (conscious), the patient can then apply realistic, logical reasoning to modify them. Thus, Lois is able to counter the automatic thought, "They don't care for me," with the rational response, "It doesn't matter if they don't care for me. I don't have anything in common with them anyhow."

Patients tend to attach absolutistic meanings to events and to view them in all-or-nothing terms. The therapist's role is to show the patient that the importance of events or people can be placed on a continuum. Thus, Lois can see that when she ranks her acquaintances on a continuum of "how important" they are to her, they rank much lower than her real friends. Once she has made this objective rating, she may no longer be so concerned about being liked by her acquaintances.

Of course, in most situations casual acquaintances usually are neutral rather than rejecting, but because patients are prone to interpret neutrality as rejection, they need to articulate the core beliefs and experience the associated affect in order to change this dysfunctional way of thinking. Techniques for dealing with negative automatic thoughts and the underlying beliefs are dealt with elsewhere (Beck et al. 1979; Freeman, Pretzer, Fleming, & Simon, 1990).

Confronting the Schemas

In discussing or elucidating the schemas with the patient, the diagnostic labels of paranoid, histrionic, or borderline may induce a bias in the therapist's view of the patient. The patient's style can be translated into operational terms. The schizoid style, for example, can be described and discussed as the patient's being "very individualistic" or not being "dependent on other people." The dependent personality disorder can be discussed in terms of "having a strong belief in the value of attachment to others," or of "placing a large emphasis on the importance of being a more social person." In every case, a nonjudgmental description modified to fit the particular belief system can be offered to the patient.

A comprehensive therapeutic program addresses all cognitive, behavioral, and affective schemas. The density, breadth, activity, and valence of the targeted schemas (Chapter 2) are all factors in determining the therapeutic mix.

Using the patient's cognitive biases or distortions as the signposts that point to the schemas, the therapist first helps the patient to identify the dysfunctional rules that dominate his or her life, then works with the patient to make the modifications or alterations necessary for more adaptive functioning. The therapist has several options in working with the schemas. The choice of a particular option is based on the goals and the conceptualization of the case.

The first option we will call "schematic restructuring." This may be likened to urban renewal. When a conclusion is reached that a particular structure or complex of structures is unsound, a decision is made to tear down the old structures in a stepwise fashion and build new structures in their place. This has been the goal of many therapeutic approaches for many years (especially psychoanalysis and the dynamic derivatives of the psychodynamic schools). Not all dysfunctional schemas can be restructured, nor is doing so always a reasonable goal, given the time, energy, or available patient (or therapist) skills.

An example of total schematic restructuring would be the transformation of an individual with a paranoid personality disorder into a fully trusting individual. The particular schemas about the potential and imminent danger from others would be eliminated, and in their place would be other beliefs about the general trustworthiness of people, the unlikely possibility of being attacked and hurt, and the belief that generally there will be others available to offer help and succor. Obviously, this is a most difficult and time-consuming treatment option, and a compromise must be reached between the overactive schemas relevant to distrust and more benevolent schemas. In other words, the restructuring consists of attenuating the dysfunctional schemas and developing more adaptive schemas.

Many patients have never formed adequate schemas to incorporate experiences that contradict their dysfunctional basic beliefs. Hence, they are unable to integrate new positive experiences and, consequently, continue to filter events through their pre-existing schemas. As a result, their life experiences are shaped in such a way that they confirm the patients' dysfunctional—usually negative—beliefs about themselves and other people. More severely impaired patients, especially those with borderline personality disorder, may have one or more areas in which adaptive schemas are simply not available. Hence, they have to build up adaptive structures to store new constructive experiences.

A variety of techniques may be utilized to build new schemas or shore up defective ones. Diaries can be used creatively to accomplish the goal of organizing and storing new observations. For example, a person who believes, "I'm inadequate," could keep a notebook with several sections labeled *work, social, parenting, alone.* Every day small examples of adequacy could be recorded in each area. The therapist can help the patient identify adequacy examples and monitor that they are recorded regularly. The patient can also review this log to help counter his or her absolute belief in the negative schema in times of stress or "failure" when the more familiar negative schema is strongly activated (Goldfried & Newman, 1986).

A different type of diary can be used to weaken the negative schemas and support the need for alternative schemas. In predictive diaries patients writes down predictions of what will happen in certain situations if their negative schemas are true. Later, they write what actually happened and compare this to the predictions.

For example, one woman with obsessive-compulsive personality disorder believed that terrible catastrophes awaited her each day and that she was totally inadequate to cope with these. She made a diary in which she listed each predicted catastrophe in the first column. In the second column she listed whether or not the catastrophe happened, and also any unforeseen catastrophes that actually occurred. In a third column she rated her coping with any actual "catastrophes." After 1 month, this woman reviewed her diary and found that out of five predicted catastrophes, only one actually happened and that she was able to handle this one with 70% adequacy.

A third type of diary more actively analyzes daily experiences in terms of old and new schemas. Patients who have begun to believe somewhat in their new, more adaptive schemas can evaluate critical incidents during their week. For example, a patient who believed she was unlovable if she displeased others analyzed her daily experiences where this old belief was activated. In one incident she criticized an employee for poor work performance. In her diary she wrote, "He seemed annoyed at me that I criticized his work. With my old schema, I would feel this is terrible and shows I am unlovable. Now I can see that it is my responsibility to correct my work and, if he is mad at me, that is OK. I don't need everyone to be happy with me all the time to be lovable."

In these ways "schema diaries" can help build up adaptive schemas, insure that subsequent experiences reinforce the new schemas, and help counteract the old nonadaptive schemas in the processing of new events and reformulating of old events. The types of "functional schemas" to be developed vary, of course, according to the nature of the patient's problems and the diagnostic category.

While transforming an individual with a personality disorder into a fully mature person, functioning at the peak of his or her capacity, would seem to be an ideal, it is rarely achieved during therapy. However, most patients do continue to mature after therapy is completed and may ultimately approximate this ideal.

The second possibility on the change continuum is "schematic modification." This process involves smaller relative changes in the basic manner of responding to the world than does reconstruction. A relevant metaphor would be renovating an old home. A clinical example would be changing a paranoid personality's relevant schemas regarding trust into less mistrusting and suspicious beliefs, and experimenting by inducing the patient to trust *some* people in *some* situations and to evaluate the results.

The third possibility on the continuum is "schematic reinterpretation." This involves helping patients to understand and reinterpret their lifestyles and their schemas in more functional ways. For example, a histrionic person could recognize the dysfunctionality of the belief that being loved or admired is a necessity. However, the person could still receive affection as a source of gratification—for example, by choosing to teach preschool children who kiss and hug the teacher. If a narcissistic person wants to be looked up to and respected, by earning a title (e.g., Professor or Doctor), he or she could meet the desire for status without being driven by compulsive beliefs regarding the value of prestige.

Mary, a 23-year-old computer programmer (mentioned briefly in Chapter 1), came to therapy because of "tremendous work pressure, inability to enjoy life, a perfectionistic approach to virtually all tasks, and a general isolation from others" (Freeman & Leaf, 1989, pp. 405-406), as well as sleep difficulty and suicidal ideation. Not only was she getting very little satisfaction from her work; she was constantly late in getting it completed. Her obsessive-compulsive personality traits had been rewarded in school and at home. Without the school structure in her life, work took all of her time, and she was no longer rewarded for her perfectionism. She reported that if she needed extra time to complete an assignment, the teachers always gave it to her, knowing that the finished product would be well worth waiting for.

She thought that it was essential to keep her "high standards." Attempts to alter these hypervalent schemas were met with great resistance. She wanted surcease from the stress that she felt, but did not want to give up rules and standards that she considered important. One choice discussed in therapy was her finding a new position that would allow her to use her "high standards." After a brief job search, she found a position at a university research center, where a requirement of the job was that she work "slowly and carefully" without regard to time. Her coworkers found her style compatible with the aims of their project. Continued therapy worked toward modification of her rules in social situations and in the vocational arena.

Given that anxiety is likely to be aroused as schemas are changed, patients must be apprised of this possibility, so that they will not be disturbed when it surfaces. A depressed patient diagnosed at intake as having borderline personality disorder asked, "Why are you trying to teach me to control my anxiety? I'm depressed; I'm not anxious at all." At that point, the therapist told the patient of the need to master anxiety reduction skills. These skills, it was pointed out, would be an essential factor in successful therapy. One patient, as noted in Chapter 1, responded to this explanation by stating that "it's good to have that safety and I don't understand why I should ever give it up." Unless patients are able to cope with anxiety, they may slide back into the old dysfunctional patterns and leave therapy. (See Beck et al., 1985, and Freeman & Simon, 1989, for detailed discussions of anxiety treatment.)

Making Decisions

One of the areas in which therapists often enter into the "outside lives" of patients with personality disorders is helping them to make decisions. While the personality problems are being treated, joint work is required to help patients learn how to make certain important decisions that have been postponed initially. During the acute phase of depressive or anxiety disorders, the therapist focuses on getting patients mobilized and back into the pattern of confronting *immediate problems,* which may seem insoluble during the depression (indeed, this feeling may be a by-product of the depression): "Should I get out of bed today?" "How can I get the children off to school?" "What should I buy at the supermarket?" A depressed attorney, for instance, could not decide which cases she should attend to first when she got to the office. She needed help in setting priorities and then listing what needed to be done for each case. The symptoms of depression may interfere with making even the simplest routine decisions. Important long-range decisions—for example, regarding marital problems, child rearing, or career changes—may need to be put off until the depression has subsided.

When the acute symptoms have subsided, the therapist can focus on the more chronic or long-range problems regarding marriage, career, and so on. Decisions that seem to tie patients in knots—especially in the area of interpersonal relations—need to be tackled. Some patients are paralyzed into inaction, while others make impulsive decisions, when faced with questions regarding choice of career, dating, marriage or divorce, and having children (as well as more mundane issues). Helping the personality problems can promote solving the realistic problems and making decisions. The calculated procedures involved in making decisions are often blocked by the patients' personality problems. The avoidant and passive-aggressive tend to procrastinate; the histrionic is more likely to be impulsive; the obsessive-compulsive gets caught up in perfectionism; and the dependent looks for somebody else to make the decision.

It is clear that the therapist cannot treat the personality problems in a vacuum. The cognitive problems encroach on the way the individual is able to cope with "real life situations." Conversely, by helping the patient to learn and integrate new coping strategies, the therapist is able to neutralize some of the maladaptive strategies that are manifestations of the personality disorder. Incorporating a new strategy of decision making can increase the self-reliance of the dependent, improve the decisiveness of the avoidant, make the histrionic more reflective, and increase the flexibility of the obsessive-compulsive. Thus, new decision-making patterns can modify the personality styles of each disorder.

Therapists can draw on the practical techniques described in various writings on making decisions (e.g., Nezu & Nezu, 1989; D'Zurilla & Goldfried, 1971). One method used successfully by D'Zurilla and Goldfried, for example, consists of a series of steps such as defining the problem, setting the goals, brainstorming to generate ideas, and so forth.

A method that elicits the unreasonable meanings that influence people when they are confronted with an either-or choice is to list the pros and cons for each option in separate columns. With the therapist's assistance, the patient lists the advantages and disadvantages of each alternative and attempts to assign weights to each of these items.

For example, Tom, who tended to obsess about making decisions, had decided to drop out of law school because of the discomfort he felt in taking exams and his fear of not living up to expectations. His habit of obsessing about his performance generated a significant amount of tension. He was prompted to consider dropping out by his belief that this was the only way he could relieve the stress. As a way of helping him to make an objective decision, the therapist and Tom set up four columns and filled them in together as shown in Table 5.1. The first column listed the reasons for dropping out or staying. In the second

TABLE 5.1
Tom's Decision-Making Process

In Favor of Dropping Out	Value	Rebuttal	Value
I won't have to worry so much.	60%	I'm in therapy to get me over my *perfectionism*, which is what's making me miserable.	40%
I can find out whether I want to be a lawyer.	10%	I don't need to make an irreversible decision to find this out . . . I can play it by ear as I continue in school.	30%
It will be a big relief. I can take time out and knock around for a while.	40%	I will feel relieved at first, but I may feel really sad about it later.	30%
In Favor of Staying	Value	Rebuttal	Value
I've prepared myself for going to law school and have only one and a half more years to go.	40%	None	—
I might really like the practice of law. (It's the exams that are getting me down.)	30%	None	—
Even if I don't like the practice of law, it's a good jumping off point for a number of different jobs (even a college presidency!).	30%	None	—
Some of the courses turn me on.	20%	None	—
My perfectionism might work well for me in the law.	20%	None	—

column, he gauged the importance of these reasons. The third column contained rebuttals, and the fourth the value or importance of the rebuttals.

After Tom went down the list with his therapist, he was able to view the question of dropping out more objectively. He experienced some relief when he realized that his perfectionism and obsessing were the real sources of distress rather than the difficulties of law school per se, and that he could get help from his therapist with this distressing personality problem that had plagued him most of his life.

It should be noted that decisions that may be relatively simple for one patient become momentous for another because they touch on a specific personality sensitivity. Thus, Agnes, a dependent personality, had no difficulty in deciding to have a dinner party, but agonized over making a decision whether to take a trip by herself. Phil, an autonomous person, on the other hand, was able to plan trips alone, but was stymied when he had to call a friend for directions.

Behavioral Techniques

The goals of using behavioral techniques are threefold. First, the therapist may need to work very directly to alter self-defeating behaviors. Second, patients may be deficient in skills, and the therapy must include a skill-building component. Third, the behavioral assignments can be used as homework to help to test out cognitions. Behavioral techniques that can be helpful (although we do not discuss all of them in detail here) include (1) activity monitoring and scheduling, which permit retrospective identification and prospective planning of changes; (2) scheduling mastery and pleasure activities, to enhance personal efficacy and validate the successfulness of and pleasure derived from changed experiences (or lack thereof); (3) behavioral rehearsal, modeling, assertiveness training, and role playing for skill development prior to early efforts to respond more effectively, either in old problematic situations or in new ones; (4) relaxation training and behavioral distraction techniques, for use when anxiety becomes an imminent problem during efforts to change; (5) *in vivo* exposure, by arranging for the therapist to go with the client to a problematic setting, so that the therapist can help the client deal with dysfunctional schemas and actions that have (for whatever reason) not been tractable in the ordinary consultation setting; (6) graded task assignment, so that the patient can experience changes as an incremental step-by-step process, during which the difficulty of each component can be adjusted and mastery achieved in stages.

Use of Role Play

Role play may be used for skill development and overcoming inhibitions, as in "assertiveness training." When the role play involves an emotionally charged topic, dysfunctional cognitions usually are aroused. These can be "worked through" just like any other automatic thoughts can be.

In reverse role playing, the therapist can "model" appropriate behavior. Also, the therapist can more readily visualize the perspective of the other person. Such reverse role playing is a crucial component of empathy training.

An 18-year-old woman was in a continuous state of anger toward her father, whom she regarded as "critical, mean, and controlling." She claimed, "He tries to run my life for me and disapproves of everything I do." Initially, after proper briefing, the therapist played the father role in a recent scenario in which the father had questioned her about taking drugs and the patient had flared up. During the role play, she had thoughts like: "You don't like me!" "You're trying to run all over me!" "You have no right to do this!" Subsequently, they reversed roles. The patient made a strong effort to do a good job—to see the situation through her father's eyes. She was moved to tears during the role play and explained, "I can see that he really is concerned about me and is genuinely worried about me." She had been so locked into her own perspective that she had been unable to see his.

Reliving Childhood Experiences

Use of childhood material is not crucial in treating the acute phase of depression or anxiety, but is important in the chronic personality disorder. We find not infrequently that after the depression and anxiety have subsided, patients retain a residue of dysfunctional thinking that is not modified by the standard cognitive and behavioral techniques (Beck et al., 1979; Beck et al, 1985). Reviewing childhood material opens up windows for understanding the origins of nonadaptive patterns. This approach can increase perspective and objectivity. One patient who kept criticizing herself, despite consistent demonstration of the unreasonableness and dysfunctionality of her beliefs, was able to attenuate her self-criticisms when she re-experienced childhood scenes of criticism. "I criticize myself now not because it's right to do so, but because my mother always criticized me and I took this over from her."

Role playing and reverse role playing of key interactions from the past can mobilize affect and produce "mutation" of the schemas or core beliefs. Recreating "pathogenic" situations of the developmental period often provides an opportunity to restructure attitudes that were formed during this period. Cases like this are similar to "combat neurosis": The patients need to experience an emotional catharsis in order to change their strong beliefs (Beck et al., 1985).

By role-playing a figure from the past, patients can see a "bad" parent (or sibling) in more benign terms. They can start to feel empathy or compassion for the parents who traumatized them. They can see that they themselves were not and are not "bad," but that they developed a fixed image of badness because their parents were upset and vented their anger on them. They can also see that their parents had rigid unrealistic standards that they imposed arbitrarily. Consequently, the patients can soften their own attitudes toward themselves.

Their parents' behavior becomes more understandable, and they can see that their own views of themselves were not based on logic or reasoning but were products of the parents' unreasoning reactions. A parent's statement, "You are worthless," is taken as valid and incorporated into a patient's system of beliefs—even though the patient himself or herself may not actually believe the label is justified. The rationale for "reliving" specific episodes from childhood may be fitted into the more general concept of state-dependent learning. In order to "reality-test" the validity of childhood-originated schemas, these beliefs have to be brought to the surface. Re-experiencing the episode facilitates the emergence of the dominant structures (the "hot schemas") and makes them more accessible. Thus, the patient can correct them.

Use of Imagery

The use of imagery in anxiety disorders has been described at length elsewhere (Beck et al., 1985). The same methods can be used in personality disorders—to enable the patient to "relive" past traumatic events, and thus to restructure the experience and consequently the derivative attitudes.

The rationale for this procedure requires some consideration: simply talking about a traumatic event may give intellectual insight about why the patient has a negative self-image, for instance, but it does not actually change the image. In order to modify the image, it is necessary to go back in time, as it were, and recreate the situation. When the interactions are brought to life, the misconstruction is activated—along with the affect—and cognitive restructuring can occur.

A 28-year-old single woman was treated successfully for panic disorder over 12 visits. It was apparent, however, that this symptomatic condition existed in the context of an avoidant personality. The patient decided that she wanted to get further treatment for her personality disorder after the panic disorder subsided.

The patient gave a typical avoidant history. She would tend to avoid social situations and consequently had very few contacts with either sex—although she was very eager to get married. Further, she was overqualified for the various jobs she held, but was hesitant to do anything that would enable her to take on a job requiring more responsibility.

During the first few sessions with the therapist, she received the standard cognitive therapy for personality problems. In one visit, after she had been given a homework assignment that she failed to follow through with, she told her therapist that she was feeling particularly upset over not having done the homework. The therapist asked her where the feeling was localized. The patient responded that she felt it somewhere in her "stomach." The therapist then asked her whether she had an image in reference to what was upsetting her. She then said the following: "I see myself coming into the session. You are larger than life; you are critical and demeaning; you are like a big authority."

The therapist then asked when this had occurred previously. The patient responded that she had experienced this many times during childhood when she had unpleasant encounters with her mother. Her mother drank a good deal and was frequently very irritable toward the child when she had been drinking. One day the child came home from school early, and her mother "blasted" her for waking her up.

The therapist asked her to recreate this experience imaginally. The patient then had the following fantasy or image: "I came home and rang the doorbell. My mother came to the door. She looked at me. She was larger than life. She looked down on me and screamed at me for waking her up. She said, 'How dare you interrupt my sleep!' She said I was bad, wrong."

The patient extracted from this experience (and many other similar experiences) the following: "I am a bad kid," and "I am wrong because I upset my mother."

The therapist tried to elicit explanations for the mother's behavior other than that the patient was a bad kid. The patient volunteered that the mother did drink a lot, was irritable, and flew off the handle easily; nevertheless, the patient could not get away from holding herself accountable for her mother's behavior.

The therapist attempted to bring to bear the patient's "adult part" in dealing with this powerful memory. She "modeled" for the patient what would be an appropriate response to the mother if the child had all of the maturity and skills of an adult. The patient practiced these rejoinders, with the therapist playing the role of the mother. Each time that she practiced, she became less uncertain about it until she was finally able to say it with some degree of conviction: "It's not my fault—you are being unreasonable, picking on me for no good reason. I haven't done anything wrong."

The patient then attempted to relive the situation in fantasy, again ringing the doorbell, but this time—instead of cowering and feeling helpless—she answered her mother back (in the image) in an assertive way, making the statements cited above.

The "working through," using role plays, fantasy inductions, and testing and assessment of beliefs, was carried on for somewhat more than a year. In the course of time, the patient's degree of conviction in her beliefs shifted substantially. Concomitantly, she expressed a pronounced symptomatic change. She became much less self-critical and ultimately was able to leave her job for which she was overqualified, and obtain a much higher-level position that matched her qualifications.

Imagery was also used successfully with an avoidant personality who worked in his wife's family's business. The problem he presented was that his in-laws were fed up with him because he did not attend to things that he was supposed to. He stated to the therapist: "My father-in-law [who was also his boss] doesn't like me. I know he will be critical of me, so I just don't do things. I'm always afraid that he will be critical." The therapist then asked him to have an image of his last encounter with his boss, and to describe it in detail. The patient had a picture of the boss towering over him saying, "I'm so disappointed in you. Don't you see the trouble you've caused?" The emotions this scene elicited—shame, sadness, and the desire to withdraw—were the same as those he had experienced as a child when his mother berated him for his poor performance in school. As a child, he had received no help with his schoolwork; when he would fail, his mother would say to him: "You're the only child who did miserably. Now I'll have to go to that school and talk to the teacher."

The patient was able to discriminate the past from the present; that is, he was able to "see" at an experiential level that although he was reacting to his boss as he once had to his mother, they were obviously different people, and he was no longer a child. It would not have been possible for him to have achieved this degree of "emotional insight" simply by making verbal comparisons between his present and his past experiences, between his reactions to his boss and his reactions to his mother.

The strategies described in this chapter will be elaborated in subsequent chapters in the context of specific personality disorders.

Part II
Clinical Applications

Chapter 6
Paranoid Personality Disorder

Three different disorders are characterized by a "paranoid" approach to life. The DSM-III-R diagnoses of schizophrenia, paranoid type (formerly paranoid schizophrenia) and delusional (paranoid) disorder (formerly paranoid disorder) are characterized by persistent paranoid delusions, while paranoid personality disorder (PPD) is characterized by an unwarranted tendency to perceive the actions of others as intentionally threatening or demeaning but is free of persistent psychotic features (APA, 1987). Schizophrenia, paranoid type, and delusional disorder have been the subject of much theoretical attention and empirical research; however, there is no clear consensus regarding the relationship between PPD and the two psychoses that are characterized by paranoia (Turkat, 1985). Thus, it is not clear whether the findings of research conducted on psychotic samples can be generalized to PPD. Since PPD has received only limited attention until recently, clinicians have had little to guide them when working with clients who are paranoid but not psychotic.

In recent years, behavioral and cognitive-behavioral investigators have focused increasing attention on the treatment of individuals diagnosed as having personality disorders (Fleming & Pretzer, in press; Pretzer & Fleming, 1989). Several cognitive-behavioral perspectives on PPD have now been developed; these have considerable potential for providing the clinician with a basis for understanding this disorder and for intervening effectively.

Characteristics

As can be seen from reviewing the diagnostic criteria presented in Table 6.1, individuals with PPD are characterized by a persistent, unrealistic tendency to interpret the intentions and actions of others as demeaning

TABLE 6.1
DSM-III-R Diagnostic Criteria for Paranoid Personality Disorder

---

A. A pervasive and unwarranted tendency, beginning in early adulthood and present in a variety of contexts, to interpret the actions of people as deliberately demeaning or threatening, as indicated by at least *four* of the following:

   (1) expects, without sufficient basis, to be exploited or harmed by others
   (2) questions, without justification, the loyalty or trustworthiness of friends or associates
   (3) reads hidden demeaning or threatening meanings into benign remarks or events, e.g., suspects that a neighbor put trash out early to annoy him
   (4) bears grudges or is unforgiving of insults or slights
   (5) is reluctant to confide in others because of unwarranted fear that the information will be used against him or her
   (6) is easily slighted and quick to react with anger or to counterattack
   (7) questions, without justification, fidelity of spouse or external partner

B. Occurrence not exclusively during the course of Schizophrenia or a Delusional Disorder.

Note. From *Diagnostic and Statistical Manual of Mental Disorders* (3rd ed., rev., p. 339) by the American Psychiatric Association, 1987, Washington, DC: Author. Copyright 1987 by the American Psychiatric Association. Reprinted by permission.

or threatening, but they are free of persistent psychotic symptoms such as delusions or hallucinations. For example, Ann was a married secretary in her mid-30s who sought help due to problems with tension, fatigue, insomnia, and being short-tempered. She attributed these problems to job stress. When asked to describe the main sources of stress at work, she reported, "People at work are constantly dropping things and making noise just to get me," and "They keep trying to turn my supervisor against me."

Ann described a long-standing tendency to ascribe malicious intentions to others, and she was unwilling to consider alternative explanations for the actions of her coworkers. She described herself as typically being sensitive, jealous, easily offended, and quick to anger; however, there was no evidence of thought disorder, persistent delusions, or other symptoms of psychosis. Despite the clear diagnostic criteria provided in DSM-III-R, diagnosis of PPD is not easy, since these clients rarely enter therapy saying, "Doc, my problem is that I'm paranoid." In Ann's case, her paranoia was obvious from the beginning of treatment; however, the disorder often is much less apparent initially and can easily be missed. For example, Gary was a single radiologist in his late 20s who had a steady girlfriend but was living with his parents while working full-time and going to graduate school part-time. He described himself as being chronically nervous and reported problems with worry, anxiety attacks, and insomnia. He said he was seeking therapy because his symptoms had intensified due to school pressures. During the interview he talked openly and seemed forthright. The initial interview was remarkable only for his not wanting his family to know he was in therapy "because they don't believe in it," and his not wanting to use his health insurance because of concerns about confidentiality, since "at the hospital I see how much confidential information is just laying around."

Cognitive therapy, focusing both on learning skills for coping more effectively with stress and anxiety and on examining his fears, proceeded unremarkably and effectively for six sessions.[1] At the beginning of the 7th session he described a number of occasions on which progressive relaxation techniques "didn't work." In discussing these episodes, he made comments such as "It's like I don't want to relax," "Maybe I'm afraid of people just taking from me," "I don't want him stealing my idea," and "Every little thing you say is used against you." Finally, he described people in general as "out to take you for what they can get." Further discussion made it clear that a suspicious, defensive approach to interpersonal situations was characteristic of his long-term functioning and played a central role both in his problems with stress and anxiety and in his difficulty with using relaxation techniques effectively.

Paranoid individuals have a strong tendency to blame others for interpersonal problems, usually can cite many experiences that seem to justify their convictions about others, are quick to deny or minimize their own problems, and often have little recognition of the ways in which their behavior contributes to their problems. Thus, when an assessment is based on the client's self-report, it can easily appear that the client's suspicions are justified or that the problems are due to inappropriate actions by others. In addition, since the characteristics of paranoia are understood to some extent by most laypeople, paranoid individuals are likely to recognize that others consider them to be paranoid and to realize that it is prudent to keep their thoughts to themselves. When this is the case, indications of paranoia tend to emerge only gradually over the course of therapy and may easily be missed.

Often it is easiest to identify paranoid individuals by watching for characteristics other than blatantly unrealistic suspicions. Table 6.2 presents a number of possible signs of a paranoid personality style that may be early indications of PPD. Individuals with PPD are typically quite vigilant, tend to interpret ambiguous situations as threatening, and are quick to take precautions against perceived threats. They frequently are perceived by others as argumentative, stubborn, defensive, and unwilling to compromise. They also may manifest some of the characteristics

---

[1]See Pretzer, Beck, and Newman (in press) for a detailed discussion of the approach to stress management that was used.

TABLE 6.2
Possible Indications of Paranoid Personality Disorder

Constant vigilance, possibly manifested as a tendency to scan the therapist's office during the interview and/or to glance frequently out the window.

Greater than normal concern about confidentiality, possibly including reluctance to allow the therapist to maintain progress notes and/or requests that the therapist take special steps to assure confidentiality when returning telephone calls from the client.

A tendency to attribute all blame for problems to others and to see himself or herself as being mistreated and abused.

Recurrent conflict with authority figures.

Unusually strong convictions regarding the motives of others and difficulty considering alternative explanations for their actions.

A tendency to interpret small events as having great significance and thus react strongly, apparently "making mountains out of molehills."

A tendency to counterattack quickly in response to a perceived threat or slight, or a tendency to be contentious and litigious.

A tendency to receive more than his or her share of bad treatment from others or to provoke hostility from others.

A tendency to search intensely and narrowly for evidence that confirms his or her negative expectations regarding others, ignoring the context and reading (plausible) special meanings and hidden motives into ordinary events.

Inability to relax, particularly when in the presence of others, possibly including unwillingness or inability to close his or her eyes in the presence of the therapist for relaxation training.

Inability to see the humor in situations.

An unusually strong need for self-sufficiency and independence.

Disdain for those he or she sees as weak, soft, sickly, or defective.

Difficulty expressing warm, tender feelings or expressing doubts and insecurities.

Pathological jealousy.

they perceive in others, being seen by others as devious, deceptive, disloyal, hostile, and malicious.

It is often stated that persons with PPD rarely enter therapy, since they do not see their suspiciousness as a problem, are reluctant to accept help, and rarely function so poorly that they require involuntary treatment (e.g., see APA, 1987, p. 338; Turkat & Banks, 1987; Weintraub, 1981). However, it is possible that rather than avoiding therapy, individuals with PPD enter therapy without the disorder being diagnosed. It is true that these individuals rarely seek therapy presenting their paranoia as their main problem, but they may seek therapy due to other problems, such as difficulty in handling stress, conflicts with superiors or colleagues, marital problems, or substance abuse. When this is the case, their underlying suspicions of others may not be apparent. Individuals with PPD can often conceal their paranoia quite well when they choose to do so. For example, Gary's paranoia was not recognized until the seventh therapy session, despite the therapist's active interest in this disorder. The prevalence of PPD in our practice has been much higher than is generally reported (e.g., Turkat, 1985), despite our interest in the disorder not being widely known. It is not clear if this is due to more efficient detection of the disorder or to some bias in our referral network, but it raises the possibility that the disorder may be underdiagnosed.

Theoretical Perspectives

The general topic of paranoia has received extensive attention from psychodynamic writers from Freud to the present. A typical view is presented by Shapiro (1965, pp. 54–107). Following an extensive discussion of the paranoid cognitive style, he argues that the disorder is a result of "projection" of unacceptable feelings and impulses onto others. In theory, attributing unacceptable impulses to others rather than to oneself reduces or eliminates guilt over these impulses and thus serves as a defense against internal conflict. The psychoanalytic view, in essence, is that the individual inaccurately perceives in others that which is actually true of him or her, and, as a result, experiences less distress than would result from a more realistic view of self and others.

A cognitive-behavioral model of paranoia that is similar to this traditional view has been presented by Colby and his colleagues (Colby, 1981; Colby, Faught, & Parkinson, 1979). These investigators have developed a computer simulation of a paranoid client's responses in a psychiatric interview, which is sufficiently realistic that experienced interviewers are unable to distinguish between the responses of the computer and the responses of a paranoid client as long as the interview is sufficiently restricted (Kochen, 1981). Colby's model is based on the assumption that paranoia is actually a set of strategies directed toward minimizing or forestalling shame and humiliation. The paranoid individual is assumed to believe strongly that he or she is inadequate, imperfect, and insufficient. This is believed to result in his or her experiencing intolerable levels of shame and humiliation when situations such as being the object of ridicule, being falsely accused, or developing a physical disability occur.

Colby hypothesizes that when a "humiliating" situation occurs, the individual can avoid accepting the blame and the consequent feelings of shame and humiliation by blaming someone else for the event and asserting that he or she was wrongfully treated. The anger and/or anxiety that results from attributing problems to persecution or harassment by malevolent others is presumed to be less aversive than the shame and humiliation that would occur if the individual were to hold himself or herself responsible for the events. Colby (1981) also notes that the paranoid individual's attributions have an important impact on interpersonal interactions. If the paranoid takes action against the individuals to whom he or she is attributing malicious intentions, they may retaliate with actions that are potentially humiliating. Thus, in actuality, paranoid behavior may indirectly amplify the shame and humiliation it was intended to reduce. While Colby's model is quite interesting, it should be noted that the individual simulated by his computer program is delusional and thus would not qualify for a diagnosis of PPD.

PPD per se has received attention from a number of authors. Cameron (1963, 1974) sees the disorder as stemming from a basic lack of trust, which results from parental mistreatment and a lack of consistent parental love. The child learns to expect sadistic treatment from others, to be vigilant for signs of danger, and to act quickly to defend himself or herself. The individual's vigilance results in his or her detecting subtle cues of negative reactions in others and then reacting strongly to them, while at the same time having little awareness of the impact his or her own hostile attitudes have on others.

Millon (1981) argues that PPD almost invariably covaries with other personality disorders, and he discusses each of five major subtypes separately. The "paranoid-narcissistic" subtype is seen as resulting from a strong belief in one's importance coupled with deficits in social skills. Millon hypothesizes that when these individuals are confronted with an environment that does not share their belief in their own importance, they retreat into fantasies of omnipotence rather than acknowledge their own shortcomings. The "paranoid-antisocial" personality is seen as resulting from an individual's having received harassment and antagonism from his or her parents, which led to a view of the world as harsh and to rebellious, hostile behavior that provokes rejection by others. "Paranoid-compulsive" individuals are seen as having learned to strive to comply perfectly to rigid parental rules, and, as a result, to have become overcontrolled, perfectionistic, withdrawn, and self-critical. Paranoia results when the hostility inherent in their harsh self-criticism is attributed to others. Millon hypothesizes that constitutional factors contribute to the development of the "paranoid-passive-aggressive" personality, such that the infant's responses to his or her parents encourage inconsistent parental responses. These subsequently encourage the child to develop into a person who is irritable, negativistic, and unable to maintain stable relationships. This results in social isolation and the development of delusional jealousy. Finally, the "decompensated paranoid" personality is seen as being highly vulnerable to psychotic episodes in response to stress and as possibly being a link between PPD and the psychoses. Millon (1981) does not provide a theoretical model of PPD in general or discuss intervention.

Turkat (1985, 1986, 1987; Turkat & Maisto, 1985) has recently presented a cognitive-behavioral model of the development and maintenance of PPD that is based on detailed examination of clinical cases. Turkat's view is that early interactions with parents teach the child, "You must be careful about making mistakes" and "You are different from others." These two beliefs are believed to result in the individual's being quite concerned about the evaluations of others, but also being constrained to conform to parental expectations, which interfere with acceptance by peers. This results in the individual's eventually being ostracized and humiliated by peers, but lacking the interpersonal skills needed to overcome the ostracism. Consequently, the individual spends much time ruminating about his or her isolation and mistreatment by peers, and eventually concludes that the reason for the persecution is that he or she is special and the others are jealous. This "rational" explanation is hypothesized to reduce the individual's distress over the social isolation. It is argued that the resulting paranoid view of others perpetuates the individual's isolation, both because the individual's anticipation of rejection results in considerable anxiety regarding social interactions and because acceptance by others would threaten this explanatory system.

Cognitive Conceptualization

A number of the theoretical perspectives on PPD presented above share the view that the individual's suspicions regarding others and his or her ruminations about persecution and mistreatment at the hands of others are not central to the disorder, but are rationalizations used to reduce the individual's subjective distress. A different view of the role of these cognitions in PPD is presented in the cognitive analysis we have developed (Pretzer, 1985, 1988; Freeman et al., 1990). If we evaluate the cognitive and interpersonal components of the paranoid approach to life manifested by Gary, the tense radiologist discussed earlier, an interesting pattern emerges. Gary held three basic assumptions: "People are malevolent and deceptive," "They'll attack you if they get the chance," and "You can be OK only if you stay on your toes." These assumptions led him to expect deception, trickery, and harm in interpersonal interactions and led him to conclude that vigilance for signs of deception, trickery, and malicious intentions was constantly necessary.

However, this vigilance for signs of malicious intentions produced an unintended side effect. If one is vigilant for subtle indications that others are deceptive and malicious (and not equally vigilant for signs of trustworthiness and good intentions), one quickly observes many actions appearing to support the view that people cannot be trusted. This happens both because people are not universally benevolent and trustworthy, and because many interpersonal interactions are sufficiently ambiguous that they can appear to reveal malicious intentions even if the individual's actual intentions are benign. Gary's vigilance produced substantial evidence to support his assumptions about human nature and tended to perpetuate his paranoid approach to life.

In addition, Gary's expectations regarding the actions of others had an important effect on his interactions with colleagues and acquaintances. He avoided closeness for fear that the emotional involvement and openness involved in close relationships would increase his vulnerability. In addition, he was generally guarded and defensive while interacting with others, tended to overreact to small slights, and was quick to counterattack when he believed he had been mistreated. These actions did not encourage others to be kind and generous toward him, but rather tended to provoke distrust and hostility from others. Thus, Gary's expectations led him to interact with others in a way that provoked the type of behavior he anticipated, and that provided him with the repeated experience of being treated badly by others. These experiences, of course, supported his negative expectations of others and also perpetuated his paranoid approach to life.

The third factor is self-efficacy, a construct that Bandura (1977) has defined as the individual's subjective estimate of his or her ability to cope effectively with specific problems or situations as they arise. If Gary had been confident that he could easily see through the deceptions of others and thwart their attacks, he would have felt less need to be constantly on guard, and thus would have been both less vigilant and less defensive. If he had been convinced that he could not cope effectively despite his efforts, he would have been likely to abandon his vigilance and defensiveness and to adopt some other coping strategy. In either case, the cycles that perpetuated his paranoia would have been attenuated or disrupted. However, Gary doubted his ability to deal effectively with others unless he was constantly vigilant; at the same time, he was fairly confident that he could at least survive if he were vigilant enough. Thus, he maintained his guardedness and vigilance, and this perpetuated his paranoia.

In addition to the tendency of the two cycles discussed above to generate observations and experiences that strongly support the paranoid individual's assumptions, another factor results in the paranoid's world view being nearly impervious to experiences that should demonstrate that other persons are not universally malicious. Since the client assumes that people are malicious and deceptive, then interactions in which other people seem benign or helpful can easily be interpreted as being an attempt to trick him or her into trusting them in order to provide an opportunity for attack or exploitation. Once this interpretation of the other persons' acts as deceptive occurs, the "fact" that the persons have tried to deceive the client by acting nice or trustworthy seems to prove that their intentions are malicious. This leads to the commonly observed tendency of paranoid individuals to reject "obvious" interpretations of the actions of others and to search for the "real" underlying meaning. Usually, this search continues until an interpretation consistent with the paranoid individual's preconceptions is found.

The paranoid's conviction that he or she faces dangerous situations and must rely on his or her own capabilities accounts for many of the characteristics of PPD. Vigilant for signs of danger, the individual acts cautiously and purposefully, avoiding carelessness and unnecessary risks. Since the most important danger is seen as coming from others, the paranoid is alert for signs of danger or deception during interactions, constantly scanning for subtle cues of the individual's true intentions. In such a "dog-eat-dog" world, to show any weakness is to court attack, so the paranoid carefully conceals his or her insecurities, shortcomings, and problems through deception, denial, excuses, or blaming others. Since "what others know about you may be used against you," the paranoid carefully guards his or her privacy, striving to suppress even trivial information and, in particular, suppressing signs of his or her own emotions and intentions. When in a dangerous situation, any restrictions on one's freedom can leave one trapped or increase one's vulnerability. Thus the paranoid tends to resist rules and regulations unless they serve his or her plans. The more powerful other individuals are, the more of a threat they are seen as posing. Thus the paranoid is keenly aware of power hierarchies, both admiring and fearing persons in positions of authority, hoping for a powerful ally but fearing betrayal or attack. He or she is typically unwilling to "give in," even on unimportant issues, since compromise is seen as a sign of weakness and the appearance of weakness might encourage attack. However, the paranoid is reluctant to challenge powerful individuals directly and risk provoking attack. As a result, covert or passive resistance is common.

When one is vigilant for signs of threat or attack and presumes malicious intentions, it follows that any slights or mistreatments are intentional and malicious and deserve retaliation. When others protest that their actions were unintentional, accidental, or justified, their protestations are seen as evidence of deception and as proof of their malicious intentions. Since attention is focused on mistreatment by others, while any apparently good treatment by others is discounted, situations constantly seem unfair and unjust. Because the individual believes that he or she has been treated unfairly and will be treated badly in the future, there is little incentive to treat others well except for fear of their retaliation. Thus when the paranoid individual feels powerful enough to resist retaliation from others or to escape deception, he or she is likely to engage in the malicious, deceptive, hostile acts that are expected from others.

There are a number of differences between this view of PPD and those presented by Colby (1981; Colby et al., 1979) and Turkat (1985). First, the individual's attribution of malicious intentions to others is seen as being central to the disorder, rather than being a complex side effect of other problems. Thus, there is no need to assume that these suspicions of others are due to "projection" of unacceptable impulses, are attempts to avoid shame and humiliation by blaming others (Colby et al., 1979), or are rationalizations used to cope with social isolation (Turkat, 1985). Second, while the fear of making mistakes emphasized by Turkat is commonly observed in these clients, it is seen as being secondary to the assumption that others are dangerous and malicious, rather than as being central to the disorder. Finally, the importance of the individual's sense of self-efficacy is emphasized in this model. At this point, the empirical evidence needed to determine which model of PPD is most valid is not available.

In discussing PPD Turkat (1985) presents his ideas about the development of the disorder at length. We have not developed an equally detailed perspective on the etiology of PPD, since it is difficult to determine the accuracy of historical information obtained from paranoid clients. Since paranoid clients' views of others and their recollections of previous events are frequently found to be distorted in a paranoia-congruent way, their reports of childhood experiences may well be quite distorted. However, it is interesting to note that a paranoid stance would be adaptive if one were faced by a truly dangerous situation where others were likely to prove to be overtly or covertly hostile. Many paranoid clients describe growing up in families that they experienced as quite dangerous. For example, Gary described a long history of being ridiculed for any sign of sensitivity or weakness, of being lied to and cheated by parents and siblings, and of verbal and physical assaults by family members. In addition, he reported being explicitly taught by his parents that the world was a "dog-eat-dog" place where one must be tough to survive. Such accounts give the impression that growing up in a generally hostile or paranoid family where vigilance is truly necessary could contribute substantially to the development of PPD.

This hypothesis is appealing, but it will remain speculative until it is possible to obtain more objective data regarding the histories of these individuals. A comprehensive theoretical treatment of the etiology of PPD would also need to account for studies that find an unusually high incidence of "schizophrenic spectrum" disorders among relatives of individuals diagnosed with PPD (Kendler & Gruenberg, 1982). Such findings raise the possibility of a genetic contribution to the etiology of the disorder, but the mechanisms through which such a link could occur are not yet understood.

Treatment Approaches

On the basis of their computer model, Colby and his colleagues (Colby et al., 1979) suggest that it might be most effective to use interventions that focus on (1) challenging the client's belief that he or she is inadequate or insufficient, (2) restricting the scope of events that are accepted as evidence of inadequacy, and (3) counteracting the client's external attributions regarding the sources of his or her distress. They argue that directly challenging specific suspicions and allegations will prove ineffective as well as difficult, because it has little effect on the factors producing the disorder. The authors make it clear that these suggestions are based purely on their computer simulation and have not been clinically validated. Unfortunately, since the client simulated in Colby's model does not meet DSM-III-R criteria for PPD, it is not clear to what extent the recommended approach to intervention would apply to PPD.

Turkat and his colleagues have not made general recommendations about the treatment of PPD, but have provided a number of detailed discussions of clients with this disorder (Turkat, 1985, 1986, 1987; Turkat & Maisto, 1985). Of these, the case example that illustrates treatment in the most detail is Turkat and Maisto's (1985) detailed case example of Mr. E. This client's problems were conceptualized as stemming from his having developed a hypersensitivity to others' evaluations of him, but lacking the social skills necessary for him to be accepted by others. This was seen as resulting in a self-perpetuating cycle in which he was concerned about the opinions of others and attempted to gain their approval and avoid their disapproval, but did so in a way that elicited criticism instead. In response to this criticism, Mr. E withdrew and ruminated about his mistreatment at the hands of others. His cognitions about persecution by others were seen as a rationalization used to cope with his recurrent failures and ruminations about failures. On the basis of this conceptualization, Turkat and Maisto (1985) selected interventions focused on decreasing the client's anxiety regarding evaluation by others and on improving his social skills as being most appropriate, and paid only limited attention to his paranoid thought style. While treatment had not been completed at the time of publication, the authors document that considerable progress had been made after 7 months of twice-weekly therapy.

The view of PPD that has been presented in this chapter suggests an approach to treatment that is somewhat different from those advocated by Colby and Turkat. At first glance, the conceptualization may appear to provide little opportunity for effective intervention. One goal of intervention would be to modify the individual's basic assumptions, since these are the foundation of the disorder. However, how can one hope to challenge these assumptions effectively when the client's vigilance and paranoid approach to interactions constantly produce experiences that seem to confirm the assumptions? If it were possible to get the client to relax the vigilance and defensiveness, this would simplify the task of modifying his or her assumptions. But how can the therapist hope to induce the client to relax the vigilance or to treat others more nicely as long as the client is convinced that the others have malicious intentions? If these two self-perpetuating cycles were the whole of the cognitive model, there would be little prospect for effective cognitive-behavioral intervention with these clients. However, the client's sense of self-efficacy plays an important role in the model as well.

The paranoid individual's intense vigilance and defensiveness are a product of the belief that constant vigilance and defensiveness are necessary to preserve his or her safety. If it is possible to increase the client's sense of self-efficacy regarding problem situations to the point that he or she is reasonably confident of being able to handle problems as they arise, then the intense vigilance and defensiveness seems less necessary, and it may be possible for the client to relax both to some extent. This would reduce the intensity of the client's symptomatology substantially, make it much easier to address his or her cognitions through conventional cognitive therapy techniques, and make it possible to persuade him or her to try alternative ways of handling interpersonal conflicts. Therefore, the primary strategy in the cognitive treatment of PPD is to work to increase the client's sense of self-efficacy before attempting to modify other aspects of the client's automatic thoughts, interpersonal behavior, and basic assumptions.

Establishing Collaboration with Paranoid Clients

The first issue in cognitive therapy with PPD is establishing a working relationship. This obviously is no simple task when working with someone who assumes that others are likely to prove malevolent and deceptive. Direct attempts to convince the client to trust the therapist are likely be perceived by the client as deceptive and therefore are likely to increase the client's suspicions. The approach that proves most effective is for the therapist to openly accept the client's distrust once it has become apparent, and to gradually demonstrate his or her trustworthiness through action rather than pressing the client to trust him or her immediately. For example, once it was clear that Gary, the radiologist discussed previously, was generally distrustful of others, this was addressed as follows:

GARY: I guess that's what I do all the time, expect the worst of people. Then I'm not surprised.

THERAPIST: You know, it strikes me that this tendency to be skeptical about others and to be slow to trust them seems like something that would be likely to come up in therapy from time to time.

GARY: Umm . . . (*Pause*)

THERAPIST: After all, how are you to know if it's safe to trust me or not? People tell me I have an honest face, but what does that prove? I've got a degree after my name, but you know that doesn't prove I'm a saint. Hopefully, the things I'm saying make sense, but you're not dumb enough to trust someone just because he's a good talker. It seems like it could be hard for a person to decide whether to trust a therapist or not, and that puts you in a tough situation. It's hard to get help without trusting at least a little but it's hard to tell if it's safe to trust. . . . How's that sound so far?

GARY: You've got it about right.

THERAPIST: One way out of that dilemma is to take your time and see how well I follow through on what I say. It's a lot easier to trust actions than words.

GARY: That makes sense.

THERAPIST: Now if we're going to take that approach, we'll need to figure out what to work on first.

It is then incumbent on the therapist to make a point of proving his or her trustworthiness. This includes being careful only to make offers that he or she will be willing and able to follow through on, making an effort to be clear and consistent, actively correcting the client's misunderstandings and misperceptions as they occur, and openly acknowledging any lapses that do occur. It is important for the therapist to remember that it takes time to establish trust with most paranoid individuals and to refrain from pressing the client to talk about sensitive thoughts or feelings until sufficient trust has gradually been established. Standard cognitive techniques, such as the use of Dysfunctional Thought Records, may require too much self-disclosure for the client to be willing to comply early in therapy. Thus, it may be useful to select a problem that can be addressed primarily through behavioral interventions as the initial focus of therapy.

Collaboration is always important in cognitive therapy, but it is especially important in working with paranoid individuals. They are likely to become intensely anxious or angry if they feel coerced, treated unfairly, or placed in a "one-down" position. Since these clients rarely present their paranoia as a problem they wish to work on, it is important to focus on understanding and working toward accomplishing the client's goals for therapy. Some therapists fear that in focusing on the client's stress, marital problems, and so forth, the "real problem" of paranoia might be missed. However, when one uses a problem-solving approach in pursuing the client's goals, the ways in which his or her paranoia contributes to the other problems will quickly become apparent. This creates a situation where it is then possible to engage the client in working collaboratively on his or her distrust of others and feelings of vulnerability, because doing so is an important step towards attaining the client's goals for therapy.

The initial phase of therapy can be quite stressful to paranoid clients even when it seems to the therapist that the focus is on superficial topics that should not be at all threatening. Simply participating in therapy requires the client to engage in a number of activities such as self-disclosure, acknowledging weakness, and trusting another person, which paranoid individuals experience as being very dangerous. This stress can be reduced somewhat by focusing initially on the least sensitive topics, by starting with more behavioral interventions, and by discussing issues indirectly (i.e., through the use of analogies or through talking about how "some people" react in such situations) rather than pressing for direct self-disclosure. One of the more effective ways to increase a paranoid client's comfort with therapy is to give him or her even more than the usual amount of control over the content of sessions, homework assignments, and the scheduling of sessions. The client may be much more comfortable and may actually progress more quickly if sessions are scheduled less frequently than usual, and the client's input regarding how often to schedule sessions can be quite useful. With a number of paranoid clients, scheduling sessions about once every 3 weeks has seemed optimal.

Cognitive and Behavioral Interventions

As the therapist's focus shifts from working to establish a collaborative relationship to working toward the client's initial goals, it is most productive to focus particular attention on increasing the client's sense of self-efficacy regarding problem situations (i.e., to work to increase the client's conviction that he or she can cope with any problems that arise). There are two main ways in which this can be done. First, if the client is actually capable of handling the situation but overestimates the threat posed by the situation, or underestimates his or her capacity for handling it, interventions that result in a more realistic appraisal of coping ability will increase self-efficacy. Second, if the client is not capable of handling the situation, or if there is room for improvement in his or her coping skills, interventions that improve coping skills will increase self-efficacy. In practice, it often works best to use the two approaches in combination.

With Ann (the secretary mentioned above), the therapist's initial attempts to challenge her paranoid ideation directly ("They are making noise just to get me") were ineffective. However, interventions directed at helping her to re-evaluate how much danger such actions would pose if her coworkers were indeed trying to provoke her, and directed toward helping her to re-evaluate her capacity for coping with the situation, were quite helpful. For example:

THERAPIST: You're reacting as though this is a very dangerous situation. What are the risks you see?

ANN: They'll keep dropping things and making noise to annoy me.

THERAPIST: Are you sure nothing worse is at risk?

ANN: Yeah.

THERAPIST: So you don't think there's much chance of them attacking you or anything?

ANN: Nah, they wouldn't do that.

THERAPIST: If they do keep dropping things and making noises, how bad will that be?

ANN: Like I told you, it's real aggravating. It really bugs me.

THERAPIST: So it would continue pretty much as it has been going for years now.

ANN: Yeah. It bugs me, but I can take it.

THERAPIST: And you know that if it keeps happening, at the very least you can keep handling it the way you have been— holding the aggravation in, then taking it out on your husband when you get home. Suppose we could come up with some ways to handle the aggravation even better or to have them get to you less. Is that something you'd be interested in?

ANN: Yeah, that sounds good.

THERAPIST: Another risk you mentioned earlier was that they might talk to your supervisor and turn her against you. As you see it, how long have they been trying to do this?

ANN: Ever since I've been there.

THERAPIST: How much luck have they had so far in doing that?

ANN: Not much.

THERAPIST: Do you see any indications that they're going to have any more success now than they have so far?

ANN: No, I don't guess so.

THERAPIST: So your gut reaction is as though the situation at work is really dangerous. But when you stop and think it through, you conclude that the worst they're going to do is to be really aggravating, and that even if we don't come up with anything new, you can handle it well enough to get by. Does that sound right?

ANN: (*Smiling*) Yeah, I guess so.

THERAPIST: And if we can come up with some ways to handle the stress better or handle them better, there will be even less they can do to you.

Obviously this interchange alone did not transform Ann dramatically, but following this session she reported a noticeable decrease in vigilance and stress at work, which apparently was due to her perceiving the work situation as being much less threatening. This resulted in her noticing fewer apparent provocations and thus in her experiencing less anger and frustration. Additional interventions focusing on re-evaluating perceived threats, on stress management, on assertion, and on improving marital communication resulted in rapid improvement. According to her husband's report as well as her own, she continued to be somewhat guarded and vigilant; however, she no longer overreacted to minor provocations, was able to be assertive rather than hostile, no longer exploded at her husband as a result of aggravations at work, and was significantly more comfortable visiting her in-laws.

With Gary, the young radiologist, by the time that his PPD was recognized, the successful stress management interventions described previously had already raised his sense of self-efficacy substantially. However, he still felt that vigilance was necessary in many innocuous situations, because he doubted his ability to cope if he wasn't constantly vigilant. It became clear that he had very strict standards for competence in work and in social interactions and viewed competence as dichotomous—one was either fully competent or totally incompetent. The "continuum technique" was used to help him re-evaluate his view of competence:

THERAPIST: It sounds like a lot of your tension and your spending so much time double-checking your work is because you see yourself as basically incompetent and think, "I've got to be careful or I'll really screw up."

GARY: Sure. But it's not just screwing up something little; someone's life could depend on what I do.

THERAPIST: Hmm. We've talked about your competence in terms of how you were evaluated while you were in training and how well you've done since then, without making much headway. It occurs to me that I'm not sure exactly what "competence" means for you. What does it take for somebody to really qualify as competent? For example, if a Martian came down knowing nothing of humans, and he wanted to know how to tell who was truly competent, what would you tell him to look for?

GARY: It's someone who does a good job at whatever he's doing.

THERAPIST: Does it matter what the person is doing? If someone does well at something easy, do they qualify as competent in your eyes?

GARY: No, to really be competent they can't be doing something easy.

THERAPIST: So it sounds like they've got to be doing something hard and getting good results to qualify as competent.

GARY: Yeah.

THERAPIST: Is that all there is to it? You've been doing something hard and doing well at it, but you don't feel competent.

GARY: But I'm tense all the time and I worry about work.

THERAPIST: Are you saying that a truly competent person isn't tense and doesn't worry?

GARY: Yeah. They're confident. They relax while they're doing it, and they don't worry about it afterward.

THERAPIST: So a competent person is someone who takes on difficult tasks and does them well, is relaxed while he's doing them, and doesn't worry about it afterwards. Does that cover it, or is there more to competence?

GARY: Well, he doesn't have to be perfect as long as he catches his mistakes and knows his limits.

THERAPIST: What I've gotten down so far [the therapist has been taking notes] is that a truly competent person is doing hard tasks well and getting good results, he's relaxed while he does this and doesn't worry about it afterward, he catches any mistakes he makes and corrects them, and he knows his limits. Does that capture what you have in mind when you use the word "competent"?

GARY: Yeah, I guess it does.

THERAPIST: From the way you've talked before, I've gotten the impression that you see competence as pretty black and white—either you're competent or you aren't.

GARY: Of course. That's the way it is.

THERAPIST: What would be a good label for the people who aren't competent? Does "incompetent" capture it?

GARY: Yeah, that's fine.

THERAPIST: What would characterize incompetent people? What would you look for to spot them?

GARY: They screw everything up. They don't do things right. They don't even care whether it's right or how they look or feel. You can't expect results from them.

THERAPIST: Does that cover it?

GARY: Yeah, I think so.

THERAPIST: Well, let's look at how you measure up to these standards. One characteristic of an incompetent person is that he screws everything up. Do you screw everything up?

GARY: Well, no. Most things I do come out OK, but I'm real tense while I do them.

THERAPIST: And you said that an incompetent person doesn't care whether it comes out right or how they look to others. So your being tense and worrying doesn't fit with the idea that you're incompetent. If you don't qualify as incompetent, does that mean that you're completely competent?

GARY: I don't feel competent.

THERAPIST: And by these standards you aren't. You do well with a difficult job, and you've been successful at catching the mistakes you do make, but you aren't relaxed and you do worry. By these standards you don't qualify as completely incompetent or totally competent. How does that fit with the idea that a person's either competent or incompetent?

GARY: I guess maybe it's not just one or the other.

THERAPIST: While you were describing how you saw competence and incompetence, I wrote the criteria here in my notes. Suppose we draw a scale from 0 to 10 here, where 0 is absolutely, completely incompetent and 10 is completely competent all the time [see Figure 6.1]. How would you rate your competence in grad school?

GARY: At first I was going to say 3 but, as I think about it, I'd say a 7 or 8 except for my writing, and I've never worked at that until now.

THERAPIST: How would you rate your competence on the job?

GARY: I guess it would be an 8 or 9 in terms of results, but I'm not relaxed, so that would be about a 3. I do a good job of catching my mistakes as long as I'm not worrying too much, so that would be an 8, and I'd say a 9 or 10 on knowing my limits.

THERAPIST: How would you rate your skeet shooting?

GARY: That would be a 6 but it doesn't matter, I just do it for fun.

THERAPIST: So I hear several important points. First, when you think it

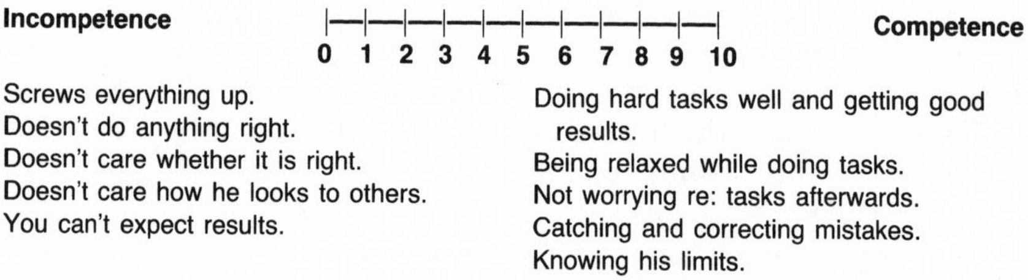

Incompetence |—|—|—|—|—|—|—|—|—|—| **Competence**
0 1 2 3 4 5 6 7 8 9 10

Screws everything up.
Doesn't do anything right.
Doesn't care whether it is right.
Doesn't care how he looks to others.
You can't expect results.

Doing hard tasks well and getting good results.
Being relaxed while doing tasks.
Not worrying re: tasks afterwards.
Catching and correcting mistakes.
Knowing his limits.

FIGURE 6.1 Continuum of competence based on Gary's dichotomous view of competence.

over, competence turns out not to be all or nothing. Someone who's not perfect isn't necessarily incompetent. Second, the characteristics you see as being signs of competence don't necessarily hang together real well. You rate an 8 or 9 in terms of the quality of your work, but a 3 in being relaxed and not worrying. Finally, there are times, such as when you're at work, when being competent is very important to you, and other times, like skeet shooting, when it's not very important.

GARY: Yeah, I guess I don't have to be at my peak all the time.

THERAPIST: What do you think of this idea—that if a person's competent they'll be relaxed, and if they're tense that means they're not competent?

GARY: I don't know.

THERAPIST: It certainly seems that if a person's sure they can handle the situation, they're likely to be less tense about it. But I don't know about the flip side—the idea that if you're tense, that proves you're incompetent. When you're tense and worried, does that make it easier for you to do well or harder for you to do well?

GARY: It makes it a lot harder for me to do well. I have trouble concentrating and keep forgetting things.

THERAPIST: So if someone does well despite being tense and worried, they're overcoming an obstacle.

GARY: Yeah, they are.

THERAPIST: Some people would argue that doing well despite having to overcome obstacles shows greater capabilities than doing well when things are easy. What do you think of that idea?

GARY: It makes sense to me.

THERAPIST: Now, you've been doing a good job at work, despite being real tense and worried. Up to this point, you've been taking your tenseness as proof that you're really incompetent and have just been getting by because you're real careful. This other way of looking at it would say that being able to do well despite being anxious shows that you really are competent, not that you're incompetent. Which do you think is closer to the truth?

GARY: I guess maybe I'm pretty capable after all, but I still hate being so tense.

THERAPIST: Of course, and we'll keep working on that, but the key point is that being tense doesn't necessarily mean you're incompetent. Now, another place where you feel tense and think you're incompetent is in social situations. Let's see if you're as incompetent as you feel there.

Once Gary decided that his ability to handle stressful situations well despite his stress and anxiety was actually a sign of competence rather than incompetence, his sense of self-efficacy increased substantially. Following this increase in self-efficacy, he was much less defensive and thus more willing to disclose thoughts and feelings, to look critically at his beliefs and assumptions, and to test new approaches to problem situations. This made it possible to use standard cognitive techniques with greater effectiveness.

Another series of interventions that was particularly effective was using the continuum technique to challenge Gary's dichotomous view of trustworthiness, then introducing the idea that he could learn which persons were likely to prove trustworthy by noticing how well they followed through when trusted on trivial issues, and raising the question of whether his truly malevolent family was typical of people in general or not. After this, he was able gradually to test his negative view of others' intentions by trusting colleagues and acquaintances in small things and observing their performance. He was pleasantly surprised to discover that the world at large was much less malevolent than he had assumed, that it contained benevolent and indifferent people as well as malevolent ones, and that when he was treated badly he could deal with the situation effectively.

When testing the client's perceptions of others as malevolent, it is important not to presume that the client's views are necessarily distorted. Paranoid individuals often turn out to have some malevolent associates or to have seriously alienated a number of acquaintances or colleagues. The goal is to enable the client to differentiate between persons who are generally safe to trust, persons who can be trusted to some extent, and persons who are malevolent or unreliable, rather than simply presuming that all persons are malevolent. It also can be important to consider the impact of significant others on the client's beliefs. It is not unusual for paranoid individuals to marry persons who are also paranoid. When this is the case, the spouse may actively oppose the changes that the therapist is working toward, and couple sessions may be needed.

Concurrently with the primarily cognitive interventions, it is important to work to modify the client's dysfunctional interpersonal interactions, so that the client no longer provokes hostile reactions from others, which would support his or her paranoid views. In Gary's case, this required focusing on specific problem situations as they arose. It proved important to address cognitions that blocked appropriate assertion, including "It won't do any good," "They'll just get mad," and "If they know what I want, they'll use that against me." It was also necessary to work to improve his skills in assertiveness and clear communication through assertion training. When this resulted in improvements in his relationships with colleagues and in his relationship with his girlfriend, it was fairly easy to use guided discovery to help him recognize the ways in which his previous interaction style had inadvertently provoked hostility from others.

THERAPIST: So it sounds like speaking up for yourself directly has been working out pretty well. How do the other people seem to feel about it?

GARY: Pretty good, I guess. Sue and I have been getting along fine, and things have been less tense at work.

THERAPIST: That's interesting. I remember that one of your concerns was that people might get mad if you spoke up for yourself. It sounds as though it might be helping things go better instead.

GARY: Well, I've had a few run-ins, but they've blown over pretty quickly.

THERAPIST: That's a change from the way things used to be right there. Before, if you had a run-in with somebody, it would bug you for a long time. Do you have any idea what's made the difference?

GARY: Not really. It just doesn't seem to stay on my mind as long.

THERAPIST: Could you fill me in on one of the run-ins you had this week?

[The therapist and Gary discussed a disagreement with his boss in detail.]

THERAPIST: It sounds like two things were different from the old way of handling this sort of situation: You stuck with the discussion rather than leaving angry, and you let him know what was bugging you. Do you think that had anything to do with its blowing over more quickly than usual?

GARY: It might.

THERAPIST: It works that way for a lot of people. If it turns out to work that way for you, that would be another payoff to speaking up directly. If they go along with what you want, there's no problem; and if they don't, at least it blows over more quickly. Do you remember how you used to feel after leaving a disagreement unresolved?

GARY: I'd think about it for days. I'd be tense and jumpy, and little things would bug me a lot.

THERAPIST: How do you think it was for the people at work?

GARY: They'd be pretty tense and jumpy too. Nobody'd want to talk to each other for a while.

THERAPIST: That makes it sound like it would be easy for a little mistake or misunderstanding to set off another disagreement.

GARY: I think you're right.

THERAPIST: You know, it seems pretty reasonable for a person to assume that the way to have as little conflict and tension as possible is to avoid speaking up about things that bug him and to try not to let his aggravation show, but it doesn't seem to work that way for you. So far, it sounds like when you speak up about things that bug you, there are fewer conflicts, and the conflicts that happen blow up more quickly.

GARY: Yeah.

THERAPIST: Do you think that your attempts to keep from aggravating people may have actually made things more tense?

GARY: It sounds like it.

Toward the close of therapy, it is possible to "fine-tune" the client's new perspective on people and new interpersonal skills by working to help him or her develop an increased ability to understand the perspectives of others and to empathize with them. This can be done through asking questions that require the client to anticipate the impact of his or her actions on others, to consider how he or she would feel if the roles were reversed, or to infer the thoughts and feelings of other people from their actions and then to examine the correspondence between these conclusions and the available data. Initially the client is likely to find these questions difficult to answer, and often to be off the mark. As the client receives feedback both from the therapist and from subsequent interactions, however, his or her ability to understand the other person's perspective is likely to increase steadily. The client discovers that aggravating actions by others are not necessarily motivated by malicious intentions, and that these actions are less aggravating if one can understand the other person's point of view.

At the close of therapy Gary was noticeably more relaxed, and was bothered by symptoms of stress and anxiety only at times when it is common to experience mild symptoms, such as immediately before major examinations. He reported being much more comfortable with friends and colleagues, was socializing more actively, and seemed to feel no particular need to be vigilant. When he and his girlfriend began having difficulties, due in part to her discomfort with the increasing closeness in their relationship, he was able to suspend his initial feelings of rejection and his desire to retaliate long enough to consider her point of view. He then was able to take a major role in resolving their difficulties by communicating his understanding of her concerns ("I know that after all you've been through, it's pretty scary when we start talking about marriage"), acknowledging his own fears and doubts ("I get pretty nervous about this too"), and expressing his commitment to their relationship ("I don't want this to tear us apart").

Conclusions

The approach to intervention outlined above is not radically different from that suggested by Colby et al. (1979) or that outlined by Turkat (Turkat, 1985; Turkat & Maisto, 1985). To a large extent, the client's paranoid views are not the main focus of therapy. Instead, standard cognitive-behavioral interventions are used to address the client's other problems. The points that distinguish the approach presented in this chapter from the other cognitive-behavioral approaches are the explicit attention paid to developing the therapist-client relationship, the emphasis on intentionally working to increase the client's sense of self-efficacy early in therapy, and the use of cognitive techniques and behavioral experiments to directly challenge the client's remaining paranoid beliefs late in therapy. Our experience has been that this strategy typically facilitates other interventions and produces improvement in paranoid symptomatology early in therapy, as increases in self-efficacy reduce the need for vigilance.

While no empirical data on the effectiveness of cognitive therapy with PPD is available, both our own clinical experience and the cases reported by Turkat and his colleagues are quite encouraging. The interventions that are recommended include increasing the client's sense of self-efficacy, improving his or her skills in coping with anxiety and with interpersonal problems, developing more realistic perceptions of the intentions and actions of others, and developing an increased awareness of the other person's point of view. These all lead to changes that would be expected to have broad intrapersonal and interpersonal impacts. It appears that major "personality change" can occur as a result of cognitive therapy with these clients. At this point, however, no data are available regarding the extent to which the improvements achieved in therapy generalize and persist.

Efforts to develop valid conceptualizations and effective treatment approaches for PPD have been hampered by a lack of empirical research on nonpsychotic paranoid subjects. In part, the lack of empirical research has been due to the difficulty of assembling samples of such individuals. Turkat and his colleagues (Thompson-Pope & Turkat, in press; Turkat & Banks, 1987) are attempting to circumvent this difficulty by identifying appropriate subjects among undergraduates enrolled in introductory psychology courses. Their initial findings indicate that it is possible to identify a small subgroup of "paranoid personality" subjects who are similar to individuals with PPD in being vigilant, keen observers who are quick to reach definite conclusions in ambiguous situations and often are quite perceptive, but who are prone to suspect that others are being deceptive and to report paranoid thoughts and experiences. If further research shows that the findings of studies using "paranoid personality" subjects can validly be generalized to individuals with PPD, this will greatly facilitate research on this disorder.

Chapter 7

Schizoid and Schizotypal Personality Disorders

Schizoid Personality Disorder

There are two striking features of schizoid personality disorder: the lack of interpersonal relationships, and the lack of desire to obtain such relationships. Others are seen as intrusive and unrewarding, and relationships are seen as messy and undesirable. As a result, these individuals are often described as withdrawn, reclusive, and isolated. Consistent with this, they show very little response to either negative or positive feedback from others. As might be expected, they report little satisfaction from relationships.

In addition, schizoid individuals are affectively constricted, showing neither strong positive nor strong negative emotional reactions. Corresponding with this, Millon (1981) suggests that they are unable to recognize subtle emotions either in themselves or in others. As a result, they often appear and feel indifferent. For many of these individuals, life is, at best, an underwhelming experience.

Although schizoid persons can be productive, they structure their lives to limit interactions with others and typically select an occupation that requires minimal social contact. Further, they pursue solitary interests even outside the work environment.

Introduction

The diagnosis of schizoid personality disorder is probably one of the most confusing of the Axis II diagnoses. The construct or label "schizoid" is a diagnostic category that has been in transition for almost 100 years. The original use of the term "schizoid" can be traced to Manfred Bleuler of the Swiss Burgholzi Clinic (Siever, 1981). It is composed of the prefix "schizo-," from the Greek word meaning "cleaving or splitting," and the suffix "-oid," which means "like or representing." Traditionally, the schizoid has been seen as an individual who is quiet, shy, and reserved and is generally withdrawn from others. Other views hold that schizoid behavior can represent either a chronic vulnerability to a schizophrenic process that may be genetically dictated or a partial state of recovery from schizophrenia. Siever (1981) utilizes the traditional definition when he states that the schizoid personality disorder resembles "the division, separation, or split of the personality that is characteristic of schizophrenia" (p. 563).

The schizoid personality can, in fact, be very creative in occupations that allow for solitary work. More frequently, the schizoid is employed at simple jobs that are below his or her level of ability. A number of early studies examined the premorbid adjustment of schizophrenics and found that a premorbid schizoid adjustment was prognostically related to the severity of the schizophrenic illness and a poorer chance of a favorable outcome though it was not necessarily a precursor to schizophrenia (Frazee, 1953; Gittelman-Klein & Klein, 1969; Longabaugh & Eldred, 1973; Mellsop, 1972, 1973; Morris, Soroker, & Burrus, 1954; Roff, Knight, & Wertheim, 1976).

Given the history of a theoretical link with schizophrenia, the view of the schizoid personality disorders presented in the past three editions of the *Diagnostic and Statistical Manual of Mental Disorders* differs markedly from earlier views. The schizoid personality disorder in DSM-I (APA, 1952) included the current diagnoses of schizoid, schizotypal, and avoidant personality disorders. Schizoid personality disorder is not presently identified with eventual movement into schizophrenia; rather, the schizoid individual is seen as chronically reclusive and isolated. In both DSM-III and DSM-III-R, the schizoid diagnosis has been separated from another diagnostic group, that of schizotypal personality disorder, which is seen as more closely related to the schizophrenic disorders (Baron, 1981; McGlashan, 1985; Siever, 1981) and which will be discussed later in this chapter.

In DSM-II (APA, 1968), the schizoid personality disorder was defined as follows:

> This behavior pattern manifests shyness, oversensitivity, seclusiveness, avoidance of close or competitive relationships, and often eccentricity. Autistic thinking without loss of capacity to recognize reality is common, as are daydreaming and the inability to express hostility and ordinary aggressive feelings. These patients react to disturbing experiences and conflicts with apparent detachment. (p. 42)

In DSM-III (APA, 1980) and, most recently, DSM-III-R (APA, 1987), the diagnostic criteria have been expanded (Table 7.1). The basic themes of emotional constriction, aloofness, and lack of desire to form relationships still remain as basic elements of this disorder. While there have been extensive theoretical musings about the nature of the schizoid individual, little clinical research has been done on this group (Freeman, 1988a,b; Freeman & Leaf, 1989; Millon, 1981). This is not surprising, given the reluctance of schizoid individuals to seek treatment.

The common link between the schizoid and schizotypal disorders can still be seen in DSM-III-R, as both include social isolation and often constricted affect. The hallmark, however, of schizoid personality is an introverted manner and lack of desire for relationships. Schizotypal personality disorder, the more severe condition, is best characterized by persistent peculiarities of cognition, behavior, and perception that are too mild to be diagnosed as schizophrenia.

Historical and Theoretical Perspective

As noted earlier, the term "schizoid" was first used by Bleuler (1924), who described a "shut-in," suspicious, dull person who directed energy inward, rather than to the external world. This person would also

TABLE 7.1
DSM-III-R Diagnostic Criteria for Schizoid Personality Disorder

A. A pervasive pattern of indifference to social relationships and a restricted range of emotional experience and expression, beginning by early adulthood and present in a variety of contexts, as indicated by at least *four* of the following:

   (1) neither desires nor enjoys close relationships, including being part of a family
   (2) almost always chooses solitary activities
   (3) rarely, if ever, claims or appears to experience strong emotions, such as anger or joy
   (4) indicates little if any desire to have sexual experiences with another person (age being taken into account)
   (5) is indifferent to the praise and criticism of others
   (6) has no close friends or confidants (or only one) other than first-degree relatives
   (7) displays constricted affect, e.g., is aloof, cold, rarely reciprocates gestures or facial expressions, such as smiles or nods

B. Occurrence not exclusively during the course of Schizophrenia or a Delusional Disorder

Note. From *Diagnostic and Statistical Manual of Mental Disorders* (3rd ed., rev., p. 340) by the American Psychiatric Association, 1987, Washington, DC: Author. Copyright 1987 by the American Psychiatric Association. Reprinted by permission.

demonstrate social withdrawal and peculiar thought, while not being overtly psychotic (Siever & Gunderson, 1983). A few years earlier, Hoch (1909) had also described a "shut-in" personality that preceded dementia praecox in patients. The premorbid personalities of these individuals were characterized by withdrawal, shyness, stubbornness, and a rich fantasy life. Later, Hoch and Polatin (1939) described this group of nonpsychotic persons who were predisposed to develop schizophrenia as "pseudoneurotic schizophrenics." Nannarello (1953) reported that the term was later popularized by Kretschmer (1925), who described "affective lameness" in two kinds of schizoid personality—"hyperaesthetic" and "anesthetic." Kretschmer's description of the anesthetic schizoid was of a dull, colorless, quiet, reserved individual who showed little or no affect or interest. In contrast, hyperaesthetic individuals were shy and so sensitive to external stimuli that they would go to great lengths to avoid it. In Kretschmer's view, the schizoid diagnosis was not necessarily synonymous with disability. Millon (1981) suggests that in current terminology, the hyperaesthetic and anesthetic classifications would correspond to the avoidant and schizoid personality disorders, respectively.

As Siever and Gunderson (1983) have noted, the term "schizoid" broadened from its original meaning to include, in general, those who avoid relationships and social interactions and who tend also to be eccentric. The broad usage of the term weakened its original meaning of a nonpsychotic form of schizophrenia. It was not until 1953, however, that Rado coined the term "schizotypal" as an abbreviation of "schizophrenic genotype." He was referring to individuals who he believed shared a genetic link to schizophrenia, but did not exhibit psychotic behavior. Rado's description of the schizotypal person included anhedonia, constricted affect, impaired empathy, and dependency. While Rado was striving to describe a nonpsychotic version of schizophrenia, his description (except for the dependency) is quite similar to the current diagnosis of schizoid personality disorder.

Meehl (1962) later described a personality type similar to schizotypal personality disorder that he also believed had a genetic similarity to schizophrenia. Characteristic of this group were cognitive slippage, social withdrawal, anhedonia, and ambivalence. This personality type tended to have a poor level of adjustment, but the eccentricities of thought, behavior, and affect were not a key component as described by Meehl. Kety, Rosenthal, Wender, and Schulsinger (1968) described "borderline schizophrenia," again similar to schizotypal personality disorder, as a nonpsychotic personality disorder including cognitive distortions, anhedonia, constricted affect, and poor interpersonal skills. Siever and Gunderson (1983) note that this personality type is best characterized as having poor interpersonal relationships, rather than as primarily exhibiting social isolation and aversiveness (consistent with current avoidant and schizoid diagnoses).

Consistent with the lack of clarity and changes in thinking about these disorders that have occurred over the years, their diagnostic labeling has changed with time. In DSM-I, schizoid personality described someone with an avoidance of relationships with others, inability to express hostility or aggressive feelings, and autistic thinking. This description of a cold, emotionally detached, fearful personality who could exhibit eccentricity seemed to combine our present diagnoses of schizoid, avoidant, and schizotypal personality disorders. It was not until DSM-III that a separation of the disorders occurred. In development of the new criteria, Millon (1969) emphasized the distinction between two of the personality types. He labeled them "passive-avoidant" and "active-detached" or "asocial" and "avoidant" to correspond to our present diagnoses of schizoid and avoidant, respectively (Millon, 1981). Although the term "schizoid" has had a confusing history, the term was retained as the "asocial" label. It was meant to be differentiated from antisocial personality disorder. The schizotypal pattern, also included in the DSM-I and DSM-II descriptions of schizoid personality, was differentiated as a distinct personality type. A further differentiation was made between schizotypal and borderline personality types (Spitzer, Endicott, & Gibbon, 1979).

While early theorists such as Bleuler and Kretschmer believed that schizoid-like personalities were a result of constitutional problems, later psychoanalytic theorists hypothesized that a schizoid character structure was the result of severely disturbed mother-child relationships. Within the psychoanalytic conceptualization, as a result of these early disturbances the schizoid individual developed a primary defensive structure, in which relationships were shunned because of an inability to give or receive love. In addition, this type of patient was considered to be so vulnerable to rejection that the value of relationships was repressed (Arieti, 1955). Fairbairn (1940) reported that the result of these unsatisfying maternal relationships was the development of depersonalization and an artificial self in which feelings were repressed. The schizoid was unable to experience love and intimacy. Klein (1952) saw a schizoid process as a developmental stage experienced by all infants. During this stage, oral and sadistic impulses, experienced as dangerous, are split off and projected to the caretaker. The caretaker is then seen as a dangerous being, and various defenses are developed to deal with the anxiety aroused thereby. The adult schizoid, retaining some of these early defenses, maintains interpersonal distance because of the anxiety interpersonal contact arouses. Guntrip (1969) also described developmental arrest in the early stages of life as infants withdraw from unsatisfying maternal relationships. These individuals then develop a primitive fear of engulfing or being engulfed by the caretaker. This results in their distant and aloof interpersonal styles as a defense against underlying terror and anger.

Psychoanalytic theorists also address, in addition to interpersonal distance, the detached, "observer" style of the schizoid as a related defense. Deutsch (1942) reported that an "as-if" personality is developed, so emotions cannot be felt. An observer might see the schizoid's life "as if" it were complete, yet on closer examination a lack of emotional reactivity would be evident.

In contrast to the complex intrapsychic mechanisms suggested by the psychoanalysts, Millon (1981) stated that the schizoid personality has a relatively simple defensive structure. He believes that the schizoid lacks the capacity to form relationships and experience affect. As a result of this insensitivity to interpersonal encounters and emotional stress, there is little need to develop elaborate defenses.

Characteristics

Not surprisingly, individuals with schizoid personality disorder consider themselves to be observers rather than participants in the world around them. They see themselves as self-sufficient loners. Others often view them as dull, uninteresting, and humorless. In fact, they are often ignored, since people frequently meet the schizoid's unresponsiveness with indifference.

Schizoids also have a cognitive style characterized by vagueness and poverty of thoughts, as well as by "defective perceptual scanning" (Millon, 1981), which eventuates in the missing of the subtle details of life mentioned earlier. Such a cognitive style further contributes to the lack of emotional responsiveness, since cues that produce affect are not perceived and are unlikely to result in emotions. The schizoid is usually either unresponsive, minimally responsive, or intellectually responsive to stimuli that would evoke pleasure, anger, sadness, or anxiety in others. These patients will often comment that they know that other people respond to particular stimuli in a particular way, but that they cannot respond in the same way or to the same degree as others.

In addition to this typical cognitive style, schizoid individuals also show a typical behavior pattern. This includes lethargic and unexpressive movements and slow, monotonous speech (Millon, 1981). Because of their lifelong lack of social involvement, schizoids usually have poor social skills. This lack of skills becomes one part of a continuous feedback loop. When rare attempts are made at social interaction or at some kind of social connection, their lack of skills predisposes them to fail; they may then give up any attempt to contact, or withdraw further.

The schizoid individual will typically not be seeking therapy to deal with his or her lack of contact. The therapeutic contact will be based on an Axis I problem. In making a diagnosis of schizoid personality disorder, the clinician should be aware of typical behaviors in the interview situation. First, the patient may appear aloof and cold, showing little affect. During the interview, it is likely that the schizoid will not speak unless spoken to, will reveal little information, will make little eye contact, and will generally appear ill at ease in the situation (Livesley, 1986). Since these observations could apply to other disorders as well, interview data and self-report information are needed to make a final diagnosis. The schizoid person will report no close friends or confidants, and little or no desire for interpersonal sexual experiences.

For example, Sam, a 65-year-old accountant, came to therapy because of his anxiety. He had a 60-year-old girlfriend whom he saw every weekend. Their pattern was that he would call her for a date on Thursday and see her on Saturday. He would pick her up at her home, go out to dinner, go to a movie, and afterwards go to her home and have sex with her. On the occasions when she asked him to stay over until Sunday, he asked, "What for?" His view, as reported to the therapist, was that he had the sex he "needed." Since he believed that he only needed sex once a week, staying over was unnecessary. His girlfriend would complain about the fact that he would have sex while wearing his shirt. His response to this criticism was that the vital parts of him were well exposed. In his opinion, he had all the physical contact he cared for. On several occasions, he went on a vacation with his girlfriend for periods of up to a week. During one 4-day vacation he reported having sex daily. Upon their return, he did not see her for 1 month.

Differential Diagnosis

A differential diagnosis must be made between the schizoid and avoidant personality disorders. Although neither will report having close friends, and both may appear withdrawn, they can be differentiated. This distinction is obvious because individuals with avoidant personality disorder desire interpersonal relationships, but avoid them because they fear criticism and disapproval. The avoidants are also keenly aware of criticism, but schizoid individuals often claim indifference to praise and criticism and thereby rarely get affectively angry, though they may report situations as "unfair."

Another distinction must be made between schizoid and schizotypal personality disorders. Here again there is similarity, as well as a critical difference that allows the differentiation. These disorders are similar in the isolated lifestyle and flat affect associated with them. However, the schizotypal person (as discussed later in this chapter) exhibits eccentric speech and behavior and will report peculiar cognitions. Further, the isolated lifestyle typical of the schizotypal individual is often due to social anxiety and inappropriateness, while with the schizoid it is due to lack of desire.

Cognitive Therapy Conceptualization

The first step in cognitive conceptualization involves the identification of the automatic thoughts that distinguish this disorder. While the cognitive therapy conceptualization of other personality disorders focuses on the types of automatic thoughts patients have, schizoid personality disorder is often marked by a paucity of automatic thoughts. It is often difficult to get a schizoid patient to identify any. Since emotions are related to thoughts, and schizoids have limited emotions, it stands to reason that they would report fewer thoughts than individuals with other personality disorders. In addition, situations such as receiving negative feedback from others, which would typically be catalysts for dysfunctional thinking in other patients, do not seem to affect the schizoid.

The few automatic thoughts that are identified reflect a schizoid's poverty of thought and apathetic outlook. It tends to take a dramatic event to evoke negative thoughts, and even then the thoughts are likely to be self-deprecating (e.g., "I'm a social outcast") rather than concern about what others think. Standard automatic thoughts of schizoids typically focus on their preference for solitude and their perception of being detached observers in life. Some automatic thoughts that are typical of this disorder are presented in Table 7.2.

From both the automatic thoughts and the lack of such thoughts, the underlying attitudes, beliefs, and assumptions can be inferred. Again, the themes of isolation and detachment are apparent. Although schizoids may feel comfortable with their lives, it becomes apparent that they

TABLE 7.2
Some Typical Automatic Thoughts in Schizoid Personality Disorder

---

I'd rather do it myself.
I prefer to be alone.
I have no motivation.
I'm just going through the motions.
Why bother?
Who cares?

---

operate in a different way from most people. One schizoid patient reported that he lacked both social graces and social interest. As he was quite intelligent, he believed that he could learn socially appropriate behavior, but he had no desire to do so. He acknowledged that his solitary interests were atypical in regard to the general population. Although usually satisfied with this, at times he would draw the conclusion that he was a misfit. This notion of being a social misfit or defective individual is a common belief of schizoids and can be triggered when it becomes apparent how very different they are from others. This realization might come from directly observing others, from a movie or TV show, or from readings that focus on relationships. The notion of being different from others will not always result in negative affect, however. The schizoid belief system is one in which other people and their responses are unimportant and often unnoticed. This belief is not manifested in any hostile fashion, but rather in a "live and let live" style. Some typical attitudes and assumptions are illustrated in Table 7.3.

There are a variety of theories concerning the development of schizoid personality. Millon (1981) notes that autonomic hyperactivity, deficits in reticular formation, congenital aplasia in the limbic system, and neurotransmitter deficits have been suggested as possible causes. In addition, disturbed maternal relationships or social learning could play a role. Because there is a paucity of research in this area, all of the current theories must remain speculative.

Some research has addressed the restricted emotional range of schizoids and their related deficits in identifying emotions of others. For example, Wolff and Barlow (1979) found that schizoid children used an unusually small number of psychological constructs (a measure of empathy) when referring to the emotional state or personality of people. The number of constructs was smaller than those used by normal controls or controls who had earlier been diagnosed as having infantile

TABLE 7.3
Attitudes and Assumptions Typical of Schizoid Personality Disorder

People are replaceable objects.
Relationships are problematic.
Life is less complicated without other people.
Human relationships are just not worth the bother.
It is better for me to keep my distance and maintain a low profile.
I am empty inside.
I am a social misfit.
Life is bland and unfulfilling.
Nothing is ever exciting.

autism. Chick, Waterhouse, and Wolff (1980) also noted that adults who had been diagnosed as schizoid during childhood could be distinguished from controls by their impaired empathy, solitariness, and abnormal style of communication.

Although schizoid personality has traditionally been thought to have a link with schizophrenia, family studies do not support a connection between the two. Kety, Rosenthal, Wender, and Schulsinger (1968, 1971) reported that "schizoid personality" (i.e., an introverted style) did not show an increased prevalence in the relatives of schizophrenics. Stephens, Atkinson, Kay, Roth, and Garside (1975) corroborated these findings, reporting no support for a genetic link between schizoid personality and schizophrenia. Other researchers (Watt, 1978; Woerner, Pollack, Rogalski, Pollack, & Klein, 1972) have been able to identify a particular personality type associated with schizophrenia.

At this time, it is unclear whether the schizoid personality is a result of constitutional differences or learning in early interpersonal relationships. Independent of the cause, the result is an individual who is not interested in others and who does not experience strong emotions. Research to determine the cause of this disorder would greatly facilitate treatment strategies.

Associated Axis I Disorders

Because of their lack of feelings, schizoids tend to experience few Axis I disorders. However, with excessive over- or understimulation, they may find themselves exhibiting Axis I symptoms. For example, although usually comfortable with a detached lifestyle, these individuals may become depressed over their awareness that they are deviants who do not fit into society. Although they do not truly desire closeness with others, they may believe that they should strive to attain a more conventional lifestyle. They may tire of being "on the outside, looking in." Further, their belief that life is meaningless and barren can lead to or exacerbate depression.

Schizoid personalities are prone to anxiety disorders when situations demand social interaction. Although typically impervious to feedback from others, they may become overwhelmed by social contact that they consider excessive.

Depersonalization may occur as a result of leading a peripheral existence, as well as feeling isolated and emotionally distant from others. In these cases, schizoids may experience a distorted sense of themselves and their surroundings. They may report that they feel "like a robot" or are "going through life in a dream."

Excessive social withdrawal can lead to an increased fantasy life and fewer chances to test reality with others. Under these circumstances, the schizoid individual may experience brief psychotic episodes. Consistent with other personality features, such a psychosis would be characterized by a lethargic style. Millon (1981) further notes that brief manic episodes may occur as a reaction to schizoids' perception of their meaningless existence.

Clinical Strategies and Techniques

Schizoid personality disorder presents a difficult challenge to the therapist, in that the patient will typically enter treatment because of an Axis I disorder and will be largely unmotivated to modify personality characteristics. The therapist must then strike a balance of treating the patient's primary problems while at the same time gaining his or her cooperation in modifying more long-standing dysfunctional patterns. It is important to note that, while many of the schizoid's long-standing patterns are antithetical to the lifestyles of others, all patterns may not be dysfunctional for the schizoid. For example, most people desire relationships with others, but if the schizoid does not desire this and is experiencing no ill effects from the lack of relationships, it is a reasonable choice for him or her not to try to build a broad social network.

When isolation is extreme and dysfunctional, the primary strategy in treating the schizoid individual is to reduce his or her isolation and establish a sense of intimacy with others. Initially, a greater sense of social connection may come only from the relationship with the therapist. From this, however, the value of relationships can be emphasized. The therapist and patient can examine the functional and dysfunctional role of isolation in the patient's life. From this analysis, the schizoid may be motivated to develop a social network. If a schizoid person agrees to work on relationships with others, a first strategy is to help the person find relationships to be reinforcing to some degree. Initially, limited self-disclosure with others may be helpful in this regard. One forum that is particularly helpful in this regard is group therapy. In such a setting, feedback from others about social interaction is readily available and, in fact, can be a central focus of the group. Further, in group therapy, a schizoid can have the experience of regularly meeting people who are interested in him or her. In a group each patient might disclose some piece of information about himself or herself, and then might make a comment about some other person in the group. When the patient is more comfortable with social interaction, the therapist or group can simulate positive, negative, or neutral reactions for the group. The schizoid can then be taught to respond to various forms of social feedback.

While increasing social connectedness may be a goal for treatment that the therapist and schizoid will agree on at some point in therapy, initially it will be important to address the problems and symptoms that brought the patient into therapy. With symptom relief, the schizoid may want to terminate rather than continue to work on interpersonal issues. If the therapeutic experience has been a rewarding one, the therapist gives the schizoid person a resource for securing help with future difficulties.

Within the framework of cognitive therapy, several specific techniques can be useful in working with schizoid personality disorder. The Dysfunctional Thought Record is useful not only to challenge dysfunctional automatic thoughts, but to educate the patient in identifying a variety of emotions and their subtle gradations in intensity. The therapist may initially provide a list of emotions, both positive and negative, on a continuum of intensity. This will allow the schizoid patient—who is typically unaware of feelings—to consider them. The Dysfunctional Thought Record is also useful in giving indications of the reactions of others as they interact with the patient. From this, it may be possible to provide feedback to the schizoid concerning the possible emotional state of others, thereby increasing his or her ability to empathize with them. In addition, feedback can be given about the appropriateness of the patient's responses, and discussion of alternatives can be generated. Teaching of social skills, however, is best done through more direct interventions, such as role playing, *in vivo* exposure, and homework assignments. After assessment of the schizoid's social skill level, the patient and therapist can collaboratively set up a hierarchy of social interaction goals that the patient wants to achieve.

Another general strategy can be to help the patient experience more positive emotions. Since the schizoid is unattentive to the emotional details that others perceive and interpret, the therapist can ask questions to help the patient attend to these emotional details. For example, if the patient reports that nothing is interesting, the therapist may help the patient identify some aspects of his or her experience that are pleasurable or interesting to a slight degree. One schizoid patient reported that he used to collect records, but no longer derived any pleasure from the activity. On closer questioning, it appeared that obtaining a new record was still a pleasurable event, although once it was added to the collection the patient lost interest in listening to it. Also, since he had an extensive collection, there were few records to add. In this case, the patient agreed that perhaps starting to collect a different kind of record might be enjoyable. In addition, he found that cataloging the old collection was interesting. These ideas had not been readily available to the patient because he was accustomed to seeing things in a global, nonspecific way. This overgeneralized view may apply to people as well. Instead of assuming that "I don't like people," the schizoid person can learn to be specific about the things he or she does not like, and may also find that there is something to like about others after all.

Case Study

Jack was a 28-year-old man who initially sought treatment for depression. He lived alone and led a very solitary life. Although he worked, he was not required to interact with others at his job. Outside of work he had no social contact; he reported that he had no friends, had dated infrequently, and considered himself a "loner." He reported that women were sometimes interested in him, but he was not interested in continuing relationships with them. There appeared to be no anxiety about this decision not to be involved with others; he was simply uninterested in developing that part of his life. In fact, he described people as being "replaceable" and found nothing unique about them. Typically, relationships were just "more trouble than they were worth." When he was not working, Jack would stay at home and occupy himself with computers or collecting old books.

Jack reported that he had led a solitary existence all his life. As a child, he enjoyed reading and collecting stamps, and rarely played with other children. He freely acknowledged that he was different from most people in his desire for a solitary existence. He could remember no experiences from childhood that might lead him to prefer a different lifestyle as an adult. In fact, he recalled his parents as being supportive. Jack still visited his parents once a year and said they were the only people he felt were special to some degree. Jack had done well academically, and after high school went to college to study biology. After college, he got a job as a laboratory technician for a medical research institution. He had been experiencing depression for the past 2 months. While depressed, Jack maintained that there was nothing of interest to him, and he could imagine nothing that could be satisfying in the future. These thoughts may sound typical for anyone suffering from depression, but Jack said that these thoughts had been pervasive even before his bout of depression. On intake, Jack was experiencing the following symptoms:

Affective: sadness, hopelessness, feeling of "inner deadness"
Physiological: sleep disturbance
Cognitive: automatic thoughts that there was nothing in life for him
    to enjoy; image of himself sitting alone in his apartment "like a
    hermit"
Behavioral: withdrawal from previously enjoyable activities; ex-
    tremely limited social interaction

The first step in therapy was introducing Jack to the cognitive model—that is, to the concept that the thoughts and interpretations he gave to his experiences strongly influenced how he felt about them. He was then introduced to the Dysfunctional Thought Record, on which he began to record his automatic thoughts. Jack's initial goal for therapy was to eliminate the depression. At the start for therapy, he said that he had no desire for friends or sexual relationships. He was willing to consider developing some interests, but was convinced that he would be unable to find anything enjoyable in life. His hopelessness interfered with his willingness to take any steps toward meeting those goals, so the hopelessness was addressed as a central therapeutic issue. Specifically, as many thoughts about hopelessness as possible were elicited during each session. Jack was also encouraged to identify automatic thoughts outside the session when he felt hopeless. A theme in these thoughts was Jack's belief that he had already done everything in life that could be interesting. Jack tested this thought by agreeing to do some activities that had previously been enjoyable. For example, he described a newsletter about old books and agreed to renew his subscription. He found, to this surprise, that this was interesting to him. At the same time, he was working to counter some negative thoughts on his own.

Progress in reducing the depression was slow, and Jack dogmatically maintained that nothing would be satisfying in the long run even if it was momentarily satisfying. With continued work, there gradually was a reduction in his depression and hopelessness. Jack's depression was atypical in that he was not able to identify negative thoughts about himself. Even his solitude he accepted uncritically for the most part. Very infrequently he would think that he was so unlike others he would "never fit in," but he then responded that he did not want to fit in. Since the desire for relationships is so common, other patients with this diagnosis may have more difficulty accepting their view of others as unrewarding and may consider themselves "freakish" or "abnormal." It is also noteworthy that Jack's depression did not include concerns about what others thought about him. He was unconcerned about how he came across to others, and usually thought of relationships only when they intruded on his life in some way. Of more concern to Jack was his increasing perception of life as unrewarding. This was helped by his being able to recognize some of the subtleties of reinforcement, and also by his realizing that he could not always accurately predict whether something would be reinforcing or not.

When the depression had subsided, the issue of social isolation was again addressed. Surprisingly, Jack thought at this point that he might like to have a relationship with a woman. Although he agreed to work on this goal, he felt considerable ambivalence about actually starting a relationship. On the one hand, he thought it would be a desirable situation, yet on the other, he thought it was not worth the effort. As a result of this ambivalence, he did not follow through with assignments to meet women. He did agree to join a club as a way to meet women. Unlike a social phobic, Jack was not concerned about what the women would think of him. Instead, he was concerned that he would be bored and uninterested in them. He also did not believe that a long-term relationship would fit into his lifestyle. Jack and his therapist set up the initial social conversation as a "necessary evil" that could lead to a relationship he might value more later.

The following excerpt from a therapy session illustrates the difficulty Jack had trying to get involved in a relationship. He seemed to have no true desire to be in a relationship, but he also thought it could potentially add something to his life.

THERAPIST: Last week you said you would think about the possibility of getting to know some women at work. How did it go?

JACK: There's one woman who's expressed interest, but I can't get motivated to pursue it.

THERAPIST: What do you think of the woman?

JACK: She seems OK—there's nothing noteworthy about her.

THERAPIST: You've used that term with a number of women you've met.

JACK: Well, the truth is, there isn't anything that interesting or special to me in a relationship.

THERAPIST: What do you think other people value in relationships?

JACK: I have no idea. . . . No, actually, they value companionship, but I don't. Sometimes I think I should value it, but I don't.

THERAPIST: We've set up assignments for you to talk to people before, and you never seem to. What automatic thoughts are you having when you consider it?

JACK: It think it's just not worth it. It's potentially ugly, messy—in fact, all my relationships are messy. The woman wants to be involved, but I just can't maintain interest.

THERAPIST: What happens when you are making these predictions about a relationship?

JACK: Then I just don't follow through. I can't get motivated to try to get a relationship.

THERAPIST: So you're torn about whether to pursue this or not?

JACK: Yes, it seems like a reasonable goal, but when I think of following through and actually having a relationship, it's aversive.

THERAPIST: Maybe it would be helpful to make a preliminary decision one way or the other: Either decide to try the relationship, and challenge the thoughts that interfere with pursuing it, or decide not to pursue a relationship at this time and remove this from the goal list. What do you think?

JACK: I guess a decision must be made—let's give it a try again.

THERAPIST: OK, but we know from experience that certain kinds of interfering cognitions will occur and cause a problem for you, right?

JACK: Right.

THERAPIST: Let's see how we can deal with them. What would be the first thing that would come to mind as you were thinking of asking someone out?

Jack continued to state interfering thoughts to be addressed. His difficulty in feeling interested in a relationship is clear from the interaction.

Jack dated a few women whom he found uninteresting, but did find one who seemed somewhat interesting to him. There were some difficulties in the relationship, because the woman complained that Jack was not giving enough. At that time, Jack and the therapist discussed empathy and the value of it in a relationship. However, Jack reported that his experience confirmed his view that relationships are messy and undesirable. He did not derive much personal satisfaction from the relationship, and thought his involvement was basically due to his thinking he "should" try it. He thought it unlikely that he would continue in the relationship if there was further conflict.

At this point, Jack chose to terminate treatment. Since his depression had been eliminated, and he sometimes had spontaneously reported things he might find enjoyable, his primary goal had been met. In addition, he had dramatically increased his social skills (although he often was still awkward socially), and had found limited value in relationships. This case is a good illustration of how the client's idea of reinforcement can differ from the therapist's or society's. Once it is ascertained that avoidance of relationships is not a result of fear, it is important to help the schizoid person structure his or her life in a way that is most individually rewarding—keeping in mind the person's belief system about relationships.

Relapse Prevention

The most important aspect of relapse prevention is maintaining contact with booster sessions after the formal treatment is over. These booster sessions may occur more frequently than usual with schizoids, because these patients are likely to fall back into an isolated lifestyle. During these sessions, it is important to assess if there is any recurrence of the initial symptomatology, and if the patient is isolated outside of therapy. If the patient is reverting to a reclusive lifestyle, and doing so is *not* part of the patient's belief system, the therapist may choose to make boosters more frequent.

Therapist Problems

As mentioned, the schizoid individual's desire to get quick symptom relief without working on underlying assumptions or interpersonal issues may prove to be contrary to the therapist's desires for treatment outcome. Since cognitive therapy is a collaborative approach, it is important that the therapist does not impose his or her goals on the patient. It is better that the schizoid be in therapy a short time and leave with a positive experience.

During therapy, the patient's unresponsiveness to praise reduces the leverage available to the therapist. This problem can be compensated for by using other means of motivation, such as explanation of the value of the treatment procedure and connection with the patient's therapeutic goal.

As might be expected from the schizoid's belief system, it is unlikely that he or she will value the therapeutic relationship. The patient will likely see the therapist as intrusive, and this may trigger the automatic strategy to stay away from people. Unlike the avoidant patient, who eventually will come to trust and value the therapist, the schizoid will probably never do so. This, of course, could lead to a number of reactions on the therapist's part. Being seen as part of an unrewarding interaction may be trying.

The combination of these patients' restricted affect, unresponsiveness, and poor social skills can make sessions difficult for the therapist. Despite this, it is essential to maintain a warm, empathic stance throughout, and to postpone comments on a patient's interactive style until rapport has been established.

On a positive note, over the course of treatment the schizoid patient can establish a relationship with the therapist and others. In addition, it is possible for such a patient to find a more fulfilling life. It is important, however, for the therapist to realize that slight gains can take a long time to occur.

Schizotypal Personality Disorder

Introduction

While social isolation, constricted or inappropriate affect, and unusual behavior are characteristic of schizotypal personality disorder, the most striking features are the oddities of cognition. The cognitive distortions in this disorder are among the most severe of any in the personality disorders. They generally fall within four themes. First, these individuals often have suspicious or paranoid ideation. Second, they experience ideas of reference, such as believing that unrelated events are related to them in a significant way. The third theme revolves around odd beliefs and magical thinking. For example, they may believe that a dead relative is present or that others know what they are thinking. Finally, people with this disorder often experience illusions—for example, thinking that they see people in shadows or in the pattern of the wallpaper.

These types of cognitions are further reflected in odd speech. Although the speech is coherent, and there are no loose associations, the schizotypal person is often tangential, circumstantial, vague, or over-elaborate. As might be expected, affect is often peculiar as well, being constricted or inappropriate to the situation.

Consistent with this constellation of features, the schizotypal person often behaves inappropriately. For example, one schizotypal patient spent hours each day organizing closets. Inappropriate behavior contributes to the extreme social isolation associated with this disorder. The patients' distorted cognitions concerning others, and their awkward and uncomfortable social interactions, lead them to develop social anxiety. Although there may be the lack of desire or appreciation for relationships seen in schizoids, it is far more likely to be the case that relationships are avoided because of anxiety. The DSM-III-R criteria for schizotypal personality disorder are listed in Table 7.4.

Differential Diagnosis

These patients are fairly easy to diagnose, although a common differential diagnosis needs to be made between schizotypal personality disorder and schizophrenia. If there are any indications of hallucinations, delusions, or loose associations, the diagnosis of schizophreniform disorder or schizophrenia should be considered. While it would be expected that oddities of speech, inappropriate or flat affect, and strange behavior would be evident with both, a diagnosis of schizophrenia would call for more severe and acute symptomatology. Baron, Asnis, and Gruen (1981) have designed a schedule for assessing this disorder that can be helpful for diagnosis. This interview schedule, called the Schedule for Schizotypal Personalities, has shown high interrater and test-retest reliability.

Cognitive Therapy Conceptualization

As with any disorder, one of the first steps in cognitive therapy of schizotypal personality disorder is identification of the typical automatic

TABLE 7.4
DSM-III-R Diagnostic Criteria for Schizotypal Personality Disorder

A. A pervasive pattern of deficits in interpersonal relatedness and peculiarities of ideation, appearance, and behavior, beginning by early adulthood and present in a variety
   of contexts, as indicated by at least *five* of the following:

   (1) ideas of reference (excluding delusions of reference)
   (2) excessive social anxiety, e.g., extreme discomfort in social situations involving
       unfamiliar people
   (3) odd beliefs or magical thinking, influencing behavior and inconsistent with sub-
       cultural normal, e.g., superstitiousness, belief in clairvoyance, telepathy, or "sixth
       sense," "others can feel my feelings" (in children and adolescents, bizarre fantasies
       or preoccupations)
   (4) unusual perceptual experiences, e.g., illusions, sensing the presence of a force or
       person not actually present (e.g., "I felt as if my dead mother were in the room with
       me")
   (5) odd or eccentric behavior or appearance, e.g., unkempt, unusual mannerisms, talks
       to self
   (6) no close friends or confidants (or only one) other than first-degree relatives
   (7) odd speech (without loosening of associations or incoherence), e.g., speech that is
       impoverished, digressive, vague, or inappropriately abstract
   (8) inappropriate or constricted affect, e.g., silly, aloof, rarely reciprocates gestures of
       facial expressions, such as smiles or nods
   (9) suspiciousness or paranoid ideation

B. Occurrence not exclusively during the course of Schizophrenia or a Pervasive Developmental Disorder.

Note. From *Diagnostic and Statistical Manual of Mental Disorders* (3rd ed., rev., pp. 341–342) by the
American Psychiatric Association, 1987, Washington, DC: Author. Copyright 1987 by the American
Psychiatric Association. Reprinted by permission.

thoughts. Although there are many individual differences in the exact
form of these cognitions, they consistently fall within the aforemen-
tioned themes. In addition to suspicious ideation, ideas of reference,
magical thinking, and illusions, other typical automatic thoughts describe fears and concerns of a social nature. As with the specific content
of automatic thoughts, there are individual differences in cognitive style.
Some schizotypal individuals may focus on details and lose sight of
the overall situation, while others may exclude attention to detail.
Many schizotypals will engage in the cognitive distortions of emotional
reasoning and personalization. In emotional reasoning, a person believes that because he or she feels a negative emotion, there must be a
corresponding negative external situation. With personalization, the
individual believes that he or she is responsible for external situations
when this is not the case. These patients are often very concrete, and
are unable to assess accurately the probability of an imagined outcome

TABLE 7.5
Some Typical Automatic Thoughts in Schizotypal Personality Disorder

---

Is that person watching me?
I know what he is thinking.
I have a feeling something bad is going to happen.
I know they are not going to like me.
I can feel the devil in her.
I am a nonbeing.
Am I dead?

(Stone, 1985). Some examples of automatic thoughts are presented in Table 7.5.

As with the other characteristics of this disorder, the underlying attitudes and assumptions tend to be bizarre. Some typical themes might include ideas that people are basically untrustworthy, or that they need to be watched at all times. But, by and large, the themes will be unique to the individual. For example, a specific belief such as "I can predict the future" or "I have a sixth sense" must be determined on a case-by-case basis. Some example of attitudes and assumptions are presented in Table 7.6.

Research and Empirical Findings

Kendler, Gruenberg, and Strauss (1981) found the prevalence of schizotypal personality disorder to be greater in the biological relatives of schizophrenic adoptees than in biological relatives of controls or adopted relatives of controls or schizophrenics. Other studies indicated that the "borderline schizophrenia" category, most similar to our present schizotypal personality disorder, was familially connected to schizophrenia (Kety et al., 1968, 1971). Reider (1979), however, applied the DSM-III criteria for schizotypal personality disorder to data from some past studies that had used the "borderline schizophrenia" label, as well as to his own data; he found that of the 73% who met the diagnosis for schizotypal personality disorder, only one also met the DSM-III-R criteria for schizophrenia. In addition, as noted earlier, no firm evidence has been found for a single personality type that results in schizophrenia.

Associated Axis I Disorders

Schizophrenia can be a concurrent diagnosis with these patients. In fact, schizotypal personality disorder is often considered to be at the opposite end of a continuum from schizophrenia. Expression of schizophrenia

TABLE 7.6
Attitudes and Assumptions Typical of Schizotypal Personality Disorder

I feel like an alien in a frightening environment.
Since the world is dangerous, you have to watch out for yourself at all times.
People will get you if they can.
There are reasons for everything. Things don't happen by chance.
Sometimes my inner feelings are an indication of what is going to happen.
Relationships are threatening.
I am defective.

can occur with a combination of genetic predisposition and environmental stress. These patients can then move from the schizotypal personality disorder to a psychotic disintegration, particularly if they are socially isolated or if they encounter increased stress. As these individuals become further removed from the opportunities to test reality with others, they are more likely to resort to fantasy. The peculiar behavior and social isolation create a predictable spiral, in that the more eccentric the behavior, the more they experience ridicule and social rejection; this experience further exacerbates the social anxiety and inappropriate behavior, leading to more and more withdrawal.

Broad Clinical Strategies

One of the first strategies with schizotypal patients is the establishment of a sound therapeutic relationship. Since these patients are likely to have a number of dysfunctional beliefs related to people, the importance of the therapeutic relationship must not be underestimated. Once established, it is an initial step toward reducing social isolation. This is even more important than with the schizoid individual, because the schizotypal patient has a greater risk of losing good reality testing without social contact. In addition, the schizotypal individual also typically desires social relationships and experiences great pain as a result of social isolation. In order to improve social interactions and to intervene in the spiral described above, increasing the patient's overall social network can be an effective strategy.

Directly related to this, the second therapeutic strategy should include increasing social appropriateness. While this might also be a goal of treatment, it is important for the therapist to reinforce appropriateness in all contact with the patient. Social skills training can be done, in addition to the modeling of appropriate behavior and speech. The therapist must also teach these patients to identify their own inappropriate responses.

With social skills training, the combination of both cognitive and behavioral interventions is most effective. Capturing and identifying the automatic thoughts and underlying assumptions about interacting with others can lead to an evaluation of these cognitions. For example, a schizotypal patient may believe that "Others will not like me" or "I am a social misfit." During the actual interaction, thoughts about how the patient is being perceived and whether others have scrutinized him or her can be identified and challenged. It will also be necessary to role-play appropriate responses, as well as to set up a hierarchy of social situations on which to work. The group setting is ideal for these interventions, as the patient can observe both his or her own and others' interactions in a supportive environment.

Another important strategy is keeping the therapy sessions structured. Because of their rambling cognitive styles, it is easy for these patients to accomplish very little during a therapy session. In addition to setting an agenda, the therapist may help the patient identify one small goal to be accomplished during that session. For example, if working on social anxiety, the patient may learn to ask open-ended questions by the end of the session.

The critical aspect of treatment is to teach patients to look for objective evidence in the environment to evaluate their thoughts, rather than relying on emotional responses. In addition, since inappropriate thoughts are likely to continue to be an aspect of these persons' life experience, it is important to teach them to disregard such thoughts, and to consider the consequences that responding emotionally or behaviorally according to such thoughts would have. As with all patients learning cognitive therapy, it is important to remember that these patients will experience an unusually high number of distorted cognitions, all of which cannot be expected to diminish with rational responding.

In the case of these cognitions, the bizarre thought can be treated as a symptom, and rational responding can focus on the thoughts that the schizotypal person has about the bizarre thought. For example, one patient who sometimes thought he wasn't real learned to discount the thought "I am not real" when it occurred. Another patient was able to address paranoid thoughts in this way: When she would drink out of a glass at home, the thought would come to mind that there might be small pieces of glass in the drink. Since there was no objective evidence of this, she was able to discount these thoughts after some practice. The procedure helps such patients to attach little significance to the actual bizarre notion. In these cases, the patients must realize that it is not necessary to respond emotionally or behaviorally to these thoughts. Instead, predesigned coping statements can be made, such as "There I go again. Even though I'm thinking this thought, it doesn't mean that it's true."

The therapist may also find it beneficial to design ways to allow patients to consider evidence contrary to their beliefs. One intervention is to keep track of predictions they make. One patient, for example, believed that if he vividly imagined something it would happen. He was typically frightened in an elevator, as he would imagine the cables snapping. Although his belief in this notion was complete, he was willing to entertain it as only a hypothesis. Based on this and other hypotheses, he made predictions about what would happen if he imagined certain things. During sessions, and for homework, he tested these and found no evidence to support his hypotheses. Although he still maintained some degree of belief in his assumptions, he gained some emotional relief by realizing that he had typically been inaccurate in his past predictions, and therefore whatever he now imagined would not necessarily happen.

In addition to addressing specific cognitions, once the therapist and patient identify the patient's cognitive style, an intervention can be designed. These styles are reflected verbally and interfere with the patient's adequate communication, both in and out of session. If the patient tends to omit details from his or her interpretation of situations, the therapist can have him or her elaborate in response to questions about the situation. On the other hand, if the patient loses the point of the situation in extraneous details, he or she can be asked to make a summary statement. If the patient agrees to work on communication style, a signal (perhaps visual) can be agreed upon. For example, in the case of overelaboration, when the therapist gives the signal the patient will summarize. It is also important to get his or her rationale for overincluding or excluding details. One patient reported that he gave excessive details because he wanted to be understood. When he realized that he was actually understood less because people could not follow his point, he was able to decrease his circumstantiality.

Another general strategy for treatment is helping to make the patient's life better in practical ways. Often these patients have difficulty in obtaining and maintaining employment, finding housing, or meeting people. Any concrete intervention the therapist can make (e.g., self-help skills, personal hygiene education, or social skills) can be very beneficial to improving a schizotypal person's lifestyle.

Case History

Frank, a 45-year-old man with a long history of emotional disturbance, sought treatment. He had been hospitalized twice previously for episodes that he said he did not remember; he claimed that his brother had said he had threatened him, although Frank denied these incidents. He lived alone and described a very solitary existence. He had not worked in years, although he had had dreams of finishing his college education and getting a job. Frank reported no social contact except for belonging to an extreme political group. At meetings, he would sometimes make contact with others who seemed similarly isolated. Occasionally he would leave his home during the day, but he usually stayed in and slept or watched television. He preferred going out at night, when he would not be exposed to the scrutiny of others. He would eat or go to the library, where he read about a variety of topics. His apartment was dirty and disorganized. Frank reported that he had "lived on the fringes" all his life, never participating fully in life. On intake, he reported the following symptoms:

Affective: sadness, social anxiety
Physiological: palpitations and sweating in social situations
Cognitive: automatic thoughts about what a failure his life had been; fearful thoughts about others' reactions to him
Behavioral: almost complete social isolation, tangential speech, infrequent eye contact

Frank's initial goals for treatment were reducing his social anxiety and finding a job. Although his social inappropriateness was apparent from the outset, the therapist felt it would be better to wait until rapport was established and some progress made on other goals before addressing this. Regarding his social anxiety, Frank was introduced to the cognitive model and taught how to collect automatic thoughts. Often these were rambling. He was taught to evaluate the accuracy of thoughts. In the process, some thoughts were bizarre; these were labeled "inappropriate automatic thoughts." When these would occur, Frank would simply label them and assume they were not worth further consideration. This would be in contrast to other automatic thoughts, which he would be able to evaluate using standard rational responding.

The following is representative session material in which some of Frank's odd ideas about social interactions were addressed:

THERAPIST: How have things been going this week?
FRANK: Ups and downs. I went to a meeting this week with one of the other [political group] members.
THERAPIST: How did it go?
FRANK: It went OK. Joe is a nice guy and seems to like me. In the meeting, though, I couldn't keep my mind off of Anna. I kept imagining living with her.
THERAPIST: Did the thinking interfere with your interacting at the meeting?

FRANK: Yes. I didn't want to talk to her because I knew she'd know what I was thinking.

THERAPIST: What evidence do you have for that?

FRANK: It's really just an odd suspicion. I would look at her and she would look at me, and then I'd sense that she was "reading me."

THERAPIST: Frank, did she say anything to you?

FRANK: She said hello after the meeting, but then went on to talk to others. I think she was disgusted with my anxiety.

THERAPIST: So she didn't say anything negative to you, and she gave you a friendly greeting. What makes you think she was having this negative reaction?

FRANK: I really could sense it.

THERAPIST: Let's remember what we've said about sensing things from others. It's true we pick up cues about others' reactions that sometimes are hard to verbalize, but remember that often this feeling is just a reflection of what we've been thinking. Do you know what I mean?

FRANK: I guess, but it feels real.

THERAPIST: Well, the feelings were real, but were they based on accurate data?

FRANK: I guess I assumed that's why I felt that way.

THERAPIST: Sure, you made an assumption about your feelings, but might not those anxiety feelings have been a result of being fearful about her reaction to you?

FRANK: I see how it could be, but how can I tell if her reaction is negative or not?

THERAPIST: That's a good question. Let's see how you could tell. Let's write down the legitimate cues—not your feelings, because they result from what you think—that give us an indication of others' reactions. Remember, though, Frank, that we don't know for sure what someone is thinking, even though we use legitimate cues to make an assessment. OK, what would be a cue?

FRANK: I suppose what they say. If they tell me they like me, or don't talk to me, I'd know what they thought.

THERAPIST: That sounds pretty good, but let's look at it carefully. If someone tells you something directly positive or negative, it is most plausible to assume that this is what they think. Is that what you mean?

FRANK: Yeah—and if they don't, I can assume they don't like me.

THERAPIST: It's that second part that needs further examination. If they don't say anything to you, you assume they don't like you?

FRANK: Yes.

THERAPIST: Are there other possibilities for this response?

FRANK: It's hard to imagine.

THERAPIST: What if the other person is shy?
FRANK: Do you think so?

The therapist and Frank went on in this vein to outline what the other specific cues were that Frank could rely on, what cues were ambiguous, and what cues were not reliable. The transcript is illustrative both of his peculiar belief that he knew what others were thinking, and his lack of information about how others respond in social situations.

As Frank learned to identify and modify thoughts, the therapist also set up a series of homework assignments in which he could make contact with others. This began with going to the grocery store or library during the day and speaking to someone. Later, he asked someone to have dinner with him. Over the course of treatment, Frank became more socially appropriate, although he continued to express many inappropriate automatic thoughts. When these occurred in session, the therapist and Frank would identify them and then continue with the topic at hand.

There were difficulties in helping Frank get a job. He had large blocks of time of hospitalization or unemployment, and he lacked the education and experience for a number of jobs that he wanted. After a very long struggle, Frank got part-time work in a used-book store. He found the work interesting, although he was still anxious around customers. Frank continued in therapy on a weekly basis until an appropriate group was found. Unlike many patients, who learn skills they can apply on their own in a relatively short period of time, Frank needed to continue to benefit from the contact of weekly therapy sessions.

Therapist Problems

The primary therapist problem with schizotypal patients is gaining compliance with the treatment plan. It is necessary that the therapist develop a good relationship with the patient, so that he or she will be willing to address some of the dysfunctional patterns. Even though the patient may agree on the value of changing a behavior or belief, the therapist may find that homework assignments are not done. Often the schizotypal person is isolated between therapy sessions, and may thus continue to resort to a fantasy life. It is sometimes useful to increase the frequency of sessions at the beginning of therapy, or to have the patient call the therapist to "touch base" each day. The therapist must also be willing to break assignments into very small, manageable units, so that the schizotypal individual will be willing to undertake them and thus will have a successful experience.

Another therapist problem is that of the peculiar behavior, speech, and affect exhibited by these patients. Because of these, they will often have difficulty staying on track in session, and therapy is likely to move quite slowly. The therapist must be willing to reduce goals and to modify traditional cognitive therapy techniques. These patients will also interpret therapist behavior in unusual ways; the therapist must be alert to patients' affective changes and inappropriate behavior, and identify the thinking involved with them. In addition, the patients may develop a deep attachment to the therapist, because he or she may be one of their sole contacts in an isolated existence. As such, inappropriate thoughts about social contact with the therapist may occur. The therapist must gently address these thoughts, while, of course, maintaining the limits of the therapeutic relationship.

Provided that the therapist has realistic expectations about what can be accomplished with these patients, working with them can be a positive experience. Many individuals with this disorder can learn to control a large portion of their inappropriate behaviors and thoughts, and can derive much more fulfillment from life.

Chapter 8
Antisocial Personality Disorder

Antisocial individuals may present in a variety of treatment settings, depending upon their particular mixture of criminal behavior and clinical psychopathology. They may be inmates in a prison or correctional institution, inpatients in a psychiatric hospital, or (less frequently) outpatients in a clinic or private practice. Whether inmate, inpatient, or outpatient, the motivation for coming to treatment usually results from someone else pressuring the patient to change. Employers or teachers may insist that the antisocial person seek treatment because of performance problems or strained interpersonal relations. Often such directions are really an ultimatum for seeking treatment or else losing a job or being expelled from school. Courts will often require that antisocial criminals obtain treatment. In many cases, probation is contingent upon their attendance in psychotherapy. Given their typical exploitive attitude toward others, it would not be surprising for antisocial persons to be brought to treatment by chronic conflict in their marriage or with their children. Antisocial patients also may come voluntarily to outpatient facilities with various contrived forms of psychopathology in order to obtain a prescription for some controlled substances. In the latter case, it is most important to spot the attempted manipulation and to provide appropriate treatment or referral for substance abuse problems.

Antisocial personality disorder (ASPD) is a perplexing and socially malignant problem. Notable for its specific behavioral reference points in the DSM-III and DSM-III-R diagnostic criteria (see Table 8.l), this disorder incorporates criminal acts that threaten people and property. The objective diagnostic criteria have produced the highest reliability among all of the DSM-III personality disorders in field trials with psychiatric inpatients (κ = .49; Mellsop, Varghese, Joshua, & Hicks, 1982), but possibly at the cost of some clinical validity.

Research in antisocial psychopathology has been built upon the

TABLE 8.1
DSM-III-R Criteria for Antisocial Personality Disorder

A. Current age at least 18.

B. Evidence of Conduct Disorder with onset before age 15, as indicated by a history of *three* or more of the following:
 (1) was often truant
 (2) ran away from home overnight at least twice while living in parental or parental surrogate home (or once without returning)
 (3) often initiated physical fights
 (4) used a weapon in more than one fight
 (5) forced someone into sexual activity with him or her
 (6) was physically cruel to animals
 (7) was physically cruel to other people
 (8) deliberately destroyed others' property (other than by fire-setting)
 (9) deliberately engaged in fire-setting
 (10) often lied (other than to avoid physical or sexual abuse)
 (11) has stolen without confrontation of a victim on more than one occasion (including forgery)
 (12) has stolen with confrontation of a victim (e.g., mugging, purse-snatching, extortion, armed robbery)

C. A pattern of irresponsible and antisocial behavior since the age of 15, as indicated by at least *four* of the following:
 (1) is unable to sustain consistent work behavior, as indicated by any of the following (including similar behavior in academic settings if the person is a student):
  (a) significant unemployment for six months or more within five years when expected to work and work was available
  (b) repeated absences from work unexplained by illness in self or family
  (c) abandonment of several jobs without realistic plans for others
 (2) fails to conform to social norms with respect to lawful behavior, as indicated by repeatedly performing antisocial acts that are grounds for arrest (whether arrested or not), e.g., destroying property, harassing others, stealing, pursuing an illegal occupation
 (3) is irritable and aggressive, as indicated by repeated physical fights or assaults (not required by one's job or to defend someone or oneself), including spouse- or child-beating
 (4) repeatedly fails to honor financial obligations, as indicated by defaulting on debts or failing to provide child support or support for other dependents on a regular basis
 (5) fails to plan ahead, or is impulsive, as indicated by one or both of the following:
  (a) traveling from place to place without a prearranged job or clear goal for the period of travel or clear idea about when the travel will terminate
  (b) lack of a fixed address for a month or more
 (6) has no regard for the truth, as indicated by repeated lying, use of aliases, or "conning" others for personal profit or pleasure

(continued)

TABLE 8.1 *(continued)*

---

(7) is reckless regarding his or her own or others' personal safety, as indicated by driving while intoxicated, or recurrent speeding

(8) if a parent or guardian, lacks ability to function as a responsible parent, as indicated by one or more of the following:

    (a) malnutrition of child

    (b) child's illness resulting from lack of minimal hygiene

    (c) failure to obtain medical care for a seriously ill child

    (d) child's dependence on neighbors or nonresident relatives for food or shelter

    (e) failure to arrange for a caretaker for young child when parent is away from home

    (f) repeated squandering, on personal items, of money required for household necessities

(9) has never sustained a totally monogamous relationship for more than one year

(10) lacks remorse (feels justified in having hurt, mistreated, or stolen from another)

D. Occurrence of antisocial behavior not exclusively during the course of Schizophrenia or Manic Episodes.

Note. From *Diagnostic and Statistical Manual of Mental Disorders* (3rd ed., rev., pp. 344–346) by the American Psychiatric Association, 1987, Washington, DC: Author. Copyright 1987 by the American Psychiatric Association. Reprinted by permission.

assumption that there is a systematically definable disorder that is distinguishable from criminal behavior alone. However, the degree of importance that criminality is accorded is a controversial issue. Building upon the work of Cleckley (1976) and Millon (1981), Hare (1985a, 1986) asserts that DSM-III overemphasizes delinquent and criminal behavior and neglects the issue of personality traits that may underlie those behaviors. As Hare points out, avoidance of early contact with the judicial system may enable an individual to avoid diagnosis by DSM-III, even though other essential traits of psychopathy might be well established.

The early work of Cleckley (1976) and Robins (1966) helped to map out certain personality traits that frequently occur in antisocial individuals. Hare (1985b) has revised a checklist originally developed by Cleckley (1976) for distinguishing these essential traits (see Table 8.2). Like most trait-based assessments, the psychopathy checklist includes some apt descriptions, but it requires more subjective judgments than the behavioral criteria of DSM-III-R diagnosis.

Historical Perspective

The terms "psychopathy," "sociopathy," and "antisocial personality disorder" are often used interchangeably. Unfortunately, there is no single set of defining criteria that is common to the three terms. Much of the

TABLE 8.2
Items in the Revised Psychopathy Checklist

1. Glibness/superficial charm
2. Grandiose sense of self-worth
3. Need for stimulation/proneness to boredom
4. Pathological lying
5. Conning/manipulative
6. Lack of remorse or guilt
7. Shallow affect
8. Callous/lack of empathy
9. Parasitic lifestyle
10. Poor behavioral controls
11. Promiscuous sexual behavior
12. Early behavior problems
13. Lack of realistic, long-term plans
14. Impulsivity
15. Irresponsibility
16. Failure to accept responsibility for own actions
17. Many short-term marital relationships
18. Juvenile delinquency
19. Revocation of conditional release
20. Criminal versatility

Note. From "A Checklist for the Assessment of Psychopathy" by R. Hare, 1985, in M. H. Ben-Aron, S. J. Hucker, and C. Webster (Eds.), *Clinical Criminology.* Toronto: M. & M. Graphics. Copyright 1985 by M. & M. Graphics. Reprinted by permission.

existing literature is limited by the interchangeable use of these terms, along with differing methods for determining the population of study. As a result, studies of psychopathy and sociopathy can only be tentatively linked to patients with ASPD, since there may be fundamental differences among these populations. Nevertheless, the treatment literature for ASPD has been based primarily on empirical research involving subjects (usually criminals rather than psychiatric patients) defined as psychopaths or sociopaths. For this reason, it is important to review briefly the major trends of this literature.

The literature on psychopathy has devoted considerable attention to a distinction between "primary" and "secondary" psychopathy (Cleckley, 1976). The primary psychopath is distinguished by an apparent absence of anxiety or guilt about his or her illegal or immoral behavior. Because of his or her ability to do things such as lying purposely for personal gain, or physically harming another person without feeling any nervousness, doubt, or remorse, the primary psychopath is regarded as lacking a moral conscience. The secondary psychopath is an individual who might engage in the same exploitive behavior, but reports feelings of guilt over having harmed someone else. He or she might fear possible consequences of wrongdoing, but continues to behave in antisocial ways, supposedly due to poor impulse control and emotional lability. Inmates classified as primary psychopaths on the basis of significantly lower trait anxiety evince more frequent and severe aggressive behaviors (Fagan & Lira, 1980) and report less somatic arousal in situations where they perceive malevolence from others (Blackburn & Lee-Evans, 1985) than do secondary psychopathic inmates.

Numerous laboratory studies have pursued the hypothesis that primary psychopaths suffer from a central nervous system dysfunction resulting in a higher than normal threshold for autonomic responses to threat (Lykken, 1957; Quay, 1965). However, as Hare (1986) points out, there is evidence that, under many conditions, psychopaths as a group do not differ from normals on autonomic and behavioral responses. For example, psychopaths have been shown to learn from experience when the contingencies are immediate, well-specified, tangible, and personally relevant—such as obtaining or losing access to cigarettes. Thus, according to Hare, laboratory findings regarding the electrodermal underactivity of primary psychopaths may have been overinterpreted, especially since such responses can be influenced by a wide range of cognitive activities. Alternatively, distinguishing motivational and cognitive features may further clarify response characteristics of psychopaths.

In reviewing several studies of cognitive development, Kagan (1986) concludes that sociopaths show a developmental delay in moral maturity and cognitive functioning. Kagan describes the sociopathic moral and cognitive development as organized at Kohlberg's (1984) second epistemological level, similar to that of a latency-age child. At this level, cognitive functioning is governed by the Piagetian concept of concrete operations. Such individuals are typically incapable of subordinating the actual to the realm of the possible. Their view of the world is a personal rather than an interpersonal one. In social-cognitive terms, they cannot hold another's point of view at the same time as their own. As such, they cannot take on the role of another. They think in a linear fashion, anticipating the reactions of others only after responding to their own desires. Their actions are not based on choices in a social sense because of these cognitive limitations.

Kagan also refers to Erikson's (1950) latency-age issue of psychosocial development involving industry. Individuals dealing with issues of industry are "on the make" and "full of plans," and they do not have concerns about how they are viewed by others, which are more characteristic of adolescence and young adulthood. Kagan goes on to suggest that treatment interventions for sociopathy might be best guided by a strategy of setting protective limits on the patient's efforts at independence and encouraging a greater awareness of the rights and feelings of others.

Treatment Interventions

General Considerations

Treatment intervention with people having ASPD obviously presents significant challenges. There is very little evidence of treatment effectiveness with such clients beyond better management of their disruptive behaviors within an institutional setting. However, interventions for ASPD have been applied to various populations, without the benefit of systematic diagnostic evaluations (Barley, 1986; Templeton & Wollersheim, 1979). A pessimistic theme runs through the literature, depicting primary psychopaths as individuals who are devoid of guilt or love (McCord & McCord, 1964), and thus unresponsive to therapy because of an absence of conscience. Psychoanalytic psychotherapy has generally been considered inappropriate and useless for ASPD, unless a degree of narcissism is also present (Kernberg, 1975; Person, 1986).

Rationale for Cognitive Therapy

The remainder of this chapter will outline a clinical application of Beck's (1967; Beck, Rush, Shaw, & Emery, 1979) model for cognitive therapy to the problems of ASPD. In this treatment model, it is assumed that changes in affect and behavior can be effected by engaging patients in a process of evaluating and testing their basic assumptions regarding key problem areas. Furthermore, it is assumed that cognitions, affect, and behavior are reflective of underlying schemas or rules. Dysfunctional schemas may be related to problems in psychosocial development, and these must be addressed if long-term improvement is to occur (Freeman, 1986).

　　Rather than attempting to build a better moral structure through the induction of affect such as anxiety or shame, cognitive therapy of ASPD can be conceptualized as improving moral and social behavior through enhancement of cognitive functioning. Drawing generally from major theories regarding moral development in men and women (Kohlberg, 1984; Gilligan, 1982), and psychosocial development (Erikson, 1950), we propose that the treatment plan be based on the strategies suggested by Kagan (1986) for furthering cognitive growth. This would involve fostering a transition from concrete operations and self-determination toward more formal cognitive operations of abstract thinking and interpersonal consideration. Moral functioning is regarded as a dimension within the broader context of epistemology, or ways of thinking and knowing.

　　Instead of separating patients into primary and secondary categories of the disorder, with the resultant dismissal of primary patients as amoral, the cognitive viewpoint is that patients vary in skills for anticipating and acting on possible negative outcomes for their actions. In addition, antisocial patients' actions are heavily influenced by a variety of dysfunctional beliefs about themselves, the world, and the future that are typically maintained through selective, confirming experiences. Cognitive therapy is designed to help an ASPD patient make a transition from thinking in mostly concrete, immediate terms, to consider a broader spectrum of possibilities and alternative beliefs.

Diagnostic Signs

When the ASPD patient presents for treatment, the clinician faces the initial task of screening the patient for disorders that are present and initiating a treatment contract. In formulating a treatment contract, the clinician needs to be explicit in informing the patient about his or her diagnosis of ASPD, and setting clear limits for his or her involvement in treatment. Otherwise, the antisocial patient is not likely to see any reason or purpose in continuing psychotherapy. Such individuals see their problems as other people's inability to accept them, or desire to limit their freedom.

A thorough discussion of the patient's life history is necessary for establishing the diagnosis of ASPD. This should include a review of relationships, academic and vocational achievement, military service, and arrest and conviction record, as well as living circumstances, physical health, history of substance use, and self-concept. Attempts also should be made to review additional sources of data, so as not to rely entirely on the patient's viewpoint. Within the spirit of a collaborative investigation, the therapist can invite the patient to bring significant others into a therapy session so that they can provide a different source of information on the patient's functioning. Significant others might include a spouse or other immediate family members, relatives, or friends. With written permission from the patient, the therapist should also obtain a copy of other relevant documents, such as previous treatment records or documents from legal proceedings.

From this life history review, a list of problem areas can be developed. This list can then be used to direct the content and focus of subsequent therapy sessions. By the time that a specific problem list is developed, it is also desirable to have established a moderate amount of cooperation and rapport and to have socialized the patient to the basic structure of therapy. Keeping in mind the antisocial patient's frequently low tolerance for boredom, it is also important not to spend too much time on just gathering information and building a relationship without developing some specific treatment interventions. Thus, an overview of history and current functioning and a tentative "try therapy out" attitude may be all that the therapist is able to obtain before treatment needs to proceed.

Within each problem area, it is helpful to identify cognitive distortions that would be amenable to intervention. A patient with ASPD typically holds a number of self-serving beliefs that guide his or her behavior. These frequently include, but are not necessarily limited to, the following six beliefs:

1. Justification—"Wanting something or wanting to avoid something justifies my actions."
2. Thinking is believing—"My thoughts and feelings are completely accurate, simply because they occur to me."
3. Personal infallibility—"I always make good choices."
4. Feelings make facts—"I know I am right because I feel right about what I do."
5. The impotence of others—"The views of others are irrelevant to my decisions, unless they directly control my immediate consequences."
6. Low-impact consequences—"Undesirable consequences will not occur or will not matter to me."

Thus, antisocial patients' automatic thoughts and reactions are frequently distorted by self-serving beliefs that emphasize immediate, personal satisfactions and minimize future consequences. The underlying belief that they are always right makes it unlikely that they will question their actions. Patients may vary in the degree of trust or mistrust they have in others, but they are unlikely to seek guidance or advice on any particular course of action. Because their behavior tends to be objectionable and even infuriating to others, ASPD patients may frequently get unsolicited counseling from others who want them to behave differently. Instead of evaluating the potential helpfulness of such input, ASPD patients tend to dismiss input from others as irrelevant to their purposes. In addition, antisocial distortions tend to show a loss of future time perspective. Antisocial patients' lack of concern for future outcomes might be placed on the opposite end of a continuum from obsessive-compulsive patients' excessive striving toward perfectionistic future goals.

Cognitive Therapy Objectives

The process of cognitive therapy for ASPD can be conceptualized in terms of a hierarchy of cognitive functioning, in which the clinician attempts to guide the patient toward a higher, more abstract process of thinking by means of guided discussions, structured cognitive exercises, and behavioral experiments. We begin with a broad hierarchy that is based on theories of moral and cognitive development. Specific steps are graded according to the individual patient's problematic ways of thinking and acting. At the lowest level on the hierarchy, the patient thinks only in terms of self-interest, basing choices on obtaining rewards or avoiding immediate punishments, without regard for others. This is where the antisocial patient functions most of the time prior to treatment. The dysfunctional beliefs previously described operate as unqualified rules at this level. Antisocial patients at this level do whatever they feel like doing, firmly believe that they always act in their own best interest, and remain impervious to corrective feedback.

At the next major level, a patient recognizes implications of his or her behavior and has some understanding of how it affects others, with an eye toward longer-range self-interest. This is the level toward which the clinician typically attempts to guide the ASPD patient. This is accomplished by helping the patient to grasp the concept of dysfunctional thoughts and behavior, and encouraging him or her to test alternative solutions that might modify earlier rules for living. For example, ASPD patients might come to realize that the views of others do have an effect on their getting what they want in the long run, even if such views do not directly control the immediate outcome of a specific situation. Gradually, such patients gain skill in considering something that is "possible" at the same time as something that is immediate or "actual." They are not so firmly convinced that they are always "right," and they are able to take in some new information and alter their behavior accordingly.

The third major level of the hierarchy is more difficult to define, since there is controversy among theorists regarding what constitutes the highest level of moral development. In moral or interpersonal terms, the individual demonstrates either a sense of responsibility or caring for others that includes a respect for the needs and wants of others, or a commitment to laws as guiding principles for the good of society. At the second level, the individual shows some concern for specific people under certain conditions where there is something he or she stands to gain or lose. At the third level, the person shows a greater ability to consider the needs of others or the needs of society in general. He or she may show respect for rules of order, or commitment to others because he cares about their welfare, and considers relationships an important part of his or her life.

A brief example may help to illustrate the general outline of the cognitive hierarchy just described. Consider an antisocial man seeking to fulfill a sexual desire. At the first level, he pursues a partner of his choice without regard for her interests or the consequences of his actions. For example, one young man described his typical relationships as consisting strictly of sexual activity that occurred at his convenience. His current girlfriend repeatedly asked him to accompany her to a public place such as a fast-food restaurant because she wanted him to take her out on a "date." The young man had no intention of responding to any of her interests in expanding their relationship or even her requests for certain sexual techniques. He felt quite comfortable in pursuing his own sexual purposes, regardless of her feelings.

At the second level, this antisocial young man might be influenced in a limited way by interests or wishes of others. For example, he might occasionally concede to some of his girlfriend's requests in order to maintain his advantage. "Make her happy once in a while and she will keep giving me what I want" might be his reasoning. At the third level, he might focus more on mutual interests as well as more long-range aspects of his behavior. For instance, he might make an effort to satisfy rather than to frustrate his girlfriend, because that is a better way of treating other people generally, and because it would contribute to a more stable and satisfying relationship for them both.

Specific Interventions

To initially counter the patient's defensive attitude toward treatment, the therapist might briefly summarize his problem as a lifestyle disorder that has roots in childhood or early adolescence, develops over a long period of time, and has serious negative consequences. It may also be pointed out that ASPD is a silent menace because persons suffering from this disorder usually can't recognize the symptoms in themselves, and typically do not feel any discomfort until the disorder is quite advanced. Once the disorder is explained, the therapist may suggest a trial of therapy during which the patient learns how treatment works and decides whether or not he or she wishes to participate. Patients should also be advised that after the initial trial, the length of treatment might extend to as many as 50 sessions or more, depending on the severity of their disorder and their progress in treatment.

As a general strategy in socializing the patient to treatment, therapy can be explained as a series of meetings that take place with an interested observer for the purpose of evaluating situations that might be interfering with the patient's independence and success in getting what he or she wants. By working with this sense of autonomy, the therapist begins to educate the patient in a process of abstract thinking—the realm of "possibilities." The therapist does this by helping the patient recognize how dysfunctional beliefs distort his or her time perspective and insulate him or her from critical information. In turn, this makes it very difficult for the ASPD patient to set clear priorities and effectively pursue them. In order to be more successful in getting what he or she wants, the patient can be encouraged to slow down the process of coming to conclusions and broaden his or her views to include a range of possibilities.

Guidelines for patient involvement in treatment include regular attendance at sessions, active participation in discussion, and involvement in homework planning and completion. By explaining these guidelines, the clinician attempts to socialize the patient toward a view of therapy as a noncoercive, beneficial activity. If the patient's behavior suggests an initial noncompliance with treatment guidelines, such as failing to keep scheduled appointments, being hostile or noncommunicative during sessions, or not attempting homework, then the therapist should directly inquire about his or her views on treatment. If encouragement or clarification of the treatment contract does not help to foster a better response, then the therapist should, by approximately the fourth session, discuss the patient's choices in whether or not to continue this course of treatment.

Other treatment options might include an additional 2-week trial for "slow starters," referral for alternative services such as family therapy, an intensive inpatient treatment program, a partial hospitalization program, or referral back to a probation officer. Therapists are advised to continue treatment only when it is reasonably clear that the patients are benefitting from it. At times, ASPD patients will come to psychotherapy in order to avoid going to jail; their participation in treatment may be very marginal. Therapists who feel compelled to continue treatment in order to keep their noncompliant patients out of jail may be operating under the assumption that such persons need to be rescued. In this case, what the therapists may not recognize is that they could be supporting antisocial behavior by protecting the patients from the legal consequences of their actions.

In attempting to discuss the problem list, the therapist is once again likely to encounter the patient's denial of problems. Attempting to coerce the patient into admitting that he or she does have problems will probably damage rapport and cause treatment avoidance, dropout, or ongoing power struggles. Instead, the therapist can review the criteria for ASPD and compare this with the patient's history. The patient can be reminded that this is a serious disorder affecting judgment and behavior, and that it tends to have very negative long-term consequences for the afflicted individual (such as alienation of friends and family, physical harm from others, or extended incarceration). Thus, the patient may wish to use therapy for evaluating potential changes before these consequences develop further. Patients whose problems are framed as symptoms of a disorder are less apt to feel that they are being accused of bad behavior. From there, the therapist can proceed to implement a systematic review of choices in various life areas, utilizing the process of guided discovery to help the patient determine the advantages and disadvantages of specific choices. Problems are most likely to be acknowledged by antisocial patients when they can see a distinct personal disadvantage that is tangible and relevant in daily life.

For example, Sam, a young man with ASPD, was on the verge of being expelled from dental school. Sam believed that he should do what he felt like doing, such as tell off supervisors, or not return from a weekend trip until Wednesday even when he was scheduled to provide clinical services on Monday and Tuesday. He viewed the consequences of these actions as mainly problems for other people and not himself. Sam tended either to dismiss or become belligerent toward people who tried to convince him that he should feel ashamed of his bad behavior. As an alternative, the therapist helped Sam to recognize that getting kicked out of dental school was a situation that he wished to avoid. Therapy discussion focused on ways to modify his belief that he could do whatever he *felt* like doing. Sam worked on reducing behavior that he justified on the basis of immediate feelings. He did this in order to meet his goal of graduating from dental school.

Making Constructive Decisions

Therapists may wish to use a structured format for reviewing different problem areas and evaluating the "risk-benefit ratio" of various choices. A "choice review" exercise has been developed for this purpose (see Table 8.3). Parts of the exercise may be adapted for homework, or may be modified to meet the needs of specific patients. The exercise format is designed to be used repetitively across different areas of functioning, to assist the ASPD patient in developing the capacity for considering a range of possibilities. The first step is to identify some situation in which there are current problems or tensions, and then to list all the facts about that situation. Some examples might include a specific relationship, job status, or current physical health. Then the patient rates his or her satisfaction with those facts on a scale of 0–100.

Next, as many choices as possible are listed in the second column. The choice column would typically include current maladaptive behavior, as well as presumably more adaptive alternatives. Options in the choice column incorporate the patient's immediate, "automatic" reactions, as well as other possibilities that come out of a discussion between the patient and therapist. In two adjacent columns, the advantages and disadvantages of each choice are listed. At this point, the therapist may be able to point out disadvantages to maladaptive behavior that the patient has overlooked. Advantages of more adaptive choices can also be

TABLE 8.3
Choice Review Exercise

Problem[a]	Choice[b]	Advantages	Disadvantages
Job. Demoted and placed on probation at work. S = 10. Want to keep job.	Tell boss to shove it and quit. E = 20.	Easy. Get revenge.	Have to start job search again. Don't want to leave this company.
	Demand old job back. E = ?.	Show I'm no patsy. Might work.	Risk getting fired now. Shows disrespect for boss's decisions.
	Find a way to make boss look bad for revenge. E = 25.	Feel better about what they've done to me.	Boss might find out I made him look bad. His bad mood won't help me.
	Do as little as possible until they show more faith in me. E = 50.	Low risk on my part. Get to take it easy for a while.	Boring. Probably won't get old job back very fast.
	Take a positive attitude and work my way back up the ladder. E = 60.	Shows my interest in the company. Gives me something to do that's not so boring.	Company will get extra mileage out of me when they've already screwed me over once.

[a] "S1 = 1___" ratings in this column indicate the patient's satisfaction with the facts of the situation, on a scale of 0–100.
[b] "E1 = 1___" ratings in this column indicate the patient's estimation of the effectiveness of each choice, on a scale of 0–100.

pointed out. Finally, the patient rates how effective each choice is likely to be, using the 0–100 scale.

An appropriate follow-up for this exercise would include an ongoing review of subsequent behavioral choices made in the problem areas discussed, with a concomitant effectiveness evaluation. Repeated ineffective choices could indicate a need to review the advantages and disadvantages again, or could highlight a need to address some specific skill deficits. Alternatively, the patient may need to review why he or she continues to make ineffective choices. This may be occurring because of some previously undetected dysfunctional belief.

Specific Therapist-Patient Interactions

Clinicians are highly advised to clarify that their role is not that of arbiter or judge, but rather that of an assistant or cooperative partner in personal evaluation, and a specialist in this evaluation process. The stated purpose of therapy is to review the personal effectiveness of the patient's current choices and to teach a cognitive strategy for obtaining success. Instead of moralizing, the therapist tries to point out consequences that might otherwise be unrecognized problems from the patient's point of view. Ultimately, the definition of personal success is left to the patient. The therapist concentrates on assisting the patient in clarifying his or her personal priorities. The cognitive therapist endeavors to teach the patient how to think and act differently, with more deliberation, rather than pushing him or her to feel different about past behavior.

To structure this role further, therapists are advised not to take on responsibility for dispensing important reinforcements to these patients. This is likely to be an issue mainly in inpatient settings, where therapists often have responsibility for determining access to privileges. Staff resources permitting, it may be useful to have one clinician determining privileges based mainly on a patient's overt behavior, and another conducting the cognitive therapy. If this strategy is used, then the cognitive therapist should conscientiously avoid arbitrating any disputes or intervening with third parties on the patient's behalf. Other staff members can direct the patient to review the problem with the cognitive therapist.

Developing and maintaining rapport with the antisocial patient is a difficult but crucial component of treatment. Adequate cognitive therapy requires a reasonably positive and cooperative rapport as necessary, but not sufficient, for intervention. One main reason for the therapist to stay out of a position of control with the patient is to maintain rapport by avoiding power struggles. Another method for circumventing nonproductive power struggles is to admit vulnerability to manipulation (Frances, 1985). The therapist may actually gain credibility by acknowledging the effectiveness of this skill in the antisocial patient. These patients are likely to lie to their therapist. The therapist can deal with this obstacle by admitting that it can happen, and thus avoid entrapment in the role of arbiter of truth. If the therapist were to try to present an impenetrable facade of toughness, an antisocial patient would likely feel challenged to prove that the therapist can be manipulated.

Therapists can use the following guidelines for assistance in managing their approach to antisocial patients:

1. The therapist needs to behave in ways that foster rapport and do not alienate the ASPD patient. He or she needs to be viewed by the patient as a knowledgeable, friendly professional rather than a punitive authority figure. The following characteristics may help therapists to have the desired impact on the therapeutic relationship:

   a. Self-assurance
   b. Reliable but not infallible objectivity

    c. A relaxed and nondefensive interpersonal style

    d. A clear sense of personal limits

    e. A strong sense of humor

Each of these characteristics can be cultivated as an important tool in attempting rapport with an antisocial patient.

    2. These patients are apt to respond to the most direct and concrete aspects of the therapist's behavior. Therefore, interaction that conveys undue suspicion, easy suggestibility, or attitudes of superiority, aloofness, or pity is apt to diminish rapport and foster a variety of counterproductive reactions.

    3. Inasmuch as the therapist wishes to facilitate psychosocial development characteristic of adolescence, then it is important to consider ways in which ASPD patients might develop some "peer-like" identification with the therapist. One therapist was positively viewed by her ASPD patient as being "like a sister" to him, primarily because she listened and helped him prioritize his family problems rather than lecturing or admonishing him. Other therapists have accomplished this sort of rapport by spending extra time playing cards with prisoners or patients, or making a point to know the latest jokes being passed around the cellblock, and thus come to be regarded as being "one of the guys." There are no simple formulas for accomplishing this rapport, because the right combination will vary according characteristics of the therapist, patient, and setting.

    Therapists may experience a number of strong emotional reactions to working with antisocial patients, often referred to as "countertransference reactions." Prominent among these are suspiciousness and anger, as well as a frustrated hopelessness about one's efforts to intervene successfully. The first pitfall, as previously mentioned, is engaging in power struggles that put the therapist on guard against being conned or duped. Doing battle with a patient and trying to catch him or her in lies leads to the therapist's feeling angry toward this patient. These feelings may also be a sign that the therapist has activated his or her own moralism and desire to punish the patient for wrong behavior. It may be helpful in such instances for the therapist to decide that someone else will function in the role of judge and arbiter of consequences for the patient. This role should be avoided, since being judgmental and controlling makes the patient resistant and defensive. Instead, the cognitive therapist helps the patient learn how to make better choices.

    Therapists may feel frustrated and hopeless when confronted with their limitations in treating antisocial patients. Some of these individuals appear wholly untouched by the therapeutic interaction. "Hard-core" criminals, who do not see themselves as having much to lose, may be one such group of elusive patients. Another group may be outpatient drifters who lead a parasitic lifestyle (often controlled by drug abuse) and attempt to stay one step ahead of the law. They will leave treatment after a session or two when it has become clear that the therapist will not fall for some obvious attempt at deception.

Therapists may be troubled by thoughts such as "Why should I even bother to help this scumbag?" Antisocial patients can seem impossible to manage and unlikely to change, and therefore not worth the effort of therapy. Hopelessness about the impact of treatment can be tempered by focusing on fairly narrow goals involving the reduction of behavior that is dangerous to the patient or others. Therapists can take heed not to devalue humble efforts. Therapy can proceed in a graded-task fashion, beginning with greater emphasis on behavior and moving toward more focus on cognitive processes. Antisocial patients may never abide by the rules of society because of their internal attitudes concerning responsibility. They may, however, learn some of the advantages of reviewing their behavior and giving consideration to the feelings of others.

Case Example

The following case history illustrates how the cognitive treatment approach can be applied with a patient diagnosed as having ASPD. It incorporates the choice review exercise within an individually tailored treatment intervention. Despite the many complexities of this clinical presentation, treatment success was linked to a limited intervention focused upon problems of parental irresponsibility and interpersonal irritability. Over the course of treatment, this patient's cognitions gradually shifted from a predominant focus on her own self-interest and immediate emotional reactions, to a greater recognition of the implications of her behavior for other people, and how others' reactions to this behavior in turn affected her. For example, she stopped focusing as much on thoughts about how unfairly she was being treated by others, and became more aware of how her own behavior influenced the way that others treated her. In terms of her parental role, she showed evidence of moving from the first level (unqualified self-interest) to the second level (qualified self-interest) on the cognitive development hierarchy. This was evident when she was able to consider her daughter's needs, her own wishes, and the father's reactions at the same time.

Susan was a 28-year-old Caucasian female who entered outpatient psychotherapy as part of a complicated family therapy intervention. Susan's 7-year-old daughter, Candy, was initially brought to treatment by her custodial father and stepmother (Mr. and Mrs. R), due to noncompliance and moodiness that had increased since Susan had recently attempted to increase the frequency of her visits to once per month.

During the previous several years, Susan had visited her daughter very sporadically, once even letting an entire year pass without contact. At the time of referral for treatment, Susan's visitation rights were restricted to being under the direct supervision and discretion of the custodial parents. This was because Susan had previously been legally found guilty of neglect, and Candy had been removed from her care.

Susan's history, gathered via interviews with Susan and the Rs, as well as review of copies of court testimony, revealed a conduct disorder before age 15 and persistent irresponsible and antisocial behavior since age 15. At age 18, she had been convicted of selling controlled substances and served a year sentence in prison. Susan conceived her older daughter, Candy, during a brief relationship with Mr. R, but she never told him she was pregnant and did not inform him of his daughter's existence until Candy was almost 3 years old. Susan's impulsive and irresponsible behavior eventually led to her two daughters being removed from her custody because of her negligence in their care.

At the time of initial therapy contact, Susan was living in a city 150 miles from the Rs. She had been coming to town once a month for a couple of months, and visiting with her younger biological child, Carol, overnight in her own mother's house. She also wanted to resume visits with Candy, so she agreed to the Rs' stipulation of therapy.

Initially, Susan was cordial but also defensive and resentful of the circumstances of therapy. She grudgingly agreed to complete the Minnesota Multiphasic Personality Inventory (MMPI), and produced a valid profile that was characterized by defensiveness and anger, with a spike elevation on scale 4 (Psychopathic Deviance).

After interviewing Candy and Susan separately, and observing them playing together, the therapist noted a high degree of attachment and interpersonal interest between them. Susan demonstrated an increased interest in playing a role in her daughter's life by her efforts to expand visitation. The Rs reported that she behaved appropriately when she was with Candy, attending to her, playing with her, and not obviously abusing or neglecting her. Susan claimed that she had been in business school for several months, that she had worked continuously in the same job for more than 6 months, and that she was involved in a romantic relationship of more than 6 months' duration—all evidence of increased stability in her life.

Based on this information, the therapist agreed to work with Susan and Candy. The therapist informed Susan that her history and psychological test results indicated that she had ASPD. This disorder was explained as a lifestyle disorder including judgments and behaviors that resulted in negative consequences for Susan as well as others, such as Candy. The agreed-upon goals of the cognitive therapy were to assist Susan in gaining greater access to visitation with her daughter and to monitor Candy's overall adjustment. Candy responded positively to contacts with Susan, but was jealous of her half-sister Carol getting to do more things with their mother, and had trouble saying goodbye when their few hours of visitation were up. Candy's moodiness and noncompliance seemed to be worse right after a visit if Carol was getting to spend that night with her mother. Candy's behavior also seemed worse in the middle of the month, when she would begin to doubt that her mother was coming back to see her again.

The choice review intervention with Susan focused on visitation with Candy, as well as other specific concerns that Susan had in handling her two daughters. The format for this exercise was introduced very early in treatment, as soon as a contract for therapy was established.

An example of Susan's choice-review exercise is illustrated in Table 8.4. In this exercise, Susan listed her immediate, "automatic" reactions to the visitation situation, as well as other possible reactions that she discussed with the therapist. Through the choice review discussion, Susan was able to see that she did have some ability to influence the future of her visitation with Candy. She decided that expressing her resentment

TABLE 8.4
Susan's Choice Review Exercise

Problem	Choice	Advantages	Disadvantages
Visitation. The Rs have a court decree giving them control over my visits. They will let me visit for only 4 hours in their home. S = 10.	Tell the Rs to shove it. E = 40.	Feel better.	May backfire and cause further restrictions.
	Give up and stop visiting altogether. E = 20.	Easy. Least amount of hassle. May be best all around.	Not what I really want. May hurt Candy
The Rs do not trust me. They think I am an unfit mother. I want to spend time alone with my daughter. S = 0.	Just take Candy when she is at school. E = 25.	Get back at the Rs and get time with Candy.	Maybe get arrested. Candy might get scared.
	Try to convince the Rs that I will do no harm to Candy. E = 50.	Rs may give in and let me have more freedom with Candy.	Pain in the ass. Too slow. Unfair to me.
	Demand that the Rs give me more time with Candy. E = 20.	Feel better faster.	Won't change their stubborn minds. Might make things harder.
	Make gradual requests for more freedom with Candy. E = 70.	May pay off in little ways real soon. Gives chance to build good faith with the Rs.	Pace too slow for my preference.

of what she believed to be the unfairness of her visitation limits was not as likely to be effective in achieving her goal as was trying to build up a "good-faith" relationship with the Rs. The therapist helped her to determine when and how to test their development of "good faith" through gradual requests to expand her range of privileges with Candy.

Over the course of approximately 8 months, Susan's privileges with Candy expanded gradually from driving to therapy in a separate car to having lunch alone with Candy after therapy; having half of an 8-hour visit on their own, then most of the visit on their own, and finally having an overnight visit together at Candy's maternal grandmother's house. Susan made all of her own requests for privileges to the Rs, after first practicing her approach with the therapist.

Initially, negotiation between Susan and the Rs was conducted in the therapist's presence, in order to facilitate communication. The Rs aired their reservations, to which Susan attempted to respond in a reassuring rather than a hostile manner, as she had practiced with the therapist. When Susan did respond with hostility, the Rs backed off and temporarily refused to expand privileges. This was helpful in that Susan could then see how her attitude had interfered with getting what she wanted. The therapist was careful not to step in and reassure the Rs on Susan's behalf, but instead worked with Susan to help her keep her priorities in mind and review the effectiveness of her behavior.

Candy showed improvement in her overall mood and in her cooperation at home and at school. A critical factor in the progress that was made with Candy and with Susan was the latter's being responsible enough to continue showing up for visits to the Rs and acting in an appropriate manner when Candy was in her care. Apparently, Susan valued her relationship with her daughter enough to work for it. She was able to function reasonably well in a structured, time-limited parental role. At the same time, that structure had to become flexible enough to allow enjoyable contact with her daughter, rather than emphasizing limitations as punishment for being a poor mother in the past.

Treatment interventions helped Susan to pursue her goal of increased visitation more effectively, and helped her to recognize that stepwise efforts were more effective than all-or-nothing demands. Her thinking and reasoning showed movement up the cognitive hierarchy as she came to recognize that her attitude toward others influenced how she might be treated, and that it was possible for her to be treated differently if she acted differently. She showed some potential for moving toward the third level (general social interest) of the hierarchy by considering several people's wants and needs at once. These considerations, however, were still motivated by a qualified self-interest, rather than a commitment to being a good mother because that was important to Candy's adjustment. For instance, she tended to emphasize what she would enjoy doing with Candy, rather than what Candy might enjoy doing with her. In another instance near the close of therapy, Susan raised the possibility that she might go to live in Europe with her boyfriend. She was mainly concerned with the possibility that Candy would get angry and reject her, rather than being sensitive to how much Candy might miss her, or concerned with how she could fulfill her responsibilities as Candy's mother. However, treatment was terminated when the agreed-upon goals of therapy were met. A mutually satisfying visitation schedule was established and maintained for 3 months without incident, and Candy showed significant improvement in her mood and cooperation at home and at school.

Treatment of Antisocial Personality Disorder with Associated Axis I Disorders

General Considerations

Several DSM-III-R Axis I disorders may be manifested along with ASPD, complicating the diagnostic accuracy as well as treatment intervention. The most frequent of these are alcohol or substance abuse, somatization disorder (Hare, 1985a; Lilienfeld, VanValkenburg, Larntz, & Akiskal, 1986), and major affective disorder (Frances, 1985). When other disorders are also present, each one can be addressed by a specific treatment plan, drawing upon methods typically used to treat that disorder. The cognitive psychotherapy methods described for ASPD would usually be applied after the Axis I disorder has improved. If patients do not acknowledge having ASPD, it is unlikely that they will remain in treatment long enough to work on their personality problems.

Although it might seem as if the consequences of their actions don't bother them, ASPD patients can become quite despondent over losses, failed relationships, or being exploited themselves. In some cases, clinical depression can result. For instance, an antisocial businessman became depressed and sought treatment after he discovered that his bookkeeper was embezzling from his business; he was charged with tax evasion; his wife discovered his extramarital affair and left him; and his daughter, disgusted with his lying to her, refused to see him any more. Generally, the depressogenic cognitions of the antisocial patient will reflect a view of having gotten a raw deal from life.

Special consideration needs to be given to the simultaneous manifestation of substance abuse and major affective disorder in an antisocial personality, because this combination makes for a very high suicide risk (Frances, 1985). In this instance, both Axis I disorders need immediate treatment. Because of the ASPD patient's poor impulse control, disregard for the consequences of actions, and loss of future time perspective, suicide potential needs to be continuously monitored. Depression and substance abuse typically require more intensive efforts earlier in treatment, with the ASPD becoming more of a focus as treatment progresses. However, the major distortions of the ASPD may be identified and dealt with throughout treatment. Treatment would be expected to take longer than that for an Axis I disorder alone, and the course of treatment is not apt to progress at a smooth or rapid pace when ASPD is present. This is because the ASPD patient is more likely to act in ways that alienate others, but is unlikely to admit his or her own role in such problems. As a result, the patient has difficulty using past experience to avoid future difficulties.

Case Example

Joe was a 34-year-old welder, voluntarily admitted to a Veterans Administration hospital for treatment of alcoholism after an incident of battering his wife. Joe had the requisite history of conduct disorder before age 15, and as an adult had shown considerable aggression, irresponsibility, and disregard for the rights of others. Currently, his wife, Becky, and four daughters were living on a combination of public assistance and the help of relatives.

On several occasions, Joe had been hospitalized for brief detoxification, but he had never continued with a rehabilitation program. This time, he completed 2 weeks of detoxification and then committed himself to a 6-week alcohol rehabilitation program. Following detox, he completed a psychological evaluation that included a valid MMPI profile with elevations on scales 2 (Depression), 4 (Psychopathic Deviance), and 8 (Schizophrenia). Joe cooperated with all aspects of this standard, comprehensive, milieu treatment program for substance abuse. He also agreed to work on his antisocial personality problems in individual cognitive therapy. Therapy sessions occurred three times a week, for a total of 18 sessions.

The list of target areas for Joe's cognitive therapy included behavior toward other people (irritability and aggression), regard for his own personal safety and health (drinking, drug taking, and associated recklessness), and functioning as a parent (irresponsibility).

The target area of behavior toward other people was the focus for discussion of Joe's spouse-battering incident. The therapist introduced the concept of a battering cycle (Walker, 1979, 1980), in which escalating personal and family tensions lead to angry outbursts and verbal harangues, culminating in a more severe battering incident that is typically followed by discomfort and a desire to re-establish equilibrium. This model appeared to fit Joe's spouse abuse. He disliked the tension between him and Becky after the abusive incidents. He didn't want to alienate his wife, and he did not want to be separated from his four daughters. It was pointed out to Joe how he seemed to minimize the consequences of being irritable and aggressive toward Becky, until she threatened to divorce him.

Joe was asked to give concrete descriptions of the typical family tensions that bothered him. This included details on exactly what each person did and said, and his automatic thoughts about the situation. For instance, it would bother him to come home after work and have his children continue to play outside or watch TV instead of rushing in to wait on him. He would think to himself, "They don't care that I've been working hard all day." His next automatic thought was "Their mother doesn't teach them any respect for me." Throughout the evening, Joe would continue to be irritated by such behaviors as the children's not eating all the food on their dinner plates, or arguing over which television program to watch. He attributed this apparent misbehavior to Becky's mismanagement, and he would feel more and more angry toward her. Exactly when Joe might lash out and physically abuse Becky was unpredictable. Practically anything that happened to irritate Joe further might become the triggering incident in which he decided that he "had enough," and Becky would become the target of abuse. Even simple domestic events such as one of the children asking for lunch money, the dog barking, or Becky saying she was going out to the store for milk might be the triggering event, because Joe would interpret it as meaning malevolence or disrespect for him.

Each circumstance in which Joe felt anger or irritation was listed as a problem situation in a choice review exercise. Joe and his therapist then tried to think of all of the different ways that he might react to the situation, listing the advantages and disadvantages for each way. The point of the intervention was not only to help Joe see his choices in the battering incident, but to assist him in making better choices about dealing with tensions prior to battering, and to help him see the pattern developing from his unchecked irritability and aggressiveness. A crucial component of this process was helping him to recognize his negative thoughts as triggers for his angry feelings and aggressive behavior, instead of blaming his actions on something Becky did or said. A second major component was clarifying for Joe how his underlying beliefs reflected rules for living that dictated mistrust of others, and a conviction of personal infallibility. These attitudes included the notions that "Others are always trying to screw you over," "No one really gives a damn about me," and "I should always have the final say-so because I am right."

Joe's automatic negative thoughts were characterized by over-generalization and emotional justification of his actions. For instance,

Joe came home late one evening (after drinking) and found that Becky had already cleaned up from the evening meal and put the food away. He automatically thought, "That bitch never fixes a decent meal for me." When he attempted to confront her about this, he thought, "She is ignoring me," so he proceeded to force her to pay attention to him by hitting her. When he was asked by the therapist to evaluate the validity of his first statement ("That bitch . . . ") and to identify other possible reactions, Joe recognized that this thought was a distortion, since Becky was in fact a very responsible homemaker. Joe and his therapist then discussed different ways that he might have handled this situation more peacefully. This discussion helped Joe to see that Becky and his children also had needs that had to be taken into consideration. Although he didn't accept it wholeheartedly, Joe agreed to consider the therapist's suggestion that his heavy drinking interfered with more rational thinking and made Becky want to withdraw from him.

Joe's choices to act automatically on his irritable and aggressive feelings were evaluated within other interpersonal situations. His tendency to get into fist fights was a form of automatic retaliation. If he felt challenged even in a small way, Joe believed that he should physically defend himself. In reviewing the consequences of this choice, Joe acknowledged that being injured was a definite disadvantage. Even when he supposedly "won" a fight, he typically sustained some injuries. He was asked to weigh the advantage of blowing off steam, acting on his immediate reflex reactions, and sometimes "winning" against the disadvantages of getting physically injured, possibly being arrested, and possibly setting himself up for future injury (because his opponents sometimes rechallenged him). It was up to Joe to decide if it was worth it to let the random comments of casual acquaintances or even strangers provoke him into exposing himself to even temporary physical pain, at the very least. Alternative strategies were discussed for those times when Joe might choose to avoid physical pain or not use emotional reasoning. His preferred choices were to tell himself to "blow it off" and not react, and to just "ease on out" by walking away from the situation without having physical contact.

Joe's inpatient treatment program for alcohol and substance abuse emphasized awareness of the negative consequences of addiction, and maintenance of sobriety through total abstinence. Since he was involved in an extensive program for the treatment of this Axis I disorder, individual therapy focused on selective problems he might anticipate in maintaining abstinence outside of the hospital. He listed low-, medium-, and high-risk situations for substance abuse, and identified thoughts that might trigger drinking or taking pills. These included automatic thoughts such as "I really need a drink," or "What the heck, I can handle it just this once."

In discussing his alternative choices, Joe recognized that challenging these thoughts and planning alternative behaviors would both be important in preventing a relapse of substance abuse. He saw that he could choose to avoid or to leave a high-risk situation such as going to a bar after work. He also planned to counter the thoughts that might lead to a relapse by reminding himself that a body needs only water, and that a felt "need" for an alcoholic drink was a confusion of wants and needs. Joe acknowledged that he was going to need considerable practice and support in order to keep making choices that would help him to achieve his goals of staying out of the hospital or jail and keeping his family together. Therefore, he planned to continue in outpatient therapy and attend regular meetings of Alcoholics Anonymous.

This ASPD patient showed a good response to treatment by his general compliance to the treatment program, and by a shift in his behavior from being testy and hostile to more friendly and positive. The positive rapport that he maintained with the therapist was an important influence in development of his ability to consider alternative viewpoints. A report of this patient's continued progress came 2 years later, when he and his wife contacted the therapist to thank her for her help and ask her advice on starting a support group for Viet Nam veterans. Joe had remained abstinent from alcohol and had worked steadily; the family remained together in their home, and severe battering had not recurred.

Treatment of Antisocial Personality Traits

The strategies of cognitive therapy can also be used with people who may present with traits of antisocial personality, but may not meet the full criteria for ASPD. Brett was such a young man, who came for outpatient therapy after being arrested for the possession of stolen goods. He was 29 years old and had shown several characteristics of irresponsible and antisocial behavior since the age of 15, but there was no evidence of his having a conduct disorder before age 15. Brett presented as a very glib, handsome young man with charismatic charm. The MMPI profile that he produced was valid, but had a moderate clinical elevation on scale K (Correction) as well as on scales 4 (Psychopathic Deviance) and 9 (Mania), with a subclinical elevation on scale 2 (Depression).

For most of his late adolescence and early adult years, Brett had lived by various schemes to cheat systems and avoid having to pay for things. For instance, he charged hundreds of dollars of phone calls to random numbers, on a telephone listed in the name of one of his roommates. Brett had been a student at a major university more or less continuously since leaving high school. He never completed a course of studies leading to a bachelor's degree, but had talked his way into a graduate program in communications. Recently, Brett had been caught red-handed with stolen goods as well as a small quantity of unprescribed drugs.

The following dialogue between Brett and his therapist illustrates how he was guided toward thinking about the consequences of his actions, and his impact on others, in the context of evaluating whether he was actually meeting his own goals.

THERAPIST: How well has the "beat-the-system" approach actually worked out for you over time?

BRETT: It works great . . . until someone catches on or starts to catch on. Then you have to scrap that plan and come up with a new one.

THERAPIST: How difficult was it, you know, to cover up one scheme and come up with a new one?

BRETT: Sometimes it was really easy. There are some real pigeons out there.

THERAPIST: Was it always easy?

BRETT: Well, no. Sometimes it was a real bitch. Like beating the phone system. That really ended up in a big hassle. There was really no way to cover it up, and everyone gave me such a hard time.

THERAPIST: Was it very easy to come up with an alternative plan?

BRETT: Not for the phones. I never did come up with another plan.

THERAPIST: How about at other times? Did beat-the-system plans come to you very easily—I mean, ones that actually worked?

BRETT: Well, I came up with lots of good ones, but it was tough coming up with something that would really pay off.

THERAPIST: Did a good plan last a long time, or were new ones frequently required?

BRETT: Seems like I'm always needing a good plan to beat the system.

THERAPIST: Do you think it's ever easier to go with the system instead of trying to beat it in some way?

BRETT: Well, after all that I have been through, I would have to say yes, there have been times that going with the system would have been easier in the long run. By the time I'm done paying legal fees, I will have shelled out more than my tuition would ever have cost me. But . . . it's such a challenge to beat the system. It feels exciting when I come up with a new plan and think I can make it work. Going *with* the system might not even occur to me.

THERAPIST: So what you choose to do is dictated by how excited you feel about your idea, your plan?

BRETT: Yeah.

THERAPIST: Yet several of your plans have actually ended up costing you and creating hassles in the long run.

BRETT: Yeah.

THERAPIST: How does that fit with your goal of having an easy, carefree life where you don't have to work too hard?

BRETT: It doesn't. (*Pause*) So how do I get the easy life, Doc?

THERAPIST: Well, when do you actually start to come up with beat-the system plans?

BRETT: When I need to pay for something, or when I want something that will cost me money.

THERAPIST: Do you ever think about what all your choices are, and weigh them out, according to what consequences each one would have?

BRETT: Not usually. Usually, I just go for beating the system.

THERAPIST: What do you think would happen if you thought about other options, rather than just acting on an idea that you feel excited about at the moment?

BRETT: I don't know.

THERAPIST: Is there some situation that you are dealing with right now in your life that you have to come up with money for, and you have to figure out how you are going to do it?

BRETT: Yeah . . . how I'm going to afford rent on my apartment, the lease on the nightclub property, getting the place ready to open for business, and still pay my lawyer.

THERAPIST: What are your options for dealing with that, your choices?

BRETT: Well, my lawyer made me give him a retainer up front, and you make me pay for each session, so I'm not getting much slack.

THERAPIST: Given the limits that you have to work with, what are your options?

BRETT: Well, I've been trying to figure out a way to get out of the rent on my apartment. If I can just come up with a good angle, maybe I can get the landlord to postpone it for a while.

THERAPIST: Would that possibly backfire on you?

BRETT: As a matter of fact, it did once, and I got sued in small-claims court. I sure wouldn't want that to happen now, because he could sue me for the remainder of my lease, even if I go to jail.

THERAPIST: What other options or choices do you have to deal with your rent and your nightclub plans?

BRETT: I have thought of trying to find a roommate. Or I have even thought of subletting my apartment or giving up my deposit to break my lease and just moving into the upstairs space at the night-club. That would make it easier to work on the place, and it would take some financial pressure off until I get the business off the ground.

THERAPIST: Would there be any negative consequences in doing that?

BRETT: For me . . . I'd be living in kind of a pit. But other than that, not really. My landlord has already told me that all he really needs is a month's notice.

THERAPIST: Can you do anything about that living space to make it better? Fix it up a bit or something?

BRETT: Oh, sure. It's not really that bad. And I wanted to fix it up anyway, to have a nice private office at the club.

THERAPIST: So it sounds like you have several options for dealing with your current financial situation. Most of the time in the past, you have dealt with financial demands by getting involved in some beat-the-system scheme. It sounded like you would react emotionally to the excitement of your idea, and perhaps the feeling of getting away with something or just making it work, and then that excitement would carry you through, without thinking about possible consequences or alternatives. This time, you have discussed several possibilities. Which do you think will be the easiest and best for you in the long run?

BRETT: Fix up the space at the club and move in.

At another session, Brett discussed his relationship with a young woman, Sara, whom he tended to blame for most of his current difficulties. The therapist encouraged Brett to take stock of the choices he made in relating to women in general, and whether or not that helped him to meet his goals. Brett was guided toward changing his self-defeating behavior and learning how to think about his choices in terms that included consideration of other people and social order.

BRETT: I talked to Sara last night. I'll bet she would still go to bed with me.

THERAPIST: Wait a minute. I thought Sara was pressing legal charges against you.

BRETT: She is. But she still loves me. And I want to be friends. Maybe I can get her to drop some of the charges.

THERAPIST: It sounds like you're saying that you would go to bed with Sara in order to get her to drop the legal charges.

BRETT: That, and just to see if I can do it . . . if I have what it takes, you know?

THERAPIST: What do you know about Sara's feelings and expectations?

BRETT: Oh, she's very traditional. She probably still hopes that we might get married. She's from a very small town, you see, and where she comes from, people deal with each other by calling the sheriff on them. Whenever she got in trouble as a teenager, her father would call the sheriff to come out and give her a lecture. That's how she thinks you're supposed to keep people in line and make them do what you want.

THERAPIST: Do you think that Sara might feel even more involved with you if you get back together and you can get some of the charges dropped?

BRETT: Well, I guess she might.

THERAPIST: Do you think you might want to get married to Sara and have the kind of relationship that she would want?

BRETT: Oh, no way. No.

THERAPIST: So what might happen when you let Sara down again, when she realizes that you still intend to date other women?

BRETT: Hard to say. She might get pissed. I try not to think that far ahead.

THERAPIST: Would she think that you had just been using her to save your own neck, without regard for her feelings?

BRETT: She might.

THERAPIST: And you know already that Sara deals with her anger in pretty dramatic ways, such as calling the sheriff. How dangerous might it be to you to make her angry again?

BRETT: I guess it would be risky. (*Pause*) I just never believed that a woman would do anything like that to me.

THERAPIST: What are the chances of Sara doing something like that to you again?

BRETT: I guess about 95%.

THERAPIST: Those are pretty high odds. With that in mind, how would you evaluate the option of resuming a sexual relationship with her?

BRETT: Not worth the risk.

THERAPIST: Considering her interest in a traditional, monogamous relationship and your interest in dating different women, what do you think is the best way to handle contacts with Sara?

BRETT: Well, I wouldn't look the other way if I saw her on the street. But I don't think I need to bother going out looking for her, you know. It's probably best to just leave her alone and not let her get her hopes back up, because she's never going to get what she wants from me.

Brett and the therapist continued discussing his relationships with women by looking at the advantages and disadvantages of habitually chasing new women, and sometimes gaining sexual gratification by force. He had never really viewed this behavior as "date rape," and he seemed unaware that this could result in prosecution. Other potential drawbacks were examined, such as how he frequently alienated women, and how he was exposing himself to retaliation or sexually transmitted diseases. There were smaller, annoying drawbacks, too, such as lack of a reliably available partner, and a surprisingly large number of very boring dates. On the other hand, Brett said that he enjoyed the thrill of the chase, and that getting the attention of so many women made him feel good about himself.

Brett was asked to scale the degree of this thrill in terms of all the thrilling events in his life, and then apply the rating to individual "conquests." What he found was that the thrill was not very intense or reliable. Feeling good about himself was identified as a form of hedonism. He felt good about himself because he got what he believed he wanted at one particular moment. This was contrasted with another way to feel good about oneself—by working to meet one's overall goals and priorities in life. Brett gradually acknowledged that feeling good in the short term often made it more difficult to reach his main long-term goal of an easy life. The therapist made a point of trying to illustrate how consideration of the feelings of others and the long-range effects of his behavior would really work in his favor.

Conclusion

Once intervention takes place, one can never really know how destructive the antisocial patient might have been if no treatment had been provided. Likewise, one cannot predict or promise how many times the antisocial person might decide not to lie, con, cheat, beat, rape, steal, harass, default, or otherwise disrupt social harmony because he or she sees some greater personal advantage in not doing so. However, each of the case histories described in this chapter illustrates how cognitive therapy can have a positive impact on the life course of an antisocial person. While optimal functioning might remain an unrealistic goal for treatment, improvements in prosocial behavior have obvious benefits for the stability of the patient and the well-being of his or her significant others, as well as society at large.

Chapter 9
Borderline Personality Disorder

Introduction

Joan, a woman in her mid-30s called seeking therapy. She said that her main problem was that she had just finished graduate school and had no motivation for looking for work. She felt that she should be writing job letters and setting up interviews, but ended up spending all her time sitting around the apartment reading. This had been going on for several months now, and she was feeling increasingly desperate because "I'm the last one from my class who doesn't have a job."

She had recently married as well as having completed a master's degree in finance at a prestigious university. She and her husband had planned to move to Philadelphia so he could finish his PhD there, and she had spent several months actively job-hunting in Philadelphia with good results. Unexpectedly, Joan's husband was offered an opportunity to attend a much better graduate school in Chicago, and they moved immediately to Chicago without really discussing the decision. From that point on, Joan was unable to get herself to do any job hunting.

The clinician who conducted Joan's initial interview diagnosed her problems as adjustment disorder with mixed emotional features, and it appeared that therapy with Joan would be fairly simple and straightforward. However, the picture grew considerably more complicated during the first therapy session. When Joan's therapist discussed Joan's goals for therapy with her, she emphasized her lack of motivation for job hunting but also described an "identity crisis" regarding her career and her marriage, periods of intense depression, panic attacks, a history of conflict with employers, unrealistically high standards for herself, and anticipation of hostility from others. In short, Joan began to manifest many of the characteristics of persons with borderline personality disorder (BPD), and it became clear that therapy would be anything but straightforward.

BPD is a relatively common disorder that results in considerable impairment in the individual's life. Psychotherapy with individuals with BPD is typically quite complicated, and there is a significant risk of negative psychotherapy outcome, regardless of the treatment approach used (Mays, 1985). Straightforward application of behavioral techniques is less effective with borderline clients than with other clients (Mays, 1985), and until quite recently it was believed by some authors that these clients could not be treated effectively with cognitive therapy (Rush & Shaw, 1983). However, with the development of cognitive-behavioral conceptualizations of BPD (Freeman, Pretzer, Fleming, & Simon, 1990; Linehan, 1981, 1987a,b; Millon, 1981, 1987; Pretzer, 1983; Young, 1983, 1987; Young & Swift, 1988), it has been possible to develop guidelines for using cognitive therapy effectively with this difficult population.

The History of the "Borderline" Concept

It is important to note that the term "borderline" has been used in a number of ways that are quite different from the DSM-III-R criteria for BPD, and that the misuse of this diagnostic label has long been criticized (e.g., Knight, 1953). Originally, this term was used when the clinician was unsure of the correct diagnosis because the client manifested a mixture of neurotic and psychotic symptoms. Many clinicians thought of these clients as being on the border between neurotic and psychotic, and thus the term "borderline" came into use. In some circles, "borderline" is still used as a "garbage can" diagnosis for individuals who are hard to diagnose or is interpreted as meaning "nearly psychotic," despite a lack of empirical support for this conceptualization of the disorder.

Another usage of the term "borderline" is the reference to a borderline "personality structure" in the voluminous literature generated by psychodynamically oriented authors (e.g., Gunderson & Singer, 1975; Kernberg, 1975, 1977; Masterson, 1978). While these authors differ among themselves to some degree in their definitions of borderline personality structure (see Stone, 1985), this personality structure is seen as being characterized by "poorly integrated identity," "primitive defensive operations," "relatively firm self-object boundaries," and "reasonably intact reality testing" (Masterson, 1978). It is important to note that in addition to being difficult to operationalize, these characteristics do not specify any particular set of behaviors or symptoms. Thus, a particular individual could manifest borderline symptomatology with or without a borderline personality structure, or could manifest a borderline personality structure with or without borderline symptoms. For example, Stone (1985) describes an individual as "a schizotypal borderline (in the DSM-III sense), [who] exhibited a psychotic structure."

Finally, with the recent popularity of "borderline" as a diagnostic category and the reputation of these clients as being difficult to treat, "borderline" is often used as a generic label for difficult clients or as an excuse for therapy going badly. For example, consider the following imaginary conversation, which concisely summarizes a number of actual conversations:

SUPERVISOR: Why are you having trouble with Mr. Schultz?
THERAPIST: Because he's borderline.
SUPERVISOR: Why do you consider him borderline?
THERAPIST: Because I'm having so much trouble with him.

While it is true that borderlines can be both difficult to diagnose and difficult to work with, they are by no means the only difficult clients. Use of "borderline" as simply a pejorative label for difficult clients robs it of any utility.

The DSM-III-R criteria provide a clear, widely accepted definition of what is meant by BPD; throughout this chapter, the term "borderline" will be used only to refer to individuals who satisfy the DSM-III-R criteria. The distinction between the various usages of "borderline" is not trivial or academic. Attention to the way in which authors are defining "borderline" is particularly important when referring to the extensive literature generated by psychodynamically oriented authors. Many individuals who are labeled "borderline" by those authors would meet DSM-III-R criteria for personality disorders other than BPD. For example, in one study only 40% of a sample of patients who had been classified as "borderline" using personality structure criteria met DSM-III criteria for BPD.

Characteristics

In DSM-III-R (APA, 1987, pp. 346–347), BPD is defined as an enduring pattern of perceiving, relating to, and thinking about the environment and oneself in which there are problems in a variety of areas including interpersonal behavior, mood, and self-image. As can be seen from Table 9.1, these individuals experience a wide range of difficulties. The most striking features of BPD are the intensity of clients' emotional reactions, the changeability of their moods, and the great variety of symptoms they present. These individuals may abruptly shift from a pervasive depressed mood to anxious agitation or intense anger, or they may impulsively engage in actions that they later recognize as irrational and counterproductive. They typically present an erratic, inconsistent,

TABLE 9.1
DSM-III-R Diagnostic Criteria for Borderline Personality Disorder

A pervasive pattern of instability of mood, interpersonal relationships, and self-image, beginning by early adulthood and present in a variety of contexts, as indicated by at least *five* of the following:

(1) a pattern of unstable and intense interpersonal relationships characterized by alternating between extremes of overidealization and devaluation
(2) impulsiveness in at least two areas that are potentially self-damaging, e.g., spending, sex, substance use, shoplifting, reckless driving, binge eating (Do not include suicidal or self-mutilating behavior covered in [5].)
(3) affective instability: marked shifts from baseline mood to depression, irritability, or anxiety, usually lasting a few hours and only rarely more than a few days
(4) inappropriate, intense anger or lack of control of anger, e.g., frequent displays of temper, constant anger, recurrent physical fights
(5) recurrent suicidal threats, gestures, or behaviors, or self-mutilating behavior
(6) marked and persistent identity disturbance manifested by uncertainty about at least two of the following: self-image, sexual orientation, long-term goals or career choice, type of friends desired, preferred values
(7) chronic feelings of emptiness or boredom
(8) frantic efforts to avoid real or imagined abandonment (Do not include suicidal or self-mutilating behavior covered in [5].)

Note. From *Diagnostic and Statistical Manual of Mental Disorders* (3rd ed., rev., p. 347) by the American Psychiatric Association, 1987, Washington, DC: Author. Copyright 1987 by the American Psychiatric Association. Reprinted by permission.

unpredictable pattern of problems, and may function competently and effectively in some areas of life while manifesting dramatic problems in other areas.

Borderline individuals are not necessarily in constant turmoil and may experience extended periods of stability, but they typically seek therapy at times of crisis and present a complex and somewhat chaotic clinical picture. In addition, they often manifest other problems, such as generalized anxiety disorder, panic disorder, obsessive-compulsive disorder, somatoform disorders, psychogenic fugue states, major depression, bipolar disorder, schizoaffective disorder, brief reactive psychosis, or additional personality disorders (Millon, 1981). Clarkin and his colleagues (Clarkin, Widiger, Frances, Hurt, & Gilmore, 1983) found that even when consensus of three raters on the presence or absence of each of the DSM-III-R criteria was required for diagnosis, 60% of their borderline sample met the criteria for other personality disorders as well. These diagnoses included paranoid, schizotypal, histrionic, narcissistic, avoidant, and dependent personality disorders.

Assessment

Since no single feature or pattern of characteristics is invariably present, and variability is one of the hallmarks of BPD, assessment and diagnosis of this disorder are more complex than with many other diagnostic categories. It would be very useful if psychological testing could provide a simple index of BPD. Research to date with traditional psychological tests has provided evidence that borderline clients tend to score high on both "neurotic" and "psychotic" scales on the Minnesota Multiphasic Personality Inventory (MMPI), especially on scales 2, 4, 6, 7, and 8 (Widiger, Sanderson, & Warner, 1986). Empirical studies have also provided some support for the hypothesis that borderline clients tend to perform well on structured tests such as the Wechsler Adult Intelligence Scale (WAIS), while performing poorly and showing signs of thought disorder on unstructured projective tests. However, no simple "borderline profile" has been identified. Traditional psychological testing can provide information that is useful in identifying clients with BPD, but it does not provide a simple, reliable way to identify borderlines.

A number of measures designed specifically to assess BPD are included by Reich (1987) in his recent review of instruments designed to assess personality disorders. These include self-report questionnaires (Bell, 1981; Edell, 1984; Hurt, Hyler, Frances, Clarkin, & Brent, 1984), personality inventories (Millon, 1982), and structured interviews (Baron, 1981; Frances, Clarkin, Gilmore, Hurt, & Brown, 1984; Kolb & Gunderson, 1980; Perry & Klerman, 1980; Stangl, Pfohl, Zimmerman, Bowers, & Corenthal, 1985). Each shows potential for use in screening, but all will need further development and validation before they are ready for clinical use. Thus, the clinician cannot rely on these new measures to make the diagnosis for him or her, but they may well prove useful.

Despite these problems, the diagnosis of BPD need not be difficult. The DSM-III-R criteria are sufficiently clear to permit reliable diagnosis if the clinician considers a diagnosis of BPD and obtains the necessary information. For many clinicians, the primary difficulty lies in recognizing indications that it might be appropriate to consider a diagnosis of BPD. Table 9.2 lists a number of characteristics that often serve as indications of BPD. These are not intended as additional diagnostic criteria, but may be useful in reminding the clinician to consider whether the client may have an undiagnosed personality disorder.

It is particularly useful to be alert for six possible indications of BPD: (1) intense, unstable relationships; (2) a lack of a clear sense of identity (confusion or inconsistency regarding goals, priorities, and values); (3) episodes of intense, uncontrolled anger; (4) impulsive behavior; (5) chronic feelings of emptiness, boredom, or loneliness; and (6) "acting-out" behaviors. Clarkin and his colleagues (Clarkin et al., 1983) have

TABLE 9.2
Possible Indications of Borderline Personality Disorder

In Presenting Problems and Symptoms:

1. A diverse assortment of problems and symptoms, which may shift from week to week
2. Unusual symptoms or unusual combinations of symptoms
3. Intense emotional reactions that are out of proportion to the situation
4. Self-punitive or self-destructive behavior
5. Impulsive, poorly planned behavior that is later recognized as foolish, "crazy," or counterproductive
6. Brief periods of psychotic symptoms that meet DSM-III-R criteria for brief reactive psychosis (but that may have been misdiagnosed as schizophrenia)
7. Confusion regarding goals, priorities, feelings, sexual orientation, etc.
8. Feelings of emptiness or void, possibly localized in the solar plexus

In Interpersonal Relationships:

1. Lack of stable intimate relationships (possibly masked by stable nonintimate relationships or relationships that are stable as long as full intimacy is not possible)
2. Tendency to either idealize or denigrate others, perhaps switching abruptly from idealization to denigration
3. A tendency to confuse intimacy and sexuality

In Therapy:

1. Frequent crises, frequent telephone calls to the therapist, or demands for special treatment in scheduling sessions, making final arrangements, etc.
2. Extreme or frequent misinterpretations of therapist's statements, intentions, or feelings
3. Unusually strong reactions to changes in appointment time, room changes, vacations, or termination of therapy
4. Low tolerance for direct eye contact, physical contact, or close proximity
5. Unusually strong ambivalence on many issues
6. Fear of change or unusually strong resistance to change

In Psychological Testing:

1. Good performance on structured tests such as the WAIS, combined with poor performance or indications of thought disorder on projective tests
2. Elevation of both "neurotic" and "psychotic" MMPI scales (2, 4, 6, 7, 8) or indications of an unusually wide variety of problems

found that approximately 80% of individuals who met DSM-III criteria for BPD (which are quite similar to the DSM-III-R criteria) showed either a combination of intense, unstable relationships and identity disturbance or a combination of intense, unstable relationships, impulsivity, and intense and uncontrolled anger. Nurnburg and his colleagues (Nurnburg, Hurt, Feldman, & Suh, 1987) found that two sets of criteria provided the optimal balance of sensitivity, specificity, and predictive power in identifying individuals with BPD. These two sets of criteria were the combination of unstable, chaotic relationships and impulsive behavior, or any three of the following: (1) unstable, chaotic relationships, (2) impulsive behavior, (3) chronic feelings of emptiness, boredom, or loneliness, and (4) acting-out behavior.

In Joan's case, a thorough review of the information obtained in the initial evaluation and in the initial therapy session revealed many indications of BPD. In addition to the lack of motivation that was her presenting problem, Joan had long-standing problems with anxiety, panic attacks, depression, and anger, and had difficulty communicating clearly and being assertive with others. She described herself as "hyper" and reported that she would sometimes stay up for nights on end when she was very busy; however, she denied any other symptoms of manic episodes. Joan considered herself to be "sensitive" to many foods and was on a "semivegetarian" diet due to her belief that she was allergic to a number of quite ordinary foods. She also described a history of psychic experiences, including dreams that foretold the future.

As far as relationships with peers went, Joan said that she "partied a lot" in college but otherwise never had a large circle of friends. Most of her long-term relationships were with persons who had either physical disabilities or emotional problems. Her husband was blind, her most recent boyfriend had been a poorly controlled diabetic, and several friends were depressed and/or alcoholic. Her relationships with others tended to be on and off, often ending abruptly in a blow-up when she felt that the friend had betrayed her trust. Joan was recently married and reported finding adjustment to marriage difficult, saying, "It's like you're not in control of your life any more."

Joan appeared to be quite bright and had done her work well in school and on previous jobs. However, she had experienced considerable difficulty choosing a career: She had spent a year in law school and a year in a social work program, and then worked in local government before settling on finance. Joan reported that she experienced recurrent interpersonal difficulties on the job. She resented schedules and rules; felt that she was constantly mistreated by superiors; and eventually would become quite angry, confront her boss, and either resign impulsively or be fired.

Joan had sought treatment on five previous occasions and had received both traditional psychotherapy and medication. She had been involved in angry conflicts with most of her previous therapists and reported that neither therapy nor medication had been very helpful. She also described having a strong negative reaction to Elavil, reporting that it made her feel disoriented and "out of control."

Following this review of the available information, it appeared that in addition to BPD, Joan met DSM-III-R criteria for panic disorder and cyclothymic disorder.

Conceptualization

A remarkable number of books and papers have been written presenting theoretical and clinical analyses of BPD. By far the majority of these works have been based on object relations theory or other contemporary psychoanalytic approaches. Unfortunately, the vocabulary used in these analyses renders these conceptualizations inaccessible to many clinicians who are not fluent in psychoanalytic terminology. When translated into cognitive-behavioral terminology, the core of the object relations view is the assertion that the borderline individual holds extreme, poorly integrated views of relationships with early caregivers and, as a result, holds extreme, unrealistic expectancies regarding interpersonal relationships. These expectancies are seen as consistently shaping both behavior and emotional responses and as being responsible for the wide range of symptoms these individuals experience. It is assumed by psychodynamic writers that the most appropriate way to resolve this situation is to conduct therapy in such a way that these expectancies will be manifested in the client's relationship with the therapist, where they may be resolved through the application of psychoanalytic techniques in long-term therapy.

BPD has received much less attention from behavioral and cognitive-behavioral authors. However, in recent years Linehan (1981, 1987a,b), Millon (1981, 1987b), Pretzer (1983; Freeman et al., 1990), and Young (1983, 1987; Young & Swift, 1988) have presented a variety of cognitive-behavioral perspectives on this disorder.

Millon (1981, 1987b) provides a view based on social learning theory in which he attributes a central role to the borderline individual's lack of a clear, consistent sense of his or her own identity. He argues that this lack of a clear sense of identity is a product of biological, psychological, and sociological factors that combine to impair successful development of a sense of identity. Since one aspect of the borderline individual's lack of a clear sense of identity is a lack of clear, consistent goals, this problem results in poorly coordinated actions, poorly controlled impulses, and a lack of consistent accomplishment. As a result of this lack of a consistent strategy for dealing with problems that arise, these individuals cope poorly both with their own emotions and with problems that arise. Millon suggests that, as a result, borderlines become dependent on others for protection and reassurance, and become very sensitive to any signs of possible separation from these sources of support. He argues that this situation is complicated by intense conflicts regarding dependency and assertion, and by a realization that their anger over being trapped by dependency could result in their losing the security they gain from dependency.

Linehan (1981, 1987a,b) presents a more behavioral conceptualization of therapy for BPD, which she terms "dialectical behavior therapy." Her view is that a "dysfunction in emotion regulation" is a core characteristic of BPD that is probably physiologically based. This dysfunction is believed to be responsible for borderline individuals' dramatic overreactions to events and for their impulsive acts. She also hypothesizes that, in the course of their development, these individuals have extensive experience with significant others who discount their emotional experiences and insist that the borderlines-to-be manifest a "positive attitude" despite their distress. As a result, the individuals (who already are physiologically prone to disproportionate emotional responses) receive inadequate training in emotion regulation skills, and at the same time learn to take a disparaging, punitive attitude toward their own emotions.

This disparaging, punitive attitude and the individuals' realistic fears of being unable to control intense emotions block them from being able to tolerate strong emotions long enough to grieve significant losses. Thus, as additional losses occur, the individuals experience "bereavement overload" as well. The combination of intense emotional responses, inadequate emotional regulation skills, impulsive behavior, and a disparaging attitude toward their own emotions results in a series of unrelenting crises, and frequent occasions when the individuals are unable to cope effectively despite their best efforts. This leads the individuals to conclude that they must rely on others in many situations. However, having learned that it is necessary to maintain a "positive attitude," the individuals are unable to ask assertively for help, or to seek help by revealing their neediness. This results in their maintaining a facade of competence while trying to obtain the help of others subtly and indirectly. However, the individuals' strong emotional responses and their impulsive acts make it difficult for them to be consistently subtle in seeking help from others.

Young (1983, 1987; Young & Swift, 1988) has been developing a general cognitive-behavioral approach to the treatment of personality disorders, which he terms "schema-focused cognitive therapy." His approach differs from the standard cognitive therapy model in postulating that extremely stable and enduring patterns of thinking—which he labels "early maladaptive schemas"—can develop during childhood and result in maladaptive behavior patterns that reinforce the schemas. These schemas are then elaborated throughout development and into adulthood. He sees each of the personality disorders as being characterized by a subset of the 18 early maladaptive schemas he has identified thus far, and advocates making these particular schemas a major focus of therapy.

The early maladaptive schemas that Young sees as being characteristic of BPD are shown in Table 9.3. While Young does not present a detailed model of BPD, he assumes that when these early maladaptive schemas are activated by relevant events, distortions in thinking, strong emotional responses, and problematic behaviors result. One could assume that the large number of early maladaptive schemas postulated for borderlines (the other personality disorders average 2.5 early maladaptive schemas apiece) might account for the wide range of symptoms experienced by borderlines and their frequent crises. However, Young does not present a detailed description of how the schemas in Table 9.3 produce BPD.

The three preceding perspectives focus on very different aspects of BPD. Millon (1981, 1987b) emphasizes the borderline individuals' identity disorder as playing a central role in the rest of their problems,

TABLE 9.3
"Early Maladaptive Schemas" Hypothesized by Young to be Characteristic of Borderline Personality Disorder

Early Maladaptive Schema	Possible Expression
Abandonment/loss	"I'll be alone forever. No one will be there for me."
Unlovability	"No one would love me or want to be close to me if they really got to know me."
Dependence	"I can't cope on my own. I need someone to rely on."
Subjugation/lack of individuation	"I must subjugate my wants to the desires of others or they'll abandon me or attack me."
Mistrust	"People will hurt me, attack me, take advantage of me. I must protect myself."
Inadequate self-discipline	"It isn't possible for me to control myself or discipline myself."
Fear of losing emotional control	"I must control my emotions or something terrible will happen."
Guilt/punishment	"I'm a bad person. I deserve to be punished."
Emotional deprivation	"No one is ever there to meet my needs, to be strong for me, to care for me."

Note. Adapted from *Schema-Focused Cognitive Therapy for Personality Disorders* by J. Young, 1987, unpublished manuscript. Adapted by permission of the author.

Linehan (1981, 1987a,b) hypothesizes that a defect in emotion regulation and three "dialectics" on which the individual vacillates are the core of the disorder, and Young (1983, 1987; Young & Swift, 1988) sees the disorder as being based on strongly held assumptions that are acquired early in development and that play an important role throughout life. While our own views (Pretzer, 1983; Freeman et al., 1990) have developed independently of these theories, the model of BPD that follows incorporates each of the above-described factors into a comprehensive understanding of BPD based primarily on Beck's view of psychopathology (Beck, 1976; Beck, Rush, Shaw, & Emery, 1979).

In Beck's theory, the individual's basic assumptions play a central role in influencing perception and interpretation of events and in shaping both behavior and emotional responses. Three key basic assumptions are often uncovered in cognitive therapy with borderline individuals and appear to play a central role in the disorder. These are "The world is dangerous and malevolent," "I am powerless and vulnerable," and "I am inherently unacceptable." In Joan's case, she held a strong conviction that employers, therapists, and mechanics, among others, were universally authoritarian, manipulative, controlling, unfair, deceptive, and hostile. She consistently perceived herself as being helpless in the face of mistreatment by others and as not being capable of performing adequately at work and in her personal life. She also held a strong conviction that she had to "perform" both professionally and socially to be accepted, but believed that she was not capable of consistently performing well enough to be accepted.

Obviously, an individual's belief that the world is generally dangerous and that he or she is relatively powerless has important consequences that are more pervasive than more specific fears. It leads directly to the conclusion that it is always dangerous to relax vigilance, to take risks, to reveal one's weakness, to be "out of control," to be in a situation where one cannot escape easily, and so forth. This results in chronic tension and anxiety, vigilance for signs of danger, guardedness in interpersonal relationships, and discomfort with emotions that are difficult to control, among other things. The individual's vigilance for signs of danger results in his or her noticing many apparent signs of danger, and thus tends to perpetuate the view of the world as a generally dangerous place as well as providing support for additional specific fears. The tendency to be cautious, avoid risks, and be guarded and vigilant rather than simply tackling problems as they arise supports the individual's belief that this behavior is necessary and blocks him or her from discovering that a more direct, confident approach could also be effective. As a result, the individual's experiences tend to support the view that he or she is relatively powerless and vulnerable and must continue to be vigilant and defensive.

Some persons who view the world as a dangerous, malevolent place believe that they can rely on their own strengths and abilities in dealing with the threats it presents (see the discussion of paranoid personality disorder in Chapter 6 of this volume). However, borderline individuals' belief that they are weak and powerless blocks this solution. Other individuals who believe that they are not capable of dealing effectively with the demands of daily life resolve their dilemma by becoming dependent on someone who they see as capable of taking care of them (and develop a dependent pattern). However, borderlines' belief that they are inherently unacceptable blocks this option, since this belief leads them to conclude that dependence entails a serious risk of rejection, abandonment, or attack if this inherent unacceptability is discovered. Borderline individuals face quite a dilemma: Convinced that they are relatively helpless in a hostile world but without a source of security, they are forced to vacillate between autonomy and dependence without being able to rely on either.

A cognitive factor that has received little attention from the other cognitive-behavioral views of this disorder greatly aggravates the predicament of borderlines. As Beck (1976; Beck et al., 1979) has demonstrated, individuals often experience errors in thinking that he terms "cognitive distortions" and that often contribute to unrealistic evaluations of situations. Borderline individuals can experience the full range of cognitive distortions, but one particular distortion that Beck refers to as "dichotomous thinking" is particularly common and is particularly problematic. Dichotomous thinking is the tendency to evaluate experiences in terms of mutually exclusive categories (e.g., good or bad, success or failure, trustworthy or deceitful) rather than seeing experiences as falling along continua. The effect of this "black-or-white" thinking is to force extreme interpretations on events that would normally fall in the intermediate range of a continuum, since there are no intermediate categories. According to the cognitive view, extreme evaluations of situations lead to extreme emotional responses and extreme actions.

In addition, a dichotomous view of experience can easily result in abrupt shifts from one extreme view to the opposite. For example, a person who proved reliable would be likely to be seen as completely trustworthy *until the first time he or she falls short of expectations.* Then the person would suddenly appear to be completely untrustworthy, since there are no categories for intermediate levels of reliability or trustworthiness. The idea that a person might be trustworthy *most of the time* would be incompatible with dichotomous thinking. Since dichotomous thinking can produce extreme emotional responses and actions and can produce abrupt shifts from one extreme mood to another, it could be responsible to a considerable extent for the abrupt mood swings and dramatic shifts in behavior that are a hallmark of BPD. Linehan (1987b) is correct in observing that borderlines' inability to exercise adaptive control over extreme emotional responses plays a major role in their difficulties, but it does not appear that one need hypothesize a physiological basis for this problem.

The combination of dichotomous thinking and borderlines' basic assumptions is particularly potent. Most people recognize that daily life presents a variety of risks and threats, but are able to cope with this knowledge. However, dichotomous thinking results in a view of the world as either completely benign or deadly. Similarly, all persons have their faults and shortcomings, and most individuals can accept this fact to some extent. However, the borderlines' dichotomous categorization of themselves (as well as others) as either flawless or completely unacceptable leads to the conclusion that if they have any shortcomings, they are irrevocably "not OK." The conviction that they are inherently unacceptable leads quickly to the conclusion that they must hide this fact from others in order to be accepted. Unfortunately, this means that the individuals must avoid intimacy and openness for fear of being "found out." When this blocks the individuals from fulfilling their desire for closeness and security, dichotomous thinking leads easily to the conclusion "I'll never get what I want—everything is pointless." In addition, since the borderlines' conviction that they must hide significant shortcomings or face rejection blocks them from ever letting others get to know them as they are, borderlines never discover that they are not inherently unacceptable.

The dichotomous thinking also creates and perpetuates some of the conflicts of borderlines. For example, frustration (or anticipated frustration) of the borderlines' desire for closeness and dependency often leads to intense anger, which the individuals view as being so devastating that it would destroy any chance of a close relationship if expressed. However, satisfaction of the desire for closeness and dependency is seen as being intolerably dangerous, because, in a hostile world, to be dependent is to be helpless and vulnerable. This intense conflict over dependency and anger would vanish if it were possible for borderlines to take a more moderate view and say, "It would be good to be diplomatic in expressing my dissatisfactions, so that this doesn't cause additional problems," and "Depending on someone opens me to the possibility of being hurt or disappointed, so I should try to use good judgment about whom to depend on and how much to rely on them." As Linehan (1987b) has emphasized, borderline individuals often vacillate between seeking dependence and actively avoiding it, rather than being able to rely on others to a moderate degree.

As emphasized by Millon (1981), the final factor that seems to play an important role in BPD is a weak or unstable sense of identity. Confusion regarding goals and priorities makes it difficult for these individuals to work consistently and effectively toward long-term goals, especially in the face of abrupt emotional shifts. This results in ineffectiveness and a low sense of self-efficacy. This, in turn, leads to a lack of motivation and low persistence, and results in even more limited success in the face of adversity. A lack of a clear sense of self makes it difficult for borderlines to decide what to do in ambiguous situations and results in a low tolerance for ambiguity. It also makes it difficult for the individuals to challenge their belief that they are inherently unacceptable, and to maintain a clear sense of their own identity when involved in relationships with others who express opinions and feelings freely.

The basic assumptions, dichotomous thinking, and weak sense of identity do not simply each contribute separately to BPD. They form a complex system. This system includes a number of cycles that tend to be self-perpetuating and that are resistant to modification by the individual's experiences. For example, Joan's conviction that persons in positions of authority had malevolent intentions resulted in her being vigilant for signs of mistreatment. As a result, she noticed and could cite many slights, instances of unfair treatment, and so forth, which seemed to confirm her view that persons in positions of authority were basically manipulative and controlling. Her view of employers as malevolent was one of the factors that contributed to her procrastination about job hunting. However, she saw the procrastination itself as one more indication that she was not capable of performing adequately on a job; this, in turn, exacerbated the procrastination. Not only are the borderline individual's key assumptions strongly held, but these self-reinforcing cycles result in a system that can be quite resistant to change unless it is approached strategically.

Intervention Strategy

The conceptualizations presented by Millon (1981, 1987b), Linehan (1981, 1987a,b), and Young (1983, 1987; Young & Swift, 1988) suggest, respectively, that intervention should focus on establishing a clearer sense of identity, improving skills at controlling emotions, or changing maladaptive beliefs and assumptions. Each of the three approaches to intervention advocated by the other authors would be compatible with the model. However, the conceptualization of BPD presented in this chapter suggests that none of these three interventions should be the initial focus of therapy. It is argued that dichotomous thinking plays an important role in the extreme reactions and abrupt mood swings characteristic of BPD, amplifies the impact of individuals' dysfunctional assumptions, and contributes to many of the dilemmas borderline individuals face. If it is possible to reduce or eliminate dichotomous thinking early in therapy, this should reduce the intensity of clients' symptoms, simplify the task of modifying their underlying assumptions, and make it easier to help them find satisfactory resolutions for the dilemmas they face. Once the dichotomous thinking has been addressed, the interventions advocated by Millon, Linehan, and Young should prove easier to implement.

However, the therapist cannot simply attack dichotomous thinking in the first session. In order to deal effectively with it, it is necessary to establish a collaborative therapeutic relationship and to establish enough of a shared understanding of a client's problems so that working to challenge dichotomous thinking "makes sense" to the client. This is not easily done, because the borderline's world view greatly complicates the process of establishing a therapeutic relationship and adopting the stance of "collaborative empiricism" characteristic of cognitive therapy. After all, the therapist is a part of the world that the borderline sees as dangerous and malevolent; therefore, simply trusting the therapist is seen as potentially quite dangerous. In addition, the conflict between the borderline's desire for both help and acceptance, and his or her fear of vulnerability and rejection results in a strong ambivalence about participating in therapy that is not easy to overcome. While interventions designed to reduce or eliminate dichotomous thinking can be quite effective, it is necessary to invest considerable effort in establishing trust and a collaborative relationship before working on dichotomous thinking. Fortunately, the time invested in the therapeutic relationship is not wasted, because if it is possible to establish a good therapeutic relationship, this in itself challenges the borderline's assumptions regarding the dangers presented by others and regarding his or her inherent unacceptability.

Specific Interventions

Developing a Working Relationship

The relationship between therapist and client plays a much more important role in therapy with borderline clients than is usually the case in cognitive therapy. Many of a borderline client's problems involve interpersonal relationships, and are played out in the client's relationship with the therapist just as they are outside of the therapy session. While this greatly complicates therapy, it also provides the therapist with the opportunity to observe interpersonal problems as they occur rather than relying primarily on the client's description of the problems, and to use the relationship to challenge the client's preconceptions about others and develop more adaptive interpersonal behavior.

Establishing a collaborative therapeutic relationship is a complex process with borderline clients. Collaboration requires some degree of trust and intimacy; however, trust and intimacy initially seem intolerably dangerous to most borderline individuals. Strategic, problem-focused psychotherapeutic approaches such as cognitive therapy and other cognitive-behavioral therapies require the therapist and client to agree on specific goals and maintain a consistent focus from session to session. However, the borderline individual's problems with lack of a clear, stable identity include confusion regarding goals and priorities; thus these are likely to fluctuate from week to week. Cognitive-behavioral therapists are generally accustomed to establishing rather straightforward, businesslike relationships with their clients, which minimize "transference" and other interpersonal complications. Borderline individuals, however, are known for their intense emotional reactions within the therapy session and are likely to react strongly to the therapist despite the his or her straightforward and direct approach. Cognitive therapists anticipate helping their clients change quickly and efficiently, but borderline individuals often fear and resist sudden changes and typically need much more than 15 or 20 sessions of therapy. Therapists who attempt to work with borderline individuals without taking these features into account run the risk of providing an ineffective treatment, having the clients terminate therapy prematurely, or precipitating a serious crisis (May, 1985; Rush & Shaw, 1983).

Since the borderline has discovered through painful experience that it can be very dangerous to trust other people and realizes that the therapist-client relationship is a relationship in which he or she will be quite vulnerable at times, it rarely is productive to try to establish trust through persuasion, argument, or pointing to one's credentials. The borderline is not foolish enough to trust others simply because they say they can be trusted or because they have diplomas. Trust is most effectively established through explicitly acknowledging and accepting the client's difficulty in trusting the therapist (once this becomes evident), and then being careful to behave in a consistently trustworthy manner. It is important to exercise more than the usual amount of care in communicating clearly, assertively, and honestly with the client; in avoiding misunderstandings; in maintaining congruence between verbal statements and nonverbal cues; and in following through on agreements. Over time, this approach will provide the evidence on which trust can be based. It is important not to press the client to take risks in therapy until a sufficient level of trust has been established, and to make it clear that the client has the option of not talking about sensitive topics until he or she feels ready to do so. (For a more detailed discussion of these issues, see the section on establishing collaboration with paranoid clients in Chapter 6 of this volume.)

Crises, emergency telephone calls, and requests for special arrangements are common during the early stages of therapy with many border-line clients. Traditionally, this behavior has been viewed as a "test" of the therapist's reliability and caring. While there is no evidence that crises early in therapy are intentionally staged as tests of the therapist, they often function as such. After all, how can a skeptical client determine if a therapist will really act as he or she says except by observing the therapist's behavior? It is important for the therapist to handle emergency phone calls and requests for special treatment effectively if he or she wishes the client to continue in treatment. This does not mean that it is necessary for the therapist to agree to the client's requests or to encourage midnight telephone calls. It is important for the therapist to consider how far he or she is willing to go in being responsive to the client and to set clear, consistent limits.

If the therapist is unresponsive, the client is likely to become angry or terminate therapy abruptly. If the therapist is inconsistent in setting limits, the client will need to test the therapist repeatedly to determine what the limits actually are. If the therapist fails to set suitable limits and begins to resent the client's demands, this resentment is likely to interfere with therapy. However, if the therapist is able to set clear limits and to be responsive to the client within those clear limits, most border-line clients can adapt to those limits. It often works well to set a policy of keeping emergency telephone sessions brief and limiting them to crisis intervention, and then offering to schedule a therapy session as soon as possible as an alternative to lengthy phone contacts. Also, it is generally advisable for the therapist to make no special arrangements that the therapist would not be willing to extend to other clients in the same situation. Therapists repeatedly discover that exceptions to their standard policies frequently turn out to be counterproductive unless they are well thought out, and that special arrangements are often followed by requests for additional special treatment.

Often a borderline individual's discomfort with intimacy will extend to some aspects of the therapy setting; when this occurs, subtle aspects of the interpersonal interaction between therapist and client can elicit intense anxiety in the client. Something as simple as a handshake, direct eye contact, changes in the therapist's posture, or self-disclosure on the part of the therapist can sometimes be quite uncomfortable for border-lines. It can be useful to avoid physical contact, familiarity, or therapist self-disclosure early in therapy in order to avoid exceeding a client's tolerance for intimacy. However, it is difficult for the therapist to anticipate which actions might be uncomfortable for the client, and it may be more productive for the therapist simply to be attentive for signs of discomfort on the part of the client and to respond sensitively if this discomfort arises.

It can be particularly valuable explicitly to involve clients in the process of avoiding uncomfortable levels of intimacy. If the therapist solicits clients' feedback and makes it clear that he or she will seriously consider any suggestions for making therapy more comfortable, this gives clients some control over the level of intimacy during the session. Once the clients realize that they have some control over the seating arrangement, the topics discussed, and so forth, this control in itself renders the intimacy of the therapeutic relationship less threatening, since it is clear that the intimacy is not inescapable or beyond the clients' control.

The phenomenon of "transference," a client's responding to the therapist on the basis of experiences in previous relationships, has received considerable attention from psychodynamic authors but is rarely discussed from a behavioral or cognitive-behavioral perspective. The client's emotional reactions to the therapist generally do not play a prominent role in cognitive therapy or in other cognitive-behavioral therapies, but are likely to do so in cognitive therapy with BPD clients. This can be problematic for therapists who are not used to dealing with strong, unprovoked emotional responses from their clients.

"Transference" reactions can easily be understood in cognitive terms if we hypothesize that the client is responding on the basis of generalized beliefs and expectancies rather than responding to the therapist as an individual. In an ambiguous interpersonal situation, such as psychoanalytic psychotherapy, many of the individual's responses are based on his or her beliefs and expectancies because the therapist's behavior is difficult to interpret. An active, directive therapeutic approach such as that used in cognitive therapy avoids this situation to a large extent, because the therapist takes a straightforward, unambiguous role. However, this does not completely eliminate these strongly emotional responses, particularly with clients such as borderlines, who have strong convictions about human nature and who are vigilant for any indication that their hopes or fears may be realized.

For example, Joan held a strong conviction that persons in positions of authority were malicious, manipulative, and controlling. This had been based initially on her interactions with her parents and had been supported over the years by many experiences in interactions with her teachers and bosses. As noted earlier, she had a long history of resenting schedules, rules, and treatment by superiors. She would eventually become explosively angry, have a major confrontation with her superior, and either quit or be fired.

Despite the therapist's efforts to develop homework assignments collaboratively and to explain the rationale behind policies regarding fee payment and cancellation of sessions, Joan was quick to jump to the conclusion that the therapist was attempting to control or manipulate her. However, she did not express the resentment she felt as a result of this misperception of the therapist. It was clear that her anger could have easily built to the point where she expressed it quite explosively. In the past, this had happened at least once with a previous therapist and had resulted in her prematurely terminating an otherwise productive course of therapy.

When strongly emotional responses do occur, it is essential to deal with them promptly and directly by first developing a clear understanding of what the client is thinking and feeling, and then clearing up the misconceptions and misunderstandings directly and explicitly. It is particularly important for the therapist to make it clear through words and actions that the client will be neither exploited nor rejected by the therapist because of his or her reactions.

Joan's therapist was largely successful in avoiding explosive confrontations by being alert for nonverbal indications of anger and resentment, such as clenched fists, a flushed face, and a defiant attitude regarding noncompliance. It was then possible to defuse the situation by inquiring about feelings of anger and resentment, encouraging Joan to express her reactions to the assignment or policy in question, and making it clear that he was not trying to control or manipulate her. However, Joan's anger could build quite quickly, and the therapist was not always perceptive enough to avert explosions. He was able to keep the explosions brief and keep them from disrupting therapy by making a point of neither defending himself nor retaliating. Instead, he focused on tolerating Joan's intense expression of anger, trying to understand the misperceptions that elicited the anger, and clarifying his true intentions and feelings. On those occasions when the therapist had been inconsiderate or noncollaborative, he acknowledged his mistakes openly.

This approach not only kept Joan's inappropriate anger from disrupting therapy, but, over time, it provided experiences that contradicted her preconceptions about authority figures and provided many real-life examples to use when working to help Joan handle anger more adaptively.

Due to their strong anticipation of rejection, borderline clients are likely to experience strong emotional reactions and potential crises when breaks in therapy occur, particularly if it is necessary to terminate therapy before treatment is completed. It is important for the therapist to initiate discussion of a client's expectations, fears, and feelings well in advance of the break in therapy, and to return to this discussion on several occasions even if the client initially insists that termination is not a major concern. Clinical experience suggests that it is often advisable to allow at least 3 months for this process. When terminating therapy because the client's goals have been achieved, it is often quite helpful to taper off treatment gradually, moving from weekly appointments to biweekly sessions and then monthly sessions.

Therapists working with borderline clients are likely to discover that, from time to time, interactions with clients elicit strong emotional reactions in themselves. These can range from empathic feelings of depression to strong anger, fear, hopelessness, or attraction. It is important for therapists to be aware of these reactions and to look at them critically so that they do not unduly bias their responses. In particular, many therapists find that they become very angry with their borderline clients at times when the clients are engaging in behavior that appears manipulative, are not complying with homework assignments, or are not responding to interventions that the therapists feel should be effective. At these times, it can be particularly valuable for the therapists to attend to their automatic thoughts (perhaps by completing a Dysfunctional Thought Record). It is not unusual for therapists to discover that they are ascribing malicious intentions to clients or are assuming that they "don't want to get better." If therapists are able to step back and better grasp the clients' point of view, this often can make these frustrating and problematic interactions much less upsetting.

For example, after several weeks of attempting to persuade Joan to follow through on a particular homework assignment, her therapist found himself thinking, "If she doesn't want to change, why the hell should I bother?" and feeling increasingly frustrated. However, after reflecting on what the homework assignment meant for Joan, he realized that completion of the assignment would lead to further assignments of which Joan was very frightened. He also realized that Joan's tendency to rebel indirectly against authority figures whom she saw as controlling was being manifested, and that she faced quite a dilemma. She feared that he would be angry over her noncompliance, but found herself unable to comply because of the intensity of her anger and avoidance. She also feared that if she objected to the assignment openly, this would anger her therapist as well. Rather than its being true that she "doesn't want to change," the therapist realized that she was afraid to comply with the assignment but also was afraid to raise her objections directly.

Whenever a therapist is having difficulty understanding his or her responses to a client, or is uncertain about how to handle a problematic situation, it is important to seek consultation from an unbiased colleague.

Far from being an impediment, strong feelings can be quite useful if the therapist is able to understand them. Emotional responses do not occur randomly. If a therapist experiences an unusually strong response to a client, this is likely to be a response to some aspect of the client's behavior, and it may provide valuable information if it can be understood. It is not unusual for a therapist to respond emotionally to a pattern in the client's behavior long before that pattern has been recognized intellectually. Accurate interpretation of emotional responses can speed recognition of these patterns. However, judgment must be exercised in deciding whether to express these emotional reactions. Self-disclosure by the therapist increases the level of intimacy and may be threatening to the client; on the other hand, denial of an emotional response that is apparent to the client from nonverbal cues may decrease trust and encourage the fear.

It is advisable for the therapist to strive for a calm, methodical approach throughout therapy, and to resist the tendency to respond to each new symptom or crisis as an emergency. Many of these new symptoms and crises will turn out to be transitory problems that vanish as quickly as they appear, particularly if the therapist receives them calmly. For those problems which do become a focus of therapy, it is important to evaluate the situation in detail before intervening, rather than hurriedly trying "standard" interventions that may be off the mark. In particular, if the borderline client begins to manifest extreme agitation, signs of thought disorder, or other indications of a brief reactive psychosis, a calm, measured response from the therapist may be sufficient to calm the client and avert the psychotic episode.

If it is not possible to prevent the psychosis from developing, this need not be tragic. Although a brief hospitalization may be necessary and psychotropic medication may be useful, these psychotic reactions rarely produce lasting effects as long as the client and therapist do not decide that this is a sign of "craziness" and give up on therapy. While the symptoms manifested during a brief reactive psychosis may resemble schizophrenia, a duration of at least 6 months is required for the diagnosis of schizophrenia. A brief reactive psychosis often lasts only a few days (APA, 1987).

Selecting Initial Interventions

The wide range of problems and symptoms presented by borderline clients presents a problem in deciding on the initial targets for intervention in therapy, particularly since confusion regarding goals and priorities is a symptom of the disorder. While the process of deciding on the priorities for therapy should be collaborative, the therapist will want to advocate an initial focus for therapy that is likely both to permit some immediate progress in therapy and to serve as a good base for initial interventions. An initial focus on concrete behavioral goals can be very useful in minimizing the problems caused by the borderline's difficulties with intimacy and trust. For most borderline individuals, working on problems where little introspection is required, and where the focus is on behavior rather than on thoughts and feelings, is less threatening than focusing directly on the therapeutic relationship or on deeply personal problems. This provides an opportunity gradually to build trust and increase the client's tolerance for intimacy while making demonstrable progress toward goals, and thereby increasing motivation for persisting with therapy.

In working with a borderline client, there is a conflict between being responsive to the client's immediate concerns and maintaining a focused strategic approach. The client's concerns and problems are likely to shift from week to week, but if each session deals with a different issue, little will be accomplished. On the other hand, if the therapist insists on sticking to a fixed set of goals and priorities, he or she risks either seeming unresponsive and alienating the client, or becoming engaged in a power struggle over the agenda. It is particularly important to maintain a collaborative approach, even if this means revising goals and priorities periodically and being more flexible than usual. It may be possible to maintain a consistent focus in therapy simply by discussing the pros and cons of maintaining a steady focus, or by agreeing to set aside part of the session for current issues and then shifting to ongoing goals.

However, with some clients it is necessary to focus on a different immediate crisis each week and to maintain continuity by addressing the issues underlying the immediate crisis. For example, when Joan insisted on setting aside her work on reducing procrastination to focus on her conflict with her employment counselor or mistreatment by her mechanic, it became clear that her perception of authority figures as hostile and herself as powerless was an important issue in all three situations. Consequently, it was possible to maintain a consistent focus while responding to this series of different but related problems by addressing this underlying issue while working on each specific problem.

In working with borderline clients, it is particularly important to maintain a collaborative, strategic approach based on guided discovery rather than on theoretical preconceptions. With cognitive therapy's wealth of specific techniques designed to address specific problems, it is easy to slip into a "cookbook" approach, in which the therapist starts to think in terms of matching techniques to problems rather than basing interventions on a conceptualization of the individual client. While this approach may work adequately in many situations, it can lead to significant problems when working with a "nonstandard" client. Borderline clients often have idiosyncratic cognitions underlying apparently commonplace problems, and interventions based on the therapist's preconceptions can easily miss the mark. When the therapist adopts a guided-discovery approach rather than a cookbook approach, the therapist and the client are constantly obtaining new data. This alerts the therapist to any unusual patterns behind apparently ordinary symptoms, and provides the information needed to select key problems for intervention.

Minimizing Noncompliance

Borderline clients are often quite sensitive to issues of control. In an active, directive therapy, it is quite easy for therapist and client to become locked in a power struggle over agenda setting or homework assignments. However, it is difficult for a client to stage a power struggle if the therapist refuses to participate actively in it. If the therapist adheres to the collaborative model underlying cognitive therapy and allows the client to have a part in developing agendas and homework assignments, is responsive to requests, and is careful to work with the client, power struggles are less likely. It is important for the therapist to refrain from rigidly insisting on using "standard" homework assignments. There is no magic to one particular format for monitoring and challenging thoughts, learning to relax, and so on, and clients are often much more compliant if they have an active role in tailoring standard techniques to suit their own needs and preferences.

When problems with noncompliance do occur, it is rarely productive for the therapist to take an authoritarian role and simply insist that the clients do the assignments. Often, it is much more productive to acknowledge explicitly that the clients have the power to refuse to do whatever they wish, but then to explore with the clients the pros and cons of choosing to do homework versus choosing not to do it. If the rationale behind the assignment is clear, and the clients recognize that they are choosing to do it rather than being forced to do it, then there is much less chance of problems with noncompliance. If noncompliance persists, exploration of the clients' thoughts at moments when they decide not to do the homework should be useful in identifying additional issues that need to be addressed.

Fear of change is a factor that often contributes to problems with noncompliance, and that can also produce increased distress during therapy or lead to premature termination. Given borderlines' world view, it is not surprising that they fear change. When persons are in a dangerous situation (or one that they view as dangerous), they tend to rely heavily on their usual "tried and true" coping responses because at least they work well enough to get by, they are familiar, and the outcomes are predictable. Trying a new response involves taking a step into the unknown, accepting a risk of failure, and tolerating uncertainty about the outcome. Borderline clients' usual coping responses may be quite unsatisfactory, but they may find it much less frightening to maintain dysfunctional behavior than to try new, unproven responses.

The borderline client's fear of change can be reduced to some extent by addressing it openly when it becomes apparent, and by examining the risks involved in trying new responses. However, it is generally necessary to be careful to make changes in a series of small steps and to be careful not to press for change too quickly. Therapists often experience a desire to "go for the kill" when they see an opportunity to make a dramatic intervention that could produce sudden change. With borderline clients, it is generally better to err on the side of caution. It is much easier to work with a client who sees gradual change and is eager to continue than it is to work with a client who is terrified by sudden changes and is reluctant to continue therapy. Clients can be valuable guides in pacing therapy if the therapist solicits their feedback and is attentive to signs of increased distress or reluctance.

Fear of change can be intensified by a client's assuming that therapy will end as soon as the problems are overcome and fearing an abrupt abandonment by the therapist. When such fears are present, it is important to make it clear to the client that therapy will not be terminated abruptly because he or she has improved, but that termination of therapy will be a joint decision.

Decreasing Dichotomous Thinking

Typically, dichotomous thinking is such a pervasive component of borderline individuals' cognitive functioning that it is difficult for them to conceive of thinking in terms of continuous dimensions rather than discrete categories. In order to work effectively to reduce dichotomous thinking, it is first necessary to demonstrate to the clients that they engage in dichotomous thinking and to convince them that it is in their interest to modify such thinking. Some borderline clients such as Joan realize that they "see everything in black and white" while others see "shades of gray," but with many other such clients it is necessary to help them recognize this pattern by pointing out examples of dichotomous thinking as they occur. It is then necessary to help the clients to consider whether thinking in terms of continua could prove more realistic and more adaptive than dichotomous thinking. This can be done by choosing a relevant dimension, such as trustworthiness, and asking the clients to provide clear enough operational definitions for the two extremes so that it will be possible to clearly categorize people if the categories are valid. It is then possible to ask the clients to classify individuals they know in terms of the two categories, and to test whether a dichotomous view is reality-based or not. For example:

THERAPIST: From the way you're talking, it sounds like you see trust as an all-or-nothing thing. Either it's safe to trust someone completely, or it's not safe to trust them at all.

CLIENT: Sure, that's the way it is.

THERAPIST: Well, since one of the situations which really gets to you is when someone you trust lets you down, maybe we should take a closer look at this. As you see it, what are the characteristics of someone who's really, truly trustworthy? One way to think of it is if a Martian came down knowing nothing of humans and wanted to tell whom he could trust, what should he look for?

CLIENT: They follow through on what they say.

THERAPIST: All the time?

CLIENT: Yeah.

THERAPIST: Is there more to it than that?

CLIENT: Umm . . . They don't ever lie, they don't let things interfere with what they say, and they don't let you down or hurt you.

THERAPIST: Does that cover it, or is there more to being really trustworthy?

CLIENT: I guess that's it.

THERAPIST: What would be a good label for the people who aren't trustworthy?

CLIENT: "Treacherous," I guess.

THERAPIST: And what would be the characteristics of a truly treacherous person?

CLIENT: They don't follow through on things they say.

THERAPIST: How are they on lying?

CLIENT: They lie and deceive all the time, and they try to take advantage of you when they get a chance.

THERAPIST: You said trustworthy people don't let anything interfere with doing what they say. How does that apply to treacherous people?

CLIENT: When they try to hurt you, they come up with all sorts of excuses about why it happened.

THERAPIST: Does that pretty much cover treacherous people?

CLIENT: I guess so. . . . Wait, one more. They get your hopes up then let you down. That really burns me up.

THERAPIST: OK, let's check out how well this way of looking at trustworthiness works. Let's start with your sister-in-law, since I know a bit about her. Would she be trustworthy or treacherous?

CLIENT: Oh, I can trust her.

THERAPIST: But let's look at the criteria. The first one was that trustworthy people always follow through on what they say they'll do. Don't I remember that last week you were mad because she didn't call when she said she would?

CLIENT: Yeah, but she apologized later.

THERAPIST: But now she doesn't completely qualify as trustworthy. Does that mean she's treacherous? Does she lie and deceive all the time?

CLIENT: No, she's pretty reliable.

THERAPIST: So she's not absolutely trustworthy by your standards, but isn't completely treacherous either. What do you make of that?

CLIENT: That it's not black or white?

THERAPIST: Well, let's check that out. Imagine a rating scale where 10 is absolutely, completely trustworthy and 0 is completely treacherous. Where would you rate your sister-in-law?

CLIENT: About an 8, I guess. She gets busy and forgets things.

THERAPIST: Where would you rate your mother?

This approach avoids much of the resistance that is encountered if the therapist simply tries to convince the client that things are not really black or white. Since it is unlikely that all of the client's acquaintances truly fall at the extremes of any continuum, it is usually easy to demonstrate that a continuous view is more realistic, and thus has significant advantages in figuring out how to deal with people and situations. With a little practice, borderline clients can become skilled at challenging their own dichotomous thinking, which gradually declines. However, it may be necessary for the therapist to use this approach on several concepts before the clients fully incorporate the method and challenge such thinking without prompting.

Increasing Control over Emotions

A decrease in dichotomous thinking often results in a notable decrease in the frequency of sudden mood swings and a decrease in the intensity of clients' emotional reactions, due to their evaluating problem situations in less extreme terms. However, the clients can attain additional control over emotional responses through increasing their ability to look critically at their thoughts in problem situations, by developing alternative ways to respond to such situations, and by learning adaptive ways to express emotions. While the techniques used in monitoring and challenging thoughts and developing active, assertive responses are no different with borderline clients from those used with other clinical groups (see Beck et al., 1979; Coché, 1987; Linehan, 1979; D'Zurilla & Goldfried, 1971), it is particularly important not to rush the borderline clients and to be alert for complications.

Many borderline clients believe that if they express certain feelings, such as anger, this will lead to immediate rejection or attack. As a result, they often attempt to suppress any expression of these emotions and are extremely reluctant to consider an active, assertive approach that might include expressing annoyance or mild levels of other problematic emotions. In either individual or group therapy, the therapeutic relationship provides an excellent opportunity for *in vivo* work on handling emotions adaptively. Therapy is a situation in which a client can experiment with expressing feelings without having to fear devastating consequences. The therapist can implement this process by periodically asking how the client is feeling when situations occur that might produce annoyance or other unpleasant emotions in the average client. The therapist can then explicitly acknowledge and accept the emotions that the client is willing to express, model appropriate responses to the client's expression of emotion, and provide the client with feedback about the impact of his or her responses. It might seem that one could speed this process by intentionally provoking aggravation or other emotions; however, it is better for the therapist either to take advantage of naturally occurring situations or to provoke reactions with the client's consent through role plays or imagery, since the therapist's genuineness and honesty are important for maintaining a trusting working relationship.

Improving Impulse Control

The same types of interventions that are useful for improving control over emotions are also useful for improving impulse control. However, consideration of the sequence of steps necessary for an individual to control an impulse to act (see Figure 9.1) suggests a variety of additional intervention points. Often the first step in improving impulse control is to deal with the client's covert response: "Why the hell should I?!" Many borderline clients have been told by many authority figures over the years that they had better control themselves "or else!" By the time the therapist broaches this topic to them, they may be quite oppositional. It is important for the therapist to make it clear that he or she is not trying to force clients to control their impulses and is not trying to enforce society's norms, but is trying to help the clients to develop the ability to *choose* whether to act on an impulse or not, so that they need not act in ways that they will regret later.

Once this has been established, it is often much easier to get the clients to focus on specific problem situations, to explore the advantages and disadvantages of controlling the impulse in question, and to develop methods for doing so. It may be necessary to work explicitly on very basic steps, such as noticing mild impulses before they build to the point where they are difficult to control and identifying adaptive alternatives. Once adaptive alternatives have been identified, self-instructional training (Meichenbaum, 1977) can be useful in helping clients implement these new behaviors.

Self-destructive impulsive behavior can be particularly problematic, since it may be necessary to eliminate this behavior quickly and since it often elicits very strong emotional reactions in the therapist. It is impor-

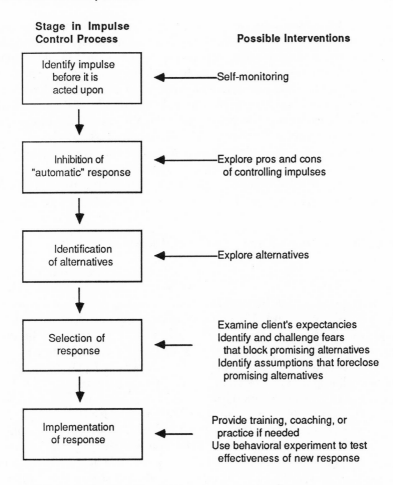

FIGURE 9.1   Possible points for intervention in the impulse control process.

tant to develop a clear understanding of a client's motivation for self-destructive behavior—first by examining the thoughts and feelings leading up to the self-destructive impulses or behavior, and then by asking directly, "What do you want to accomplish through this action?" or "What's the point to X?" Suicide attempts, self-mutilation, and other self-destructive acts can be the product of many different motives: desire to punish others at whom the client is angry, desire to punish oneself or obtain relief from guilt, desire to distract oneself from even more aversive obsessions, and so forth.

Once the motivation is understood, it is possible to work with the client to find other ways to accomplish the same result that are likely to be more adaptive or have fewer bad side effects. For example, as a stopgap measure, it is sometimes possible to substitute a minimally self-destructive behavior (such as marking oneself with a marking pen) for a more self-destructive act (such as slashing oneself). This less destructive act can then be replaced with a more adaptive alternative when time allows. Obviously, if the risk of the client's performing seriously self-destructive acts is high, and the above-described interventions do not prove effective in the limited time available, hospitalization may be needed in order to allow sufficient time for effective intervention. For an excellent account of five borderline clients' perspectives on their episodes of self-mutilation, the reader is referred to Leibenhuft, Gardner, and Cowdry (1987).

Strengthening the Client's Sense of Identity

To some extent, a clearer sense of one's goals, priorities, competencies, and accomplishments is a side effect of cognitive therapy's approach of choosing specific goals for therapy and working to adopt an active, assertive approach toward achieving them. However, it is possible to further facilitate clients' developing a clearer sense of identity by helping them to identify their positive characteristics and accomplishments, by providing positive feedback about good decisions and effective coping, and by helping them to evaluate their own actions realistically. It is generally wise to practice moderation and avoid effusiveness, since borderline clients may be very uncomfortable with positive feedback at first. It is especially important for feedback to be honest, since unrealistic positive feedback simply lowers the therapist's credibility and makes it appear that he or she is trying to "humor" a client. When a BPD client is functioning poorly, it can be difficult to give honest positive feedback. However, if an appropriate frame of reference is used and the therapist is attentive to small steps forward and sincere attempts on the client's part, it is possible to find opportunities for honest positive feedback long before the client is doing well from day to day. For example, it is very difficult for a borderline client to risk revealing an act of which he or she is truly ashamed, or to risk expressing anger at the therapist. However, steps such as these contribute in important ways to progress in therapy. A therapist can appreciate the client's risk taking, even if the way in which the shame was acknowledged or the anger was expressed leaves much room for improvement.

Addressing Assumptions

The process of identifying and challenging borderline clients' underlying assumptions or schemas differs from the "standard" cognitive therapy approach to depression (Beck et al., 1979), primarily because of the intensity of these clients' belief in their assumptions. As a result, it is generally most effective (1) to rely on developing "behavioral experiments" to test the validity of the beliefs, and (2) to think in terms of "chipping away" at the beliefs, rather than hoping to intervene intensively and eliminate them in a few sessions.

Clients' beliefs that daily life is full of danger and that they are helpless can be gradually challenged through testing their expectancies against previous experience, developing behavioral experiments that can be used to test expectancies, and helping them to develop new competencies and coping skills. For example, Joan's conviction that she was helpless in the face of unfair treatment was modified slightly by a review of her experiences on jobs and in graduate school, where she had had to cope with unfair treatment on occasion. It was further reduced by her use of much-enhanced skills at assertion and problem solving, but it was not eliminated until she had started a new job and had dealt successfully with several instances of unfair treatment.

Borderline individuals' conviction that they are inherently flawed in some way that will inevitably lead to rejection if it is discovered can be particularly difficult to modify. Clients are typically quite resistant to test this belief by risking openness and observing the reactions of others. It can be useful to talk explicitly about this dilemma, to help the clients try to determine if they have any flaws that are immutable and universally unacceptable, and to help the clients consider the costs entailed by avoiding intimacy in order to be sure of not being "found out." However, the client-therapist relationship presents the single most powerful opportunity for addressing this assumption. Over the course of therapy, clients will gradually reveal the full range of their "craziness," many of the acts about which they feel ashamed or guilty, and the emotions that they believed were intolerable. If the therapist can honestly accept these clients as they are and communicate this acceptance through empathy and concern, this provides the clients with powerful evidence that they can be accepted "as is" even when their worst secrets are known. It is also important for the clients to understand that not everyone will accept them, and to be able to cope with rejection as well as acceptance as they go on to risk greater openness and closeness in relationships outside of therapy.

Conclusions

Cognitive therapy with borderline clients can be quite demanding, and the clinician is well advised to limit the number of borderline clients in his or her caseload if at all possible; however, it also can be quite rewarding.

For example, Joan was seen weekly for a total of 5 months. At the close of therapy she had no longer been having problems with mood swings, anxiety, or depression for 2 months. She had overcome her procrastination over job hunting; had found a good job in her field; was doing well at it; and was free of resentment over the schedules, rules, and unfair treatment that typically go with working for a major corporation.

Joan was also more comfortable with her marriage, reacted more moderately when problems arose, and was able to be assertive with her husband. She was experiencing only fairly ordinary problems, was able to deal with them effectively when they arose, and had clear ideas regarding how she wanted to deal with any larger problems that might arise in the future.

At the close of therapy, Joan continued to be rather high-strung and was still working to relax her high standards for herself. She also had not yet made many friends in Chicago, because she was devoting her time and energy to improving her marriage. However, she felt ready to continue working on these issues on her own and to recontact her therapist if she stopped making progress.

Progress with Joan was faster than usual because she had achieved considerable benefit from previous therapy, despite her initial claims to the contrary. Our experiences suggest that it may be realistic to expect cognitive therapy with a borderline client who has not had extensive previous therapy to require 1½ to 2½ years of weekly sessions. (More limited goals often can be accomplished in a shorter period of time as long as care is used in preparing the client for termination.)

This is a very different time frame from the 15 to 20 sessions typical for cognitive therapy with an uncomplicated unipolar depression, and can hardly be considered short-term therapy. However, it does not compare badly with the leading alternative treatment approach, psychoanalytic psychotherapy. Because psychoanalytic psychotherapy for BPD is primarily a transference-based treatment that does not focus on treating specific symptoms or cognitions (Kernberg, 1977), cognitive therapy typically produces improvement in important symptoms much more quickly. Psychoanalytic authorities on the treatment of BPD report that therapy typically requires 5 to 7 years (Masterson, 1982). Cognitive therapy with borderline clients is hardly quick and easy, but it shows promise of proving to be an effective treatment approach that is more efficient than the currently available alternatives.

Empirical research on the effectiveness of cognitive therapy or other cognitive-behavioral therapies with BPD is in its initial stages, and little is known regarding the effectiveness of cognitive therapy with this population. Linehan and her colleagues (Linehan, Armstrong, Allmon, Suarez, & Miller, 1988; Linehan, Armstrong, Suarez, & Allmon, 1988) have recently examined the effectiveness of dialectical behavior therapy versus "treatment as usual" with a sample of chronically parasuicidal borderline subjects. Patients receiving dialectical behavior therapy had a significantly lower dropout rate and manifested significantly less self-injurious behavior than control subjects. However, over 12 months of treatment, only small improvements in depression and other symptomatology resulted from either treatment approach, with neither being clearly superior overall. These results are modest; however, it is encouraging to find that 1 year of cognitive-behavioral treatment can produce lasting improvement in parasuicidal behavior in a sample of subjects who not only met diagnostic criteria for BPD, but also were chronically parasuicidal, had histories of multiple psychiatric hospitalizations, and were unable to maintain employment due to their psychiatric symptoms. Obviously, much additional research examining alternative treatment approaches and testing the various cognitive-behavioral conceptualizations of this disorder is needed.

Our clinical experience using the present approach with borderlines has been quite encouraging, particularly considering the poor results reported when cognitive-behavioral interventions are used without taking the characteristics of borderline clients into account (Mays, 1985; Rush & Shaw, 1983). Still, it goes without saying that extensive empirical research is needed. There are obvious practical problems with attempting to assemble a large sample of borderlines for a traditional treatment outcome study or for hypothesis testing. The sophisticated type of single-case design that has been used by Turkat and Maisto (1985) in their research on the behavioral treatment of personality disorders may provide a practical way to develop an empirically validated approach to understanding and treating these complex individuals.

Chapter 10

Histrionic Personality Disorder

The concept of "hysteria" has a long history, spanning over four thousand years (summarized by Vieth, 1977). The use of this term is controversial, and the concept of hysteria has been rejected by feminists as a sexist label, often used to discount the problems of women whenever they present complaints that are not easily explained or when they have made demands that seem excessive. The term "hysteria" has been used to refer to phenomena as diverse as transient loss of control resulting from overwhelming stress, conversion disorder, Briquet's syndrome, a personality disorder, and a personality trait. Perhaps most commonly, it has been used to describe excitable female patients who are difficult to treat. In their review of this phenomenon, Temoshok and Heller (1983) state that " 'Hysteria' as a diagnostic label is as impressionistic, labile, diffuse, unstable, and superficially appealing as the various phenomena with which it has been associated" (p. 204). In an attempt to reduce the confusion (and possible sexist connotations) regarding the use of the term "hysteria," the American Psychiatric Association did not include the term anywhere in DSM-III (APA, 1980). Instead, separate categories of somatization disorder, conversion disorder, hypochondriasis, dissociative disorders, and histrionic personality disorder (HPD) were designated.

Historical Review

The concept of hysteria began with the Egyptian idea that if the uterus were unmoored, it would wander throughout the body, lodging in one place and producing hysterical symptoms there. Treatment consisted of luring the uterus back to its normal position by fumigating or anointing the vagina with sweet-smelling or precious substances, or chasing the womb away from its new location by inhalation or the application of foul-smelling, noxious substances at the distressed site. Hippocratic prescriptions often included marriage and childbirth—recommendations expressed by physicians to their hysterical patients ever since.

Millon (1981) provides an excellent review of early German descriptions of hysterical character, providing an outline of the long-standing controversy over the use of the term. For example, according to Millon, even as early as 1923 Schneider used the label "attention-seeking" as a substitute for "hysterical," claiming that the latter term implied a moral judgment and had acquired too broad and vague a meaning.

Although psychoanalytic theory had its origins in Freud's explication of hysterical symptoms, his primary interest focused on conversion hysteria, not on hysterical personality traits. Early psychodynamic descriptions emphasized unresolved Oedipal conflicts as the primary determinant of this disorder, with repression seen as the most characteristic defense. Abraham (1927/1948), Fenichel (1945), and Reich (1945) all stressed the prominence of the Oedipus complex, and of castration anxiety and penis envy, in the development of the hysterical personality. They viewed oral fantasies as a defensive regression against the dominant Oedipal features. Based on the belief that the discharge of repressed sexual emotions would result in a cure, early analytic treatment of hysteria consisted of suggestion and hypnosis in order to facilitate abreaction. Later, Freud modified his method to include the use of free association and the interpretation of resistance and transference in order to develop insight and abreaction. Although the treatment of hysteria has been characterized as the foundation of the psychoanalytic method, few empirical, controlled studies have been published.

Marmor (1953) challenged classic psychoanalytic thinking by raising the question of whether the fixation involved in hysterical personality is primarily oral rather than phallic in nature, suggesting a more pervasive and primitive disturbance. Several psychoanalytic thinkers have reached a compromise between these two views by suggesting differentiations within the spectrum of hysterical personality (Easser & Lesser, 1965; Kernberg, 1975; Zetzel, 1968). More recently, Baumbacher and Amini (1980–1981) propose three subgroups among HPD: (1) hysterical character neurosis, associated with classical triadic Oedipal issues; (2) hysterical personality disorder, stemming from the initial phallic phase and thus associated with dyadic (mother-child) issues; and (3) borderline personality organization with hysterical features, utilizing more primitive defenses characteristic of pre-Oedipal phases.

In factor-analytic studies, Lazare, Klerman, and Armor (1966, 1970) found that four of seven traits classically associated with hysterical personality clustered together as expected. The traits of emotionality, exhibitionism, egocentricity, and sexual provocativeness were strongly clustered together, while the traits of suggestibility and fear of sexuality did not cluster together. Dependency fell into an intermediary position. Unexpected traits that fell into the hysterical cluster were aggression, oral expression, obstinacy, and rejection of others. On the basis of these findings, Lazare et al. concluded that their hysterical sample may have corresponded to the more primitive, pregenital variant of hysteria.

As early as DSM-I (APA, 1952), a discrimination had been made between what were considered neurotic aspects of hysteria (conversion reaction) and the personality aspects (then called emotionally unstable personality). In DSM-II (APA, 1968), the distinction was made between the hysterical neuroses (including conversion reaction and dissociative reaction) and hysterical personality. Although psychoanalytic theories of hysterical personality have been more prominent than any other perspective, they appear not to have had much impact on the official categorizations. For example, the diagnosis of hysterical personality in DSM-II relied on clusters of traits and behaviors, defining hysterical personality as a behavior pattern "characterized by excitability, emotional instability, overreactivity, and self-dramatization. . . . These personalities are also immature, self-centered, often vain, and unusually dependent on others" (p. 43). As noted earlier, in DSM-III (APA, 1980) the term "hysteria" was not used at all, and the separate category of histrionic personality disorder was delineated.

Clinical Assessment

According to DSM-III-R (APA, 1987), HPD is characterized by excessive emotionality and attention seeking (Table 10.1). Individuals with HPD are constantly seeking or demanding reassurance, approval, or praise from others. Unlike people with dependent personality disorder, they actively pursue the attention of others through dramatic, attention-seeking behavior. They are overly concerned with physical attractiveness, often overtly seductive, and most comfortable when they are the center of attention. Their emotionality seems to be inappropriately exaggerated, labile, and shallow, and they tend to have a global, impressionistic style of speech. They are seen by others as self-centered and lacking the ability to delay gratification. These patients are lively, dramatic, and, as the diagnosis implies, histrionic in style. Their behavior is overly reactive and intense. They are emotionally excitable and crave stimulation, often responding to minor stimuli with irrational, angry outbursts or tantrums. Their interpersonal relationships are impaired, and they are perceived by others as shallow, lacking in genuineness, demanding, and overly dependent.

TABLE 10.1
DSM-III-R Diagnostic Criteria for Histrionic Personality Disorder

A pervasive pattern of excessive emotionality and attention-seeking, beginning by early adulthood and present in a variety of contexts, as indicated by at least *four* of the following:

(1) constantly seeks or demands reassurance, approval, or praise
(2) is inappropriately sexually seductive in appearance or behavior
(3) is overly concerned with physical attractiveness
(4) expresses emotion with inappropriate exaggeration, e.g., embraces casual acquaintances with excessive ardor, uncontrollable sobbing on minor sentimental occasions, has temper tantrums
(5) is uncomfortable in situations in which he or she is not the center of attention
(6) displays rapidly shifting and shallow expression of emotions
(7) is self-centered, actions being directed toward obtaining immediate satisfaction; has no tolerance for the frustration of delayed gratification
(8) has a style of speech that is excessively impressionistic and lacking in detail, e.g., when asked to describe mother, can be no more specific than, "She was a beautiful person."

Note. From *Diagnostic and Statistical Manual of Mental Disorders* (3rd ed., rev., p. 349) by the American Psychiatric Association, 1987, Washington, DC: Author. Copyright 1987 by the American Psychiatric Association. Reprinted by permission.

DSM-III-R describes the interpersonal relationships of histrionic individuals as usually being stormy and ungratifying. Due to their dependence on the attention of other people, individuals with HPD are especially vulnerable to separation anxiety, and may seek treatment when they become intensely upset over the breakup of a relationship. In their study of 32 patients who had been admitted to a psychiatric hospital with the diagnosis of histrionic personality, Slavney and McHugh (1974) found that almost 80% had been admitted because of suicidality, depression, or both. Most of the suicide attempts were not life-threatening, and most had occurred after anger or disappointment. Anxiety disorders such as panic disorder, with and without agoraphobia, are also common presenting problems. Other common complications of HPD that may lead to the seeking of treatment include alcoholism and other substance abuse, conversion disorder, somatization disorder, and brief reactive psychosis.

For example, Debbie was a 26-year-old woman who worked as a salesclerk in a trendy clothing store and who sought therapy for panic disorder with agoraphobia. She was dressed flamboyantly, with an elaborate and dramatic hairdo. Her appearance was especially striking, since she was quite short (under 5 feet tall) and at least 75 pounds overweight. She wore sunglasses indoors throughout the evaluation and constantly fiddled with them, taking them on and off nervously and waving them to emphasize a point. She cried loudly and dramatically at various points in the interview, going through large numbers of Kleenex. She continually asked for reassurance ("Will I be OK?" "Can I get over this?"). She talked nonstop throughout the evaluation. When gently interrupted by the evaluator, she was very apologetic, laughing and saying "I know I talk too much"; yet she continued to do so throughout the session.

As the name implies, the strongest indication of HPD is an overly dramatic, or histrionic, presentation of self. Asking house officers and faculty members to rank-order the diagnostic importance of trait items describing hysterical personality, Slavney (1978) found that self-dramatization, attention seeking, emotional instability, and seductiveness were ranked as most diagnostically important and most confidently recognized. Vanity, immaturity, and conversion symptoms were seen as relatively unimportant and less certainly recognized.

The direct measurement of self-dramatization has been difficult, but there has been research on the trait of emotional lability. In a series of studies, Slavney and his colleagues demonstrated that variability of mood was positively correlated with self-ratings on hysterical traits in normal men and women, and that patients diagnosed as having HPD had greater variability of mood than did control patients (Rabins & Slavney, 1979; Slavney, Breitner, & Rabins, 1977; Slavney & Rich, 1980). Standage, Bilsbury, Jain, and Smith (1984) found that women with the diagnosis of HPD showed an impaired ability to perceive and evaluate their own behavior as it is perceived and evaluated by others in the same culture.

The patient with HPD has been conceptualized as a caricature of what is defined as femininity in our culture: vain, shallow, self-dramatizing, immature, overdependent, and selfish. When asked to rate the concepts "woman," "man," histrionic personality," "antisocial personality," and "compulsive personality" using a semantic differential technique, psychiatric residents and psychiatrists showed a stronger connection between the connotative meanings of the concepts "woman" and "histrionic personality" than was found between the concepts of "man" and either "antisocial personality" or "compulsive personality" (Slavney, 1984).

HPD is most frequently diagnosed in women, and when it is diagnosed in men it has been associated with homosexuality. This gender differential, however, may be more a product of our societal expectations than a true difference in occurrence. It has been suggested that HPD is more appropriately seen as a caricature of sex roles in general, including extreme masculinity as well as extreme femininity (Kolb, 1968; MacKinnon & Michaels, 1971; Malmquist, 1971). The extreme of femininity is fairly commonly diagnosed as histrionic, whereas a caricature of masculinity (an overly "macho" male who is dramatic, sensation-seeking, shallow, vain, and egocentric) is rarely diagnosed as having HPD even though he would meet the DSM-III-R criteria. Such a man would not be likely to seek treatment.

The relationships among HPD, antisocial personality, and somatization disorder have been studied by Lilienfeld, VanValkenburg, Larntz, and Akiskal (1986). They found the three disorders to overlap considerably within individuals, with the strongest relationship being between antisocial personality and HPD. In addition, they reported that HPD appeared to moderate the relationship between antisocial personality and somatization disorder, since it was only in individuals without HPD that the relationship between antisocial personality and somatization disorder was significant. This led the authors to suggest the possibility that histrionic individuals develop antisocial personality if they are male and somatization disorder if female.

Emotions of the histrionic individual are expressed intensely, yet seem exaggerated or unconvincing, as if the patient is dramatically playing a role. In the assessment of HPD, the clinician can use his or her own reactions as a useful of indicator of when to consider this disorder. If a patient is expressing extreme distress, yet the clinician has the sense of watching a performance rather than having a feeling of empathy for the individual, it may be helpful to explore further for possible HPD. These patients appear quite warm, charming, and even seductive, yet there seems to be something missing. Their feelings seem to lack depth or genuineness.

In a group therapy session, for instance, one of the therapists commented on the fact that Debbie always brought a large glass of water. Debbie responded by saying, "The water is nothing; look what else I have to carry with me!" She then dramatically grabbed her large handbag and pulled out a Bible, salt, a washcloth, a paper bag, and a medicine bottle, explaining how she would use each of these items in case of a panic attack. Although she was describing how anxious she was, and how she could not stand to go out without all of these items, she seemed proud of her display of equipment and seemed to enjoy the "show and tell."

These patients often present their symptoms, thoughts, and actions as if they were external entities involuntarily imposed upon them. They tend to make all-inclusive statements, such as "These things just always seem to be happening to me!" Their speech is often strong and dramatic, including a great deal of hyperbole. They tend to use phrases that seem quite powerful and striking at the time, yet later the clinician realizes that he or she does not really have any idea what the patients meant. They use theatrical intonation, with dramatic nonverbal gestures and facial expressions. They often dress in ways that are likely to attract attention, wearing striking and provocative styles in bright colors, and overusing cosmetics and hair dyes.

Although indications of a dramatic portrayal of the self can serve as useful cues to the presence of HPD, a dramatic style or unusual clothing alone are not sufficient data upon which to base a diagnosis of HPD. In order for the term to do more than just substitute for "hysteric" with all its biases, clinicians must be careful to use the full DSM-III-R diagnostic criteria, and not to classify patients as histrionic merely on the basis of indications of dramatic flair. However, if these characteristics are used as indications that the clinician needs to probe carefully for further information that will be useful in arriving at a diagnosis, then appropriate diagnosis of HPD will be enhanced.

It is helpful to explore interpersonal relationships in depth. Details should be obtained as to how relationships started, what happened, and how they ended. Indications to watch for include a romantic view of relationships that is soon shattered, relationships that start out as idyllic and end up as disasters, and stormy relationships with dramatic endings. Another area to ask about is the way that these individuals handle anger, fights, and disagreements. The clinician should ask for specific examples and look for any signs of dramatic outbursts, temper tantrums, and the manipulative use of anger.

For example, Debbie had a history of stormy relationships with men. When she was 16 years old, she had a boyfriend who was very jealous and followed her without her knowledge. This relationship finally ended with a knife fight, although Debbie still saw him on and off at the time she began treatment. In her early 20s, when her boyfriend suddenly stopped calling her, she found another boyfriend whom she "married for spite." When asked what was good about the marriage, she said that they were compatible in that "we both like clothes." She reported that the relationship was great before marriage, but that soon after the marriage, "he began to control me." However, this report was contradicted by later descriptions of how she had begged him not to marry her on the night before the wedding, with him threatening to kill her if she didn't go through with the wedding. Only when she was questioned carefully as to what she meant by being "controlled" by him did she specifically mention that he was an alcoholic and a compulsive gambler, and that he physically abused her and was unfaithful to her. They were divorced a few months later.

Most people would not readily acknowledge possessing many of the negative traits of HPD, but it is often possible to obtain some relevant material regarding these factors by asking patients how other people tend to view them. One way to do this is to discuss previous relationships that did not work out well, asking what complaints the other persons made about them. With any patient, details should be gathered about suicidal ideation, threats, and attempts in order to determine whether there is currently suicidal risk. With a patient who is potentially histrionic, this information is also useful to help determine whether there is a dramatic or manipulative quality to the current threats or attempts. It can also be useful to ask for details of the types of activities the patient most enjoys, to see if he or she seems especially to enjoy being the center of attention or shows a craving for activity and excitement.

Cognitive Conceptualization

Although Shapiro (1965) sees repression as being significant in the development of hysterical pathology, he views the "neurotic style" of the hysteric as stemming from more than just the exclusion of specific ideational or emotional contents from consciousness. He sees the hysteric's general mode of cognition as being global, diffuse, and impressionistic, regardless of content. He views the hysteric as being incapable of intense or consistent intellectual concentration, which he sees as leading to a general distractability and suggestibility and to a deficiency of general knowledge even in areas that cannot reasonably be assumed to have come under repressive influence.

Among cognitive and behavioral therapy theorists, Beck (1976) presents a cognitive conceptualization of hysteria, but examines hysteria in the sense of conversion hysteria rather than HPD. Millon (1981) presents what he refers to as a "biosocial learning theory" view of HPD, seeing this disorder as fitting into the active-dependent personality pattern.

One of the underlying assumptions of the individual with HPD is "I am inadequate and unable to handle life on my own." Individuals with many other disorders may hold a similar assumption; however, the way that the person copes with this assumption is what distinguishes HPD from other disorders. For example, depressives with this basic belief might dwell on the negative aspects of themselves, feeling worthless and hopeless. Individuals with a dependent personality disorder may choose to emphasize their helplessness and passively hope that someone will take care of them. Histrionic persons tend to take a more pragmatic approach, without leaving anything to chance. They conclude that, since they are incapable of caring for themselves, they will need to find ways to get others to take care of them. Then they actively set about seeking attention and approval, in order to find ways to insure that their needs are sufficiently met by others.

Since other people are seen to hold the key to survival in the world, histrionic patients tend also to hold the basic belief that it is necessary to be loved by virtually everyone for everything they do. This leads to a very strong fear of rejection. Even entertaining the notion that rejection is possible is extremely threatening to these individuals, since this reminds them of their tenuous position in the world. Any indication of rejection at all is devastating, even when the person doing the rejecting is not actually that important to a patient. Feeling basically inadequate, yet desperate for approval as their only salvation, people with HPD cannot relax and leave the acquisition of approval to chance. Instead, they feel constant pressure to seek this attention in the ways they have best learned to achieve them, which is often by fulfilling an extreme of their sex-role stereotype. Female histrionics (as well as some of the males) seem to have been rewarded from an early age for cuteness, physical attractiveness, and charm rather than for competence or for any endeavor requiring systematic thought and planning. The more "macho" male histrionics have learned to play an extreme masculine role, being rewarded for virility, toughness, and power rather than actual competence or problem-solving ability. Understandably, then, both male and female histrionics learn to focus attention on the playing of roles and "performing" for others.

For example, Debbie's parents were divorced when she was still an infant, after which her father moved to New York City and went into show business. As a child, she saw him once a year, and clearly felt that she had to compete with all his exciting show business friends and "all the women" he had around. She reported that he had always wanted her to be "the perfect little girl," and she had been constantly worried that she would disappoint him.

In the discussion of one case of HPD, Turkat and Maisto (1985) formulated her problems as "an excessive need for attention and a failure to use the appropriate social skills in order to achieve attention from others" (p. 530). Thus, although winning approval from others may be the primary goal, these individuals have not learned effective ways to achieve this. Instead of learning to observe and analyze the reactions of other people and systematically plan ways to please or impress them, the histrionic person has been more frequently rewarded for the global enactment of certain roles, so it is only in the enactment of these roles that he or she learns to excel. The striving to please others would not necessarily be dysfunctional in and of itself. Histrionic people, however, get so involved in this strategy that they take it far beyond what is actually effective. Carried away with dramatics and attracting attention, they lose sight of their actual goal and come to seek stimulation and drama for its own sake.

People with HPD view themselves as sociable, friendly, and agreeable. In fact, they are often perceived as very charming at the beginning of a relationship. However, as the relationship continues, the charm seems to wear thin, and they gradually are seen as overly demanding and in need of constant reassurance. In their attempts to gain acceptance and approval from others, they tend to engage in a variety of maneuvers to elicit positive responses from other people. Since being assertive and asking directly for what they want involve the risk of rejection, they often use more indirect approaches such as manipulation to try to achieve their ends, but will resort to threats, coercion, temper tantrums, and suicide threats if more subtle methods seem to be failing.

Histrionic people are so concerned about eliciting external approval that they learn to value external events over their own internal experience. With so little focus on their own internal life, they are left without any clear sense of identity apart from other people and see themselves primarily in relation to others. In fact, their own internal experience can feel quite foreign and uncomfortable to them, and at times they actively avoid self-knowledge, not knowing how to deal with it. Having some vague sense of the superficial nature of their feelings may also encourage them to shy away from true intimacy with another person for fear of being "found out." Since they have paid little attention to their own internal resources, when any depth is required in a relationship, they have no idea how to respond. Thus, their relationships tend to be very shallow and superficial.

The focus on the external and the dramatic could lead to the characteristic thought style that has been described by Shapiro (1965). The thinking of the histrionic patient is seen as impressionistic, vivid, and interesting, but lacking in detail and focus. This seems to result not only from the histrionic's lack of introspection, but also from the fact that he or she simply does not attend to details and specifics in the first place. If something is not clearly noticed, it cannot be remembered in a specific manner; thus histrionics' memories of events remain global and diffuse. This results in an actual deficiency in knowledge of specific details and facts, which, along with a lack of experience in systematic problem solving, can lead to serious difficulty in coping constructively with problem situations. Being unable to cope effectively only serves to strengthen their belief that they are inadequate to cope with life alone and need to rely on the help of others.

Their vague style of cognition leads to an impressionistic sense of self, rather than one based on specific characteristics and accomplishments. If one does not view one's own actions and feelings in a sufficiently detailed fashion, it is difficult to maintain a realistic impression of oneself. In addition, since cognitive theory argues that thoughts exert a strong influence on emotions, then it follows that global, exaggerated thoughts would lead to global, exaggerated emotions. These global emotions can be very intense and labile, so that histrionic patients get carried away by affect even though it does not feel totally connected to themselves. Without the availability of complex cognitive integration, these undifferentiated emotions can be very difficult to control, leaving the persons subject to explosive outbursts.

The histrionic patient's characteristic thought style leads to several of the cognitive distortions outlined by Beck (1976). Since these patients tend to be struck by impressions rather than thinking things through, they are especially susceptible to dichotomous thinking. They react strongly and suddenly, jumping to extreme conclusions, whether positive or negative. Thus, one person is seen immediately as wonderful, while someone else is seen as a totally awful person. Because they feel their emotions so strongly, and lack sharp attention to detail and logic, histrionic patients are also prone to the distortion of overgeneralization. If they are rejected once, they dramatically conclude that they always have been rejected and always will be. Unlike depressives, however, they can be equally extreme in their positive conclusions about people and relationships, and can easily switch between the two extremes. Since they are not capable of looking at responses critically, they are also subject to the distortion of emotional reasoning—taking their emotions as evidence for the truth. Thus, histrionic individuals tend to assume that if they feel inadequate, they must be inadequate; if they feel stupid, they must be stupid.

Treatment Approaches

Little has been written about the treatment of hysteria from a behavioral point of view, and most of the limited behavioral research has been confined to the treatment of conversion hysteria and somatization disorders (summarized by Bird, 1979). Even less has been presented about behavioral treatment specifically for the patient with HPD. Kass, Silvers, and Abrams (1972) describe an inpatient behavioral group treatment of five women diagnosed (according to the authors' idiosyncratic criteria) as having a hysterical personality. Four of the five had been admitted from the emergency room because of suicide attempts. The group members were responsible for specifying each other's hysterical behaviors (which had been operationally defined), making up daily schedules most likely to evoke each individual's maladaptive behaviors, and contingently providing the rewards and penalties that had been agreed upon. Specific therapy techniques included positive and negative feedback, assertion training, desensitization, and contingency management. The authors state that each patient's maladaptive behaviors increased, peaked during the program, and subsequently decreased in frequency. There was no control group, and although the authors report that multiple measures of progress were kept, none of these were reported in the published study. All but one of the patients were reported to be functioning well at the time of discharge, showing symptomatic improvement and more adaptive behavioral responses at the end of treatment and after an 18-month follow-up, but no data were reported to support this assertion.

Similarly, Woolson and Swanson (1972) present an approach to the treatment of four "hysterical women" (again, diagnosed according to the authors' idiosyncratic criteria) that was primarily psychodynamic in nature, but also included some behavioral components. Charts and graphs were used to teach the patients empathic behaviors, and patients were taught to reinforce important others in their lives selectively, in order to improve their interpersonal relationships. The authors report that all four patients made substantial progress toward their stated goals within 4 months of initiating therapy; again, though, no objective measures were reported. Thus, fairly positive results were reported in two studies using at least partly behavioral treatments with a population generally acknowledged to be very difficult to treat.

The above-described approaches focused on modifying the histrionic's interpersonal behavior; however, the cognitive model of HPD presented earlier suggests that helping the patient shift from a global, impressionistic thought style to more systematic, problem-focused thinking would also be an important goal of therapy. It has been said that we need to "teach the hysteric to think and the obsessive to feel" (Allen, 1977, p. 317). Since the characteristic thought style of patients with HPD is clearly dysfunctional in many ways, cognitive therapy could be seen as a particularly appropriate treatment. However, the very nature of the histrionic patient's dysfunctional thought style means that he or she comes to the session with an approach to life diametrically opposed to the systematic, structured nature of cognitive therapy.

With such different basic styles, both the therapist and the patient can find cognitive therapy quite difficult and frustrating at first; if this conflict in styles can be gradually resolved, the cognitive changes facilitated by therapy can be particularly useful to the patient. The primary challenge in doing cognitive therapy with the histrionic patient is for the therapist to maintain steady, consistent effort and to be sufficiently flexible to enable patients gradually to accept an approach that is initially so unnatural to them. Cognitive therapy exposes the histrionic patient to an entirely new approach to the perception and processing of experience. Thus, skills acquired just by learning the process of cognitive therapy can constitute the most significant part of the treatment.

Obviously, in the course of working on specific problem situations, the full range of cognitive-behavioral techniques (outlined in Beck, Rush, Shaw, & Emery, 1979) can be useful. Depending on the goals of the patient, it may be helpful to use a variety of specific techniques, including pinpointing and challenging automatic thoughts; setting up behavioral experiments to test thoughts; activity scheduling; and training in relaxation, problem solving, and assertiveness. The conceptualization of HPD presented above would suggest that the underlying assumptions, "I am inadequate and unable to handle life on my own" and "It is necessary to be loved (by everyone, all the time)," will need to be challenged in order to make changes that will persist long after the treatment has ended.

Therapist-Patient Relationship

At least initially in therapy, the patient is likely to view the therapist as the all-powerful rescuer who will make everything better, so the more active a role the patient is required to play in the treatment, the less this image can be maintained. The consistent use of collaboration and guided discovery is especially important, given the tendency of the histrionic patient to play a dependent role in relationships. Whenever the patient begs the therapist for help, the therapist needs to be careful not to be seduced into the (sometimes tempting) role of savior, but rather to use questioning to help the patient arrive at his or her own solutions to the problems.

The unwary therapist can easily be maneuvered into taking on the role of "rescuer," taking on too much of the blame if the patient does not work toward change, and giving in to too many demands. This may lead to the therapist's feeling manipulated, angered, and deceived. A therapist who strongly wants to be helpful to others may inadvertently reinforce the HPD patient's feelings of helplessness and end up embroiled in a re-enactment of the patient's usual type of relationship. When the therapist becomes aware of having strong emotional reactions to the patient, and of being less than consistent in reinforcing only assertive and competent responses, it may be time to monitor his or her own cognitions and feelings. Adapting cognitive therapy procedures for the therapist's own use can be helpful in recognizing inconsistencies in behavior that may be interfering with the process of the treatment.

For instance, Debbie's therapist found himself having mixed feelings about her. On the one hand, he found her to be quite likable and could see how it could be fun to know her as a friend. As a therapist, however, he found himself getting very frustrated with her. For example, when he would try to probe for thoughts and feelings before or during a recent panic attack, all he could get were repeats of the superficial thought "I'm going to faint," over and over again. He experienced a sense of futility and frustration, and felt an urge to throw up his hands and give up. He had thoughts such as "Why bother with this? Nothing sinks in. It won't make any difference. Nothing is going to change anyway." At times like these, he needed to counter some of those thoughts by thinking, "I can't be certain of the effect of what we're doing. She is getting better, so things are in fact progressing. This is just a challenge. I simply need to continue to help her process events, since the idea is so foreign to her."

Since individuals who have HPD have previously been rewarded for extreme emotionality and manipulation, it is important to reinforce them for competence and for attention to specifics within the therapy sessions. Learning that attention to details and assertiveness can pay off in the sessions is the first step toward teaching these individuals that being assertive and doing active problem solving can pay off. Thus, it is important for the therapist to avoid falling into the patterns of so many of a patient's previous relationships. This can be quite a challenge even to the experienced therapist, since the style of the histrionic patient can be very appealing and attractive, and dramatic renditions of experience can be quite absorbing, entertaining, and amusing. It is crucial for the therapist to avoid getting too wrapped up in the drama of the patient's presentation, and to be aware of attempts at manipulation within the therapy, so that clear limits can be set by the therapist without rewarding these attempts.

Debbie tried for months to get special fee arrangements of various kinds, at times trying to go "over the head" of the therapist and contacting administrators throughout the hospital to make special "deals" without the therapist's knowledge. Fortunately, all such attempts were brought to the attention of the therapist promptly, so that he could clearly and repeatedly enforce the same fee arrangements for Debbie as for other patients. When she viewed refusals to comply with her requests as rejection, her feelings were discussed, but no exceptions to the fee arrangements were made. She tested the limits by insisting that she would need to schedule appointments only every other week because she could not afford treatment, and was surprised and angry when the therapist agreed to this instead of making exceptions so that she could come weekly. After coming to therapy biweekly for a few weeks and seeing no hopes of special considerations, she returned to weekly therapy. Later in the treatment, when her income actually did change and she assertively raised the issue with her therapist, her assertiveness was rewarded and an appropriate fee adjustment was made.

Specific Cognitive and Behavioral Techniques

Even before the actual work of cognitive therapy can begin, the individual with HPD needs to learn how to focus attention on one issue at a time. The setting of an agenda is an excellent place to begin teaching the patient to focus attention on specifics in the therapy session. The natural tendency of the histrionic patient is to spend most of the session dramatically relating all the exciting and traumatic events that occurred throughout the week. Rather than fighting this tendency, it may be important to schedule a part of each session for that purpose. Thus, one agenda item could be to review how things went during the week (with a clear time limit), so the therapist can be supportive and the patient can feel understood; then the rest of the session can be spent on working toward goals.

One of the biggest problems in the treatment of individuals with HPD is that they usually do not stay in treatment long enough to make significant changes. As with other activities and relationships, they tend to lose interest and move on to something more exciting. One key to keeping histrionic patients in treatment is to set goals that are genuinely meaningful and important to them, and that present the possibility of deriving some short-term benefit as well as longer-term gain. They have a tendency to set broad, vague goals that fit their image of what is expected from a therapy patient, but that do not seem particularly genuine. It is crucial that the goals be specific and concrete.

The therapist can help patients to operationalize their goals by asking questions such as "How would you be able to tell if you had achieved your goal?" "What exactly would look and feel different, in what ways?" and "Why exactly would you want to accomplish that?" It may be useful to have patients fantasize in the session about how it would feel to have changed their lives, in order to help them begin to fit their ideas together into a tentative model of who they would like to become. Once the goals have been set, they can be enlisted as an aid to help teach a patient to focus attention during the session. When the patient wanders off the subject or goes into minute detail about some extraneous topic, the therapist can gently but persistently ask how that is related to the goal that the two of them had agreed to discuss.

Debbie originally came into treatment with the very practical goals of going back to work, being able to drive alone, and staying alone in her own apartment. However, she was much more able to get excited about treatment when the goals were expanded to include being able to go into situations that were more immediately rewarding. Working on goals such as going to shopping malls ("especially to buy shoes!"), going to rock concerts, eating out at restaurants, and going to church (since she considered herself a born-again Christian) kept her interest longer than her more practical goals. One of the most powerful motivators for Debbie came when she had the opportunity to fly on an exotic vacation trip. This was such a compelling goal for her that she made more progress in the short period of time before the trip than she had at any other point in therapy.

After the initial stages of the treatment, the actual interventions will depend to some extent on the patient's particular presenting problem and goals. However, it is important to address each of the various elements of the cognitive conceptualization of HPD in order to make a lasting change in the overall syndrome.

Since histrionic patients' problems are exacerbated by a global, impressionistic thought style (which includes an inability to focus on specifics), teaching them to monitor and pinpoint specific thoughts will be an important part of treatment, regardless of the presenting problem. In teaching these patients to monitor thoughts using Dysfunctional Thought Records (DTRs), it is likely that a great deal of time will have to be spent specifying events, thoughts, and feelings in the first three columns. Although many other types of patients may be able to go home and monitor thoughts accurately after a simple explanation and demonstration in the session, this is an unrealistic expectation for histrionics. It is much more likely that they will forget the purpose of monitoring automatic thoughts and will instead bring in a lengthy narrative of exactly what happened to them throughout the week. The therapist needs to reward them for all attempts to do the homework, but the DTRs will probably need to be explained several times before the patients understand and remember that the goal is not just to communicate with the therapist, but to learn the skill of identifying and challenging thoughts in order to change emotions. Some histrionic patients strongly feel the need to communicate all their thoughts and feelings to the therapist. If so, it can be suggested that they write unstructured prose *in addition* to the DTRs (but not as a substitute).

The process of identifying thoughts and feelings is the first step toward making gradual changes in the problematic thought style of histrionics, while also serving the function of focusing attention on their emotions, wants, and preferences. The DTRs can be used to help patients challenge any of a wide range of thoughts that prove to be dysfunctional for them, as well as to help pinpoint and modify cognitive distortions. DTRs can be especially useful in helping patients to distinguish reality from their extreme fantasies and in helping them begin to make more accurate attributions regarding cause and effect.

Debbie would attribute any slight change in her physical condition to a terrible disease, and would immediately conclude that she had cancer or AIDS and was about to die. It made no difference to her whether she became dizzy and had trouble breathing because the room was hot and crowded, or because she was having a panic attack. Whatever the actual cause of her dizziness, she immediately concluded that she was going to faint or die. Teaching her to stop and explore the possible alternative causes for her physical symptoms helped her to make more appropriate causal attributions and interrupt her cycle of panic.

Since the idea of writing down homework assignments is likely to strike histrionic patients as boring and dull, some extra time may need to be spent in the therapy sessions to convince them of the usefulness of the approach. Rather than fighting the sense of drama in the histrionic patient, the therapist can use the vivid imaginations of histrionic patients to their benefit in the challenge of dysfunctional thoughts. For example, patients can be encouraged to be dramatic when writing their rational responses, making the rational responses more compelling and powerful than the automatic thoughts. Since histrionic patients have such colorful imaginations, their cognitions often take the form of imagery rather than verbal thoughts, so vivid imagery modification can also be encouraged. Dramatic types of verbal challenges to automatic thoughts—such as externalization of voices, where the therapist role-plays the patient's automatic thoughts and the patient role-plays more adaptive responses—can be particularly convincing to histrionic patients.

Debbie's therapist found that she paid more attention when he was able to use her own dramatic words when setting up homework assignments. They therefore ended up with unusual-sounding assignments, such as "meeting with The Creep," instead of more mundane terminology such as "meeting with my boss." Debbie found externalization of voices to be a dramatic and therefore powerful method of rational responding to thoughts. After having done a dramatic externalization of voices in a session, she was more able to go home and challenge her automatic thoughts on her own in writing.

Setting up dramatic behavioral experiments can be another powerful method of challenging automatic thoughts. For example, every time Debbie felt dizzy, she had thoughts such as "I'm going to faint and make a total fool of myself." To challenge these thoughts, it was important to set up exposure to the interoceptive cue of dizziness, which could be done in a dramatic way in group therapy.

THERAPIST: Debbie, it seems like the main symptom that frightens you is the dizziness.

DEBBIE: Yeah, I hate it. It's awful, isn't it?

THERAPIST: Well, I know that it feels that way to you. But I can't help but wonder if you've convinced yourself that it's awful, when it may simply be unpleasant. Can you tell us what makes feeling dizzy seem awful?

DEBBIE: It's just terrible. You know, I'll pass out and I'll embarrass myself.

THERAPIST: So you believe that if you become dizzy you will pass out. And if you do pass out, what is it that you find frightening about that?

DEBBIE: I just have a picture of myself getting up and passing out again and again, forever.

THERAPIST: You picture that happening continuously? For how long?

DEBBIE: Just forever, like I'll never snap out of it. (*Debbie laughs.*)

THERAPIST: You're laughing as you say that. Are you doubting your prediction?

DEBBIE: Well, I know it sounds a little silly, but that's the way it *feels* to me at the time.

THERAPIST: So you are making a prediction based on your feelings at the time. And how many times have you felt dizzy?

DEBBIE: Oh, thousands of times. You know I'm always talking about it.

THERAPIST: Then, how many of the thousands of times that you felt dizzy, and assumed that you would faint, did you actually faint?

DEBBIE: None. But that's only because I fight the dizziness. I'm sure if I didn't fight it I'd faint.

THERAPIST: That's exactly what we need to test out. As I see it, the problem here is not the dizziness per se, but rather the fear that you've come to associate with it. The more accepting you become of the dizziness and the less you catastrophize it, the less your life will feel ruled by the agoraphobia. So the job we have is of working on your becoming more comfortable with the dizziness. Does that make sense?

DEBBIE: Yeah, I guess it makes sense. But I don't see how to do that. We talk about it, but it seems just as scary to me.

THERAPIST: That's right, and that's because you need real evidence that nothing catastrophic will happen if you become dizzy. The evidence we have at this point is too weak. You also need to intentionally expose yourself to the dizziness rather than just let it hit you whenever. Are you willing to try an experiment that will be useful to you?

DEBBIE: Not if you're going to tell me to do something ridiculous.

THERAPIST: Do you agree with everything I've said so far?

DEBBIE: I guess.

THERAPIST: Then, while what I'm going to ask you to do may seem a little awkward, it will fit with what you've already said makes sense. I'd like for you to go to the center of the group and twirl until you get very dizzy.

DEBBIE: I don't want to do that.

THERAPIST: Here, I'll demonstrate. (*Therapist gets up and twirls a number of times.*) There, like that. I was able to get dizzy quickly. I used to do that all the time when I was a kid. Didn't you?

DEBBIE: Yeah. Except now it's different. Then it was fun, and now it scares me.

THERAPIST: If you are unwilling to twirl until you become very dizzy, would you be willing to do it a more limited number of times?

DEBBIE: I'll go around twice. No more.

THERAPIST: Great!

DEBBIE: (*She reluctantly gets up and very tentatively rotates two times.*) I hate that feeling!

THERAPIST: All the more reason to do it. As you directly face the feeling, rather than try to avoid it, I expect that you will eventually become more accepting of it. What did you discover today?

DEBBIE: I didn't faint. But that's probably only because I know I'm in a hospital and help is right around the corner. (*Debbie laughs.*)

THERAPIST: That's why I'm going to ask that you practice twirling daily, first at home, so you can face the dizziness in your natural environment. Then in the next group, we'll see if you can twirl a bit longer.

DEBBIE: You mean I have to do this again?

THERAPIST: I think it's the quickest way to work on your problems. Your hesitancy gives an even stronger indication that we're right on track. But we can work on this at a pace that you can tolerate.

DEBBIE: It seems crazy, but I guess it make sense.

Another advantage of teaching histrionic patients to pinpoint automatic thoughts is that the process of monitoring thoughts can be used to help the patients begin to control their impulsivity. As long as they automatically react in an emotional, attention-seeking, and manipulative manner, it is very difficult to make any change in their behavior. If they can learn to stop before they react long enough to record their thoughts, they have already taken a major step toward self-control. Thus, even before they learn to challenge their cognitions effectively, the simple pinpointing of cognitions can serve to begin to reduce impulsivity.

One cognitive technique that is valuable in improving the coping skills of the individual with HPD is the listing of advantages and disadvantages. This technique is best introduced early in the treatment, as soon as the patient resists efforts to focus on the agreed-upon topic. If the therapist simply tries to insist that the patient focus attention on goals, a power struggle may ensue, with the patient deciding that the therapist is "mean" and "doesn't understand." On the other hand, if the therapist consistently points out that it is the patient's choice how to spend the therapy time, but that the advantage of focusing on the goal is that there will be more likelihood of achieving it, the patient is left to make his or her own decision. Whatever is chosen then feels more as if it has come from the patient than from the therapist. Helping the patient to make conscious choices within the therapy session by examining the "pros and cons" of various courses of action is a useful antecedent to learning to make such choices and to do active problem solving in daily life.

Although Debbie had listed "being able to stay alone in my own apartment" as one of her primary goals, she never seemed to follow through on homework assignments involving spending even short periods of time in her apartment (e.g., 5 minutes). Rather than trying to push her into increased compliance, her therapist raised the issue of whether Debbie really wanted to work on this as a goal. Writing a list of the advantages and disadvantages of staying at her mother's house, versus staying at her own apartment, helped her to make a decision that she did indeed want to pursue this goal (see Table 10.2). After coming to this decision on her own, she began to work more consistently on homework assignments.

In addition to these cognitive strategies, these patients can also improve their ability to cope by being trained in specific problem-solving skills. Since they are rarely aware of the consequences before they act, it is helpful for them to learn to do what has been called "means-ends thinking" (Spivack & Shure, 1974). This problem-solving procedure involves teaching the patient to generate a variety of suggested solutions (means) to a problem and then to evaluate accurately the probable consequences (ends) of the various options.

Treatment of patients with HPD is rarely complete without attention to their problematic interpersonal relationships. These individuals are

TABLE 10.2
Debbie's Analysis of the Pros and Cons of Staying Alone in Her Apartment

Staying at Mother's Home	
Advantages	Disadvantages
A lot of things are done for me (meals, cleaning).	My grandmother likes it warm and I like it cooler, so it is uncomfortable for me.
There is someone here for companionship.	I don't have the independence I have in my own place.
We've been doing a lot of craft projects together.	My mom can nag a lot of times (re: losing weight, smoking).
I'm not as frightened when I'm here than when I am alone.	I feel like a failure not being in my own apartment.
My mom is fun to be with most of the time.	No stereo.
	Mom's VCR is acting up, so I can't tape while I'm away.

Staying at My Own Apartment	
Advantages	Disadvantages
I love the way the apt. looks and feels.	I don't feel comfortable in my apartment now.
I have call waiting.	The rent is high and I'm not using it now.
I can have my TV or stereo loud as I want.	I think of how I was before agoraphobia and I feel bad that I don't enjoy it like that now.
I can keep my apt. cool.	
I feel independent.	
My VCR is working so I can tape while I'm away.	

so concerned about maintaining attention and affection from others that they dominate relationships, albeit in indirect ways that seem to carry less risk of rejection. The methods that they most generally use to manipulate relationships include inducing emotional crises, provoking jealousy, using their charm and seductiveness, withholding sex, nagging, scolding, and complaining. Although these behaviors may work well enough to be maintained, they have long-term costs that are often not apparent to patients, due to their focus on the short-term gains.

Challenging patients' immediate thoughts may not be sufficient, however, since these individuals so often use emotional outbursts to as a way to manipulate situations. Thus, if a woman with HPD has a tantrum because her husband came home late from work, her immediate thoughts may include "How can he do this to me? He doesn't love me any more! I'll die if he leaves me!" As a result of her tantrum, however, she may well receive violent protestations of his undying love for her, which satisfy her desire for reassurance. Thus, in addition to challenging her thoughts when she gets emotionally upset, she also needs to learn to ask herself, "What do I really want now?" and explore alternative options for achieving this.

Once patients can learn to stop reacting and to determine what they want out of the situation (which, with histrionic patients, is usually reassurance and attention), they can apply their problem-solving skills by exploring the various methods for achieving that goal and looking at the advantages and disadvantages of each. Thus, rather than automatically having a temper tantrum, they are confronted with a choice between having a temper tantrum and trying other alternatives. Rather than asking them to make permanent changes in their behavior (such as giving up temper tantrums completely), the therapist can suggest that they set up brief behavioral experiments to test which methods are the most effective and have the least long-term cost. This can be much less threatening to patients than the idea of making lasting behavior changes, and may help them to try out some behaviors that they would be unwilling initially to do.

Once patients are able to delineate various means of trying to get what they want, the therapist can help them to consider the advantages of a method that is likely to be quite new to them: assertiveness. The process of assertiveness training with histrionic patients involves more than just helping them learn to communicate their wishes to others more clearly and effectively. Before they can communicate their wishes to others, they need to learn to identify those wishes and attend to them. Having spent so much time focusing on how to get attention and affection from others, these patients have lost sight of what it actually is that they want, and have very little sense of their own identity. Thus, effective assertiveness training with histrionic patients will involve using cognitive methods to help them pay attention to what they want and begin to develop a sense of identity, in addition to the more behavioral methods of teaching them how to communicate more adaptively.

For example, in one group therapy session, the group leader encouraged Debbie to take on a difficult homework assignment. She agreed to the assignment, but than skipped the next group session and sat pouting in the following session. When another group member confronted her on her behavior, she became very anxious and had a full panic attack. At first, she was unable to pinpoint what she was thinking and feeling, but just reported vague feelings of not liking being in group any more. Eventually she was able to identify her thoughts and assertively tell the group leader that she felt he was pushing her too hard, and had set too difficult a homework assignment. She was strongly rewarded for her assertiveness by the other group members as well as by the group leaders, and concluded that it had been worth enduring the anxiety.

The concept of "identity" or a "sense of self" is likely to be a source of many dysfunctional thoughts for histrionic patients. They tend to see identity as a big, magical thing that other people somehow have but that they are lacking. The idea of exploring their sense of self seems totally overwhelming, and they tend to see identity as something one either already has or doesn't have. Once the patients have started using some of the cognitive techniques discussed above, they are already paying some attention to their emotions, wants, and preferences, but they may not see these as important parts of an identity. It can be helpful to describe the development of a sense of self as simply the sum total of many varied things one knows about oneself. The therapist and patient may begin listing some of these in the therapy session, starting with mundane, concrete items such as favorite colors, types of food, and so forth. The elaboration of this list can be an ongoing homework assignment throughout the rest of the therapy, and every time a patient makes any type of statement about himself or herself during the sessions (such as "I really hate it when people keep me waiting"), the therapist can point it out and have it added to the list.

In addition to working to improve their interpersonal relationships, it is important that these patients eventually challenge their belief that the loss of a relationship would be disastrous. Even if their relationships improve, as long as they still believe that they could not survive if the relationship ended, they will have difficulty continuing to take the risks of being assertive. Fantasizing about the reality of what would happen if a relationship should end, and recalling how they survived before this relationship began, are two ways to begin helping a patient to "decatastrophize" the idea of rejection. Another useful method is to design behavioral experiments that deliberately set up small "rejections" (e.g., with strangers), so the patient can actually practice being rejected without being devastated.

Ultimately, patients need to learn to challenge their most basic assumption: the belief that "I am inadequate and have to rely on others to survive." Many of the procedures discussed above (including assertiveness, problem solving, and behavioral experiments) are designed to increase patients' ability to cope, thereby increasing self-efficacy and helping them to feel some sense of competence. Given the difficulty these patients have in drawing logical conclusions, however, it is important to point out to them systematically how each task they accomplish challenges the idea that they cannot be competent. It can also be useful to set up small, specific behavioral experiments designed with the explicit goal of testing the idea that they cannot do things by themselves.

Even patients who come to see the advantages of thinking more clearly and using assertiveness may become frightened by the idea that if they learn to become more "reasonable," they will lose all the excitement in their lives and become drab, dull people. Histrionics can be lively, energetic, and fun to be with, and they stand to lose a lot if they give up their emotionality completely. It is therefore important to clarify throughout the treatment that the goal is not to eliminate emotions, but to use them more constructively. In fact, the therapist can encourage the adaptive use of patients' vivid imaginations and sense of drama throughout treatment, by helping them use dramatic and convincing means for challenging automatic thoughts. Other constructive avenues for sensation-seeking can be encouraged, including involvement in theater and drama; participating in exciting activities and competitive sports; and occasional escape into dramatic literature, movies, and television. For Debbie, her new-found Christianity provided a more constructive avenue for some of her sensation seeking, and she was able to get very absorbed in the drama of her baptism and the laying on of hands that was part of her church.

For patients who feel reluctant to give up the emotional trauma in their lives and insist that they have no choice but to get terribly depressed and upset, it can be useful to help them gain at least some control by learning to "schedule a trauma." Patients can pick a specific time each day (or week) during which they will give in to their strong feelings (of depression, anger, temper tantrum, etc.). Rather than being overwhelmed whenever such feelings occur, they learn to postpone the feelings to a convenient time and keep them within an agreed-upon time frame. This often has a paradoxical effect. When patients learn that they can indeed "schedule depression" and stick to the time limits without letting it interfere with their lives, they rarely feel the need to schedule such time on a regular basis. It always remains as an option for them, however, so that long after therapy has been terminated, if they convince themselves that they simply have to "get it out of their system," they have learned a less destructive way to accomplish this.

Since the histrionic patient is so heavily invested in receiving approval and attention from others, a structured cognitive therapy group can be a particularly effective mode of treatment. Kass et al. (1972) demonstrated that group members can be enlisted to assist in the reinforcing of assertiveness and the extinction of dysfunctional, overly emotional responses.

For example, most of Debbie's treatment took place in an agoraphobia group. Being the most histrionic member in the group, she quickly took on the role of "social director" and set the tone for dramatic reinforcement of progress on exposure heirarchies. With Debbie's encouragement, group members applauded and, at times, gave each other standing ovations for accomplishing particularly difficult items. The group provided an ideal arena for her to work on assertiveness and her need to entertain and please the group. For example, in one session, Debbie made a joke that did not get the response she had expected. In the following session, the group decided that they wanted to spend some time discussing assertiveness. Debbie responded, "Well, since we are talking about assertiveness, I want to share how I felt last session." She was able to pinpoint thoughts such as "I said something funny, so now they'll kick me out," "I did something wrong," and "People want me to be different than I am." In discussing this, she was able to clarify for herself that she was especially concerned about how the male group leader would react. This discussion, and the challenging of these thoughts, led to her working for the next several sessions on the goal of deciding what she wanted and what was best for her, separate from other people, including men in authority.

For patients who are currently involved in significant relationships, couple therapy can also be especially useful. In couple treatment, both spouses can be helped to recognize the patterns in the relationship and the ways in which they each facilitate the maintenance of those patterns.

Conclusions

The efficacy of cognitive therapy for the treatment of HPD has not yet been tested empirically. In the absence of controlled, empirical data, clinical reports are the only evidence available. The Kass et al. (1972) study described above showed some promise, but was an uncontrolled case report using idiosyncratic diagnostic criteria that did not correspond to those of DSM. More recently, several colleagues have used cognitive therapy with a variety of histrionic patients, and informally report it to be an effective treatment that results in less frustration on the part of both therapist and patient than more traditional approaches to treatment. As in the cognitive therapy of most personality disorders, treatment tends to be longer in duration than with Axis I diagnoses.

For example, Debbie was seen for a total of 101 sessions over the course of 3 years. When she began therapy, she was unable to work due to her agoraphobia and had a Beck Depression Inventory score of 24. After six sessions, she was back at work and her Beck Depression Inventory score had dropped to 11 (within the normal range). Although she showed rapid symptomatic improvement in the early stages of therapy, it took a much longer period of time to make lasting changes not only in her agoraphobia and depression, but also in her HPD. Two years after she completed therapy, Debbie reported that she had not had any recurrence of agoraphobia or serious depression, despite having to go through several major crises: the breakup of a relationship, putting her dog (and beloved companion) to sleep, and the serious illness of her grandmother. When dealing with these major stresses, she reported that she continually told herself, "If I can get over the phobia, I can deal with anything." She had ended a problematic relationship and was engaged to be married to a man who, she reported, was stable and mature and treated her well. She reported that, for the first time in her life, she had a good, solid relationship with great sex.

While 101 sessions over a period of 3 years is hardly short-term therapy, it should be noted that Debbie was treated for agoraphobia and recurrent depression in addition to HPD. Although changes in the Axis I symptoms can be achieved in a much shorter period of time, our experience has been that changing the characteristics of HPD itself often requires 1 to 3 years. Clearly, uncontrolled case reports are limited in their usefulness. Empirical research is urgently needed in order to substantiate the effectiveness of this treatment with this population, to clarify the necessary components of the treatment, and eventually to determine which types of patients are most appropriate for which variations of the treatment.

Chapter 11

Narcissistic Personality Disorder

A new patient, David, sought therapy for what at first sounded like an adjustment disorder or a mild depressive episode. During the initial interviews, David expressed considerable blame and hostility toward his wife, and strong desires to get even with her and put her in her place. He complained about his quality of life as "beneath" him, and he spoke about the rest of the world in negative, condescending terms. He seemed preoccupied with fantasies of exceptional achievement and recognition, but had done very little toward actualizing any of these goals. Although he assured the therapist that he didn't want to kill himself, he nevertheless elaborated on an extremely graphic and detailed plan for shooting himself in a way that would make the cleanup easy. The therapist was alarmed by how vividly he described his plan, but also wondered why he was detailing such a dramatic, striking scenario. The nature of David's current presentation and his premorbid history suggested the possibility of an Axis II disorder that predated his current depression. As the therapist pursued the hypothesis that David might have a personality disorder, these and other pieces of clinical information began to fit together, pointing toward the narcissistic pattern of grandiosity, hypersensitivity to evaluation, and lack of empathy for others.

The concept of narcissistic personality disorder (NPD), as defined by DSM-III and DSM-III-R (see Table 11.1), is primarily based on psychoanalytic case literature (Akhtar & Thomson, 1982; Frances, 1985). As with other personality disorders, considerable subjectivity and inference are involved in judging the presence or absence of the diagnostic criteria for clinical narcissism (Stangl, Pfohl, Zimmerman, Bowers, & Corenthal, 1985; Widiger & Frances, 1985; APA, 1980, p. 7). Diagnostic reliability for this personality disorder is low (Spitzer, Forman, & Nee, 1979). Increased diagnostic reliability and demonstration of conceptual validity would require more specific designation of a representative sample of

TABLE 11.1
DSM-III-R Diagnostic Criteria for Narcissistic Personality Disorder

A pervasive pattern of grandiosity (in fantasy or behavior), lack of empathy, and hypersensitivity to the evaluation of others, beginning by early adulthood and present in a variety of contexts, as indicated by at least *five* of the following:

(1) reacts to criticisms with feelings of rage, shame, or humiliation (even if not expressed)

(2) is interpersonally exploitative: takes advantage of others to achieve his or her own ends

(3) has a grandiose sense of self-importance, e.g., exaggerates achievements and talents, expects to be noticed as "special" without appropriate achievement

(4) believes that his or her problems are unique and can be understood only by other special people

(5) is preoccupied with fantasies of unlimited success, power, brilliance, beauty, or ideal love

(6) has a sense of entitlement: unreasonable expectation of especially favorable treatment, e.g., assumes that he or she does not have to wait in line when others must do so

(7) requires constant attention and admiration, e.g., keeps fishing for compliments

(8) lack of empathy: inability to recognize and experience how others feel, e.g., annoyance and surprise when a friend who is seriously ill cancels a date

(9) is preoccupied with feelings of envy

Note. From *Diagnostic and Statistical Manual of Mental Disorders* (3rd ed., rev., p. 351) by the American Psychiatric Association, 1987, Washington, DC: Author. Copyright 1987 by the American Psychiatric Association. Reprinted by permission.

independent, observable behaviors, along with specific criteria for chronicity and consistency across situations, and perhaps a measure of case prototypicality (Widiger & Frances, 1985). Research delineating multiple behavioral acts that are linked to specific traits (e.g., Buss & Craik, 1983; Livesley, 1986) offers promise in this endeavor. A cognitive focus may also enhance the specification of observable indications of narcissism.

Historical Overview

Evolution of the Psychoanalytic View

The term "narcissism" has its origins in a classical Greek myth about Narcissus, a young man who fell in love with the image he saw of himself reflected in a pool. His fate was to waste away from unsatisfied desire and to be transformed into the narcissus flower. The first reference to this myth in the psychological literature appeared in a case report by Havelock Ellis (1898), describing the masturbatory or "autoerotic" practices of a young man.

Freud subsequently incorporated the term "narcissistic" into his early theoretical essays on psychosexual development (1905/1953), and later developed ideas about narcissism as a distinct psychological process (1914/1957). He conceptualized narcissism as a phase of normal development that would follow an autoerotic phase, and eventually mature into object love. Erratic, unreliable caretakers in early life, or parents who overvalued their child, were viewed as the major disruptions to development of object love, therefore causing a fixation at the narcissistic phase of development. Narcissists were thus thought to be unable to form lasting attachments because of a fixation at this stage of self-involvement.

Subsequent psychoanalytic theorists focused on interpersonal aspects of narcissism, and the concept of a "narcissistic personality" began to emerge (e.g., Waelder, 1925). However, as Akhtar and Thomson (1982) point out, there was disagreement as to whether narcissism was a component of the neuroses, psychoses, or character disorders. The work of a current generation of object relations theorists has advanced narcissism as a character or personality disorder. Prominent among these are the writings of Kernberg (1967, 1970) and Kohut (1966, 1971).

Kernberg views the characteristic narcissistic grandiosity and exploitation as evidence of "oral rage," which is a pathological process in libidinal (psychosexual) development. This is presumably due to emotional deprivation caused by a chronically indifferent or covertly spiteful mother. At the same time, some unique talent or role provides the child with a sense of being special that is an emotional escape valve in a world of perceived indifference or threat. The sense of grandiosity or entitlement serves to shelter a "real self" that is "split off," or outside conscious awareness. The real self is believed to contain strong but largely unconscious feelings of envy, fear, deprivation, and rage. Since Kernberg's theory holds that the grandiosity is a pathological process, his approach to treatment requires confrontation and interpretation of unconscious conflicts in order to repair damage to the intrapsychic structure caused by the developmental arrest.

Kohut, by contrast, has conceptualized narcissism as a form of libido with a normal course of development of its own, rather than as a pathological deviation in the process of normal libidinal development. In Kohut's theory, pathological narcissism is the result of a developmental arrest that occurs when the major personality structures of "grandiose self" and "idealized parent imago" are not properly integrated. This would result from a traumatic disappointment caused by a mother who was not sufficiently confirming in her emotional responses to her child, or, conversely, failed to permit appreciation of her real limits. Thus, the archaic grandiosity and idealized parent imago are "split off" and become subject to repetitive, unconsciously motivated searching for fulfillment. Kohut's approach to treatment requires an empathic therapist who works to complete the developmental tasks of toning down the grandiosity and accepting the disappointment that comes with the realization that idealized people have realistic limits.

Other analytic writings have detailed various emotional and behavioral manifestations of clinical narcissism (e.g., Bursten, 1973; Modell, 1976; Svrakic, 1985). Some have provided observations that have relevance to a cognitively oriented treatment. Bach (1977), for example, has discussed a "narcissistic state of consciousness," which alludes to a variety of cognitive distortions. These include a predominance of self-oriented reality perception and a tendency toward excessive self-stimulation. Narcissistic language and thought fluctuate between abstract and concrete extremes. Engaging in a learning process is difficult for narcissistic individuals because of their emotional reactions to being in a state of ignorance. Narcissists tend to rely on certain external circumstances, such as repeated praise or attention from others, to regulate their moods. Time, space, and causality are also interpreted in a personal rather than impersonal way. Horowitz (1975) has referred to a faulty information-processing style of too much attention to sources of praise and criticism, resulting in incompatible psychological attitudes. These attitudes apparently contribute to a subjective sense of uncertainty and need for confirmation.

Thus, the theme of self-love and self-involvement has evolved from an explanation for masturbation to a broad-spectrum disorder of character called "narcissism." The psychoanalytic literature on narcissism provides extensive detail regarding the phenomenology of this disorder. However, the psychoanalytic theory of narcissistic etiology appears to be limited by an overemphasis on presumed inadequacies in emotional nurturance by mothers.

It is important to note that there is no empirical evidence that clearly links nurturant deprivation in childhood with characteristics of adult narcissism. Studies evaluating nurturant deprivation during early development in both animals and humans indicate effects of emotional apathy, withdrawal, inadequate social behavior (Harlow, 1959; Provence & Lipton, 1962; Yarrow, 1961), and a retarded growth syndrome referred to as "failure to thrive" (Cupoldi, Hallock, & Barnes, 1980; Gagan, Cupoldi, & Watkins, 1984; Oates, Peacock, & Forest, 1985). These effects are incompatible with narcissistic features of exploitation, grandiosity, and striving for constant admiration.

Prospective studies of adult personality adjustment in children deprived of nurturance have, by and large, not been conducted. One longitudinal, prospective study of 456 men at risk for juvenile delinquency (Vaillant & Drake, 1985) recently reported that the "immature defenses" associated with personality disorders in adulthood were independent of the quality of a man's childhood in terms of clinical ratings of home atmosphere and classification as having come from a "problem family." Thus, psychoanalytic assumptions about narcissistic etiology have no direct empirical support beyond case history reports. Indeed, related research appears to contradict assumptions about the causative role of maternal inadequacy.

The possibility of sex bias also needs to be noted as a factor in the psychoanalytic theory of narcissistic etiology. Existing observations are based on male patients (Akhtar & Thomson, 1982) and are primarily provided by male authors. It may be that men are somehow particularly vulnerable to narcissism, as Akhtar and Thomson suggest. Thorough investigation of this and other possibilities regarding narcissism is likely to be impeded by a lack of awareness and uncritical acceptance of traditional theoretical assumptions. For instance, mothers continue to be singled out as the responsible figures. Recent analytic work advances the idea that the future narcissist is born as a replacement following the death of a significant other in the mother's life; she thus regards the child as "special," but unresolved grief renders her mothering inadequate (Volkan, 1981).

Mother-blaming is a serious and pervasive problem that clearly biases professional clinical literature (Caplan & Hall-McCorquodale, 1985). In the area of deprivation, it has become clear that parental rather than maternal deprivation is a more appropriate concept for study, and that a lack of support and nurturance for the mother is a critical aspect of the problem (Gagan et al., 1984). Thus, the psychoanalytic theory of narcissistic personality disorder may be limited by sexual bias in the population of theorists, in the subjects of clinical study, and in the basic assumptions regarding cause. Alternatives that correct this apparent bias need to be developed.

Application of Social Learning Theory

A social learning theory of narcissism advanced by Millon (1969) dispenses with the maternal deprivation hypothesis and focuses primarily on parental overvaluation. According to Millon, when parents respond to their child in such a way as to overinflate the child's sense of self-worth, the child's internalized self-image is enhanced beyond that which external reality can validate. This overinflated self-image is the source of the narcissistic personality style. Parents (not just the mother) still play the primary role. But their impact centers around the information that they give their child directly, through feedback, and indirectly, through modeling. Inferred intrapsychic structures are limited to the child's self-image.

Cognitive Conceptualization

Cognitive theory can extend the social learning approach to narcissism. Utilizing the concept of the cognitive triad proposed by Beck, Rush, Shaw, and Emery, (1979), we propose that NPD can be conceptualized as stemming from a combination of dysfunctional schemas about the self, the world, and the future. The early foundation of these schemas is developed by direct and indirect messages from parents, siblings, and significant others, and by experiences that mold beliefs about personal uniqueness and self-importance. The composite result is a number of distorted beliefs that are very compelling and overactive. Narcissists regard themselves as special, exceptional, and justified in focusing exclusively on personal gratification; they expect admiration, deference, and compliance from others, and their expectations of the future focus on the realization of grandiose fantasies. At the same time, beliefs about the importance of other people's feelings are conspicuously lacking. Behavior is affected by deficits in cooperation and reciprocal social interaction, as well as by excesses in demanding, self-indulgent, and sometimes aggressive behaviors.

The sense of being unique, important, and different from others in some special way may be developed by a variety of experiences. Obviously, pointed flattery, indulgence, and favoritism can foster the development of narcissism. A belief in oneself as unique or exceptional could also develop from the experience of deficits, limitations, exclusion, or rejection. Some examples of such experiences might include being specifically singled out as the target of abuse from a parent; being labeled as weak or sickly by parents; or having one's whole family labeled as "different" from most of the community on the basis of ethnic, geographic, racial, or economic status. This deficit- or rejection-based self-image could be likened to the pattern of narcissism that Frances (1985) notes as a more subtle form, characterized by feelings of inferiority, envy, use of fantasy, and attachment to omnipotent others. The common denominator for either an inferior or superior belief about the self may simply be perceiving oneself as different from others in some important way. That difference may then be associated with exaggerated emotional reactions as it is labeled either a wonderful or terrible difference.

The actual presence of some culturally valued (or devalued) talent or physical attribute will tend to elicit social responses that reinforce the "superior/special" schema. Feedback that would modify the special schema may be lacking or distorted. For example, narcissists may get very little feedback regarding their similarities to others. Parents also may systematically deny or distort negative external feedback to their child. Insulation from negative feedback could contribute to the hypersensitivity to evaluation so common among narcissists. Conversely, in the more subtle case, continuous negative feedback could be an experience that supports extreme, catastrophic reactions to perceived criticism, and hypervigilance toward attention from others. Problems emerge mainly when these self-schemas become overactive and are not balanced by more integrative judgments.

Cognitive Assessment

General Clinical Context

Narcissistic people typically seek treatment when they develop an uncomfortable Axis I disorder, or when they are confronted with some severe relationship problem. Depressive disorders are probably the most common symptomatic disturbance that leads to the narcissist's entering treatment. These include adjustment disorder with depressed mood, dysthymic disorder, and occasionally major depression. Narcissistic individuals do not tolerate discomfort very well, so they are apt to seek treatment for depression. The more serious the presenting depression is, however, the more difficult it will be to evaluate accurately the presence of a personality disorder.

Precipitating factors for depression often include some relationship disturbance or breakup, trouble at work, or some crisis that punctures the grandiosity with discouragement or humiliation. Sometimes unmet grandiose expectations accumulate over time, triggering the dysphoric conclusion that great dreams will never come true. A sense of grandiosity and uniqueness may continue to be expressed via an emphasis on the exceptional quality of the despair.

Narcissistic depression typically involves a discrepancy between expectations/fantasies and reality. Automatic thoughts reflect a repetitive focus on unmet expectations, the shortcomings and inferiorities of others, and the uniqueness of the patient's problems. There may be a concomitant sense of hopelessness about things ever being "really good," along with withdrawal from pleasurable activities and contacts. The narcissistic patient also may be preoccupied with a sense of humiliation about being depressed.

Other symptomatic disorders or problem behaviors may cause narcissists to enter treatment. Significant others may get fed up with them and issue an ultimatum that forces them into psychotherapy. Or the narcissists may seek treatment in order to end the discomfort of a symptomatic disorder other than depression. These commonly include social phobias, hypochondriasis, and substance abuse. A hypersensitivity to evaluation by others may become manifest in the form of social phobia. Overconcern with presumed flaws in appearance precipitates phobic behavior, as the individuals simultaneously seek attention yet fear evaluation.

With hypochondriasis, excessive self-involvement becomes focused upon protection and nurturance of the physical self. This provides a socially acceptable way to focus time and energy on oneself, and allows the classic secondary gains of attention and sympathy from others. Physical vulnerability provides a reason why special consideration is needed, and why reality may not match fantasized capabilities. Illness, or potential illness, provides a tolerable explanation for having failed to accomplish what "could have been."

Substance abuse can develop as part of the overall narcissistic pattern of self-involvement and indulgence. "High-status" drugs such as cocaine are also particularly attractive to the narcissist. Immediate relief from personal discomfort, and a sense of self-importance and power, can sometimes be achieved with the use of chemical substances. Unacknowledged tensions created by hypersensitivity to evaluation can be readily soothed with a few drinks or pills. The notion that they are unique and special serves to insulate narcissists from recognition of their reliance on alcohol or drugs. It also keeps them believing that they will escape the negative effects of addiction, and that they can easily quit using chemicals.

In some cases, the narcissistic patients may develop paranoid trends in their thinking. A "me against the world" attitude predominates, as the narcissists perceive others to be jealous of their special talents, and therefore out to "get" them, or diminish them in some way. Information discrepant with the narcissists' grandiose fantasies may provoke intense rage, verbal or physical abuse of others, and major self-protective maneuvers. In extreme instances where reality testing is curtailed, paranoid narcissists may be capable of violently assaulting others whom they perceive as a threat to their superiority.

A tragic example of this occurred when a man who was later characterized as having NPD, suffered a series of stresses that produced hardship and isolation from others. He was separated from his wife but had retained custody of their four small children, two of whom were named after him. He had suffered layoffs and physical stress in his job as a freight clerk. Financial hardship had resulted in the repossession of his furniture, and his home was without beds or chairs. He worked sporadically at night and cared for his children during the day.

This man's estranged wife had reportedly telephoned him on several occasions, taunting him with stories of her new boyfriend's sexual prowess and material possessions, such as a new gun. The man became increasingly angry and preoccupied with the idea that the boyfriend "had a bigger gun than mine," and that his wife and her boyfriend were plotting to steal his children during a weekend holiday. To prevent this, he purchased a rifle from a discount store and planned to murder his wife and her boyfriend. On the day he set out to do this, however, he also "took care of" his four children by murdering each of them so as not to leave them alone, available for his wife and boyfriend. He proceeded to murder his wife, and in his frenzy murdered her mother, too. He then waited for 6 hours outside the boyfriend's place of employment and wounded him when he emerged.

After extensive evaluation, it was finally concluded that this extreme act of violence was primarily an effort to ward off further blows to the man's self-esteem, to retaliate against those who threatened to diminish him, and to re-establish his sense of superiority and dominance. He was judged to be legally sane for the killing of his wife and mother-in-law and the wounding of the boyfriend, and temporarily insane for the killing of his children. This case highlights the need to be alert to the possibility of violent behavior, particularly when the suspicious, angry narcissist plots to seek revenge.

The presence of underlying NPD will generally complicate standard treatments for the associated Axis I disorders. Quite often, the additional diagnosis of the personality disorder is made when the treatment for the symptomatic disorder stalls, or fails to show the expected improvements. We recommend that simultaneous consideration be given to the Axis I and Axis II disorders when both are present. In practice, this might mean spending some time developing cognitive interventions for both disorders within a given session. The Axis I disorder definitely needs to be addressed in standard fashion, with increasing amounts of time spent on it relative to the severity of symptoms. However, if the narcissism isn't directly and systematically dealt with at the same time, the patient's overall improvement is apt to remain marginal.

Specific Assessment Procedures

Accurate assessment of NPD is difficult, especially when an Axis I disorder is also present. In addition, a patient may present with features that are characteristic of other personality disorders. The personality disorders most likely to overlap with narcissism are histrionic, antisocial, and borderline (Stangl et al., 1985). The most important assessment tool for distinguishing narcissism is probably a careful clinical interview. Including a collateral informant in the interview process is also very helpful.

Standard symptomatic measures such as the Beck Depression Inventory can be used to assess the presenting level of distress. Other standard psychometric instruments can help to clarify the level of discomfort and the presence of certain personality characteristics. The MMPI profile is likely to show clinical elevations that are consistent with presenting distress. Scale 4 (Psychopathic Deviance) is likely to show some significant elevation, due to narcissists' view of themselves as different, exceptional, and intent on having their own way. Scales 6 (Paranoia) and 9 (Mania) also are sometimes moderately elevated by the characteristic hypersensitivity and grandiosity. Data from nonclinical student samples suggest that scales 8 (Schizophrenia), 9 (Mania), and the validity scales constitute the profile elevations most representative of narcissistic personality style (Raskin & Novacek, 1989). The Dysfunctional Attitude Survey is likely to show extreme endorsement of beliefs about achievement, perfectionism, and approval.

Direct inquiry about narcissistic features is limited by the patient's ability to evaluate such characteristics objectively (e.g, "Do you exaggerate your achievements?") or willingness to admit to certain behaviors (e.g., exploiting others). Alternatively, the therapist can systematically assess the narcissistic features that are revealed by a patient's presentation in the sessions, self-report of social relationships, and self-reported functioning in areas of work or vocational achievement. The following descriptions present some general guidelines for what to look for in each of these areas.

Behavioral Presentation

The alert therapist may pick up potential signs of narcissism in his or her very first impression of a new patient. Frequently, new patients reveal their sense of entitlement in the demanding way that they negotiate their first appointment. Upon physical presentation, the therapist may first notice a very polished or eye-catching appearance that is the result of constant attention to grooming, fitness, and wardrobe. Hyperconcern for personal appearance and comfort is, however, more diagnostic than good looks or grooming per se. The patients will show this hyperconcern in numerous small verbal and nonverbal behaviors. Some patients will show it by frequent fluffing, patting, adjusting and checking their appearance. Others might hold either an exceptionally relaxed or exceptionally upright posture, and maintain what looks like a haughty facial expression. Minor physical flaws, such as a broken fingernail, or minor physical discomforts, such as being hungry, produce characteristic overreaction. A brief inquiry into a patient's thoughts and feelings when one of these behavioral signs is detected can help to establish if this may be an indication of narcissism, or is simply a coincidental feature of some other circumstance (e.g., being hungry can be an urgent problem if one is diabetic).

The narcissist may complain about or resist diagnostic testing, both because it requires effort, and because it classifies a problem—implying that it is ordinary, just like anyone else's. Resistance to testing procedures or feedback may also be an indication of hypersensitivity to evaluation and potential negative feedback. Narcissistic individuals take feedback poorly, responding with characteristic anger or shame. The patients may be very comfortable with talking on about themselves, sometimes to the point of obvious self-aggrandizement. Frequent references may be made to talents, accomplishments, connections, or material possessions. A self-righteous stance toward difficulties, and a tendency to complain about the shortcomings of others, are also characteristic of narcissism.

How the patient interacts with the therapist provides important diagnostic information. In more obvious instances, patients will readily describe themselves as haughty, arrogant, or cocky. They may emphasize their high position, notable family name, or celebrity status, and expect special consideration in return. Narcissists may also attempt to manipulate the therapist to support their sense of grandiosity or entitlement. Beyond fishing for compliments, possible indicators of this include extensive questioning of the therapist's qualifications ("Are you sure you can treat someone as unique or tough as me?") and persistent attempts to negotiate therapy appointment times and fees. The patients may act indignant when appointments and fees are not arranged to their preference or convenience.

The narcissistic tendency to idealize or devalue others will commonly be evident in interaction with the therapist, too. Therapists can be aware of when they are being treated as unusually special. Conversely, therapists' interventions may be criticized or rejected in an automatic sort of way. Narcissistic patients may even personally insult a therapist. They may also reveal these attitudes in description of previous therapists' attempts to help. Inquiry into previous therapeutic contacts can discern how the patients view the experience, and how they handled the termination. One might expect a pattern of high expectations followed by disappointment and abrupt termination.

Social Relationships

Relationships of the narcissist are typically a source of tension. While the patient may have a wide circle of acquaintances, stable, long-term relationships are lacking. Only vague references can be made to specific friends. During initial interviews, significant others are either not mentioned, or described as the source of the patient's problems. Multiple divorces or breakups are common, although some narcissists will never have found someone "good enough" for even an initial commitment. Narcissists can readily list characteristics they seek in a partner, and they will quickly lose interest in someone who doesn't have all of the requisite features of looks, personality, and position.

Within marriage, narcissists are prone to problems of competition with their spouses. After having chosen mates because of their "special" characteristics, the narcissists then resent it when their partners get more attention. They want to be married to someone special, but they become angry when they lose the spotlight. This anger may be evident in a variety of aggressive and passive-aggressive behaviors.

In a general social context, narcissists may be adept at making a smooth, favorable first impression. Further contact, however, reveals a range of rudeness and impropriety. Narcissists can be abrasive, abrupt, and notably lacking in gratitude. Courtesy is a one-way street. They expect others to let them take the right of way in traffic, cut in lines, avoid waiting, and be served immediately by clerks or waiters. Social interactions are at their command and convenience. If a favor or social obligation is reciprocated, it is likely to be done in a manner that is more attention-getting than actually considerate of the recipient.

Frequently, the reports of significant others are what reveal this demanding, insensitive interpersonal style. For example, a mother reported that her young adult son would demand she relinquish the telephone to him, and then scream obscenities at her if she didn't immediately slam the receiver down, terminating her conversation in midsentence. Another example was reported by a secretary whose boss wanted her to return to work the day that she suffered a miscarriage. When she told him her doctor recommended several days of rest at home, he bristled about all the work that needed to get done, and chided her for obstructing his deadline.

Temper tantrums, verbal harangues, and emotional, physical, or sexual abuse all may be evidence of narcissists' belief that others should be primarily concerned with making them happy or comfortable. Others may describe their relationships with narcissists as "love-hate": They are simultaneously taken in by charm and exploited in some way. Narcissists are apt to become most resentful and contemptuous of anyone who tries to hold them accountable for their exploitative, self-centered behavior.

Work and Achievement

Commitment to hard work may be evident, but the purpose of it is self-centered. The goal of personal recognition motivates narcissists far more than the social value of the work they do, the relative contribution it may make to their family security, or simply pleasure and enjoyment in the work itself. Otherwise, the narcissistic person tends to believe that he or she should be exempted from difficult or dull tasks.

On the job, narcissists may overstep the boundaries of authority in a number of ways. They may make decisions that they are not qualified to make, or they may fail to be appropriately respectful of superiors. They generally dislike and resent subordinate positions. When in a position of authority, the narcissist may misuse power to exploit those under his or her influence. One likely example of this is sexual harassment. Another example is a stockbroker who excessively buys and sells or otherwise "churns" a client account to generate commissions, regardless of whether money is made or lost for the client. Other public examples might be found among political figures who behave as if their authority exempts them from generally accepted norms of conduct. Numerous examples could illustrate exploitative behavior reflecting a narcissistic belief that "All that really matters is my getting what I want or what I think is right."

Narcissists live according to the rule that they are above or exempt from the ordinary rules that govern everyone else. For instance, a beauty queen thought she should be exempted from charges of driving under the influence of alcohol, even though she was clearly inebriated and had bumped into a parked car. Her rationale for exception was that it would destroy her career and everything she'd worked for as a beauty pageant contestant about to compete in a national contest. When she was found guilty as charged, the judge cautioned her to remember that "pretty girls can kill too."

Case History

The following case history of David, the patient introduced at the start of the chapter, provides a composite illustration of many of these diagnostic signs of NPD. David was an attorney in his early 40s when he sought treatment for depressed mood. He cited business and marital problems as the source of his distress, and wondered if he was having a midlife crisis.

David appeared to be an outgoing man who paid meticulous attention to his appearance. He made a point of asking for the therapist's admiration of his new designer suit, his winter tan, and his new foreign convertible. He also asked the therapist what kind of car he drove and how many VIP clients he dealt with. David wanted to make sure that he was dealing with someone who was the best in the business. But he was also apprehensive of anyone important seeing him at the therapist's office. Although he expressed some general doubts about psychotherapy, David decided to continue because his therapist offered a unique treatment—cognitive therapy.

David had grown up in a comfortable suburb of a large city, the oldest of three children and the only son of a successful businessman and a former secretary. Always known to have a bit of a temper, David usually provoked his parents and sisters into giving in to his wishes. Even if they didn't give in to his demands, he reported that he usually just went ahead and did what he wanted anyway. David spoke of being an "ace" student and a "super" athlete, but could not provide any details that would validate a superior performance in these areas.

David recollected that he had his pick of girlfriends, as most women were "thrilled" to have a date with him. His strategy was to act quite cool initially; nevertheless, he had a pattern of short-lived, intense involvements. If a girl broke off a relationship before he did, or if she even showed some interest in someone else, he was apt to respond with a temper tantrum. When he was 17, he slapped a girlfriend for dating another boy, causing some facial bruises. Because she worked as a professional model, she threatened to sue David, and he was stunned that she had the nerve to question his anger.

David went to college, fantasizing about being famous in a high-profile career. He majored in communications, planning to go on to law school and eventually into politics. He met his first wife during college, the year she was the university homecoming queen. They married shortly after their joint graduation. He then went on to law school, and she went to work to support the couple.

During law school, David became a workaholic, fueled by fantasies of brilliant work and international recognition. He spent minimal time with his wife, and after their son was born, even less time with either of them. At the same time, he continued a string of extramarital affairs, mostly brief sexual encounters. He spoke of his first wife in an annoyed, devaluing way, complaining about how she just did not live up to his expectations. He waited until he felt reasonably secure in his first job so that he could let go of her financial support, and then he sought a divorce. He continued to see his son occasionally, but he rarely paid his stipulated child support.

After his divorce, David decided that he was totally free to just please himself. He loved spending all his money on himself, and he lavishly decorated his condominium and bought an attention-getting wardrobe. He constantly sought the companionship of different, attractive women. He was very successful at making initial contacts and getting dates, but he rarely found anyone good enough to date more than once or twice. Sometimes he played sexual games to amuse himself, such as seeing how fast he could make sexual contact or how many women would agree to have sex with him. He was somewhat bewildered by the fact that he did not really feel triumphant when he finally managed to "score" five women in one day. David began to long for the convenience and the attention that a single, steady mate could provide. So he screened his dates with a shopping list of requirements, and he eventually married Susan, the daughter of a well-known politician.

David had trouble identifying automatic thoughts or problems that precipitated his negative moods, so initial treatment interventions centered around tracking his mood fluctuations. He found that he frequently felt worse when he went into his office to work, when he had consultations with certain colleagues, and when he was with his wife. He felt better when he could fantasize about his future plans, when he could drive around in his sports car by himself and get attention from women, or when he was socializing with a group such as at a party or cocktail lounge.

Feeling worse at work was associated with a heightened sense of discomfort in doing routine work, and the thought that such work was beneath him. He would think about how he really deserved better, and how he was not getting appropriate recognition for his talents and aptitudes. Consultations with colleagues often triggered thoughts of their failure to give him appropriate recognition, or their "nerve" in saying something even marginally critical about him. David believed that because he was "different" from other people, they had no right to criticize him. But he had every right to criticize others. He also believed that other people were weak and needed contact with someone like him in order to bring direction or pleasure into their lives. He saw no problem in taking advantage of other people if they were "stupid" enough to allow him to do so.

David admitted that when he felt worse with his wife, he was usually focusing on some negative aspect of her looks or her intelligence. Typically, he was thinking about her not being worthy of him. Whenever Susan made requests of him, he was apt to become irritated with her. He thought that she was lucky to have him and therefore did not really have the right to make demands. He knew that there were plenty of other, prettier women who would be glad to cater to his needs.

David felt better when someone flattered him; when he was in a group social situation where he could easily grab the center of attention; and when he could fantasize about obtaining a high-level position, being honored for his great talent, or just being fabulously wealthy. The composite picture produced by the assessment of David's clinical history, his current symptoms, and his attitudes and automatic thoughts thus indicated a major depressive episode, of mild severity, with concomitant NPD. Further details of David's therapy will be discussed throughout the remainder of this chapter.

Cognitive Therapy Objectives

The initial clinical objectives for cognitive therapy of NPD involve the development of a collaborative relationship; the teaching of, or "socializing" the patient to, the cognitive model of treatment; and mutual agreement regarding problem conceptualization and treatment approach.

Major difficulties may be encountered in trying to meet these objectives with narcissistic patients. Developing collaboration can be exceedingly difficult, since narcissists have a strong investment in being superior, as well as significant deficits in the area of cooperative interaction. The therapist's authority may be questioned, resented, devalued, or otherwise disqualified. The patients may regard the therapy as a competitive game in which they must fight to maintain their superiority. In responding to such challenges, therapists need to make a point of supporting the importance of understanding the patients' subjective responses, but also of consistently guiding them toward a broader way of making decisions. The consideration of alternatives can be clearly linked to goals such as more comfortable moods or stable, tension-free relationships. Specific suggestions for patient-therapist interactions to facilitate collaboration will be discussed in a subsequent section.

Beyond the initial objectives of collaboration, problem conceptualization, and socialization to the cognitive model of treatment, goals of treatment can range from resolution of the specific presenting complaints to more long-term development of alternative behavior and attitudes. A resolution of symptoms or crises can obviously be accomplished much more quickly than an alteration of lifestyle, and the relative pace of treatment needs to be clarified with the patient in terms of short- and long-term goals. Long-term goals might include adjustment of the patient's grandiose view of self, limiting cognitive focus on evaluation by others, better management of affective reactions to evaluation, enhancing awareness about the feelings of others, activating more empathic affect, and eliminating exploitative behavior.

Specific Treatment Interventions

As soon as the therapist gathers enough data to indicate the presence of NPD, he or she can take the lead in conceptualizing the patient's presenting problem (depression, relationship problem, procrastination, work difficulty, etc.) as complicated by lifestyle problems. Using the cognitive model, the therapist can discuss these problems with the patient in terms of specific situations with associated feelings, thoughts, assumptions, and behavior.

Treatment interventions will typically alternate focus among increasing behavioral responsibility, decreasing cognitive distortions and dysfunctional affect, and formulating new attitudes. More specific long-range goals might include behavior that is reciprocal and sensitive to the feelings of others (e.g., more courtesy); cooperating with others and taking on a share of the work; more reasonable expectations of others; greater self-control of habits and moods; and more discriminating self-appraisals that recognize the commonalities between self and others. Motivation to pursue longer-range goals can come from the desire to obtain more stable moods, to maintain certain relationships or careers, or to resolve persistent, recurring symptoms.

It is helpful to tailor clinical strategies according to the three major components of narcissism: grandiosity, hypersensitivity to evaluation, and lack of empathy. For grandiosity, an emphasis can be placed on utilizing cognitive techniques to adjust patients' distorted view of themselves and to manage the associated extremes of affect. The patients' belief in themselves as special individuals is typically quite tenuous, and tends to swing between the extremes of positive and negative evaluation. They automatically compare themselves with others, and tend to over-enhance their differences as superiority and uniqueness, or as inferiority. Another common error that contributes to grandiosity is all-or-nothing categorization. In their dualistic reasoning, narcissists are either wonderfully superior or totally worthless. Adjustment of this form of reasoning can help to limit the exaggeration of self-importance. Another adaptive alternative is to have patients make comparisons within themselves, or to seek commonalities in their view of themselves vis-a-vis others (see Table 11.2).

Imaginal restructuring may be useful for altering preoccupations

TABLE 11.2
Alternative Beliefs

Be ordinary. Ordinary things can be very pleasurable.
One can be human, like everyone else, and still be unique.
There can be rewards in being a team player.
I can enjoy being like others, rather than always having to be better.
I can choose to be a member of a group and not always the exception.
I can go for long-term respect from others instead of short-term admiration.
Other people have needs and opinions that matter too.
Colleagues can be resources, not just competitors.
Feedback can be valid and helpful. It's only devastating if I take it that way.
No one owes me anything in life.
Thinking about real situations can be healthier than being preoccupied with exaggerated dreams.
I don't really need constant attention and admiration from everyone to exist and be happy.
Superiority and inferiority among people are value judgments and thus always subject to change.
Everyone has flaws.
Everyone is special in some way.
I can choose to be accountable for my own moods. To let the evaluations of others control my moods makes me dependent on them and out of control.

with fantasies of unlimited or ideal attributes. A replacement fantasy that emphasizes gratifications and pleasures in immediately attainable, everyday experiences can be developed as a form of distraction from the narcissistic images. Such a fantasy can also serve the purpose of covert rehearsal of activities that, if pursued, could help raise self-esteem. For instance, instead of fantasizing about singing a hit song to an audience of thousands, a patient might also fantasize about finding pleasure in singing in the church or community choir. An important technical aspect of this intervention is helping the patient develop a sense of pleasure in the imagined activity itself, and focus away from idealizing the joys of attention and recognition.

Systematic desensitization that incorporates cognitive methods of coping and adaptation can be used to address the narcissistic problem of hypersensitivity to evaluation. In this, the therapist would help structure a hierarchy of gradual exposure to feedback from others. The patient's role would be to confront catastrophic thinking and dichotomous reasoning, and to develop skills in tolerating, using, and benefitting from evaluation. An important question for the narcissistic patient to test is whether he or she can maintain a positive (nongrandiose) view of self without constantly basing this on positive reactions from others.

As a specific exercise, the patient could purposely plan to request feedback from others. In structuring this exposure, it would be beneficial to start with feedback that is likely to be positive. Positive feedback is a more tolerable point from which to begin taking emotional risks and examining the role of personal thoughts and interpretations. The patient's task isn't to fish for compliments; it is to ask directly for specific feedback.

The exposure can then continue into more critical sources of feedback, so that the patient can utilize cognitive skills for managing emotional reactions, and make a discriminating judgment about how to use the feedback. We would caution against simple desensitization to "feeling less than great," mentioned by Frances (1987), as a potentially limited behavioral application. The point is not for the patient to learn to accept feeling bad; it is to learn more effective ways of interpreting situations that tend to provoke bad feelings.

Narcissists can also learn to be more discriminating in the attention they pay to evaluation. These patients compulsively focus on how they are being evaluated by others, often without regard for the importance of that evaluation. They do a lot of mind reading, and indirectly solicit confirmation of a positive opinion. Thought stopping and distraction are sometimes useful techniques for breaking these habits of thinking about what others are thinking. Different situations or experiences can be rated or ranked for importance as a source of feedback, so that the narcissists can work on moderating their sensitivity to what others might be thinking about them. Eventually, the patients should be able to stop preoccupations with others' thoughts, directly seek feedback when appropriate, and be discriminating in their reactions to feedback.

The development of empathy for others is the third major area of specific clinical focus. Three strategies are useful in this endeavor. First, the lack of empathy needs to be brought to the patient's attention. Sometimes a simple question about the recognition of others' feelings will suffice. Other times, the disregard and exploitation need to be specifically pointed out and labeled. Second, emotional schemas relevant to the feelings and reactions of others need to be activated. This can probably be most effectively accomplished by role reversals and role plays in which the patient assumes the role of another. Emphasis needs to be placed on how the other person is likely to feel, not just on how the patient would react in the circumstances of the other person. Third, alternative, adaptive ways to treat others can be suggested and discussed. New statements of belief can be formulated to articulate the affective recognition of others' reactions—for instance, "Other people's feelings matter too." Specific ways to act on this new alternative can be mapped out (e.g., "Let someone go ahead of you in line," "Give someone else a compliment," "Call up someone who is out of touch with you and find out what that person is feeling"). Together, these three strategies provide cognitive, affective, and behavioral points of focus for intervention.

The use of a specific problem list will help focus therapy discussion around concrete problems. In the case of David (the attorney described above), the problem list included moodiness, as well as difficulties in the areas of work, relationships with colleagues, and the marital relationship. With each problem, David's therapist looked for thoughts and behaviors that reflected the pathologically narcissistic pattern of grandiosity, lack of empathy, and hypersensitivity to the evaluation of others.

In working with David's automatic thoughts, simply shifting the focus of attention from "I" to "we" or "they" was often helpful in redirecting his self-involvement. Like many narcissistic patients, David tended to personalize situations and events. He placed himself at the center of action, and generally did not consider that others might be reacting to something besides him. Role plays and role reversals were quite useful in helping David to see beyond his personal emotional reactions. He also tended to use emotion-based, dichotomous reasoning, and he overgeneralized his conclusions. He was able to develop logical arguments in his adversarial legal work, but he had a great deal of trouble seeing alternatives in his personal life. Persistent testing of dysfunctional automatic thoughts within therapy sessions helped David to internalize the habit of questioning the reasonableness of his thoughts about himself.

Even though his generalization of changes outside the therapy consultation was limited and slow, David was encouraged by the therapist to focus on testing a few basic alternative beliefs, such as "Other people matter too," or "Everyone is unique in some way." It was made clear to him that these alternatives were not just "better ways to think," but were options that might be more beneficial to him in the long run. Table 11.2 outlines some of the alternatives developed by different narcissistic patients. A major component of trying out these new, alternative attitudes was specifying the ways of thinking and acting that would be consistent with the belief. Thus, concrete ways to think, act, and feel were tied to each belief. For instance, David tested the belief that "Everyone is unique in some way" by making a point to notice something special about everyone he came in contact with for 2 weeks. Further, he acted on this belief in several ways, including giving compliments on what he noticed and recommending colleagues because of their special skills. Finally, the therapist helped David to focus on positive feelings he might gain from the new belief, and discouraged him from disregarding or trivializing these feelings.

Guidelines for Therapist-Patient Interactions

Careful attention to the therapeutic relationship is an important part of cognitive therapy for NPD. Narcissism is defined by deviations in the way these individuals relate to other people, and how they think about themselves vis-a-vis others. Cognitive psychotherapy provides an excellent opportunity to introduce some corrective elements into narcissists' interpersonal relationships.

Therapists' personal reactions to narcissistic patients deserve particular attention. As with most personality disorders, work with a narcissistic patient can be challenging, as well as quite stressful. While issues of transference and countertransference are not central mechanisms of treatment in cognitive therapy, consideration of the therapeutic relationship is an integral part of the cognitive approach. To manage the limits of the therapeutic relationship effectively, and to use their personal reactions in the process of treatment, cognitive therapists must first be sensitive observers of their own thoughts, feelings, and beliefs.

Second, cognitive therapists need to become practiced in using carefully timed, selective self-disclosure of personal reactions. These reactions can sometimes be framed as "experimental evidence" for patients' probable impact upon other people in their environment.

Third, the therapists have to find ways to cope with personal reactions that may be strong and quite negative toward this type of patient. They need to deal with those reactions, perhaps by tracking and testing automatic thoughts, so that they can avoid undue personal stress and can further the progress of the therapy. Therapists also need to remain aware of the vulnerabilities that they bring into the therapy relationship, such as confidence problems, or approval and omnipotence concerns.

There are some predictable therapist reactions to narcissistic patients. These reactions can even sometimes be the major signal for considering narcissism as part of the clinical picture. Initially, therapists may experience pleasure and enjoyment in the company of narcissists. This primarily occurs when the patients flatter the therapists with idealization and regard them as very special and important. This can obfuscate the nature of the patients' problem and actually hinder progress. Especially in marital or family therapy, a therapist should be alert to narcissistic flattery, which attempts to develop a special alliance with the therapist, rendering the narcissistic patient and therapist as "superior" to the other "identified patients." It is very important to distinguish between genuine patient gratitude for a therapist's assistance, and manipulative flattery that is part of the patient's pathology.

The sense of potential teamwork that comes with initial narcissistic flattery may be followed by growing annoyance and frustration as the patient does not follow through on agreed-upon plans. Narcissistic patients will typically have trouble taking responsibility for treatment efforts in or out of the office. They will expect things to go their way, with someone else doing the actual work. Their behavior is directed by a pair of assumptions: "No one is doing enough for me," and "I deserve to have things taken care of for me." They may adamantly claim that they are making every effort to do what is required, yet evidence of their following through on specific assignments is lacking. When the therapist attempts to clarify expectations for mutual efforts, the patients may discredit the therapist or the treatment, and show overt indifference, disdain, or anger.

Narcissistic patients may claim that the therapist is unable to understand the unique nature of their problem, thus rejecting the therapist's attempts to help. One patient demonstrated this by placing several calls to the clinic director, asking for a therapist "higher up" who could deal with her "tough case"; she was unable to grasp the fact that she was already working with someone at the top level of authority for that agency. Other narcissistic patients may foil collaboration by being passive or tangential, or persistently failing to follow through on an agreed-upon plan. Or they may abruptly leave therapy because of unmet expectations, without discussing their intent to terminate with the therapist. In maneuvering these pitfalls, it is important to point out that mutual efforts are necessary for smooth progression of therapy.

The therapist may, at this point, be vulnerable to working harder to gain a patient's approval. Frustration mounts as the therapist tries various strategies for engaging the patient, such as increasing or decreasing the structure of sessions. Sometimes this pleases the patient enough that he or she continues coming for therapy, but little change seems to be taking place. Both patient and therapist are apt to feel disappointed with therapy progress as long as the essential narcissistic problems of grandiosity, hypersensitivity to evaluation, and lack of empathy are not directly pinpointed. Therapists need to be attentive to their own dichotomous attributions that blame therapy stagnation on bad or "resistant" patients, or on themselves as "bad" therapists. Therapy may be stuck because the personality problems are not being adequately addressed by either party.

Specific relationship limits are required in order to discourage narcissistic attitudes and behavior within therapy. Therapists need to clarify limits and expectations of acceptable or productive therapy behavior, and not allow violations of their personal rights. Protection of personal rights frequently centers around maintaining the limits of therapist-determined schedules and fees. It might also include insisting on compliance with other general rules, such as no smoking in the office. In some cases, therapists need to protect their physical rights, as narcissistic patients might violate personal space or make sexual advances (e.g., rearranging furniture to sit closer, insist on touching). Selective use of feedback regarding the therapist's thoughts and reactions as a "real person" can be an important component of the corrective experience. Such in-therapy behavior can be directly limited; at the same time, possible links to dysfunctional schemas can be explored. From there, alternatives can be discussed.

Being hypersensitive, narcissists are apt to overreact to any feedback. Therapists are cautioned to avoid a critical, accusatory tone of voice, and to check patient reactions and thoughts. Overreaction to therapy interaction often presents a prime opportunity for clarifying the cognitive model and intervening with core issues. Even small cooperative interactions can be therapeutic steps out of the patients' demanding self-involvement.

We agree with Frances's (1987) comment on the absolute necessity of maintaining one's own sense of self-esteem and objectivity when treating narcissistic patients. Neither flattery nor devaluation should be taken too personally. The temptation to label and discard a narcissistic patient has to be resisted. Such labeling usually reflects the therapist's hopelessness about treatment progress. The therapist may think that with NPD, the patient's attitudes and behavior are so entrenched that he or she will never change. Or the therapist may think that valuable time is just going to be wasted on someone who is so self-centered and rotten to other people. Instead of giving up, the therapist can review his or her overall conceptualization and try to identify some reasonable, short-term goals.

An example of this would be to work on one specific belief in one particular context, such as trying to help the patient be more cognizant of a friend's or spouse's feelings, or even the therapist's feelings, instead of trying to get him or her to be more thoughtful toward all people.

Additional Treatment Interventions

Behavior therapy techniques and other adjunctive interventions can play an important role in cognitive therapy of narcissism. Such patients often exhibit behaviors that are destructive to others, such as physical or verbal abuse or sexual harassment, and these need to be limited and changed. Therapy would be, at the least, incomplete if no attempt is made to alter these harmful actions. Behavioral response prevention or contingency management plans can help to decrease destructive habits (e.g., drinking, overspending, not working). Cognitive interventions can be useful for assessing thoughts that function as antecedents to the destructive habit, or as obstacles to the more desirable behavior. Specific cognitions can also serve as cues to elicit and guide more adaptive or desirable behavior. For example, David used the phrase, "Some work is better than none," as a cue for focusing on his work.

Other adjunctive interventions frequently include marital or family therapy. In David's case, marital therapy provided an important forum for helping him to develop empathy for and cooperation with a significant other. Therapists need to recognize that a narcissistic patient will sometimes enter treatment as the reluctant member of a marital or family unit, while insisting that the problems reside within someone else. Marriage or family partners can help to emphasize the interactive nature of the shared problems. They can also emphasize to the narcissistic patient the necessity for certain behavioral changes, and assist in implementing contingency management plans. In some instances, obvious behavioral changes are absolutely necessary to keep significant others involved with the narcissist.

One stepfamily with three sons, ages 14, 19, and 20, grappled with numerous problems, including the eldest son's narcissistic personality. Amy and John, the parents, sought family therapy within the first year of their marriage; they cited many family tensions, particularly with the oldest son, Roy.

Since his graduation from high school, Roy had worked erratically, only when he "felt like it." He contributed no money to the household, did no chores, and expected groceries, meals, and laundry service to be provided. His room was decorated with pictures of himself. With money saved from graduation gifts, Roy made a down payment on an expensive, flashy new truck. He spent his free time "cruising for chicks," rarely calling to let the family know of his whereabouts. Amy and John were worried about his lack of direction in life, and they resented the way that he took advantage of their home, without contributing anything in return.

Initial changes in the family involved requiring Roy to contribute a certain amount of money to his room and board and to be financially responsible for his truck payments, or face the logical consequence of losing these privileges if he did not work to support them. Roy was also expected to do his own laundry, help clean up after meals, and take his turn with home and yard maintenance chores. Roy thought that these expectations were unreasonable, and he was hostile and grudging in response to his parents' statement of these limits.

John and Amy were consistent in following through, and they refused to bail Roy out when he got behind in his truck payments. They pointed out that he was not entitled to free room and board, and assigned him extra house chores when he used "rent" money for his truck payment. Extra chores were used as "interest" on the "rent overdue," and unpaid funds continued to accrue. If Roy reached a certain level of overdue room and board, then eviction was to follow. Fortunately, Roy responded by working steadily and beginning to be responsible for his obligations. Some time later in treatment, Amy voiced her annoyance with his continuing self-centered attitude, as he repeatedly focused on himself and failed to show concern for other family members. However, both Amy and John were soothed by the recognition that at least Roy's behavior had changed in significant ways, and he was being more responsible at home.

Conclusion

Narcissistic patients are usually difficult to treat. Not all of them will be amenable to the procedures outlined in this chapter. Patience, persistence, and confidence in setting appropriate limits will probably prove to be important allies to therapists who work with narcissistic individuals. The same tools can also be offered to the significant others who may appear in treatment as the "victims" of narcissists' behavior. Cognitive therapy offers much promise as a specific modality for modifying the essential psychological features of clinical narcissism.

Chapter 12
Avoidant Personality Disorder

Introduction

Most people, including those with a variety of clinical syndromes, some-times use avoidance to relieve anxiety or to forestall facing difficult situations. Avoidant personality disorder (APD) is characterized by a pervasive behavioral, emotional, and cognitive avoidance. This avoid-ance is fueled by cognitive themes such as self-deprecation, an expecta-tion of interpersonal rejection, and a belief that unpleasant emotions and thoughts are intolerable.

In therapy, APD patients express a desire for affection, acceptance, and friendship, and yet frequently have few friends and share little intimacy with anyone. In fact, they may experience difficulty even talk-ing about these themes with the therapist. Their frequent loneliness and sadness is maintained by a fear of rejection, which inhibits the initiation or deepening of friendships.

A typical patient with APD will believe, "I am socially inept and undesirable," and "Other people are superior to me and will reject or think critically of me if they get to know me." As the therapist elicits thoughts and uncomfortable feelings stemming from these beliefs, patients will frequently initiate avoidance or "shut down" by changing the topic, standing up and walking around, or reporting that their minds have "gone blank." As therapy proceeds, the therapist may find that this emotional and cognitive avoidance is accompanied by beliefs such as the following: "I can't handle strong feelings," "You'll think I'm weak," "Most people don't have feelings like this," and "If I give in to these feelings, they'll go on forever; if I ignore them, it might get better someday." These patients have a low tolerance for dysphoria both in and out of therapy, and use a variety of activities (sometimes even addictions) to distract them from negative cognitions and moods.

Historical Perspective

The term "avoidant personality" was first used by Millon (1969). He described this personality as consisting of an "active-detached" pattern representing "a fear and mistrust of others."

> These individuals maintain a constant vigil lest their impulses and longing for affection result in a repetition of the pain and anguish they have experienced with others previously. Only by active withdrawal can they protect themselves. Despite desires to relate, they have learned it is best to deny these feelings and keep an interpersonal distance. (Millon, 1981, p. 61)

Millon's formulation of APD is largely based on social learning theory. Objects relations theorists Burnham, Gladstone, and Gibson (1969) have presented a theory that stresses motivation, attributing the symptoms of APD to the "need-fear dilemma:"

> He has an inordinate need for external structure and control. . . . [His] existence depends upon his maintaining contact with objects. . . .
> The very excessiveness of his need for objects also makes them inordinately dangerous and fearsome since they can destroy him through abandonment. Hence, he fears and distrusts them.
> [One way] to avert or alleviate the pain of his need-fear dilemma [is] . . . object avoidance. . . .
> Attempts by others to engage him in interaction are regarded as intrusions which carry the threat of disorganization. (pp. 27–31)

A more cognitive perspective can be found in the writings of Karen Horney (1945), who described an "interpersonally avoidant" person over 40 years before the current DSM-III-R formulation: "There is an intolerable strain in associating with people, and solitude becomes primarily a means of avoiding it. . . . There is a general tendency to suppress all feeling, even to deny its existence" (pp. 73–82). In a later book (1950), Horney wrote a description of such an avoidant person that is consistent with cognitive formulations:

> On little or no provocation he feels that others look down on him, do not take him seriously, do not care for his company, and, in fact, slight him. His self-contempt . . . make[s] him . . . profoundly uncertain about the attitudes of others toward him. Being unable to accept himself as he is, he cannot possibly believe that others, knowing him with all his shortcomings, can accept him in a friendly or appreciative spirit. (p. 134)

Since the advent of cognitive therapy, little has been written about APD from a cognitive perspective. In this chapter we will demonstrate how examination of the automatic thoughts, underlying assumptions, and schemas of APD patients can lead to a parsimonious conceptualization that describes the development and maintenance of this disorder. Following this conceptualization, clinical strategies are suggested that can help modify the problematic thoughts and behaviors, as well as the underlying assumptions and core beliefs, that maintain the disorder.

Differential Diagnosis

Table 12.1 summarizes the DSM-III-R criteria (American Psychiatric Association, 1987) for APD. It is apparent that features of this disorder overlap with other diagnostic categories, most notably schizoid personality disorder, social phobia, and agoraphobia. Therefore, to make a differential diagnosis it is important that the therapist inquire about the beliefs and meanings associated with various symptoms.

For example, both APD and schizoid personality disorder are characterized by a lack of close relationships. However, avoidant patients desire friendships and are bothered by criticism—two attributes not shared by schizoid patients, who are satisfied with little social involvement and are indifferent to being criticized by others.

APD shares some of the cognitive and behavioral features of social phobia and agoraphobia. However, while persons with social phobias are

---

TABLE 12.1
DSM-III-R Diagnostic Criteria for Avoidant Personality Disorder

A pervasive pattern of social discomfort, fear of negative evaluation, and timidity, beginning by early adulthood and present in a variety of contexts, as indicated by at least *four* of the following:

(1) is easily hurt by criticism or disapproval
(2) has no close friends or confidants (or only one) other than first-degree relatives
(3) is unwilling to get involved with people unless certain of being liked
(4) avoids social or occupational activities that involve significant interpersonal contact, e.g., refuses a promotion that will increase social demands
(5) is reticent in social situations because of a fear of saying something inappropriate or foolish, or of being unable to answer a question
(6) fears being embarrassed by blushing, crying, or showing signs of anxiety in front of other people
(7) exaggerates the potential difficulties, physical dangers, or risks involved in doing something ordinary but outside his or her usual routine, e.g., may cancel social plans because she anticipates being exhausted by the effort of getting there

Note. From *Diagnostic and Statistical Manual of Mental Disorders* (3rd ed., rev., pp. 352–353) by the American Psychiatric Association, 1987, Washington, DC: Author. Copyright 1987 by the American Psychiatric Association. Reprinted by permission.

fearful of humiliation and have low confidence in their social skills, they do not avoid close relationships—just certain social circumstances (such as public speaking or large parties). Patients with agoraphobia may present behaviors similar to those with APD. However, agoraphobic avoidance is associated with fears of being in a place where help for a personal disaster may not be available, rather than fears of intimacy.

Another diagnostic consideration is that patients with APD often seek treatment for related Axis I disorders. These include anxiety disorders (e.g., a phobia, panic disorder, generalized anxiety disorder), affective disorders (such as major depression or dysthymia), substance abuse disorders, and sleep disorders.

It is important that proper diagnosis of APD be made early in therapy. As will be discussed below, the Axis I disorders may be treated successfully with standard cognitive methods, as long as the therapist includes strategies to overcome the characteristic avoidance that might otherwise cause roadblocks to treatment success.

Somatoform disorders and dissociative disorders may also accompany APD, although less commonly. Somatoform disorders may develop because physical problems can have secondary gain in providing a reason for social avoidance. Dissociative disorders occur when the cognitive and emotional avoidance patterns of patients are so extreme that they experience a disturbance in identity, memory, or consciousness.

Conceptualization

Patients with APD wish to be closer to other people, yet they generally have few social relationships, particularly intimate ones. They are fearful of initiating relationships or of responding to others' attempts to initiate relationships with them, because they are certain they will be rejected. They view such rejection as unbearable. Their social avoidance is usually apparent. Less obvious, though, is their cognitive and emotional avoidance, in which they avoid thinking about things that cause them to feel dysphoric. Their low tolerance for dysphoria also leads them to distract themselves behaviorally from their negative cognitions. This section will explain social, behavioral, cognitive, and emotional avoidance from a cognitive perspective.

Social Avoidance

Schemas

Avoidant patients have several long-standing dysfunctional beliefs or schemas that interfere with their social functioning. These beliefs may not have been fully articulated, but reflect patients' understandings of themselves and others. As children, they may have had a significant person (parent, sibling, peer) who was highly critical and rejecting of them. They developed certain schemas from interactions with that person, such as "I'm inadequate," "I'm defective," "I'm unlikable," "I'm different," "I don't fit in." They also developed schemas about other people: "People don't care about me," "People will reject me." Not all children with critical, rejecting significant others, however, become avoidant. Avoidant patients must make certain assumptions to explain the negative interactions: "I must be a bad person for my mother to treat me so badly," "I must be different or defective—that's why I have no friends," "If my parents don't like me, how could anyone?"

Fear of Rejection

As children, and later as adults, avoidant patients make the error of assuming that others will react to them in the same negative fashion as the critical significant person did. They continually fear that others will find them lacking and will reject them. They are afraid they won't be able to bear the dysphoria that they believe will arise from the rejection. So they avoid social situations and relationships, sometimes severely limiting their lives, to avoid the pain they expect to feel when someone inevitably (in their judgment) rejects them.

This prediction of rejection causes dysphoria which in and of itself is extremely painful. But the prospect of rejection is all the more painful, because avoidant patients view others' negative reactions as justified. They interpret rejection in a very personal manner, as being caused solely by their personal deficiencies: "He rejected me because I'm inadequate," "If he thinks I'm unintelligent [unattractive, etc.], it must be true." The attributions are generated by their negative self-schemas and, in turn, reinforce these dysfunctional beliefs, leaving patients feeling all the more inadequate and hopeless. So they seek to avoid the dysphoria produced by predictions of rejection and attributions of self-inadequacy by avoiding relationships.

Self-Criticism

Avoidant patients often have a string of self-critical automatic thoughts, both when they are in social situations and when they are contemplating future encounters. These thoughts produce dysphoria, but are rarely evaluated, as patients assume them to be accurate. They arise from the negative schemas described previously. Typical negative cognitions are "I'm unattractive," "I'm boring," "I'm stupid," "I'm a loser," "I'm pathetic," "I don't fit in."

In addition, both before and during social encounters, the avoidant patient has a stream of automatic thoughts that predicts—in a negative direction—what will happen: "I don't have anything to say," "I'll make a fool of myself," "He won't like me," "He'll criticize me." Patients initially may or may not be fully cognizant of these thoughts. They may primarily be aware of the dysphoria that these thoughts evoke. Even when they do recognize their cognitions, they accept them as valid, without testing them to determine whether they are perceiving themselves and others accurately. Their method of coping with the dysphoria is avoidance. They actively avoid situations that they believe may engender negative cognitions and dysphoria.

Underlying Assumptions about Relationships

Avoidant patients' schemas also give rise to dysfunctional assumptions about relationships. They may believe that they are basically unlikable, but that if they can hide their true selves they may be able to deceive others, at least a little or for a while. They believe they can't let anyone get close enough to discover what they "know" to be true about themselves—that they are inadequate, different, and so on. Typical underlying assumptions are as follows: "I must put on a facade for others to like me," "If others really knew me, they wouldn't like me," "Once they get to know me, they'll see I'm really inferior," "It's dangerous for people to get too close and to see the real me."

When they do establish a relationship with someone, avoidant patients make assumptions about what they must do to preserve the friendship. They may go overboard to avoid confrontation and may be quite unassertive. Typical assumptions are as follows: "I must please her all the time," "He'll like me only if I do whatever he wants," "I can't say no." They may feel as if they're constantly on the brink of rejection: "If I make a mistake, he'll change his whole view of me in a negative direction," "If I displease him in any way, he'll end our friendship," "He'll notice any imperfection in me and reject me."

Misevaluation of Others' Reactions

Avoidant patients have difficulty evaluating others' reactions. They may misread a neutral or positive reaction as a negative one. They may look for positive reactions from people whose opinions are irrelevant to their lives, such as store clerks or bus drivers. It is very important to them that no one think badly of them, because of this belief: "If anyone judges me negatively, the criticism must be true." It seems dangerous for them to be in a position where they can be evaluated, because negative or even neutral reactions of other people confirm their belief that they are unlikable or defective. They don't have inner criteria with which to judge themselves in a positive manner; instead, they rely solely on their perception of others' judgments.

Discounting Positive Data

Even when faced with evidence, incontrovertible to others, that they are accepted or liked, avoidant patients discount it. They believe that they have deceived the other person, his or her judgment is faulty, or he or she has inadequate information with which to view them clearly. Typical automatic thoughts are these: "He thinks I'm smart but I've just fooled him," "If she really knew me, she wouldn't like me," "He's bound to find out I'm really not very nice."

Case Example

Jane exemplified just such a patient. She was raised by an alcoholic mother who had borderline personality disorder and who abused her verbally and physically. As a child, she made sense of her mother's abusive treatment by believing that she (Jane) must be an intrinsically unworthy person to be treated so badly. She couldn't even explain away the abuse by accounting for it by her own bad behavior; in fact, she was an extremely well-behaved child who tried desperately to please her mother. Therefore, Jane concluded that her mother treated her so badly because she (Jane) was bad at heart. (She never thought to attribute her mother's behavior to problems within her mother.) As an adult in her late 20's, Jane still expected to be rejected when others found out that she was inherently unworthy and bad.

Jane had a host of automatic thoughts before every social encounter. She was highly self-critical and predicted that she would not be accepted. She thought that people would not like her, that they would see she was a loser, and that she would not have anything to say. It was very important to Jane that everyone she met should respond to her positively. She became upset if she perceived that someone in even the most fleeting encounter was reacting negatively or neutrally. If a newspaper vendor failed to smile at her, or a sales clerk was slightly curt, Jane automatically thought it must be because she (Jane) was somehow unworthy or unlikable. She then felt quite sad. Even when she was receiving positive feedback from a friend, she discounted it. She believed she was putting on a facade, and her friend would cut off the relationship as soon as she discovered what Jane was really like. As a result, Jane had few friends and certainly no close ones.

Cognitive, Behavioral, and Emotional Avoidance

In addition to social avoidance, most avoidant patients also demonstrate cognitive, behavioral, and emotional avoidance. They avoid *thinking* about matters that produce dysphoria, and act in ways that permit them to continue this avoidance. A typical pattern emerges:

Avoidant patients become aware of a dysphoric feeling. (They may or may not be fully aware of the thoughts that precede or accompany the emotion.) Their tolerance for the dysphoria is low, so they take a "fix" to distract themselves and make them feel better. They may discontinue a task or fail to initiate a task they had planned to do. They may turn on the television, pick up something to read, reach for food or a cigarette, get up and walk around, and so forth. In short, they seek a diversion in order to push the uncomfortable thoughts out of mind. This pattern of cognitive and behavioral avoidance, having been reinforced by a reduction of dysphoria, eventually becomes ingrained and automatic.

Patients are aware, to some extent at least, of their behavioral avoidance. They invariably criticize themselves in global, stable terms: "I'm lazy," "I'm resistant," "I'm passive-aggressive." Such pronouncements reinforce beliefs about being inadequate or defective and lead to hopelessness. Patients don't see that their avoidance is their way of coping with uncomfortable emotions. They generally are not aware of their cognitive and behavioral avoidance until such a pattern is made clear to them.

Attitudes about Experiencing Dysphoria

Avoidant patients may have certain dysfunctional attitudes toward experiencing dysphoric emotions: "It's bad to feel bad," "I shouldn't have to feel anxious," "I should always feel good," "Other people rarely feel scared or embarrassed or bad." Avoidant patients believe that if they allow themselves to feel dysphoric, they will be engulfed by the feeling and will never be able to recover: "If I let my feelings get unbottled, I'll be overwhelmed," "If I start feeling a little bit anxious, I'll go to my worst point," "If I start feeling down, it'll get out of control and I won't be able to function." Unlike anorexics, who fear the behavioral consequences of losing control (eating too much), avoidant patients fear the overwhelming emotion they expect to feel if they lose control. They are afraid they'll be bogged down in dysphoria and will always feel bad.

Excuses and Rationalizations

Avoidant patients have a strong desire to reach their long-term goal of establishing closer relationships. In this respect, they differ from schizoid patients, for whom a lack of intimacy with others is ego-syntonic. Avoidant patients feel empty and lonely and want to change their lives, to make closer friends, to get a better job, and so on. They generally are aware of what they must do to realize their desires, but the short-term cost of experiencing negative emotions seems too high. They make a myriad of excuses for not doing what is necessary for them to do to reach their goals: "I won't enjoy doing it," "I'll be too tired," "I'll feel worse [more anxious, bored, etc.] if I do it," "I'll do it later," "I don't feel like doing it now." When "later" comes, they invariably use the same excuses, continuing their behavioral avoidance. In addition, avoidant patients may not really believe that they are capable of reaching their goals. They make certain assumptions: "There's nothing I can do to change my situation," "What's the use of trying? I won't be able to do it anyway," "It's better to lose by default than to try and inevitably lose."

Wishful Thinking

Avoidant patients may engage in wishful thinking about their future. They may believe that one day the perfect relationship or perfect job will arise from the blue, with no effort on their part. In fact, they often don't believe they will be able to reach their goals through their own efforts: "One day I'll wake up and everything will be fine," "I can't improve my life by myself," "Things may get better, but it won't be my doing." Here avoidant patients differ from obsessive patients, who don't really believe they will ever emerge from their difficulties.

Case Example

Jane, the patient described earlier, worked at a level below her capabilities. Yet she avoided taking the steps that could result in a better position: talking to her boss about a promotion, investigating other job opportunities, circulating her resumé. She continually clung to the hope that something would happen to propel her out of her current situation. Attitudes such as these carried over to therapy, too. Jane expected that her therapist would "cure" her with little or no effort on Jane's part. In fact, Jane believed that the "cure" had to come from the outside, since she was completely ineffectual in making changes herself.

Conceptualization Summary

Avoidant patients thus hold deep-seated negative beliefs about themselves, probably stemming from childhood, when interactions with a rejecting, critical significant person led them to view themselves as inadequate and worthless. Socially, they avoid situations in which other people could get close and discover the "real" them. Behaviorally, they avoid tasks that would engender thoughts that make them feel uncomfortable. Cognitively, they avoid thinking about matters that produce dysphoria. Their tolerance for discomfort is quite low, and they rely on distracting "fixes" whenever they begin to feel anxious, sad, or bored. They are unhappy with their current state of affairs, but feel incapable of changing through their own efforts.

Treatment Approaches

Trust Issues

As with most patients with personality disorders, the therapy relationship with the APD patient itself provides a fertile testing arena for dysfunctional thoughts, assumptions, and schemas. Unlike some personality disorder patients (e.g., borderline, paranoid) with whom the issues of trust center on fear of harm from the therapist, avoidant patients distrust the therapist's genuine caring and fear rejection. They often have a host of negative cognitions about the therapy relationship, just as they do about their other relationships. The process of identifying and testing these dysfunctional thoughts during therapy can serve as a model for doing so in other relationships as well.

Even when avoidant patients are aware of their automatic thoughts about the therapist or their relationship, they are usually unwilling at first to reveal them. They often infer criticism ("You must think I didn't do the homework very well") and disapproval ("You must be disgusted when I cry like this"). Avoidant patients may also discount the therapist's direct expression of approval or caring: "You like me only because you're a therapist and you're trained to like everybody," or "You may think now that I'm OK, but if I told you about my relationship with my mother, you'd dislike me."

These automatic thoughts may be elicited when patients display a change of affect ("What is running through your mind right now?"), in the midst of a discussion ("Are you predicting what you think I must be feeling or thinking now?"), or toward the end of a session ("Were you aware of doing any mind reading during our session today? . . . How about when we discussed your difficulty completing today's assignment?").

Once elicited, the automatic thoughts can be evaluated in several ways. Initially, the therapist can tell patients directly what he or she was thinking, and help them discover patterns of thinking errors they may be committing with other people as well. It is helpful for patients to rate how much they believe the therapist's feedback (using a 0–100% scale), and to monitor changes in their degree of belief as their trust in the therapist grows. After several such direct expressions, patients can be encouraged to evaluate their negative cognitions about the therapy relationship in light of these past experiences with the therapist ("Do you remember how I reacted the last time you didn't complete the assignment?"). Patients can also test out their automatic thoughts by engaging in small experiments. As the following example demonstrates, patients might be asked to relate part of some event they are sure the therapist will find unacceptable and to evaluate the validity of this belief in small stages.

One patient felt certain that the therapist would feel disgusted because she had begun an extramarital affair. This therapy excerpt demonstrates how the therapist worked with the automatic thought, and then shifted the discussion to identifying and evaluating the patient's assumption about the therapeutic relationship.

PATIENT: I can't tell you this part.

THERAPIST: What do you think will happen if you tell?

PATIENT: You won't want to see me any more.

THERAPIST: And if you don't tell me, what will you think?

PATIENT: I'll think you care about me only because you don't know this bad thing about me.

THERAPIST: Can you think of any other possible responses I might have? [Patient and therapist explore this for a few minutes; patient decides, based on history, that the therapist may have a reaction other than rejection, although this is hard for her to imagine. They agree that she will test this out by revealing the information in small steps.]

PATIENT: Well, you know I've been unhappy in my marriage.

THERAPIST: Yes.

PATIENT: Well, I enjoy spending time with Mark at work more than time with my husband.

THERAPIST: Tell me about what you enjoy about the time with Mark. [In small steps, the patient reveals her affair and then bursts into tears.]

PATIENT: So now you see I'm not the good person you thought I was.

THERAPIST: So you are convinced I'm seeing your relationship with Mark in absolute terms of your being a good or bad person?

PATIENT: (*Pause*) Yes, aren't you? (*Sobbing quiets down*)

THERAPIST: Well, that would be one way of seeing it. Is that how you see it?

PATIENT: Yes, of course.

THERAPIST: Have you ever had a friend who had an affair?

PATIENT: (*Pause*) Yes, my friend Ann.

THERAPIST: And did you evaluate it solely in moral terms?

PATIENT: No. I guess I could understand why she did it. She was so unhappy.

In this example and the dialogue that continued, the therapist was able to help this patient recognize that her thinking about the affair was dichotomous and that she expected this same type of thinking from the therapist. By helping the patient recall her reactions to a friend's similar behavior, the therapist guided the patient to a view that such behavior was complex. The patient was able to recall that she continued caring for Ann, even though she thought Ann's affair might not have been the best thing for her friend to do with her unhappiness. Therefore, it was possible that the therapist could continue to care for her, whether the therapist thought the affair was wise or not.

At the end of the session, the therapist pointed out a similar theme in an earlier session, during which they had uncovered a "rule" in her family of origin that "Defying convention leads to rejection." She was able to see that some people might reject her for having an affair and others would not.

Because avoidant patients are reluctant to relate things that they believe may lead the therapist to think badly of them, it is important for the therapist to ask occasionally if indeed the patients have been afraid to reveal something. Unless these patients do express these suppressed topics, they may continue to believe that the therapist would reject them (or, at the very least, view them negatively) if this piece of information were known, as the following example illustrates:

THERAPIST: We've gotten to know each other a lot better since our first session. Is there anything you've been afraid to tell me?
PATIENT: I'm not sure.
THERAPIST: Sometimes patients are afraid to tell their therapist something, especially if they think it'll put them in a bad light. Could that be true for you?
PATIENT: Yes. There is something. But I don't want to tell you.
THERAPIST: How are you predicting I'll react?
PATIENT: You'll think I'm terrible.

The therapist and patient then discussed alternative reactions, based on past experience in their therapeutic relationship. The patient revealed a pattern of childhood sexual abuse, the therapist related her true reaction, and together they examined how the patient's initial fear was unfounded.

Avoidant patients often assume that once they establish a relationship, they must continually try to please the other person. They believe that if they assert their own desires, the other person is bound to sever the relationship. In therapy this can lead to extreme compliance and an unwillingness to give the therapist negative feedback.

One way to encourage patient assertiveness in therapy is the use of a therapist feedback form at the end of sessions. Patients can rate the therapist on a checklist of qualities including process (e.g., "The therapist listened well and seemed to understand me today") and content (e.g., "The therapist explained the homework clearly enough"). In the next session the therapist can review the ratings and discuss relatively low ratings. By taking a nondefensive stance and discussing possible changes in session content and process, the therapist can reward patients for assertive criticism, correct legitimate dissatisfactions, and demonstrate the change potential of relationships. Later, patients can be encouraged to give more direct verbal feedback. Experiments can be designed for practicing assertiveness within other relationships. Role-playing assignments and guided-imagery practice are very helpful prior to *in vivo* assertiveness.

Specific Interventions

Standard cognitive therapy approaches (Beck, Rush, Shaw, & Emery, 1979; Beck & Emery with Greenberg, 1985) can be used with these patients to help them manage depression, anxiety, panic attacks, phobias, and insomnia. Socratic methods and standard written behavioral techniques for testing automatic thoughts and underlying assumptions can help them begin to counter self-criticism, negative predictions, maladaptive assumptions about relationships, and misevaluations of others' reactions.

Special techniques, outlined below, can help APD patients overcome the cognitive and emotional avoidance that otherwise may hamper these standard approaches.

Overcoming Cognitive and Emotional Avoidance

Although patients with APD experience a range of dysphoric moods, it is not desirable or possible simply to teach them to eliminate depression and anxiety. One of the complications that could interfere with standard cognitive therapy treatment is that these patients avoid thinking about things that cause unpleasant emotions. They also, as described above, have many negative assumptions about experiencing negative emotions. Since cognitive therapy *requires* a patient to experience such emotions and to record the thoughts and images accompanying various emotional experiences, this cognitive and emotional avoidance can prove a serious impediment to treatment.

Avoidant patients not only avoid experiencing negative emotions between sessions (e.g., they often fail to start or complete therapy assignments), but also avoid feeling dysphoric during therapy sessions (e.g., they may fail to report negative thoughts or change the subject). It is desirable to diagram the process of avoidance so that patients can examine how the avoidance operates and how they can intervene to stop it. A typical example is shown in Figure 12.1; patients should be encouraged to discover similar patterns on a daily basis. It is helpful, when applicable, to reframe patients' notions of themselves as "lazy" or "resistant" (qualities that may appear more difficult to modify). Rather, in evaluating themselves in light of the figure, they can see that they avoid situations in which they have automatic thoughts that engender dysphoria. Together therapist and patient can evaluate these negative cognitions and increase the patient's tolerance for negative emotion.

Before embarking on the process of increasing such tolerance, it is helpful to provide a rationale. Through Socratic questioning, patients can confirm the disadvantages of avoidance, such as the improbability of their reaching their goals and the likelihood that positive emotions, like negative emotions, can't be fully experienced. If applicable, the therapist and patient can explore the origin of the avoidance of dysphoria. Often such avoidance was initiated in childhood, when a patient may indeed have been more vulnerable and less able to cope with unpleasant feelings.

One of the best ways to begin increasing emotional tolerance is to evoke emotions in the session by discussing experiences about which patients report discomfort. As they begin to react strongly, some cognitive avoidance may be initiated (e.g., patients may change the topic, get

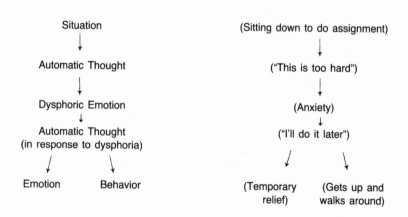

FIGURE 12.1   The process of avoidance: An example.

up and walk around, or experience their minds "going blank"). The therapist can direct them back to the feelings in order to begin to identify and test the beliefs leading to the avoidance. A therapy excerpt (Padesky & Beck, 1988, p. 124) illustrates this process.

PATIENT: (*In the middle of an imagery exercise*) I don't want to talk about this anymore.
THERAPIST: What are you feeling right now?
PATIENT: Depressed . . . and scared—real scared.
THERAPIST: What do you think will happen if you keep feeling this way?
PATIENT: I'll freak out—go crazy. You'll see just what a basket case I am.
THERAPIST: As we've discussed before, these feelings you avoid may lead to some useful information. Try staying with them for now. Continue imagining yourself talking to your husband about your unhappiness. Tell me what happens. (*Long pause*)
PATIENT: (*Sobbing*) He's going to leave me. I'm a rotten person for making him so unhappy. Now my children will be destroyed and it's all my fault.

In this portion of the session, the therapist helped the patient become aware of and "stay with" her distressing thoughts and images. At the same time, she was able to test out her belief that she would "go crazy" and get out of control if she allowed herself to experience strong emotions. The therapist reminded her of this prediction and allowed the patient time to reflect on how she did experience strong emotions but never really got "out of control."

Repeated experiences like this one may be necessary to build tolerance for dysphoria and to erode patients' dysfunctional beliefs about experiencing uncomfortable emotions. To desensitize patients, a hierarchy may be constructed that outlines increasingly painful topics to be discussed in therapy. The therapist can elicit patients' predictions of what they fear will happen before they discuss each succeeding topic, test out the predictions, and accumulate evidence to contradict their faulty beliefs (e.g., "It'll be too painful to discuss," "If I start feeling bad, I'll never get out of the feeling," etc.). Patients can also construct hierarchies for assignments outside of therapy to increase tolerance for negative emotions. Such assignments can be labeled "dysphoria practice" or "antiavoidance activities." They may involve initiating certain behaviors ("Work on your thesis for 30 minutes without a break") or structured reflection ("Think about telling your boss you want more time off"). Again, it is helpful for patients to predict what they fear will happen if they engage in an assigned activity, and to test out and modify these ideas.

Avoidant patients often have difficulty identifying their automatic thoughts for homework (or even in the therapy session itself). Usually, asking patients to imagine and minutely describe a situation as if it were happening right then in the session helps identify thoughts. A second technique, if applicable, involves role play: Patients play themselves, and the therapist takes on the part of the other person involved in a specific situation. While re-enacting an upsetting situation, patients are instructed to capture their automatic thoughts. If these more standard techniques are unsuccessful, the therapist can compile a checklist of hypothesized thoughts, based on a specific patient's previously identified thoughts and beliefs and on the therapist's conceptualization of the patient. Patients can be instructed to review the checklist, trying to confirm what their thoughts had been in the situation. They can also use the checklist in the future to identify cognitions while still in a distressing situation.

For patients who are able to identify their thoughts but fail to do homework assignments, it may be useful to use imagery for homework rehearsal and planning, as the following example illustrates:

THERAPIST: We've agreed that you're going to go to the library at noon tomorrow to work on the literature review for your thesis. I'd like you to take a minute to imagine yourself a few minutes before noon and see if there's anything that might get in the way of your doing that.

PATIENT: (*Pause*) OK. I'm in my apartment, getting my books ready, and I think, "I'll go later."

THERAPIST: And how are you going to answer that thought?

PATIENT: I don't know. I probably won't answer it. I'll probably just put my books down and not go.

THERAPIST: Will not going help you fulfill your goal of completing your thesis?

PATIENT: No.

THERAPIST: What could you do or say to make it more likely that you will go?

PATIENT: I could read the card we wrote today that reminds me that every time I avoid I strengthen my dysfunctional habits, and every time I follow through with my plans, I strengthen my new, better habits.

THERAPIST: OK. Imagine yourself starting to put down your books and then picking up the card. What happens next?

[Patient keeps describing process of starting and completing work, with predicted interference of specific automatic thoughts. Together they devise rational responses to each thought.]

If necessary, the therapist can employ a point-counterpoint approach at this time. First, patients argue with their "emotional" voice why they don't have to undertake the assignment, while the therapist answers with (and models) an "antiavoidance" voice. Then they switch roles so the patients have practice using the antiavoidance responses. Finally, patients may write down their predicted automatic thoughts on index cards, with the antiavoidance responses in their own words on the back. They may read these cards daily—especially before undertaking an assignment that they are likely to avoid.

The experiences in and between therapy sessions such as those described above will aid patients in identifying dysphoric thoughts and tolerating negative feelings. As such tolerance grows, they may begin to change in the way they relate to family members (e.g., they may become more assertive). They also may experience more intense sadness, fear, or anger as they bring into awareness memories and reactions they have avoided for so many years. At this point, it is helpful to teach them cognitive and behavioral approaches to manage these moods.

The therapist can point out that even though the patient now understands the importance of negative feelings and is willing to tolerate them, it is not necessary or desirable to experience intense feelings all the time. Patients can be instructed to keep diaries of feelings and thoughts when they occur, and then to use cognitive restructuring to correct distortions. If they have not yet learned cognitive restructuring methods for evaluating and correcting distorted beliefs, they can use distraction after writing the thoughts and feelings, and can then bring the diary to therapy for assistance in testing out their thoughts.

At this point, it may also be helpful to do couple or family therapy if the patient is in a relationship or living with parents. Therapy sessions can provide a "safe" forum for patients to test the validity of relevant beliefs and thoughts. One patient, for example, feared that her husband had been angry at her for some time because she didn't work outside the house. In one of their marital sessions, the therapist encouraged her to bring up this question. She did so, thereby learning that her assumption had been incorrect. In the course of the marital session, her husband revealed other situations that did distress him; their difficulties were then resolved through joint problem solving.

Couple or family therapy may also be indicated when avoidant patterns are supported by the patient's social system. For example, the husband of another patient had his own negative assumptions about the expression of emotion ("Expressing feelings leads to conflict and irreparable harm"). Therapy with the family can help deal with dysfunctional assumptions held by family members, and can provide a forum for teaching constructive skills for communication and problem solving (e.g., Beck, 1988).

Skill Building

Sometimes patients with APD have skill deficits because of their impoverished social experiences. In these cases, skill-training exercises should be included in the therapy, so that the patients will have a reasonable chance of success in social interactions designed to test dysfunctional beliefs.

For some, social skills training will begin with nonverbal cues (e.g., eye contact, posture, and smiling). These can be practiced in therapy sessions, at home, and then in low-risk social situations. Some patients with meager social experience may need educational information to evaluate their experiences more accurately (e.g., "If you wait until the last minute on weekends to make plans, most people will already be busy"). More advanced social skills training may include instruction regarding conversational methods, assertiveness, sexuality, and conflict management. Patients' negative beliefs about themselves may create obstacles to trying out newly developed skills. They may need to be encouraged to act "as if" they possessed a certain quality. For example, one patient had the thought, "I won't be able to make small talk at the cocktail party. I'm not confident enough." The patient was encouraged to act as if she were confident; indeed, she discovered that she could appropriately engage in conversation. During behavioral skills training, it is critical to elicit automatic thoughts, especially ones in which patients disqualify their progress or the training itself: "These exercises are teaching me to fool people so they don't see my inadequacy," "Only a real loser has to learn how to talk at this age." Therapist and patient can then work together to test the validity and utility of these beliefs.

Identifying and Testing Maladaptive Schemas

A major portion of the therapy involves helping patients identify and test the cognitive underpinnings of their avoidant patterns. To do this, the therapist and patient first gain an understanding of the developmental roots of the negative schemas. Next, these schemas are tested through predictive experiments, guided observation, and role-play re-enactments of early schema-related incidents. Finally, patients are directed to begin to notice and remember counterschematic data about themselves and their social experiences. A case example illustrates these points.

At age 24, Peter had no dating experience and no friends other than his brother. After nearly a year of therapy in which Peter learned to do cognitive restructuring, gained basic social skills, and even succeeded in beginning a steady relationship with a woman he met at work, Peter still clung to the negative schema "I'm unlikable."

The therapist and Peter agreed to focus on testing the validity of this belief, since it seemed to be the core theme of his negative automatic thoughts. First, the therapist helped Peter understand and review the developmental origins of this schema. He had believed he was unlikable as long as he could remember, and his abusive father underscored this conclusion by frequently yelling at him, "You're a no-good son. I wish you were never born! There's nothing I like about you!"

One powerful method that can be used when a patient recalls such vivid childhood scenes is a dyadic psychodrama. First, Peter played himself and the therapist acted as the parent. Peter was asked to re-experience his childhood feelings as if he were 4 years old, and then to describe the experience to the therapist. Next, Peter was asked to act as the parent, and the therapist played the part of 4-year-old Peter. Again, Peter related his emotional and cognitive experience.

In this case, Peter was able to empathize with his father and recognize his father's depression and frustration at being unemployed with three small children to support. For the first time, Peter realized that his father was feeling anger at himself rather than Peter. With tears in his eyes, Peter reported, "My dad had been beaten by his father, and he didn't know how to love."

Once Peter had greater understanding of the whole situation, he was able to speculate that he might not have been quite so unlikable as his father had implied. A third psychodrama allowed Peter to "try on" this new viewpoint. The therapist and Peter first discussed how a less depressed and angry adult might have comforted young Peter and countered his dad's assault. The therapist asked Peter to think of his neighbor's 5-year- old son in recalling how young children act and their level of responsibility for family problems. Then Peter was instructed to play 4-year-old Peter again; however, this time he would assertively defend himself:

FATHER: [Played by therapist] You're a no-good son! I wish you were never born! I don't like anything about you!

PETER: Don't say that, Daddy. Why are you so angry?

FATHER: I'm angry because you're such a bad son!

PETER: What did I do that was so bad?

FATHER: You make noise all day. You're a worry—just one more mouth to feed.

PETER: (*Silent—then, after prompting by therapist:*) Are you worried about money?

FATHER: Yes. I get so mad because no one will hire me. You'd think I was a good-for-nothing.

PETER: That's what you say I am. I wish you'd get mad at the people who won't hire you instead of me.

FATHER: I do. But I can't tell them. And you're here all day under foot.

PETER: I'm just playing like 4-year-olds do.

FATHER: That makes me mad. I don't get to enjoy *my* life.

PETER: I'm really sorry, Dad. I wish you did so you'd be happier. Then you wouldn't yell at me so much.

FATHER: I guess I do yell at you because I'm unhappy.

Once Peter understood that his father's invective stemmed from his father's personal unhappiness, rather than representing valid judgments of young Peter, he was able to consider that perhaps his belief that he was totally unlikable warranted closer examination. At this point, Peter and his therapist began a historical test of his schema (Young, 1984).

Using one page for every few years of his life, Peter and the therapist gathered historical evidence for and against the proposition that Peter was totally unlikable. Peter predicted that if this schema were true, there would be few items in the "evidence against" column and an increasing number of facts in the "evidence for" column as he grew older.

In fact, Peter discovered that evidence for his likability was much greater than he imagined (e.g., he had friends in grammar school, people at work were friendly toward him, his girlfriend told him she loved him). Also, the balance tipped toward likability after he left home and began therapy. He began to understand how his depression in college had isolated him and led to few opportunities for people to know him. His therapist also helped him find alternative explanations for the evidence that seemed to support his unlikability schema.

A historical review of a negative schema does not remove the power of a schema, even with strong evidence such as in Peter's case. Since Peter had lived his entire life interpreting (and misinterpreting) experiences to support his schema, he had no "likable" schema to replace the "unlikable" schema. The final stage of therapy, therefore, involved helping Peter construct and validate a more positive schema: "I am likable—at least to some people."

Some helpful techniques at this stage of therapy were prediction logs, positive-experience logs, and imagery rehearsal of new behaviors. In prediction logs, Peter recorded his outcome expectations for different social experiences (e.g., "I'll invite 10 people to the party and none will want to come") and actual outcomes ("Eight people accepted the invitation"). These helped Peter see that his negative schema did not predict his current experiences well.

In addition, Peter kept a list of social interactions that supported the new likability schema. This positive-experience log required Peter to shift his attention from rejection experiences to ones involving acceptance or social enjoyment. When he became self-critical, and the negative schema was activated, he reviewed this positive-experience log to help reactivate the more positive schema.

Finally, as Peter began changing his beliefs about his likability, he became willing to enter more social situations (e.g., inviting a few people to dinner, arranging a bigger party, asking additional women for dates). He prepared for these new experiences through imagery rehearsal with his therapist. In imagery, he would live through the experiences and report to the therapist any difficulties or embarrassment encountered. They would then discuss possible solutions to these social dilemmas, and Peter would rehearse the desired behavior and conversations in imagery before *in vivo* practice.

Treatment Summary

Treatment of APD patients involves the establishment of a trusting patient-therapist alliance, fostered by the identification and modification of patients' dysfunctional thoughts and beliefs about this relationship. This therapeutic relationship can serve as a model for patients to question their beliefs about their other relationships; it can also provide a safe environment to try out new behaviors (such as assertiveness) with others. Mood management techniques are employed to teach patients to manage their depression, anxiety, or other disorders.

The goal is not to eliminate dysphoria altogether, but to increase patients' tolerance for negative emotion. A schematic diagram to illustrate the process of avoidance, and a strong rationale for increasing dysphoria tolerance, help patients agree to experience negative feelings in the session—a strategy that may be implemented in hierarchical fashion. Tolerance of negative affect within sessions may have to precede such "dysphoria" or "antiavoidance" practice outside of therapy. An important key to increasing tolerance is the continual disconfirmation of beliefs concerning what patients fear will happen if they experience dysphoria.

Couple or family therapy may be indicated, as well as social skills training. Finally, treatment also encompasses the identification and modification of maladaptive schemas through interventions involving imagery, psychodrama, historical review, and prediction logs. More positive schemas may have to be constructed and validated through a variety of techniques, such as those described above.

Relapse Prevention

The final phase of therapy involves relapse prevention. It is essential to predict and plan for relapse, since patients with an APD can easily become avoidant again. Relapse prevention involves work in both the behavioral and cognitive realms. Ongoing behavioral goals often include activities such as the following:

Establishing new friendships
Deepening existing relationships
Taking on more responsibility at work, or changing jobs
Acting in an appropriately assertive way with family, friends, co-
workers, and others
Tackling previously avoided tasks at work, school, or home
Trying new experiences: taking a class, pursuing a new hobby,
volunteering, and so on

These goals may feel risky to the patient; even thinking about trying one might engender considerable distress. The therapist can frame the anxiety in a positive way: The emergence of anxiety signals the reactivation of a dysfunctional attitude that needs attention, just as a recurrent fever may signal a need for more medication. The therapist can teach the patient to use the anxiety as a spur to look for automatic thoughts that interfere with the ability to achieve goals. Together they can devise a system for the patient to respond to these negative cognitions and attitudes after therapy is terminated.

It is important for patients to attenuate their residual dysfunctional attitudes, and to strengthen their new, more functional beliefs. On a daily or weekly basis, they should review the evidence against the old beliefs and the evidence supporting the new ones. One way to achieve this goal is to encourage patients to keep a daily log in which they record their experiences, both positive and negative, during the period when these beliefs are active. They then develop arguments to undermine the dysfunctional belief and to strengthen the functional belief.

Two typical entries in one patient's log were as follows:

9/27—Attended a meeting with my boss and the lawyers. Made a
suggestion without being asked. It was well received. This is
evidence against my old belief that I'm stupid and incompetent.
This is evidence for my belief that I am competent.

10/1—Howard got irritated when I said I didn't want to go out to
dinner. I felt bad and thought, "I shouldn't have said that."
According to my old belief, I would have considered myself
bad—I'm bad if I make others upset. According to my new belief,
I'm not bad. It's inevitable that other people are going to get
upset sometimes, and it has nothing to do with my worth as a
person. It's undesirable to always put others first. It's good to
assert my desires, too.

It is particularly important for patients to remain vigilant of situations they are avoiding, and to become aware of cognitions that foster the avoidance. They can use either the kind of log described above, or a Dysfunctional Thought Record to uncover dysfunctional attitudes behind the desire for avoidance and to develop or strengthen more functional attitudes. One of this same patient's typical avoidance entries was as follows:

10/24—Thinking about asking boss for time off. Feeling very anxious.
A.T. [automatic thought]: "He'll get mad at me."
Dysfunctional attitude: It's terrible for people to get mad.
Functional attitude: It's OK if he gets mad. He may not even get mad, but even if he does, he won't be mad forever. This is good practice for me to act assertively. I'll never get what I want if I let my attitude get in the way. The worst that will happen is he'll say no.

A belief that is particularly troublesome to the avoidant patient is this: "If people really knew me, they'd reject me." This belief is likely to be activated as patients begin to develop new relationships and to reveal more of themselves to others. If relevant, it is often helpful for patients to review their initial fears of revealing themselves to their therapist and to trace what actually happened when they eventually did so. Then they can experiment by disclosing to someone else a relatively "safe" but previously unrevealed statement about themselves and examining what transpires. They can continue to do so in a hierarchical fashion, gradually disclosing more about themselves to others.

In addition to daily logs and Dysfunctional Thought Records, daily or weekly review of specially prepared index cards is also helpful. Patients record a troublesome dysfunctional attitude on one side of a card, with evidence against it beneath. On the other side is the more functional attitude with supportive evidence. Patients can rate their degree of belief in each attitude on a regular basis. A significantly increased degree of belief for a dysfunctional attitude, or a significantly decreased degree of belief for the new attitude, indicates that patients need to work in that area.

Toward the end of therapy, the therapist should take care to assess the benefits of spacing out sessions. Avoidant patients often need encouragement to experiment with reducing the frequency of therapy sessions, taking more time to engage in new experiences between sessions and to test out their fears. On the other hand, some avoidant patients may desire and feel prepared to terminate, but may fear hurting the therapist's feelings by making such a suggestion.

Finally, it is helpful for therapists and avoidant patients jointly to develop a plan for the patients to continue therapy on their own when formal therapy is terminated. Patients might, for example, set aside an hour each week to do activities aimed at continuing the progress made in therapy. They can review homework they had assigned for themselves in their previous self-therapy session. They can look for any situations they avoided, investigating obstacles or ideas that interfered. They can look ahead to the coming week, predict which situations may be troublesome, and devise a way to deal with likely avoidance. They can review relevant notes or Dysfunctional Thought Records from therapy. And they can assign homework and schedule their next self-therapy session.

An important goal of relapse prevention is to predict likely difficulties in the period following termination. Once predicted, patients can be encouraged and guided to devise a plan to handle these troublesome situations. Patients may find it useful, for example, to compose paragraphs to address the following difficulties:

> What should I do if I find myself starting to avoid again?
> What should I do if I start believing my old dysfunctional assumptions more than my new beliefs?
> What should I do if I have a setback?

Review of these paragraphs at relevant times is also an important part of relapse prevention for avoidant patients.

Therapist Reactions

Therapists may experience considerable frustration with APD patients because progress is usually quite slow. In fact, it is often a challenge just to keep avoidant patients in therapy, since they may begin to avoid therapy, too, by cancelling appointments. It is helpful for the therapist to realize that the patients' avoidance of behavioral assignments, or of therapy itself, provides an opportunity to uncover the automatic thoughts and attitudes associated with the avoidance.

If such avoidance is present, the therapist (and patients, too) may begin to feel hopeless about therapy. It is important to anticipate and to undermine hopelessness by focusing on progress made in sessions. A functional way to deal with avoidance of homework assignments is to focus on the thoughts that interfered with undertaking or completing a task, so as to prepare patients to answer those thoughts in the future.

Typical therapist cognitions about the avoidant patient may include the following:

> "The patient isn't trying."
> "She won't let me help her."
> "I'll try really hard and she'll drop out of therapy anyway."
> "Our lack of progress reflects poorly on me."
> "Another therapist would do better."

The therapist thinking these types of thoughts may begin to feel helpless, unable to assist the patient in effecting significant change. When these beliefs occur, the therapist can test them by reviewing what has transpired in therapy. It is important to keep expectations for progress realistic and to recognize the achievement of small goals.

Finally, therapists need to distinguish between patients' rationalizations for avoidance and real obstacles before concluding that such avoidance is not amenable to change. Emily, for example, claimed that she couldn't resume classes at college because her mother, who had become disabled, depended on her. After the therapist and Emily evaluated the situation, it became apparent that her mother was somewhat functional, that alternative arrangements for her care were possible, and that Emily could return to school (at least on a part-time basis). It is likely that therapists who fail to confront avoidant patients' excuses will feel hopeless and helpless, as their patients do.

Future Directions for Research

Given the paucity of research on APD, there are many important avenues to explore. First, it is not known if there is a genetic vulnerability for developing APD. This chapter has described a number of social and cognitive factors that seem relevant in the developmental history of patients with this disorder. Research studies are needed to examine whether these interpersonal experiences and the concomitant beliefs held by patients are a critical part of the development of APD. Determination of etiology can be an important step toward developing programs to prevent or to identify and treat this disorder in children.

Only a few studies have been published on APD, and many of these are case descriptions of treatment with either medication (e.g., Daltito & Perugi, 1988) or psychodynamic therapy (e.g., Frances & Nemiah, 1983). No empirical studies have been reported on APD from a cognitive therapy perspective.

Social anxiety has been widely studied from a behavioral perspective (Oakley & Padesky, in press). While some of these studies (Greenberg & Stravynski, 1985) note the similarity between their patients' symptoms and APD, most behavioral studies of social anxiety do not describe their subjects in terms of DSM-III-R diagnostic categories. It cannot be presumed that these studies pertain to APD. In fact, a majority of those studied in social anxiety research probably meet the criteria for social phobia rather than a diagnosis of APD.

A notable exception has been the research of Turner and his associates (Turner, Beidel, Dancu, & Keys, 1986), who directly compared individuals with social phobia with those diagnosed with APD. All patients were asked to participate in a structured role-play test and in an impromptu speaking situation. Although the two groups reported equal levels of anxiety and similar anxious thoughts, those patients with a diagnosis of APD showed poorer social skills than those with social phobia on ratings of eye contact, voice tone, and overall social skills.

These findings should be considered tentative, since there were only 18 patients in the study (10 with social phobia, 8 with APD). However, this research is an important step toward an empirical examination of APD. The cognitive conceptualization of this condition suggests that researchers should assess negative self-schemas, in addition to the situational anxiety thoughts tapped in the study by Turner and his associates.

Conclusion

We have proposed that a cognitive formulation for APD is parsimonious, and that cognitive therapy can be efficacious. While we have noted clinical support for these conclusions, they need to be experimentally demonstrated. Since a number of patients with APD have benefitted from cognitive therapy as described here, outcome studies could be devised to compare cognitive therapy to other forms of treatment for this disorder. If cognitive therapy is found to be effective, further research to determine which dysfunctional attitudes are most central to the maintenance of APD could help strengthen and streamline the therapy. The conceptualization provided here suggests cognitive themes that are likely candidates for such research.

Chapter 13

Dependent Personality Disorder

Feelings of dependency and attachment are said to be universal, and perhaps defining, mammalian behaviors (Frances, 1988). While it clearly is adaptive for individuals to rely on others to some extent, excessive amounts of dependency can be quite problematic, and the extreme of dependency was defined in DSM-III as dependent personality disorder (DPD; APA, 1980). Treatment of DPD presents an interesting dilemma to the therapist. Initially, in therapy, these patients can seem deceptively simple to treat. They are so attentive and appreciative of the therapist's efforts that they provide a welcome relief in contrast to the many other patients who do not seem to listen to or respect what the therapist has to say. They are easy to engage in treatment, and are so cooperative at the beginning of therapy, that they create the expectation that progress in therapy will be quite rapid. However, this can serve to add to the therapist's frustration in the later stages of treatment, when these patients seem to cling to treatment, resisting the therapist's efforts to encourage them toward greater autonomy.

Hill (1970) summarizes some of the frustration of working with these patients by describing the initial improvement of the dependent patient: "The patient feels encouraged by having someone new showing an interest in her, meeting her dependency needs, and offering her a more rewarding life. . . . Invariably each patient has a setback when she realizes that therapy is not a passive experience" (p. 39). Helping the patient to move beyond dependence on the therapist, and encouraging him or her to move toward autonomy from both the therapist and other significant others, is the challenge of working with DPD.

Historical Review

Early descriptions of dependent individuals were often pejorative. In the writings of 19th-century psychiatrists, the passivity, ineffectuality, and excessive docility characteristic of these patients were seen as failures in moral development, and terms such as "shiftless," "weak-willed," and "degenerate" were used to describe these individuals. Although frequently observed, the overly dependent personality type was not given its own diagnosis in most early classification systems.

A very different view was taken by early psychoanalytic theorists. Both Freud and Abraham described their "oral-receptive" character as due to either overindulgence or deprivation in the oral or sucking stage of development. Abraham (1924/1948) stated: "Some people are dominated by the belief that there will always be some kind person—a representative of the mother, of course—to care for them and to give them everything they need. This optimistic belief condemns them to inactivity . . . they make no kind of effort, and in some cases they even disdain to undertake a bread-winning occupation" (pp. 399–400).

The forerunner to the diagnostic categorization of passive-aggressive and dependent personality types was the World War II category of "immaturity reactions," defined as a "neurotic type reaction to routine military stress, manifested by helplessness or inadequate responses, passiveness, obstructionism or aggressive outbursts" (Anderson, 1966, p. 756). Dependent personality was mentioned only briefly in DSM-I (APA, 1952) as the passive-dependent subtype of the passive-aggressive disorder, characterized by inappropriate clinging in the face of environmental frustration. The dependent personality was totally overlooked in DSM-II (APA, 1968), with the closest category being the inadequate personality disorder, described as characterized by "ineffectual responses to emotional, social, intellectual and physical demands. While the patient seems neither physically nor mentally deficient, he does manifest inadaptability, ineptness, poor judgment, social instability and lack of physical and emotional stamina" (p. 44).

Using the classic polarities of active-passive, pleasure-pain, and self-other as a basis, Millon (1969) derived a classification system producing eight basic personality types. The passive-dependent pattern (originally known as the Millon submissive personality) involves seeking pleasure and avoiding pain by looking passively to other people to provide reinforcement. This classification was expanded in several drafts by Millon into DPD as it first appeared in DSM-III (APA, 1980).

The contemporary psychodynamic conceptualization of DPD states that either overindulgence or deprivation can lead to excessive and maladaptive dependency resulting from fixation in the oral-sucking stage of development. In his study of maternal overprotection, Levy (1966) saw overindulgence as leading to overdependent traits such as demandingness, lack of initiative, and the insistence that others do for these individuals what they feel unable to do for themselves. In some cases, overdependence is seen as representing a regressive expression of a female's unsatisfied phallic longings, with the individual hoping that through a dependent attachment she will get the penis she believes is necessary for self-esteem (Esman, 1986). Esman (1986) stresses the prominence of latent and unconscious hostility toward the dependent individual's primary figures, with cloying sweetness and submissiveness seen as a reaction formation against the expression of hostile feelings that could threaten the existence of what is viewed as a vital relationship.

West and Sheldon (1988) view DPD as a clear example of a disorder of the attachment system, which has been most thoroughly discussed by Bowlby (1969, 1977). The attachment pattern most characteristic of DPD is the "anxiously attached" pattern, which Bowlby views as developing from experiences leading the individual to doubt the attachment figure's availability and responsiveness. When these individuals do establish relationships, they become excessively dependent upon, and live in constant anxiety over losing, this attachment figure.

Further work on attachment and dependency has been done by Pilkonis (1988). Pilkonis has used a modified prototype methodology to develop a differentiated view of the constructs of excessive dependency and excessive autonomy as perceived by clinicians experienced in the treatment of depression. Descriptors of excessive dependency cluster into two subtypes: indicators of "anxious attachment," and features typically associated with borderline personality disorder. The characteristics of the "anxious attachment" subtype (including items such as "tends to depend too much on other people," "rejection by another person leads to a loss of confidence and self-esteem," and "feelings of helplessness are common") seem to correspond most closely to the diagnosis of DPD.

Characteristics

According to DSM-III-R (APA, 1987, p. 354), the essential feature of DPD is "a pervasive pattern of dependent and submissive behavior, beginning by early adulthood and present in a variety of contexts" (see Table 13.1). These people are unable or unwilling to make everyday decisions unless they have an excessive amount of advice and reassurance from other people, and can concur with what other people suggest. They have difficulty initiating projects or doing things on their own, feeling so uncomfortable when alone that they go to great lengths to be with other people. They feel devastated and helpless when close relationships end, and tend to be preoccupied with fears of being abandoned. They are easily hurt by disapproval, tend to subordinate themselves to others, and will go to great lengths to get other people to like them. They are so fearful of rejection that they will agree with others

TABLE 13.1
DSM-III-R Criteria for Dependent Personality Disorder

A pervasive pattern of dependent and submissive behavior, beginning by early adulthood and present in a variety of contexts, as indicated by at least *five* of the following:

(1) is unable to make everyday decisions without an excessive amount of advice or reassurance from others

(2) allows others to make most of his or her important decisions, e.g., where to live, what job to take

(3) agrees with people even when he or she believes they are wrong, because of fear of being rejected

(4) has difficulty initiating projects or doing things on his or her own

(5) volunteers to do things that are unpleasant or demeaning in order to get other people to like him or her

(6) feels uncomfortable or helpless when alone, or goes to great lengths to avoid being alone

(7) feels devastated or helpless when close relationships end

(8) is frequently preoccupied with fear of being abandoned

(9) is easily hurt by criticism or disapproval

Note. From *Diagnostic and Statistical Manual of Mental Disorders* (3rd ed., rev., p. 354) by the American Psychiatric Association, 1987, Washington, DC: Author. Copyright 1987 by the American Psychiatric Association. Reprinted by permission.

even if they believe the other person is wrong. These individuals lack self-confidence, tending to discount any of their own abilities and strengths.

Depression is one of the most common presenting problems of DPD. In fact, major depression and adjustment disorder were the Axis I diagnoses found to be most frequently associated with DPD by Koenigsberg, Kaplan, Gilmore, and Cooper (1985). Using personality questionnaire criteria, Reich and Noyes (1987) found that 54% of their depressed subjects qualified for a diagnosis of DPD. Overholser, Kabakoff, and Norman (1989) point out that the criteria for DPD contain many traits commonly found in depression, including lack of initiative, feelings of helplessness, and difficulty making decisions. Because they rely excessively on other people for support and nurturance, and feel helpless in the face of potential abandonment, they appear to have an increased predisposition to depression (Birtchnell, 1984; Zuroff & Mongrain, 1987).

Anxiety disorders are also common among individuals with DPD. Since they count on other people for their survival, they are especially prone to separation anxiety and worry over being abandoned and left to fend for themselves. Panic attacks may occur as they anticipate and dread new responsibilities that they do not believe they can handle. Phobias tend to elicit care and protection, as well as enabling avoidance of responsibilities, providing secondary gains that are fully consonant with the individuals' basic dependent orientation (Millon, 1981). In their study of panic disorder patients, Reich, Noyes, and Troughton (1987) found DPD to be the most frequent Axis II diagnosis, especially in the subgroups with phobic avoidance. Depending on the instrument used, roughly 40% of the subjects with some phobic avoidance met criteria for DPD. In addition, in a sample of psychiatric inpatients, Overholser et al. (1989) found dependent patients to display MMPI profiles suggestive of anxiety, self-doubt, and social insecurity, regardless of their level of depression.

Other common presenting problems in individuals with DPD include somatic complaints, ranging from conversion symptoms to hypochondriasis and somatization disorder. In a study of 50 women who were classified as passive-dependent and seen as outpatients, Hill (1970) found that all the women reported somatic complaints, usually leading to a great deal of attention from family and professionals. Many of these patients looked to medications as their primary source of potential help. Greenberg and Dattore (1981) found that men who developed a physical disorder (cancer, benign tumors, hypertension, or gastrointestinal ulcers) had significantly higher premorbid scores on dependency-related MMPI scales than men who remained well over a 10-year period. Similarly, Vaillant (1978) and Hinkle (1961) found a relationship between dependent personality traits and a general predisposition to disease. In a recent review of the empirical literature, Greenberg and Bornstein (1988a) conclude that "an individual with a dependent personality orientation is clearly at risk for a variety of physical disorders, rather than being predisposed to exhibit one particular type of symptom" (p. 132). In addition, they conclude that dependent people are more apt to view their problems in somatic rather than psychological terms, are more likely to seek professional help for their problems, will tend to initiate help seeking earlier, and will follow through on treatment more conscientiously than will independent people.

Alcoholism and other substance abuse are also common presenting problems in dependent individuals, since these substances are often seen as an easy, passive way either to deal with their problems or at least to escape from them. In their review of the empirical literature (comprised primarily of ratings of oral dependency indications on projective tests), Greenberg and Bornstein (1988b) conclude that an individual with a dependent personality orientation is at risk for a variety of psychopathological conditions, including depression, alcoholism, obesity, and tobacco dependence.

Diagnosis

When an individual presents for treatment with low self-confidence and a clearly high need for reassurance, the diagnosis of DPD needs to be considered. For example, Karen was a 45-year-old married woman who was referred for treatment by her physician for problems with panic attacks. During the evaluation, she appeared to be very worried, sensitive, and naive. She was easily overcome with emotion and cried on and off throughout the session. She was self-critical at every opportunity throughout the evaluation. For example, when asked how she got along with other people, she reported that "others think I'm dumb and inadequate," although she could give no evidence as to what made her think that. She reported that she didn't like school because "I was dumb," and that she always felt that she was not good enough. She needed a great deal of reassurance from the therapist before she would even attempt to count backwards from 100 by 7's as part of a mental status examination. In addition to the panic attacks and avoidance, she reported being seriously depressed on and off for at least 5 years and having severe premenstrual syndrome. She reported drinking one to three shots of liquor daily, but she did not see that as a problem for her.

In diagnosing DPD, however, it is important to go beyond initial presentation and to assess carefully the patient's relationship history, particularly noting how he or she has responded to the ending of relationships and how other people have said that they perceive the patient. It can be helpful to ask carefully about how decisions are made, exploring everyday decisions as well as major ones. Information should also be gathered about how the patient feels about being alone for extended periods of time. In addition, it can be useful to ask how the patient handles situations where he or she disagrees with someone else or is asked to do something unpleasant or demeaning. The therapist's own reaction can be helpful in alerting her to the possibility that a patient may have DPD. A therapist who feels tempted to rescue a patient, or finds himself or herself making unusual exceptions for the patient due to the patient's neediness, should suspect DPD and collect further data to substantiate or refute this diagnosis.

Karen described staying in her first marriage for 10 years, even though "it was hell." Her husband had affairs with many other women and was verbally abusive. She tried to leave him many times, but gave in to his repeated requests to return. She was finally able to divorce him, and shortly afterwards she met and married her current husband, whom she described as kind, sensitive, and supportive. Karen stated that she preferred to have others make important decisions, and agreed with other people in order to avoid conflict. She worried about being left alone without anyone to take care of her, and reported feeling lost without other people's reassurance. She also reported that her feelings were easily hurt, so she worked hard not to do anything that might lead to criticism.

Dependent features can be a part of a variety of disorders, so it is important to be careful to differentiate DPD from other disorders that share some similar features. For example, although patients with either histrionic personality disorder or DPD may appear childlike and clinging, patients with the latter diagnosis are less flamboyant, egocentric, and shallow than those with the former diagnosis. The individual with DPD tends to be passive, submissive, self-effacing, and docile; this contrasts with the actively manipulative, gregarious, charming, and seductive behaviors of the individual with histrionic personality disorder. The person with avoidant personality disorder also has a strong need for affection from others, but strongly doubts and fears that such affection will be attained; the individual with DPD tends to trust and faithfully rely on others, anticipating that his or her efforts will be rewarded with affection and nurturance. Agoraphobics are dependent on other people in a very specific way—they need a reliable person to go places with them, so that they are not in danger of having a panic attack when they are alone. Agoraphobics are generally more insistent in asserting their dependence than individuals with DPD, actively demanding that they be accompanied wherever they go. It is possible, however, to meet the criteria for both panic disorder with agoraphobia and DPD, in which case both diagnoses should be given (on Axis I and II, respectively).

Although Karen sought treatment for her panic attacks and showed extensive patterns of avoidance over the past 7 years, she acknowledged that many of her problems had existed long before the agoraphobia and panic attacks. She did not like doing things alone long before she had a panic attack, and she had been having thoughts such as "I'm no good" since at least the third grade. She clearly met criteria for both DPD and panic disorder with agoraphobia, as well as major depression.

Conceptualization

Although there has not been much discussion of DPD in the behavioral literature, individuals with DPD have been conceptualized at times as "underassertive in the extreme" (Marshall & Barbaree, 1984, p. 417). Turkat and Carlson (1984) take a different approach by formulating the problem as one of anxiety regarding independent decision making, in their case study of one patient with DPD, although they make no attempt to generalize this conceptualization to DPD as a whole. While individuals with DPD are both extremely unassertive and quite anxious about making independent decisions, a comprehensive cognitive-behavioral conceptualization needs to encompass more than these two characteristics.

DPD can be conceptualized as stemming from two key assumptions. First, these individuals see themselves as inherently inadequate and helpless, and therefore unable to cope with the world on their own. They see the world as a cold, lonely, or even dangerous place that they could not possibly handle alone. Second, they conclude that the solution to the dilemma of being inadequate in a frightening world is to try to find someone who seems able to handle life and who will protect and take care of them. They decide that it is worth giving up responsibility and subordinating their own needs and desires in exchange for being taken care of. This adaptation, of course, carries adverse consequences for the individual. For one thing, by relying on others to handle problems and make decisions, the individual has little opportunity to learn and master the skills needed for autonomy. Some people never learn the skills of independent living (such as assertiveness, problem solving, and decision making), while others do not recognize the skills they have and therefore do not use them, thus perpetuating their dependency. In addition, the idea of becoming more competent can be terrifying, because dependent individuals fear that if they are any less needy they will be abandoned without being equipped to cope on their own.

This arrangement has several additional disadvantages for the dependent person. He or she always has to be very careful to please the other person and avoid conflict for fear of jeopardizing their all-important relationship and being left alone. Thus, assertiveness and expressing one's own opinion are clearly out of the question. Also, the dependent person may seem so desperate, needy, and clinging that it can be difficult to find a partner who is willing or able to meet his or her needs for any length of time. If the relationship ends, the individual feels totally devastated and sees no alternatives unless he or she can find someone new to depend on.

Karen reported that she always had an excellent relationship with her father, saying that "I was his little angel child." She said that he got mad at her only once, over a little matter, but otherwise things were always good between them. She described her mother as more domineering and said that they tended to clash a lot, but "I went to her for everything." Karen reported that it was in school that she learned she was dumb and "not good enough." She stated that she used to "read backwards" and that the nuns in Catholic school used to ridicule her in front of others. She would get physically sick and throw up at school at times, and sometimes she avoided going.

Karen was married young and moved directly from relying on her parents to relying on her husband, without any period of time during which she lived on her own. She found it very difficult to leave her first husband, even though he was abusive and unfaithful to her, and found it devastating to be without him once they actually separated. She found a new relationship very soon after the divorce, and felt tremendously relieved once she had a partner to take care of her again.

The individual with DPD tends to have such basic beliefs as "I can't survive without someone to take care of me," "I'm too inadequate to handle life on my own," "If my spouse [parent, etc.] left me, I'd fall apart," "If I were more independent, I'd be isolated and alone," and "Independence means being completely on your own." The main cognitive distortion in DPD is dichotomous thinking with respect to independence. These individuals believe that either one is completely helpless and dependent or one is totally independent and alone, with no gradations in between. They also show dichotomous thinking regarding their abilities: Either they do things "right" or they are completely "wrong." Of course, since they do not see themselves as being capable of functioning adequately, they generally conclude that they are completely wrong, incapable, and a total failure. They also tend to show the cognitive distortion of "catastrophizing," especially when it comes to the loss of a relationship. They go far beyond the normal level of concern that it would be sad and difficult to lose a relationship; they believe that it would be a total disaster and they would completely and permanently fall apart if a relationship should end.

The basic beliefs and cognitive distortions of the DPD lead to automatic thoughts such as "I can't," "I never would be able to do that," and "I'm much too stupid and weak." When asked to do something, they also have thoughts such as "Oh, my spouse could do that much better," and "I'm sure they don't really expect me to be able to do that." For example, when asked to do serial 7's during the initial evaluation, Karen made comments like "Oh, I'm no good at math, I'll never be able to do that," and "Is that really necessary? I can just tell you right now that I can't do it." In the first therapy session, when the therapist outlined the plan for treatment, she said, "Oh, I won't be able to record thoughts," and "I'm sure that may help some people, but I'm too dumb to do that."

Treatment Approaches

It is easy to assume that the goal of treatment with DPD is independence. In fact, many dependent patients' worst fear is that therapy will lead to total independence and isolation—that they will have to face life completely on their own, with no aid or support from others. A better word for the goal of therapy with DPD would be "autonomy." Autonomy has been described as being capable of acting independently of others, yet also capable of developing close and intimate relationships (Birtchnell,

1984). To achieve this, it is necessary to help the patient to learn to become gradually more separate from significant others (including the therapist) and to increase his or her self-confidence and sense of self-efficacy. However, given the common fear that competence will lead to abandonment, this must be done gradually and with some delicacy.

As with any of the personality disorders, the early stages of treatment involve working toward achieving the patient's stated goals, using interventions such as helping him or her to pinpoint and challenge dysfunctional automatic thoughts. Although it may be obvious to the therapist from the beginning that dependence is the major issue for the patient, it is rarely acknowledged by the patient as being part of the presenting problem. In fact, even the use of the words "dependence," "independence," or "autonomy" can frighten the patient early in the treatment if he or she does not feel ready to explore these issues. Regardless of the specific goals of therapy, the issue of dependence will become obvious to both the therapist and the patient as treatment proceeds. It may, nevertheless, be more natural and less frightening to the patient to let the actual use of these terms come first from the patient when he or she is ready to bring them up.

Although specific words like "dependence" were not explicitly used in the early treatment sessions, Karen was able to articulate therapy goals, such as these: "To increase my self-confidence so I can (a) be more outgoing and initiate contacts, (b) initiate projects, (c) take on things at work, (d) be more comfortable around others, and (e) reduce my fear of failure and give myself more credit for what I do."

It is particularly important to use guided discovery and Socratic questioning when working with patients who have DPD. These patients are likely to look on the therapist as "the expert" and hang on his or her every word, and it can be tempting just to tell these patients exactly what the problem is and what they need to do, thereby taking on an authoritarian role. Unfortunately, this encourages the patient to become dependent on the therapist, rather than to develop autonomy. These patients do, at least initially, need some active guidance and practical suggestions by the therapist in order to become engaged in the treatment. A totally nondirective approach could be too anxiety-provoking for these patients to tolerate for long. However, when the patient asks the therapist to tell him or her what to do, the therapist needs to be careful to use Socratic questioning and guided discovery, and help the patient arrive at his or her own solutions.

Karen seemed to look to her therapist to come up with the answers, especially when it came to understanding and explaining her own feelings. She would walk into sessions saying, "I felt depressed and discouraged last week. Why?"—fully expecting her therapist to sit down and explain it all to her without any effort on her part. Instead, he would ask her questions about how she had felt, when her feelings had seemed to change, and details of specific thoughts and feelings she had had when particularly upset. Through this process of questioning, Karen was able to arrive at her own increased understanding of what had transpired throughout the week and how her feelings were related to her thoughts.

Therapist-Patient Relationship

It is particularly important to pay careful attention to one factor that is too often ignored in the writings of cognitive-behavioral therapists: the patient-therapist relationship. The DPD patient's dependent behavior is pervasive enough to be manifested strongly within the therapeutic relationship. This has led some to suggest that humanistic or nondirective approaches may be preferable to more directive, cognitive-behavioral approaches, which run the risk of encouraging the patient to remain submissive in relation to a dominant therapist (e.g., Millon, 1981). However, appropriate utilization of the cognitive-behavioral approach, including the use of Socratic questioning and collaborative empiricism (Beck, Rush, Shaw, & Emery, 1979), can help to circumvent any tendencies of the therapist to fall into an authoritarian role with the patient. Because individuals with DPD are coming into treatment looking desperately for someone to solve their problems, engaging them in treatment may necessitate initially allowing some dependence in the treatment; however, the therapists need to work consistently throughout treatment to wean the patients gradually away from that dependence. Collaboration does not always need to be 50–50, and at the beginning of treatment the therapist may need to do more than half of the work. However, that pattern needs to change throughout the course of therapy, with the patient gradually being asked to provide his or her own agenda items, homework assignments, and so on, so that the treatment eventually becomes more clearly the patient's own.

As long as the therapist persists in using guided discovery to help the patient to explore his or her thoughts and feelings, making use of the interactions between the patient and the therapist in the session can lead to interventions that can have a particularly strong impact on the patient due to their immediacy. In order to use the relationship between the therapist and the patient most effectively as an example of an ongoing pattern of dependent relationships, it is necessary to encourage the patient to explore his or her thoughts and feelings about the therapist as well as about other relationships. These patients may be so focused on other relationships in their lives that it may not occur to them that thoughts and feelings about the therapist are important, or even appropriate, to discuss.

At one point in the treatment, when the therapist was focusing on teaching Karen to pinpoint and examine her automatic thoughts, Karen came into a session clearly upset, apologizing profusely for not having done her homework. The therapist chose to use her current thoughts and feelings as an example of pinpointing automatic thoughts. Karen reported experiencing high levels of anxiety and guilt, with her primary automatic thought being "Sam [the therapist] is going to be so disappointed in me." They were then able to examine this thought more objectively, rerating her anxiety and guilt after their discussion. Karen felt significantly less upset after the discussion. Using her immediate thoughts and feelings about the therapist as a basis for exploring automatic thoughts not only made a powerful demonstration of how useful the process could be in changing feelings, but also gave her explicit permission to openly discuss her feelings toward the therapist.

Another important part of paying careful attention to the patient–therapist relationship is for the therapist to monitor his or her own thoughts and feelings toward the patient. The temptation to rescue this type of patient is particularly strong, and it can be very easy either to accept patients' belief in their own helplessness or try to rescue them out of frustration with slow progress. Unfortunately, attempts at rescuing these patients are incompatible with the goal of increasing their independence and self-sufficiency. When therapists find themselves making exceptions for patients (e.g., prescribing medications or doing interventions without the usual thorough evaluation) because it seems so urgent that these clearly "pathetic" patients get immediate help, it is wise for them to assess whether they are simply accepting dependent patients' view of themselves as helpless. Whenever a therapist feels tempted to be more directive and less collaborative with a patient, or to make exceptions, it may be useful to write a Dysfunctional Thought Record (DTR) to clarify whether the exception is going to be in the best long-term interests of the patient, or whether it will serve to foster dependency.

Often Karen's therapist would ask her what seemed to be a simple question about her thoughts or feelings, and she would respond by saying, "My mind is blank, I just can't think." After having dealt with these reactions many times, he would have strong feelings of frustration and annoyance at her self-deprecation and apparent helplessness. At these times, he became aware of having thoughts such as these: "Oh, c'mon! You can do this," "This is really simple stuff," "Maybe she really is stupid," and "Oh, just stop acting helpless and just do it!" Instead of impatiently lashing out at her, he was able to respond to his thoughts with challenges such as the following: "She really isn't stupid; she's just used to seeing herself that way. It may seem simple to me, but it clearly isn't simple to her. If I act impatient and aggravated with her, I'll just confirm her belief that she is stupid. I need to just slow this down, and help her look at these thoughts and think it through."

At other points in therapy, her therapist would get frustrated at her slow progress. For example, while doing an *in vivo* driving exposure, the therapist waited on the front steps while Karen drove on her own to and from work. As he waited, he was struck with frustration and pinpointed automatic thoughts such as these: "For Pete's sake, look at what we're doing here! All this fuss over driving 1½ miles to work! What's the big deal to driving a car a stupid 1½ miles! Just get in there and do it!" Rather than staying with his frustration, however, he challenged his automatic thoughts with responses such as the following: "My goals can't be her goals. I can't make her do what I want her to. She needs to move at her own pace. I just need to lower my sights. What is insignificant to me isn't insignificant to her."

Because patients with DPD are especially prone to develop overly dependent relationships, it is crucial to set clear limits on the extent of the therapist's professional relationship with them. It is our clinical experience that these patients are more likely than others to report that they have fallen in love with their therapists. Even if it is part of a therapist's usual style, it is safer to minimize physical contact with these patients (even handshaking, pats on the back, or a casual hug), and it is important not to bend the usual rules of maintaining a clearly pro-fessional relationship. If exposure to anxiety-provoking situations ne-cessitates the therapist's being outside of the office with the patient, it is important to be explicit about the goals of the exercise, keep it very professional (e.g., take notes of cognitions and write down anxiety levels at regular intervals), and minimize casual conversation. For example, when Karen was avoiding doing homework that involved driving due to her anxiety, the therapist went driving with Karen to help her get over this hurdle. However, they discussed the exercise carefully beforehand and planned out a specific route, and he monitored her anxiety levels and cognitions throughout the drive, so that she did not misinterpret this as just "going for a drive with Sam."

If the therapist notices indications that the patient is beginning to feel overly emotionally involved with the therapist, or if the patient expresses these feelings overtly, it is crucial for the therapist to handle the situation carefully and thoughtfully. If discussion of the patient's thoughts and feelings toward the therapist have been an ongoing part of treatment, it is only natural that the thoughts and feelings of over-involvement should be pinpointed and examined in a similar manner. It is important for the therapist to acknowledge the patient's feelings, and explain how these are reactions that commonly occur in therapy. However, it is also crucial for the therapist to state explicitly that despite these feelings, it is not an option for the relationship to change into a more personal rather than a professional one. The patient is likely to have strong emotional reactions to the process of discussing these feelings, as well as to the setting of clear limits by the therapist. Thus, the thoughts and feelings of the patient about this issue will need to be examined throughout the next several sessions, and possibly throughout the rest of treatment.

Cognitive and Behavioral Interventions

The structured collaborative approach used in cognitive therapy can be used to help encourage patients to take a more active role in dealing with their problems. Even the setting of an agenda can be an exercise in taking more initiative. It is common for these patients to try to delegate all the power in the therapy over to the therapist—for example, by responding to "What do you want to focus on today?" with statements such as "Oh, whatever you want," and, "Oh, how am I supposed to know? I'm sure whatever you have in mind is best." In standard cognitive therapy, the therapist gives patients the option of suggesting topics for the agenda, but provides topics for the session if the patients have nothing particular in mind. However, with DPD patients, it is important to go one step further, explaining that since this is their therapy, they will be expected to make suggestions each session about how they want to spend the time.

With Karen, the therapist was able to get her to collaborate in agenda setting by taking whatever she said at the beginning of the session and asking if they should discuss it this session. For example, when at the beginning of one session Karen blurted out, "I didn't do anything this week," the therapist said, "Oh, should we include that on our plan for this week and discuss that?"—even though Karen had not originally offered that as an explicit agenda item. Part of the written homework assignment for the week can include jotting down some ideas for topics for the following session. By making it clear that patients are expected to contribute items to the agenda, continuing to ask at the beginning of each session (even if they repeatedly offer no suggestions), and waiting until they do offer some suggestions before moving on, the therapist may be able to foster some early active involvement in the treatment. Since these patients tend to be so eager to please, they generally try to do what is expected of them. Eventually, Karen brought her own agenda items (e.g., "feeling down," "problems with daughter") into each session.

Setting clear, specific goals is a crucial early part of treatment, since progress toward goals can be used as powerful evidence to challenge the dependent person's underlying assumption that he or she is helpless.

After all, one of the best ways to challenge the belief that one is helpless is to collect concrete evidence of personal competence. With agoraphobia as her main presenting problem, Karen's goals included the following:

a. Being able to drive
b. Going to the grocery store alone
c. Going to shopping malls alone
d. Sitting anyplace I want to at church

Doing graded exposure to these anxiety-provoking situations provided an excellent challenge to Karen's belief in her helplessness. When Karen was able to go to a grocery store alone, do her shopping, and write a check, she was very proud of herself and felt a bit more capable. The patient does not need to be working on an anxiety hierarchy, however, to collect systematic evidence of competence. The accomplishment of any concrete goal will achieve the same purpose. When Karen was able to complete a sewing project, she had more confidence that she could try things even if they were somewhat challenging. As outlined in Turkat and Carlson's (1984) case example of treatment of DPD, the therapist and patient can collaboratively develop a hierarchy of increasingly difficult independent actions. For example, a hierarchy of decision making could range from what type of fruit to have for lunch to decisions regarding jobs and places to live. Every decision made increases the patient's belief that he or she can do at least some things independently.

Regardless of the specific interventions used in therapy, the patient's DPD is likely to impede progress toward his or her goals. At times when this is occurring, the patient's automatic thoughts can become a productive focus for intervention. In Karen's second session, when the concept of a hierarchy was introduced to her, she had difficulty understanding the idea and became very self-critical. She decided that it was much too complicated to rate her anxiety from 0 to 100, so she and the therapist agreed to use a scale from 0 to 10 instead. When the idea of relaxation training was introduced in the third session, she reported these thoughts: "I won't be able to do it," "It's too complicated," and "I'll fail."

In particular, automatic thoughts regarding inadequacy are likely to interfere with trying homework assignments between sessions. Therefore, these thoughts need to be elicited and evaluated very early in treatment. Behavioral experiments in the session can be very useful in challenging some of these ideas. For example, when the idea of monitoring and challenging automatic thoughts was introduced to Karen, she responded with her typical thought of "I can't do it." Rather than taking an authoritarian role and just plunging forward anyway, the therapist helped her to write a list of the advantages and disadvantages of doing DTRs. As they explored the pros and cons, she reported the thought, "I can't comprehend anything written." The therapist was able to set up a behavioral experiment to challenge this thought by pulling a book out of his bookshelf, opening it to a random page, and asking her to read the first sentence aloud. He then asked her to explain to him what the sentence meant. When she was, in fact, able to do this, they were able to write a convincing rational response to her automatic thought: "It's true that it's hard for me to understand some things that are written, but if I work at it I usually can."

Given dependent patients' tendency to feel unable to do things on their own, it makes sense for them to practice doing new tasks and potential homework assignments in the session before expecting them to do it at home. For example, with most patients it is possible to demonstrate the first three columns of a DTR and then send the patients home to pinpoint thoughts between sessions. With Karen, it was necessary for her and her therapist to agree to work together on pinpointing thoughts in the session until she felt comfortable trying it on her own. They gradually worked on giving her more responsibility for doing the thought sheets in the office, and it was not until after several sessions of practice that she was actually writing out thoughts and responses during the session and felt ready to begin doing them on her own. Although she denigrated her first attempt to do a DTR at home, it was no worse than many patients' initial efforts (see Figure 13.1). After some suggestions by the therapist, her second attempt at homework was much improved (see Figure 13.2).

When planning interventions, it is not safe to assume that the patient actually has skill deficits even when he or she appears to be quite unable to function effectively in the world. Some patients actually have many of the skills needed to function independently and successfully, but either do not recognize this or fail to use the skills they have. When there is, in fact, a skill deficit, the patient can be trained in such skills as assertiveness (e.g., Lange & Jakubowski, 1976), problem solving (D'Zurilla & Goldfried, 1971), decision making (Turkat & Carlson, 1984), and social interaction (Curran, 1977) in order to increase his or her competence.

Karen had relied on others for so long that she did have genuine skill deficits; thus, she needed training in a variety of coping skills, in addition to help in challenging her negative thoughts about her abilities. In dealing with her anxiety, she needed thorough training in relaxation skills (e.g., Bernstein & Borkovec, 1976). When discussing differing ways to deal with her husband and daughter, she needed some explicit training in assertiveness. Even in concrete areas of life, her skill level could not be taken for granted. In doing graded exposure to driving situa-

Daily Record of Automatic Thoughts

Date	Situation Briefly describe the situation	Emotion(s) Rate 0–100%	Automatic Thought(s) Try to quote thoughts then rate your belief in each thought 0–100%	Rational Response Rate degree of belief 0–100%	Outcome Re-rate emotions
4/8	Came into work and panicked	Anxious Stomach churning Shaky	Too many people. Eat slow because of stomach. Calm down. Relax.	Don't know how to finish. Stomach upset for 2 hrs. Calmed down about 3 o'clock.	

FIGURE 13.1 Karen's initial attempt at using the DTS.

Daily Record of Automatic Thoughts

Date	Situation Briefly describe the situation	Emotion(s) Rate 0–100%	Automatic Thought(s) Try to quote thoughts then rate your belief in each thought 0–100%	Rational Response Rate degree of belief 0–100%	Outcome Re-rate emotions
4/15	Banquet dinner	Anxious	People I don't know. 100	I have good qualities, even if I'm not the most educated.	
		Scared	I'm going to say something stupid. 100	Most people won't notice me. Some might, some might not.	
		Angry	I hope they don't have soup. 100		
		Sad	Everybody will see me shake if I eat it. 100		
			I'll make a bad impression and they'll wonder what's wrong with me. 100		

FIGURE 13.2 Karen's second attempt at using the DTR.

300

tions, it was necessary to do more than just reduce her anxiety. She had for so long been convinced that she was incapable of driving that she had questions about how to make basic driving decisions (e.g., "How do you decide when to stop at a yellow light?"), and these needed to be addressed.

In addition to training dependent patients in a variety of general coping and problem-solving skills, Overholser (1987) recommends that dependent patients be taught self-control skills such as those developed by Rehm (1977) for the treatment of depression. Training in self-control includes three basic components: self-monitoring, self-evaluation, and self-reinforcement. Self-monitoring involves teaching the patient to record the frequency, intensity, and duration of specific behaviors, including their antecedents and consequences. Learning to keep such records can be useful to help the patient see definite changes and improvement, rather than working simply for the therapist's approval. Self-evaluation involves comparing one's observed performance with one's standard for performance. Dependent people (such as Karen) can have unrealistically high standards for performance, or can be so focused on other people's standards that they do not have a clear image of standards for themselves. Training in more appropriate self-evaluation can help dependent patients develop such standards, and learn to distinguish when a request for assistance is necessary—not merely a sign of their own uncertainty. Self-reinforcement involves providing appropriate consequences based on one's performance in relation to one's standards. Teaching the dependent individual to reinforce his or her own desirable behavior is probably the most important aspect of self-control, since dependent people tend to rely exclusively on other people to provide all of their reinforcement. Initial self-reinforcers may include concrete rewards for desirable behavior (e.g., tokens to be redeemed for a wanted gift, going for a pleasant walk, reading a chapter of a novel), but also need to include building in positive cognitive reinforcers (e.g., "Hey, I really followed through and did a good job!").

While patients with DPD are generally cooperative and eager to please in the beginning of treatment, there is often a problem with their not following through on homework assignments. This can result from the patients' belief that they are not capable of doing the homework, or from skill deficits; however, it can also occur if patients become frightened by moving too quickly in therapy, advancing too rapidly toward their goals. If so, it can be useful to list the advantages and disadvantages of changing, seriously exploring the disadvantages of achieving goals. Often, when first asked about the disadvantages of improving in therapy, the patients will be surprised and insist that it would be completely positive to achieve their goals. On careful examination, there are disadvantages to making any type of change. Exploring reasons not to change can put a patient in the position of trying to convince the therapist that change is worthwhile, rather than the therapist's pushing him or her toward autonomy—a situation that is much more likely to lead to compliance.

As described earlier, Karen did her first *in vivo* exposure session—driving with the therapist in the car. Although the exposure went very well, her anxiety came down as expected, and she was able to drive farther than anticipated, she wasn't sure how she felt at the end of the session and reported "a lot of mixed feelings." These were addressed in the next session as follows:

THERAPIST: Even though the driving *in vivo* went quite well, you had some mixed feelings about it. What are your thoughts about it this week?

KAREN: I'm not sure how I feel about last week. I'm so confused. I've even thought about quitting therapy.

THERAPIST: That's a little surprising to me. On the one hand, the driving went well and your anxiety dropped quickly, but on the other hand you suddenly have thoughts about dropping out of therapy. What do you think is going on here?

KAREN: I don't know. Something happened to me last week. Am I fighting it because I know I can do it? Am I afraid I'm going to be independent? I like George [husband] taking care of me.

THERAPIST: This seems pretty important. Help me understand this. Does driving mean to you that you could become more independent, and that concerns you?

KAREN: Maybe.

THERAPIST: What might happen if you became more independent?

KAREN: Well, then I could fail.

THERAPIST: What do you mean?

KAREN: Independent people do things. And I might fail. I guess if I lean on George, then I can't fail.

THERAPIST: So if you're able to drive, that will mean you're more independent, and if that happens you could be more open to failing at some things.

KAREN: I think so.

THERAPIST: OK. There's a lot to talk about here, but it helps me to understand what you're going through. It looks a little like your success frightened you because it challenged how you see yourself. Can we spend some time discussing this, to try to understand better what it's all about?

KAREN: Yes, I'd like to, because it all seems so confusing to me.

[Much of the session was spent gathering and examining the network of cognitions regarding independence.]

THERAPIST: OK, to summarize, it looks a little like you weren't quite ready for all the changes greater independence could bring. I'm wondering if it would make some sense to slow things down a bit so you can feel more in control of your change and do it at a pace you can handle.

KAREN: You mean we can do that? I'm feeling more comfortable now. I'm starting to relax.

THERAPIST: Can you think of ways to slow your progress to a rate that's more acceptable to you?

Sometimes, an exploration of the advantages and disadvantages of changing will reveal that change really does not seem worthwhile to the patient. For instance, Dorothy, a 24-year-old housewife, sought treatment for depression. She had always been extremely dependent on her mother and had never learned to do things on her own. She very rigidly believed that she could not do anything successfully on her own, and was therefore terrified to try anything new because she was certain she would fail miserably. She had married her high school sweetheart and moved out of the state, immediately becoming very depressed. She felt overwhelmed by her expectations of being a wife, and felt helpless to handle her new responsibilities without her mother nearby. She ruminated about her inadequacies and believed everything would be fine again if she could only be back in her hometown. As treatment progressed, she revealed that if she became less depressed and learned to accept life away from her hometown, she was concerned that her husband would have no incentive to move back. When she acknowledged that her main goal was to convince her husband to move back to her hometown, it became clear why she had been noncompliant in treatment. In fact, her mood did not improve until her husband agreed that they could move back within the year.

Thus, there often are some compelling reasons for the dependent person to be ambivalent about changing. Although the person struggling with helplessness may feel that he or she has no power, taking the helpless role can actually be very powerful and reinforcing (as with Dorothy), and this role can be difficult to give up. If the patient can be helped to identify what would be lost if he or she were less helpless, it may be possible to find a more constructive substitute. For example, if Karen was concerned that her husband would not spend time with her if she did not need him to go shopping with her, she could schedule a weekly "date" with her husband. Therefore, she could still have time with him, without needing to be helpless to accomplish this.

The patient's dichotomous view of independence is a crucial area to explore. When the patient believes that one is either totally dependent and helpless or totally independent, isolated, and alone, any movement toward autonomy at all can seem like a commitment to complete and permanent alienation. Working with the patient to draw a continuum from dependence to independence can be very useful (Figure 13.3). Seeing that there are many steps in between the extremes of total dependence and total independence can make it less frightening for the patient to make progress in small steps. One illustration that can be useful with patients is that even independent, well-functioning adults take steps to be sure that assistance is available when needed, such as joining automobile clubs. Thus, no one needs to be totally independent at all times, and it is no disgrace to admit that one might need help from time to time.

Karen's dichotomous thinking led her to conclude that she was "stupid" or a "dope" whenever she perceived that she was less than perfect (e.g., if she made even a small, simple mistake). Challenging this cognitive distortion through highlighting the double standard inherent in her approach was very helpful to her. When asked if she would draw the same conclusions if a friend made the same mistake, she was able to see that she was setting totally different standards for herself from those she would see as appropriate for other people. Keeping her dichotomous thinking in mind when setting homework assignments, the therapist specifically assigned her to do imperfect DTRs deliberately (e.g., to use poor spelling and messy writing, not to include all thoughts, to put some items in the wrong column). This was explained to Karen as an attempt to short-circuit her tendency to begin a task, quit as soon as she saw it was not coming out perfectly, and conclude she was stupid.

At some point in the treatment, dependent patients will need to explore the belief that if they become more competent they will be abandoned. One useful way to challenge this is by setting up specific behavioral experiments in which they behave a bit more competently

Totally											Totally
Dependent	**0**	**1**	**2**	**3**	**4**	**5**	**6**	**7**	**8**	**9**	**10**	**Independent**

Doesn't do anything alone

Has someone else make all decisions

Does whatever she's told

Agrees w/what is said

Has someone else always there to handle problems

Completely helpless

Subservient, docile

Like a puppy, always acting happy and pleased

Does everything alone

Makes her own decisions without considering anyone else

Does whatever she wants

Expresses opinions no matter what anyone else thinks

Handles all problems on her own

Totally competent

Doesn't need anyone

Outspoken, aggressive, brash

Isolated and alone

FIGURE 13.3   A typical continuum of independence developed jointly with a dependent client.

and observe the reaction of others. Since this type of behavioral experiment involves other people, this truly is an "experiment" in the sense that neither the patient nor the therapist can be certain what the results will be. Although it may be irrational to believe that one will end up totally abandoned and alone forever if one is assertive, the therapist really does not know if more autonomy will, in fact, lead to abandonment by any particular individual. Without having met Karen's husband, George, her therapist had no way of knowing how he would react to changes in Karen. Many people are attracted to dependent individuals, so it is possible that a spouse (parent, etc.) will react negatively if the patient begins to change by becoming more assertive and independent. The dependent behavior may be actively reinforced by significant others, and attempts to change may be punished. However, it is also possible that the spouse could react well to these changes, even if the patient feels certain that he or she will react negatively. By starting with small steps, one can usually observe the spouse's reaction without risking serious or permanent consequences.

Karen was very concerned about how her husband would react to her increasing independence. His first wife had had an affair, and he had many times expressed his fears that she, too, would have an affair. He seemed to facilitate her dependence in many ways—by accompanying her to stores, offering to do things that she could do by herself, and worrying if he didn't know exactly where she was at any time. Although Karen was concerned about his reactions, she had been doing graded exposure to increasingly anxiety-provoking situations, including going to grocery stores and driving on her own. She tried to stay aware of her husband's reactions; to her surprise, she did not perceive anything but positive reactions to her progress. Her therapist had offered to meet with Karen and her husband for a few conjoint sessions if that seemed necessary, but when she was able to look at the situation objectively, she realized that he could handle her progress and couple sessions would not be necessary.

In cases where the spouse's reaction to increased assertiveness is, in fact, negative, it may be necessary to explore other options for treatment. Marital or family therapy can often be useful in helping both spouses begin to adjust to the changes in the identified patient—and sometimes even change together. If, however, either the patient or the spouse is not willing to pursue conjoint treatment, the patient may need to explore the advantages and disadvantages of a variety of options, including maintaining the current approach to relationships, modifying the new assertiveness to be more tolerable to the spouse, and even possibly ending the relationship. Even though the idea of ending the relationship may be very frightening to the patient, it may need to be acknowledged as one of many possible options.

Whether the person decides to stay in the relationship and work toward change, to stay in it and accept it as it is, or to get out of it, the therapist will eventually need to discuss the possibility that the relationship may end, and challenge the patient's catastrophic thinking in regard to the loss of relationships. Even if the patient insists that things are wonderful in the dependent relationship, no one can absolutely count on another person's always being there, since accidents are always possible. Of course, the therapist would never try to minimize the grief involved in losing an important relationship. The goal is not to try to convince dependent patients that other people are unimportant, but to help them to see that, even though it may be very upsetting, they could and would survive the loss of the relationship.

It is possible to foster the progression in therapy from dependence to autonomy by changing the structure of therapy itself. Moving from individual to group therapy can help to reduce the patient's dependence on the therapist and serve to dilute the intensity of the relationship. In a group setting, the patient can still get a great deal of support, but can begin to derive this more from peers than from the therapist. This serves as a good first step toward finding more natural means of support for autonomy in the patient's circle of family and friends. Modeling has been found to help increase independent behavior (Goldstein, Martens, Hubben, Van Belle, Schaaf, Wirsma, & Goedhart, 1973), and in group therapy the other patients can serve as models for the development of many skills. Watching another group member assertively express anger to a group leader, or watching a peer go carefully through the steps of problem solving to resolve a dilemma, can provide useful examples of behaviors that the patient is trying to learn. In addition, the group therapy setting provides a relatively safe place to practice new skills, such as assertiveness. For example, by practicing more open and assertive expression of feelings, first through role plays and then through sharing actual feelings with group leaders and members, and by getting constructive feedback from peers, the patient can build up the confidence to try similar behaviors in relationships outside of the group.

Termination

The termination of therapy may be extremely threatening for persons with DPD, since they may believe that it would be impossible to maintain their progress without the therapist's support. Rather than trying to challenge this belief through strictly verbal means, the process of "fading" sessions by scheduling them less frequently can serve as a behavioral experiment to test it. If sessions have typically been scheduled weekly, switching to an every-other-week schedule enables patients to see how well their changes are maintained over a 2-week interval. Once the patients see that they can function well over the 2 weeks, they may then be able to move to monthly sessions. If patients are not able to maintain progress over the course of 2 weeks, it is possible that they are not yet ready for termination, and it may be appropriate to return to weekly sessions until further problems are resolved. If patients can be given a great deal of control over the spacing of the sessions, this is likely to leave them feeling less threatened and more willing to try some fading, since the choice is not irrevocable. The therapist can fade sessions further and further, offering to meet every month, every 3 months, or even every 6 months. When given this type of free choice, however, patients usually come to realize that if they can go a full month without therapy, they really no longer need to be in treatment.

Another factor that can make termination easier for the person with DPD is the offer of booster sessions when necessary. Whenever terminating therapy with a patient, the therapist can explain that if the patient experiences any difficulties in the future, either with issues already discussed or new ones, it is a good idea to recontact the therapist for one or two booster sessions. Such booster sessions often serve to get patients "back on track" by encouraging them to resume the interventions that had helped in the past. Simply knowing that they have the option of recontacting the therapist helps to make the transition to termination easier.

Allowing the dependent patient to achieve more autonomy may mean that he or she makes independent decisions, making treatment take a different course from what the therapist had anticipated. At times, it may be necessary to let go of the patient to allow him or her to be more independent. For example, Karen had several sessions in which her motivation seemed to be waning, and she was not following through on homework assignments. Her thoughts and feelings about the assignments had been discussed at length over a number of sessions. As she came into this session, Karen said, with great hesitation:

KAREN: I don't want to do any more.
THERAPIST: Help me understand. I thought you wanted to be able to drive farther.
KAREN: I do, but not right now. I feel like you're pushing me.
THERAPIST: You almost sound a little angry.
KAREN: (*After a pause*) Well, maybe I am. Guilty too.
THERAPIST: Guilty?
KAREN: Like maybe I should do more and you'll be upset if I don't.
THERAPIST: What do *you* want?
KAREN: (*Adamantly*) I want to work on driving at my own pace.
THERAPIST: Sounds like you're pretty clear about it. What's wrong with that?
KAREN: Well, nothing, I guess. But then I wonder if I've made any progress.

THERAPIST: Would you like to spend some time reviewing progress, so we can see what the evidence tells us and what that means for where we go from here?

KAREN: Yes. That's a really good idea. I feel relieved already. I thought you were going to be mad at me.

THERAPIST: You felt some pressure to please me?

KAREN: Yes, but I guess it was coming from me and not you.

[They spent about 15 minutes reviewing progress. Karen felt she'd made important progress on seven of her eight goals.]

KAREN: I feel a lot more relaxed now. I didn't realize I'd come so far.

THERAPIST: The evidence would seem to say that you have. So where do you see yourself wanting to go from here?

KAREN: I just want to work on the driving by myself. I know that I need to just do it.

THERAPIST: Then would you like to spend some time discussing how you'll do that, and looking at what could get in the way of continued progress?

[They worked on this for 15 minutes.]

THERAPIST: OK. So now it looks like you've got a clear plan for how to continue your progress, as well as some ideas for what to do if problems crop up. How's that feel to you?

KAREN: Really good. I thought I was going to leave here upset today. But I know this is what I want.

THERAPIST: So you expected that if you were clear on what you wanted with me, it would be a disaster. What did you discover?

KAREN: Just the opposite. And that it's OK to decide on what I want.

THERAPIST: And of course you know that if you decide you want more assistance, or show signs of sliding backwards, it would make good sense to call me so we can figure out what the best course of action would be.

Although treatment of DPD can be a slow, arduous process that can be frustrating at times, it can be very rewarding as well. As demonstrated by Turkat and Carlson (1984) in their case study of a patient with DPD, recognition of the disorder, a comprehensive case formulation, and strategic planning of interventions based on that formulation are likely to make the treatment more effective and less frustrating than symptomatic treatment alone. With the proper conceptualization and careful strategic planning throughout treatment, the therapist may have the opportunity to watch the patient blossom into an autonomous adult, providing satisfaction that is remarkably similar to that of watching a child grow up.

Chapter 14
Obsessive-Compulsive Personality Disorder

Obsessive-compulsive personality disorder (OCPD) is fairly common, particularly among males, in present-day Western culture (American Psychiatric Association, 1987). This is due, in part, to the high value society puts on the more moderate expression of some of the characteristics of this personality style, such as attention to detail, self-discipline, emotional control, perseverance, reliability, and politeness. In some individuals, however, these characteristics are expressed in such an extreme form that they lead to either significant functional impairment or subjective distress. Thus, when a diagnosable personality disorder exists, the obsessive individual becomes rigid, perfectionistic, dogmatic, ruminative, moralistic, inflexible, indecisive, and emotionally and cognitively blocked.

Historical Background

According to Carr (1974), the first person to write about OCPD was Esquirol in the early part of the 19th century. Since then, OCPD has been one of the primary areas of interest in the mental health field in the 20th century. Freud (1908/1963) and some of the other early psychoanalysts (Abraham, 1921/1953; Jones, 1919/1961) were the first ones to develop an explicit theory and form of treatment for these individuals. Some confusion developed around the terms "obsession" and "compulsion," because they were used by the early analysts to refer both to specific symptomatic, pathological behaviors and to a type of personality disorder. Both the neurosis, or Axis I obsessive-compulsive disorder as it is now labeled in DSM-III-R, and the personality disorder (now Axis II OCPD) were hypothesized to have originated during the anal stage of development (ages 1 to 3) due to inappropriate toilet training.

Obsessive-compulsive disorder is characterized by the symptoms of obsessions, which consist of persistent, ritualized thought patterns, or compulsions, which consist of persistent, ritualized behavior patterns. OCPD, or anal character, is characterized by the personality traits of obstinancy, orderliness, and parsimony, or a combination of obsessions and compulsions. These personality traits were hypothesized to have developed out of the same conflicts and use of the same defense mechanisms (regression, reaction formation, ritualization, isolation, and undoing) as the symptoms in obsessive-compulsive disorder. The personality traits, though, are reflected in the general, ego-syntonic personality style of the persona and not in specific symptomatic behaviors. According to Fenichel (1945), not much is known about why one person develops OCPD while another person develops specific obsessions or compulsions, but it is possible that the personality disorder represents an arrested developmental evolution, whereas specific obsessive or compulsive symptoms represent a regression back to the anal stage of psychosexual maturation.

Wilhelm Reich was another theorist in the psychoanalytic tradition who wrote about obsessive-compulsive disorder, or, as he referred to obsessive-compulsive patients, "living machines" (Reich, 1945, p. 215). He also viewed the disorder as arising out of the obsessive's parents' being overly rigid and punitive in toilet training during the child's anal stage of development. Due to this, the child develops an overly strict superego, or conscience, which later leads to overcontol and conflict over the expression of impulses, desires, or emotions. Reich believed that this early developmental pattern resulted in a number of characteristics he saw in adult OCPD patients, including guilt, need for control, passion for collecting things, inhibition, pedantic sense of order, and emotional reserve.

Harry Stack Sullivan, a neopsychoanalyst, wrote about OCPD from a somewhat different perspective (Sullivan, 1956). Sullivan developed the theory of interpersonal psychoanalysis. He believed that people's psychological problems developed out of their relationships with others, and not out of fixations at various stages of instinctual psychosexual development, as the Freudians believed. Sullivan thought that the primary problem of people with OCPD is their extremely low level of self-esteem. This was hypothesized to occur when a child grows up in a home environment in which there is much anger and hate. The anger and hate are for the most part hidden, though, behind superficial love and niceness. Because of this, the obsessive learns what Sullivan calls "verbal magic." Words are used to disguise or excuse the true state of affairs—for example, "This spanking will hurt me more than it will hurt you." Obsessives learn to rely overly on words and external rules to guide their behavior. They do not tend to develop emotional and interpersonal skills and, in fact, usually avoid intimacy because of their fear of letting others know them.

Another neopsychoanalyst who stressed the importance of low self-esteem in OCPD was Andras Angyal (1965). Angyal, like Sullivan, believed that the basis for the obsessive's dysfunctions is the inconsistent, often contradictory behavior of the parents. The parents' actions and feelings often seem to be in contradiction to their words, or else they behave in very erratic, seemingly irrational ways—for example, affectionate one minute and then cold and rejecting the next. Confusion is created for the child by the parents' contradictory demands and by their obvious failure to practice what they preach.

A third neopsychoanalyst who has written extensively about OCPD is Leon Salzman. He states that the "primary dynamism in all instances [of obsessive-compulsiveness] will be manifested as an attempt to gain control over oneself and one's environment in order to avoid or overcome distressful feelings of helplessness" (Salzman, 1973, p. 27). Salzman believes that this pattern is exacerbated by obsessives' tendency to deal in extremes. Unless they feel they have control, they tend to experience total lack of control. Obsessives attempt to develop their intellect to the point of omniscience. This need for omniscience and perfection leads to an unwillingness to take chances, indecisiveness, procrastination (so as not to make a mistake), rigidity, grandiosity, and discomfort with their emotional life, which is experienced as being out of conscious control.

Behavioral theorists have written very little about OCPD. They have focused their attention more on the specific obsessions and compulsions that are characteristic of the DSM-III-R Axis I obsessive-compulsive disorder. This is due primarily to the behaviorists' view of psychological disorders as consisting of specific, learned, maladaptive patterns of behavior, and their general disbelief in the existence of broad, stable personality styles or traits.

Millon (1981; Millon & Everly, 1985) has written about OCPD from the perspective of biosocial learning theory. In this theory, he attempts to integrate biological, learning theory, and psychodynamic approaches to understanding personality development. Millon states that the obsessive can best be described in one work: "conforming." He believes that the obsessive is brought up by overcontrolling parents who punish the child for behaving autonomously or in any way of which the parents disapprove. The child thus never develops a separate identity, and functions in the world by conforming to strict, internalized parental standards and to the standards of those around him or her.

Research and Empirical Data

There has been little definitive research on OCPD. To date, most of the knowledge about this disorder has been derived from clinical work. There is a good deal of evidence that OCPD does indeed exist as a specific clinical entity. Several factor-analytic studies have found that the various traits hypothesized to comprise OCPD do indeed tend to occur together (Hill, 1976; Lazare, Klerman, & Armor, 1966; Torgerson, 1980). However, there is little evidence that OCPD stems from inadequate toilet training, as psychoanalytic theory proposes (Pollack, 1979). Adams (1973), in working with obsessive children, did find that the children's parents had a number of obsessive traits, including being strict and controlling, overconforming, unempathic, and disapproving of spontaneous expressions of affect. It has not been determined at the present time what percentage of children with obsessive-compulsive personality traits develop into adults with OCPD.

There is beginning to be some research into the genetic and physiological bases of OCPD. In a study by Clifford, Murray, and Fulker (1980), a significantly higher correlation of obsessive traits, as measured by the trait scale of the Layton Obsessive Inventory, was found in a sample of monozygotic twins than in a sample of dizygotic twins. In another study, Smokler and Shevrin (1979) examined obsessive and histrionic personality styles in relation to brain hemisphericity as reflected by lateral eye movements. The authors found that the obsessive subjects looked predominantly to the right, which indicated a higher degree of left-hemisphere activation, while the histrionic subjects looked predominantly to the left. The left hemisphere has been associated with language, analytic thinking, and reason—which is what would be expected for the obsessive. The right hemisphere has been associated with imagery and synthetic thinking.

Cognitive Therapy Conceptualization

According to Beck, Rush, Shaw, and Emery (1979), cognitive theory "is based on the underlying theoretical rationale that an individual's affect and behavior are largely determined by the way in which he structures the world. His cognitions (verbal or pictorial 'events' in his stream of consciousness) are based on attitudes or assumptions (schemas), developed from previous experiences" (p. 3).

The first theorist to write extensively about OCPD from a primarily cognitive point of view was David Shapiro. Shapiro, who was trained as a psychoanalyst, developed his concepts because of his dissatisfaction with the psychoanalytic theory of personality disorders. Shapiro delineated the structure and characteristics of a number of what he referred to as "neurotic styles." He wrote that a person's "general style of thinking may be considered a matrix from which the various traits, symptoms, and defense mechanisms crystallize" (Shapiro, 1965, p. 2), and later that "the view of symptomatic behavior as a reflection of how individuals characteristically think and see things is in certain ways not only different [from] but actually contrary to the traditional dynamic view" (Shapiro, 1981, pp. 3–4).

Shapiro, although not presenting a comprehensive theory of OCPD, discussed what he saw as three of its primary characteristics. The first is a rigid, intense, sharply focused style of thinking. Shapiro finds obsessives to have a "stimulus-bound" quality to their cognition, similar in certain ways to that of organically brain-damaged people. They are continually being attentive and concentrating, and rarely seem to just let their attention wander. Thus, they tend to be good at technical, detailed tasks, but rarely are surprised and are poor at discerning more global, impressionistic qualities of things, such as the tone of a social gathering. Shapiro refers to obsessives as having "active inattention." They become distracted and disturbed by new information or external influences outside of their narrow range of focus, and actively attempt to keep this distraction from happening.

The second characteristic Shapiro discusses is the distortion in the obsessive-compulsive's sense of autonomy. For the obsessive, "self-direction is distorted from its normal meaning of volitional choice and deliberate, purposeful action to a self-conscious directing of every action, to the exercise, as if by an overseer, of a continuous willful pressure and direction on himself and even, strange as it may appear, an effort to direct his own wants and emotions at will" (Shapiro, 1965, pp. 36–37). The fundamental aspect of the obsessive's experience is the cognition "I should." Obsessives experience any relaxation of deliberateness or purposeful activity as improper and unsafe. They invoke morality, logic, social custom, propriety, family rules, and past behavior in similar situations to establish what the "should" is in a given situation, and then act accordingly.

The final characteristic mentioned by Shapiro is the obsessive-compulsive's loss of reality or sense of conviction about the world. Due to obsessives' being cut off to a large degree from their wants, preferences, and affects, their decisions, actions, and beliefs tend to be held much more tenuously than most people's. This leads to varying combinations of continual doubt or dogmatism, which are reciprocal attempts at dealing with this conflict.

Guidano and Liotti (1983) are cognitive therapists who have written about OCPD. They state that perfectionism, the need for certainty, and a strong belief in the existence of an absolutely correct solution for human problems are the maladaptive components underlying both OCPD and the ritualistic behavior in Axis I obsessive-compulsive disorder. These beliefs lead to excessive doubting, postponing, over-concern for detail, and uncertainty in making decisions. Guidano and Liotti have found, as did Sullivan and Angyal, that obsessives usually grow up in a home in which they are given very mixed, contradictory messages from at least one of their parents.

Characteristics

Obsessive-compulsives are characterized by a certain content, style, and structure of their thought processes. The obsessive's thoughts are often irrational and dysfunctional, leading to maladaptive emotions, behaviors, and physiological responses. Characteristic automatic thoughts of the obsessive-compulsive include the following:

> "I need to get this assignment done perfectly."
> "I have to do this myself or it won't be done correctly."
> "I should be doing something productive rather than wasting time by reading this novel."
> "I better think about this some more before deciding what to do or I might make a mistake."
> "What if I forgot to pack something?"
> "That person misbehaved and should be punished."
> "I better do this again to be sure I got it right."
> "I should keep this old lamp because I might need it some day."
> "I should want to do this assignment."
> "I should enjoy myself at this party."

Obsessive-compulsives' automatic thoughts are based on certain assumptions that they hold about themselves and the world. McFall and Wollersheim (1979) and Freeman, Pretzer, Fleming, and Simon (1990) have identified some of the most important and problematic of these assumptions. Among the most common of these are the following:

1. *"There are right and wrong behaviors, decisions, and emotions."* Typically, there is a narrow range of acts and feelings considered to be perfectly acceptable. Anything that does not fall within this narrow domain is imperfect and therefore "wrong." For example, a young female student complained about her "loss of poise" when she experienced irritation at her ex-roommate, who had made a shambles of their apartment in the process of moving out. Even though her irritation was mild and would be considered by most to be justified, she was upset because she did not want to experience any negative emotions.

2. *"I must avoid mistakes to be worthwhile."* If obsessives do or feel anything that is imperfect, they conclude that they are bad or worthless persons. Because it is impossible to be perfect on a regular basis, the obsessives suffer from low self-esteem and depression. The prospect of being imperfect in the future generates anxiety, panic, and avoidance. An example of this is given by the obsessional artist who avoids working on his latest painting because it may be "wrong" in some way—it might not be of sufficient social relevance, or it might not be placed properly within the history of art, or a friend may not like it. Any of these shortcomings means he is worthless as an artist.

3. *"To make a mistake is to have failed,"* and *"Failure is intolerable."* Obsessives' idea that success requires perfection makes the experience of failure inevitable. Their further assumption that failure is terrible causes them to experience a great many of the normal shortcomings of life as intolerable, tragic, and horrible. An example of this kind of thinking is provided by a businessman who wanted to get a special gift for his secretary, to whom he was very attracted. After having a piece of jewelry made for her, he agonized as to whether she would like it or nor. The thought that he might have made a mistake—that is, she would not like it—made him very depressed and anxious.

4. *"To make a mistake is to be deserving of criticism."* The reasoning goes as follows: One is (inevitably) imperfect, and therefore one must feel very guilty (i.e., self-condemning). If one is not severely self-critical for one's mistakes, one is compounding the mistake and will become increasingly imperfect and worthless. For example, an obsessive woman who begins a diet in order to lose weight will feel that any deviation, however, slight, from the prescribed program means that she has failed. Thus, she may have followed the Scarsdale Diet perfectly for 11 days, but if she eats one cookie on day 12, she will feel like a failure and will tell herself she is totally out of control and is fat and disgusting. If the therapist suggests that her guilt and depression are disproportionate to her "sin," she will counter that without guilt she will become increasingly out of control and, ultimately, obese.

5. *"I must be perfectly in control of my environment as well as of myself,"* *"Loss of control is intolerable,"* and *"Loss of control is dangerous."* These are the assumptions that underlie obsessives' insistence on certainty and predictability. Without predictability of the world, how can such persons maintain total control over themselves and avoid mistakes? Thus, once again, the obsessives make impossible demands on themselves. When they fail to live up to their imperatives, they experience terror and frustration. Life must be lived with intense care so as not to risk the terrible possibility of making a mistake.

6. *"If something is or may be dangerous, one must be terribly upset by it."* Let us consider, for example, an obsessive woman who hears on the news

that some unfortunate man had a stroke while at the wheel of his car and died in the ensuing crash. The obsessive may respond by becoming terrified of driving alone because she fears having a stroke and dying. It makes no difference that the client is a healthy 34-year-old female and the man on the news was 62 and had a history of high blood pressure and strokes. Obsessives cannot simply acknowledge that something might be dangerous, take steps to reduce its risk, and put it out of mind. They feel compelled to worry about it at great length. The reason is this:

7. *"One is powerful enough to initiate or prevent the occurrence of catastrophes by magical rituals or obsessional ruminations."* Worrying is seen as functional. If one worries enough, one can forestall whatever dire consequences one may feel are waiting. Furthermore, "It is easier or more effective to carry out a ritual or to obsess than it is to confront one's thoughts or feelings directly." Also, "If you think about something long enough, the perfect decision or course of action will emerge." Ritualistic acts and obsessional rumination are seen as essential, helpful, and productive; to do anything else would seem foolhardy and dangerous.

8. *"If the perfect course of action is not clear, it is better to do nothing."* Because imperfection carries such terrible consequences, the obsessive will frequently make choices or act only when certain of success. Since there is so much uncertainty in life, the best choice is often to do nothing. If one does nothing, one cannot fail, and therefore one does not risk censure from self or others. The procrastination of the student or the lawyer may be an example of this assumption in action. The problem with this strategy is obvious when one considers that the environment more often requires productivity than perfection, and usually penalizes unproductivity.

9. *"Without my rules and rituals, I'll collapse in an inert pile."* Obsessives often do not understand that they probably have many reasons for doing what is important to them. Consequently, if the therapist suggests that some rules or rituals might be modified or abandoned, obsessives fear disaster: "I'll stop working altogether," "My work will become low-rate," "I'll become promiscuous," and so on. With these as predicted consequences, obsessives do not dare to question their rules.

These underlying assumptions account for the major and minor characteristics of OCPD, and will need to be challenged if these clients are to overcome the deleterious effects of their style. In addition to these assumptions, there are certain cognitive distortions (i.e., systematic errors in information processing) that are characteristic of OCPD. Among these is dichotomous thinking, the tendency to see things as all-or-nothing and in strictly black-and-white terms. It is this tendency that underlies the obsessive's rigidity, procrastination, and perfectionism. Without this primitive, global style of thinking, the obsessive would see the shades of gray that are obvious to others: Things may be perfect, excellent, very good, good, fair, poor, very poor, or extremely poor. The obsessive would then be able to tolerate making an imperfect decision because it could still be a good one. With dichotomous thinking, an imperfect decision is, by definition, a wrong decision, and as such cannot be tolerated.

Another cognitive distortion in which the obsessive-compulsive frequently engages is magnification or catastrophizing. For the obsessive, the importance or consequences of an imperfection or error become greatly exaggerated. Thus, the obsessive would not only view getting less than 100% on a test as a failure, based on dichotomous thinking, but would also view the failure as being horrible and having severe consequences. Obsessives often have difficulty gauging the realistic importance of events. They frequently also make the complementary cognitive distortion of minimization, or undervaluing the significance of an action or event. For example, they may get very caught up in trying to make sure all the minor details of a project are perfectly correct, while paying little attention to the fact that the overall project is very late, which is much more important and possibly detrimental.

A characteristic of many obsessives is thinking in terms of "shoulds" and "musts." This primitive, absolutistic, and moralistic style of thinking leads them to do what they should or must do according to their strict internalized standards, rather than what they desire to do or what is preferable to do. This gives tasks the force of an imperative, and substitutes pressure for personal volition as the primary source of motivation. If obsessives fail to do what they "should," then they must feel guilty and self-critical. In addition, if others do not do what they "should" do, then they are deserving of anger and condemnation. Karen Horney (1950) discussed this style of thinking in great detail, and referred to it as the "tyranny of the shoulds" (p. 65). Beck (1967, 1976) and Ellis (1962) have also written about some of the psychological problems that this mode of thinking can engender.

Diagnostic Criteria and Assessment Strategies

The DSM-III-R diagnostic criteria for OCPD are presented in Table 14.1. Assessment and diagnosis of OCPD are not usually difficult if the clinician is aware of and watchful for the various manifestations of it. On the first phone contact with the obsessive, the therapist may detect signs of rigidity or indecisiveness in making arrangements for the first session. Indecisiveness in the obsessive will be based on the fear of making a mistake rather than the fear of displeasing or inconveniencing the therapist, as would be seen in a patient with a dependent personality dis-

TABLE 14.1
DSM-III-R Diagnostic Criteria for Obsessive Compulsive Personality Disorder

A pervasive pattern of perfectionism and inflexibility, beginning by early adulthood and present in a variety of contexts, as indicated by at least *five* of the following:

(1) perfectionism that interferes with task completion, e.g., inability to complete a project because own overly strict standards are not met

(2) preoccupation with details, rules, lists, order, organization, or schedules to the extent that the major point of the activity is lost

(3) unreasonable insistence that others submit to exactly his or her way of doing things, *or* unreasonable reluctance to allow others to do things because of the conviction that they will not do them correctly

(4) excessive devotion to work and productivity to the exclusion of leisure activities and friendships (not accounted for by obvious economic necessity)

(5) indecisiveness: decision making is either avoided, postponed, or protracted, e.g., the person cannot get assignments done on time because of ruminating about priorities (do not include if indecisiveness is due to excessive need for advice or reassurance from others)

(6) overconscientiousness, scrupulousness, and inflexibility about matters of morality, ethics, or values (not accounted for by cultural or religious identification)

(7) restricted expression of affection

(8) lack of generosity in giving time, money, or gifts when no personal gain is likely to result

(9) inability to discard worn-out or worthless objects even when they have no sentimental value

Note. From *Diagnostic and Statistical Manual of Mental Disorders* (3rd ed., rev., p. 356) by the American Psychiatric Association, 1987, Washington, DC: Author. Copyright 1987 by the American Psychiatric Association. Reprinted by permission.

order. Upon first meeting, the clinician may notice that the obsessive patient is rather stilted and formal and not particularly warm or expressive. In trying to express themselves correctly, obsessives often ruminate a great deal about a topic, making sure that they tell the therapist all the details and consider all the options. Conversely, they may speak in a slow, hesitating manner, which is also due to their anxiety about not expressing themselves correctly. The content of the obsessive's speech will be much more in the realm of facts and ideas rather than feelings and preferences. In obtaining historical and current life information, possible indicators of OCPD include the following: patients' having been raised in the rigid, controlling type of family environment discussed earlier; their not having close, self-disclosing interpersonal relationships; their being in a technical, detail-oriented profession such as accounting, law, or engineering; and their either not having many leisure activities, or having leisure activities that are very purposeful and goal-directed and not merely pursued for enjoyment.

Formal psychological testing may be helpful at times in diagnosing OCPD. The Millon Clinical Multi-Axial Inventory (Millon, 1983) was specifically designed to diagnose personality disorders, and is often useful in understanding the various manifestations of OCPD. Typical responses on projective tests are a large number of small-detail responses on the Rorschach, and long, detailed, moralistic stories on the Thematic Apperception Test. It needs to be considered, though, whether the time and money spent on projective tests are worthwhile, since an accurate diagnosis and understanding of the patient can probably be obtained without them.

The simplest and most economical way to diagnose OCPD is usually just to ask patients directly, in a straightforward, noncritical manner, whether the various DSM-III-R criteria apply to them. Most obsessives will quite readily admit to such criteria as not feeling comfortable expressing affection, being perfectionistic, and having difficulty throwing old things away—although they might not understand the connection between such characteristics and their presenting problems in therapy.

Related Axis I Disorders

Patients with OCPD come to see therapists for a wide variety of problems. Obsessives rarely, if ever, ask for help with their personality disorder, although sometimes they are aware that certain aspects of their personalty, such as being very perfectionistic, contribute to their psychological problems.

The most common presenting problem of persons with OCPD is some form of anxiety. Obsessives' perfectionism, rigidity, and continued reliance on "shoulds" to govern their behavior predispose them to experience the chronic, mild anxiety that is characteristic of a generalized anxiety disorder. Many obsessives continually worry and ruminate about whether they are performing well enough or doing the right thing. This often leads to the characteristic traits of indecisiveness and procrastination that are frequent presenting complaints. For certain obsessives, their chronic anxiety can intensify to the point of panic disorder if they find themselves in a severe conflict between their obsessiveness and external pressures. For example, if an obsessive is working on a project and is progressing very slowly due to perfectionism, but has only a short time to finish the project, his or her anxiety may intensify to the point of panic. The obsessive often then begins to ruminate and worry about the various physical symptoms that accompany panic, such as rapid heart beat and shortness of breath. This may lead to the vicious cycle often seen in panic disorder patients, in which increased worry leads to increased panic-related physical symptoms, which leads to further increased worry, and so on.

Patients with OCPD also suffer from specific obsessions and compulsions more often than average. In a study by Rasmussen and Tsuang (1986), it was found that 55% of a sample of 44 patients with obsessive or compulsive symptoms had OCPD.

Another common presenting problem in OCPD is depression. This may take the form of dysthymic disorder or unipolar major depression. Obsessives often lead rather flat, boring, unsatisfying lives and suffer from chronic mild depression. Some obsessives will become aware of this over time, though they will not understand why it is occurring, and will come to therapy complaining of anhedonia, boredom, lack of energy, and not enjoying life as much as others appear to. Sometimes they will be pushed into therapy by spouses who view them as depressed and depressing. Due to their rigidity, perfectionism, and strong need to be in control of themselves, their environment, and their emotions, obsessives are very vulnerable to becoming overwhelmed, hopeless, and depressed when they experience their lives as having gotten out of control and their usual coping mechanisms as being ineffective.

A variety of psychosomatic disorders are often experienced by obsessives. Obsessives are predisposed to developing such problems because of the physical effects of their continually heightened arousal and anxiety. They frequently suffer from tension headaches, backaches, constipation, and ulcers. They may also have Type A personalities, and thus are at increased risk for cardiovascular problems, particularly if they are often angry and hostile. Patients with these disorders are often referred by physicians, since obsessives usually view these disorders as having physical causes. Getting them to understand and work on the psychological aspects of these problems can be quite difficult.

Some patients with OCPD present with sexual disorders. The obsessive's discomfort with emotion, lack of spontaneity, overcontrol, and rigidity are not conducive to a free and comfortable expression of his or her sexuality. Common sexual dysfunctions experienced by the obsessive are inhibited sexual desire, inability to have an orgasm, premature ejaculation, and dyspareunia.

Finally, obsessives may come to therapy at the urging of others, due to problems the other persons are having in coping with them. Spouses may initiate couple therapy because of their discomfort with obsessives' lack of emotional availability or with their being workaholics and spending little time with their families. Families with an obsessive parent may come for therapy due to the rigid, strict style of parenting, which can lead to chronic fighting between the parent and children. Also, employers may send obsessive employees to therapy because of their continual procrastination or their inability to function effectively in interpersonal relationships on the job.

Treatment Approaches

The general goal of psychotherapy with OCPD patients is to help them alter or reinterpret the problematic underlying assumptions so that behaviors and emotions will change. Therapy begins by focusing on the presenting problem. Cognitive therapists are generally much more willing to accept patients' complaints at face value than are psychodynamic therapists (who focus their attention much more on unconscious factors). Thus, whether a patient initially complains of anxiety, headaches, or impotence, this is frequently the problem that is addressed. Sometimes the obsessive's complaints are more externalized—for example, "My supervisors are very critical of my work with no good reason." This type of problem presentation can be more difficult to work with. The therapist can still directly address the presenting complaint, however, by clearly establishing that since the supervisor's behavior cannot be directly changed through the therapy, the goal will need to be to change the patient's behavior in ways that may lead to the supervisor's acting differently.

As in all therapies, it is important at the start to establish a rapport with the patient. This can be difficult with obsessive patients because of their rigidity, discomfort with emotion, and tendency to downplay the importance of interpersonal relationships. Therapy with the obsessive tends to be more businesslike and problem-focused, with less emphasis on emotional support and relationship issues. Usually, rapport is based on the patients respect for the therapist's competence and a belief that the therapist respects and can be helpful to the patient. Trying to develop a closer emotional relationship than the obsessive is comfortable with early in therapy can be detrimental, and may lead to an early termination. See Beck's (1983) article on the treatment of autonomous depression for a further discussion of this.

Obsessives can elicit a variety of emotional reactions from therapists. Some therapists find these patients to be somewhat dry and boring because of their general lack of emotionality, and their tendency in particular to focus more on the factual aspects of events rather than the events' affective tones. They can also be experienced as exasperating because of their slowness and focus on details, particularly to therapists who value efficiency and goal-directedness. Therapists who tend to like the idealization and dependency that many patients develop in therapy often find obsessive patients less rewarding, as they tend not to form this kind of therapeutic relationship. Some obsessives act out their needs for control in the therapy in either a direct or a passive-aggressive manner. For example, when given a homework assignment, they might directly tell the therapist that the assignment is irrelevant or stupid, or else agree to do it but then forget or not have time to get the assignment done. These patients can elicit anger and frustration from therapists and bring up conflicts related to the therapists' own needs to be in control.

Therapists' reactions to obsessive patients can provide valuable information about the patients and the sources of their difficulties. However, therapists should avoid trying to make changes in the patients based on their own values rather than influenced by the patients' needs and presenting problems. For example, an obsessive patient may be less emotionally expressive than a therapist believes is psychologically healthy, but this may not be a source of significant impairment or subjective distress for the patient.

Early in cognitive therapy, it is vital to introduce the patient to the cognitive model: that the patient's feelings and behaviors are based on the perceptions of, thoughts about, and meanings given to the events in his or her life. This can be demonstrated by watching for an affect shift in the session, and then asking the patient what he or she had been thinking just before. Another way to demonstrate this would be to describe a situation such as someone's waiting for a friend who is late, and listing the various emotions that the person waiting may be experiencing, such as anger, anxiety, or depression, and relating these feelings to thoughts that were probably producing them: "How dare he make me wait for him," "Maybe he was in an accident," or "This just proves that nobody likes me."

In addition to teaching patients the cognitive theory of emotion, it is important at the beginning of cognitive therapy to establish therapeutic goals. These obviously relate to the presenting problems and may, for the obsessive, include such things as "getting assignments at work done on time," "no longer having tension headaches," or "being able to have orgasms." It is important to try to be specific in listing goals; general goals such as "not being depressed" are harder to work with. If the patient is mainly concerned with depression, it is necessary to break that down into its various aspects, such as not being able to get up in the morning or not being able to accomplish anything, in order to be able to work with the depression effectively.

After goals have been established that the patient and therapist agree are relevant and can be worked on, they are ranked in the order they are to be worked on, as it is difficult and often nonproductive to try to work on them all at once. Two criteria to use in ranking the goals are the importance of each problem and how easily solvable it is. It is often helpful to have an early, fairly rapid success in therapy, to heighten the patient's motivation and belief in the therapeutic process. After the problem areas have been established, it is important to identify the automatic thoughts and schemas that are associated with them.

Generally, the problem being worked on is monitored each week between sessions, usually on a Dysfunctional Thought Record (Beck et al., 1979). The Dysfunctional Thought Record allows patients to list what the situation is, how they are feeling, and what their thoughts are when the problem occurs. Thus, an obsessive working on procrastination might become aware that he or she is doing a task at work, feeling anxious, and thinking, "I don't want to do this assignment because I won't be able to do it perfectly." After a number of similar examples of automatic thoughts have been gathered, it becomes apparent to the obsessive that much of the anxiety and procrastination is due to perfectionism. It is then crucial to determine the assumptions or schemas underlying the various automatic thoughts. In the example of perfectionism, the underlying assumption may be "I must avoid mistakes to be worthwhile." It is often helpful at this point to assist the patient in understanding how he or she learned the schema. Usually it developed out of interactions with parents or other significant figures, although sometimes the schemas are based more on cultural norms or developed in more idiosyncratic ways. Therapy then consists of helping the obsessive patient to identify and understand the negative consequences of these assumptions or schemas, and then to develop ways of refuting them so that they no longer control the patients feelings and behavior and lead to the problems that brought him or her to therapy.

Specific Cognitive Therapy Techniques

Within the broad general structure of cognitive therapy, a number of specific techniques are helpful with obsessive-compulsive patients. It is important to structure the therapy sessions by setting an agenda, prioritizing the problems, and using problem-solving techniques. This is useful in working with a number of characteristics of the obsessive, including indecisiveness, rumination, and procrastination. Structure forces the patient to pick out and work on a specific problem until it is improved to an acceptable level. If the obsessive has difficulty working with the structure, the therapist can have the patient look at his or her automatic thoughts about this, and relate this difficulty to the general problems of indecisiveness and procrastination. The Weekly Activity Schedule (Beck et al., 1979), a form on which patients can schedule activities on an hour-by-hour basis for a week, is also of great benefit in helping them add structure to their lives and become more productive while exerting less effort.

Because of obsessives' frequent problems with anxiety and psychosomatic symptoms, relaxation techniques and meditation are often helpful. Obsessives frequently have difficulty using these techniques at first, due to their belief that they are just wasting time by taking half an hour off to relax or meditate. A cognitive therapy technique that can be used to address issues like this is the listing of advantages and disadvantages of a specific behavior or belief. A disadvantage to relaxation techniques for the obsessive may be that they take time; the advantage would be that then the patient can actually get more done because he or she is more refreshed and less anxious.

It is often useful to conduct a behavioral experiment (another specific technique used in cognitive therapy) with obsessive-compulsive patients. For example, instead of directly trying to dispute a certain belief held by an obsessive, the therapist can take a neutral, experimental attitude toward it. Thus, if an obsessive businessman thinks that he does not have time to relax during the day, the therapist can have him try relaxation for a few days and then measure how much he accomplishes on the days he uses a relaxation tape and how much he accomplishes on days he does not. It would also be beneficial to assess to what degree the patient enjoys the days he uses the relaxation technique in contrast to the days he does not. Obsessives tend to value pleasure much less than productivity. It is often therapeutic to help them become aware of this and to evaluate with them the assumptions behind their value system concerning the place of pleasure in their lives.

Several cognitive and behavioral techniques can be useful in helping obsessive patients cope with chronic worrying and ruminating. Once patients agree that this is dysfunctional, they can be taught thought-stopping or distraction techniques to redirect their thought processes. If they continue to believe that worrying is somehow helpful or productive, they may agree to limit it to a certain time period during the day, which at least manages to free them from worrying for the rest of the day. Graded task assignments, in which a goal or task is broken down into specific definable steps, are often helpful. These serve to counter patients' dichotomous thinking and perfectionism by demonstrating that most things are accomplished by degrees of progress, rather than by being done perfectly or in their entirety right from the beginning.

Case Study

The following case study will demonstrate how cognitive therapy is used with a patient who has OCPD. Mr. S was a 45-year-old white engineer who was married and had a 10-year-old son. He came for cognitive therapy after a recent exacerbation of a long-standing problem of experiencing severe muscular pain in his back, neck, and shoulders. Mr. S had suffered from this condition since age 28. He originally considered it to be purely a physical problem, but was told by his physician that, although he did have a minor degree of arthritis in his neck, this should not cause nearly the degree of pain that he was experiencing. Over the next 10 years, Mr. S was periodically treated for the pain by osteopaths, physical therapists, and chiropractors, and was prescribed Valium and aspirin. These treatments helped to some degree, but at age 38 Mr. S had a severe episode of pain and had to miss 3 weeks of work. This was during a period when he was working on an important and complicated project. At that point, he began seriously considering that his neck and back pain might be related to the degree of psychological stress he was experiencing.

Mr. S then went into psychodynamically oriented psychotherapy for the next 18 months. He found this to be somewhat useful, as it helped him to understand how his back pain was an expression of stress and anxiety, and it also helped him gain a better understanding of some of the problems in his family background. At the conclusion of the therapy, however, Mr. S was still experiencing some degree of pain on most days. He periodically had episodes during which the muscles in his back would knot up, resulting in a great deal of pain for several days in a row. He coped with this for several years by using relaxation techniques, taking aspirin, and occasionally seeing an osteopath. It was after one of these more severe episodes of pain that Mr. S decided to come to the Center for Cognitive Therapy, which he had read about in a magazine article.

Mr. S had been born and raised in the southern United States. He was the younger of two children, with a sister 7 years older. He was from a conservative, religious, middle-class family. His father worked as a sales manager. Mr. S described him as being a nice, somewhat anxious man with whom Mr. S had a good but not very close relationship. He was much closer to his mother, who was a housewife, and stated that he was always very concerned about her opinion of him. His mother was very involved with Mr. S when he was a child. He liked that, but also experienced her as being a fairly critical, judgmental woman who had lots of "shoulds" about the way people are supposed to behave. Mr. S remembered one particular incident, when he was in first grade, in which a friend had written him a letter and he was trying to write a response. Mr. S was having some difficulty in doing this; although it wasn't explicitly stated, he got the impression that his mother was dissatisfied with him and was thinking, "Your friend can write a letter, so why can't you?"

Mr. S reported being reasonably happy during his childhood. By sixth grade, though, he started becoming concerned about how he was functioning both academically and socially. In school he coped with this by either working very hard to do well (while always worrying that he wasn't doing well enough), or else by procrastinating and trying not to think about what he was supposed to be doing. Socially, he became introverted, avoidant, and emotionally constricted. The less involved and expressive he was, the less chance it seemed that there was to be criticized or rejected. These patterns of behavior gradually increased throughout his adolescence.

During his second year of college, Mr. S experienced a great deal of anxiety over his inability to perform academically up to his expectations. It became increasingly difficult to complete written assignments, because he was concerned that they would not be good enough. In addition, Mr. S was feeling very lonely and isolated due to his being away from home, and his being unable to develop friendships or heterosexual relationships at college. He became more and more pessimistic about himself and his future. This culminated in his experiencing a major depressive episode, during which he lost interest in all activities and spent the majority of his time sleeping. This lasted a couple of months and led to Mr. S's dropping out of school and joining the Army. The increased structure and companionship in the Army were helpful, and he functioned well for the 3 years he was in the service. He then returned to school and obtained his engineering degree. Mr. S had worked as an engineer since age 27. He had been moderately successful in his career. At the time of his seeking treatment, he was performing some administrative and supervisory duties, which he was less comfortable with than the more structured, technical, detail-oriented engineering work on which he spent most of his time.

Mr. S was never comfortable or very successful with dating. At age 31, he was reintroduced to a woman he had met briefly several years before. She remembered him—which surprised and flattered him—and they started dating. They married 1 year later, and 2 years after that had a son. Mr. S described the marriage as being good, but not as close as he would like. He felt emotionally and sexually restrained with his wife, which he realized was part of the problem. Mr. S did not have any close friends, but was marginally involved with various church and civic groups.

Mr. S's goal in therapy was to eliminate, or at least greatly diminish, the pain he experienced in his back and neck. Unlike many psychosomatic patients, he had already come to accept that psychological factors played in major part in his pain. The therapist discussed the cognitive model with Mr. S, and he was quite receptive to it. The homework assignment for the first few weeks was to monitor his pain on the Weekly Activity Schedule. this consisted of ranking the severity of his pain from

1 to 10 on an hour-by-hour basis, while also noting hour by hour what he was doing. At first, Mr. S noticed that the pain was the most severe in the evening, when he was home with his family. This was difficult for him to understand, as usually he enjoyed this period of time and found it relaxing. It was determined in the therapy, though, that this was due to his having learned very well to distract himself from the pain—thus he wouldn't notice it as it was building up during the day. At times distraction is a useful technique for obsessives, particularly with their nonproductive, ruminative thinking. In Mr. S's case, though, it interfered with the assessment of the problem. As he became more aware of his pain, he noticed that it would start as a type of tingling, sunburn-like feeling and then progress from a mild to a more severe pain. Under prolonged stress, the muscles in his back and neck would knot up, and he would have to spend a couple of days at home in bed.

After Mr. S learned to monitor his pain more closely, it became clear that three types of situations were associated with his muscular tension: having tasks or assignments to do; having procrastinated and thereby having a whole list of things not completed; and being expected to participate in social situations with new people. The therapist and Mr. S decided to work initially on the first situation, as it occurred much more often than the third, and the second (the procrastination) was due in large part to it. Mr. S began filling out Dysfunctional Thought Records whenever he noticed any tension or pain in his back associated with doing a task. For example, he once noticed that he was experiencing a moderate degree of back pain while standing and rinsing off the dishes before putting them in the dishwasher. He was thinking that the dishes needed to be perfectly clean before putting them in the dishwasher. This was making the task stressful and also making it take a long time to complete. He collected a number of similar examples that in and of themselves were not that major, but helped Mr. S to see that his perfectionism caused numerous tasks during the day to become sources of stress that were eventually manifested in pain. He then began to look for the general assumptions or schemas underlying his automatic thoughts. Mr. S developed the diagram shown in Figure 14.1 as a model of his behavior.

The therapist and Mr. S then further discussed the meaning of this pattern of thinking and behavior.

THERAPIST: So you find that generally you experience a lot of stress when having to do something because you believe that no matter how well you do it, it won't be acceptable?

PATIENT: Yes, and I think that's why I always have a tendency not to make decisions or to procrastinate so I don't have to deal with these feelings.

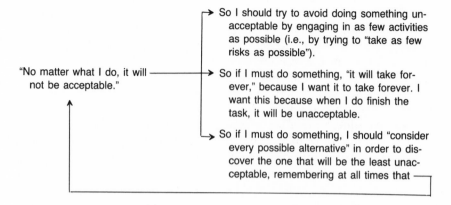

FIGURE 14.1   Mr. S's model of his behavior.

THERAPIST: Does that work as a way of reducing stress for you?

PATIENT: No, putting things off usually just makes it worse. I like to think I'm a pretty responsible person, and it really bothers me not to be getting things done. I've had some of my worst episodes of back pain after I've been procrastinating a lot.

THERAPIST: You put down on the diagram that your belief is that what you do won't be acceptable. Why would that be upsetting for you?

PATIENT: What do you mean?

THERAPIST: Do you think that some people are able to perform in a manner that isn't very good or that someone else would consider unacceptable, yet not get upset about it?

PATIENT: Yes, I've known some people like that. I guess for me, though, I feel like in some way I am personally unacceptable or deficient if I don't function up to a certain level, which often seems impossible for me to do.

Thus, Mr. S's core schema or belief was that if he didn't continuously function at a very high level, then he was personally unacceptable. Since Mr. S's belief was for the most part conditional, and there was but little chance that he could perform well enough to be acceptable, his primary symptoms were a form of anxiety (i.e., the physical stress in his back). At times, though, Mr. S would give up and conclude that no matter what he did he would be unacceptable. At these times, such as during college, he would become hopeless and depressed.

After uncovering Mr. S's core belief, the main focus in therapy was to change it, as the belief was the primary source both for Mr. S's current symptoms and for his OCPD. As the therapist and Mr. S discussed his belief over the next few sessions, he came to understand better how he had internalized the very high standards he thought his mother had for him. In addition, he became very self-critical, as he had experienced his mother to be when he did not meet her expectations; he also expected others to be very critical of him.

The therapist and Mr. S started examining the validity of his beliefs by first looking at whether they appeared to be accurate interpretations of the past. For one homework assignment, Mr. S listed all the times he could remember in the past that others had been very critical of him, and also listed possible alternatives as to why they might have acted that way. Mr. S was able to remember only a few instances of this sort, and most of them had occurred with his sergeant in the service—who had been very critical with everyone. Mr. S did have the thought, though, that probably on many occasions others had been disapproving of him but just had not said so. The therapist and Mr. S then discussed what he could do about this belief.

THERAPIST: So it still seems to you that others are disapproving of you, even though you can think of very few times in the past when you have had solid evidence that this was true?

PATIENT: Yes, I find that I still often think that others aren't pleased with what I am doing, and then I am very uncomfortable around them.

THERAPIST: How do you think you could find out if these beliefs you are having are accurate?

PATIENT: I don't know.

THERAPIST: Well, in general, if you wanted to know something from someone, what would you do?

PATIENT: I guess I would ask them about it.

THERAPIST: Why couldn't you do that in these situations to see if your belief about others' disapproving of you is true?

PATIENT: I suppose I could, but they might not like my asking them and might not tell me the truth.

THERAPIST: That is a possibility, but most of the time I have found that if you ask someone how they are feeling in a calm, receptive manner, you can get an honest answer. For example, can you think of a way you could ask your boss how he is feeling about you and your work?

PATIENT: I suppose I could say something like this: "Jack, you seem to be concerned about something. Is anything bothering you about the way my project is going?"

THERAPIST: Yes, I think that would be a good way to approach him. Why don't we set up as homework for the next week that you check it out whenever you think that someone is disapproving of you, and record both what you expected the person to say and what they did say?

PATIENT: OK, I'll try that.

This was an example of setting up a behavioral experiment to test out a specific dysfunctional belief. For the next couple of weeks, Mr. S did ask others on several occasions what they were thinking when he thought that they were evaluating him critically. He found that on all but one occasion, he had misinterpreted what others were thinking about him. On that occasion, one of his bosses at work was mildly annoyed with him, but this was due to Mr. S's being late in getting him some work. The patient was able to realize from this that it was more often his procrastination than his level of performance that caused problems and dissatisfaction for him.

Mr. S, like many obsessives, had the belief that it was often functional to put things off because this enabled him to perform better. The therapist had him evaluate this belief in a homework assignment by rating his level of performance on a variety of tasks from 1 to 10. He then compared the average level of performance on tasks on which he had procrastinated to his performance on those the had done as soon as he could after being given them. He found that his average level of performance was slightly higher on tasks that he did immediately; Mr. S attributed this to the increased stress he would feel about tasks he kept putting off.

Another technique that proved helpful to Mr. S was having him compare the values and standards he had for himself to those he had for others. He came to realize that he was much more critical and demanding of himself than he was of others, and agreed that it didn't make much sense to have two different sets of values. The therapist then used this understanding to have him ask himself, when he was being very self-critical, what he would be thinking about how he was functioning if he were someone else. Mr. S found that this technique helped him to be more understanding and less critical of himself. The technique does not work with many obsessives, though, because obsessive patients are frequently as critical and demanding of others as they are of themselves.

The therapist and Mr. S also identified the primary cognitive distortions and maladaptive modes of thought that Mr. S frequently used. These included dichotomous thinking ("If I don't do this task perfectly, I have done it terribly"); magnification ("It is horrible if I don't do this well"); overgeneralization ("If I do something poorly, it means I am an unacceptable person); and "should" statements ("I should do this perfectly"). Mr. S monitored the use of these thought patterns on Dysfunctional Thought Records, and identified how they increased his stress level and often lowered his level of performance.

As Mr. S became more and more able to recognize and understand the distortions in his thought processes, he became increasingly effective at responding rationally to his automatic thoughts and breaking the habitual cognitive and behavioral patterns that led to his muscular pain.

A couple of sessions were spent in working on his social anxiety, which was also related to his perfectionism and fears of being unacceptable. As a result of the progress he had already made in these areas, Mr. S found that he was experiencing less social anxiety, and was able to continue making progress on it by using the same techniques he had learned to help with his anxiety about doing tasks.

After 15 sessions over a 6-month period, Mr. S was experiencing little back pain, and when he did he was generally able to recognize the source of stress and his dysfunctional automatic thoughts, and then modify them. At a 6-month follow-up session, Mr. S reported having remained relatively pain-free. He had had one difficult weekend before he had to make a speech, but he had been able to cope with this and prepare the speech, and the presentation of it went well.

Relapse Prevention

For most patients it is easy to slip back into familiar, but dysfunctional cognitive and behavioral patterns. This is particularly true with personality-disordered patients, as their problems are so ingrained. Cognitive therapy has advantages over some other forms of therapy in coping with this. It is made very clear to patients on a conscious level what their problems are, and they are shown effective ways of coping with them. They are taught how to use tools such as the Dysfunctional Thought Record, which can be used outside of the therapy context to work on problem areas.

It is crucial at the end of therapy to warn patients about the possibility of relapse, and to have them watch closely for minor recurrences of the problems that brought them to therapy. These are indications that the patients need to do some more work—either by themselves, with the tools they learned in therapy, or with the therapist. It is important at the end of therapy for the therapist to tell patients that it is not unusual to need occasional booster sessions, so that they will not be ashamed to get help if a problem recurs. Most cognitive therapists build this into the therapy by scheduling periodic booster sessions after the main part of the therapy has been completed.

Summary

Based on clinical experience alone, cognitive therapy appears to be an effective and efficient treatment for OCPD. Obsessives often respond particularly well to certain aspects of cognitive therapy, including its problem-focused nature, its use of various forms in homework assignments, and its stress on the importance of thought processes. They usually prefer therapeutic approaches that are more structured and present-focused to therapies that focus more on the therapeutic process and the transference relationship as the means of effecting personality change (Juni & Semel, 1982).

At present, unfortunately, there are no research findings that substantiate the validity of cognitive therapy—or any other form of treatment—for OCPD. Due to the problem of getting a substantial number of obsessives at any one research center, and due to the variety of their presenting problems, it may be difficult to do definitive outcome studies with this group of patients.

Chapter 15
Passive-Aggressive Personality Disorder

Diagnostic Features

The most striking feature of passive-aggressive personality disorder (PAPD) is a resistance to external demands, which is typically manifested in oppositional and obstructive behaviors. These behaviors include procrastination, poor work quality, and "forgetting" obligations. These people often have a history of substandard performance in both occupational and social arenas. As might be expected, they typically resent having to conform to standards set by others. While these characteristics might be observed occasionally in many individuals, in PAPD they represent a chronic, inflexible behavior pattern. Although passive-aggressive behavior in general is usually not the most advantageous form of interaction, it is not severely dysfunctional until it becomes a pattern that interferes with achieving life goals.

People with PAPD also avoid being assertive, believing that a direct confrontation can be dangerous. Unlike the person with avoidant personality disorder, who avoids assertiveness for fear of rejection or negative evaluation by others, the passive-aggressive person sees confrontation as leading to interference and control by others. When others make requests that people with PAPD do not wish to fulfill, the combination of resentment of external demands and lack of assertiveness leads them to respond in a passively provocative manner. In addition, they become angry at people who ask them to do things, not seeing that they might be able to deny or modify a request. Regarding obligations at work or school, individuals with PAPD are again angry and resentful. In general, authority figures are seen as arbitrary and unfair. Consistent with this, they typically blame others for their problems, and are unable to see how their own behavior contributes to their difficulties.

Millon (1969) noted that, in addition to opposing external demands, these individuals are characterized by a general moodiness and pessimism. In other words, they focus on the negative elements of whatever happens to them.

The DSM-III-R criteria for PAPD (APA, 1987) are presented in Table 15.1.

Historical Perspective

Although the concept of a passive-aggressive personality style had been described in earlier writings, the term was not coined until World War II. In 1945, an "immaturity reaction" was described by the War Department as a response to "routine military stress, manifested by helplessness, or inadequate responses, passiveness, obstructionism or aggressive outbursts." Later, a 1949 U.S. Joint Armed Services Technical Bulletin used "passive-aggressive" to describe soldiers who displayed this behavior pattern. In DSM-I (APA, 1952) the passive-aggressive category was divided into three subtypes: passive-aggressive, passive-dependent, and aggressive. The passive-dependent type, similar to our present diagnosis of dependent personality disorder, was characterized by helplessness, indecisiveness, and a tendency to cling to others.

TABLE 15.1
DSM-III-R Criteria for Passive Aggressive Personality Disorder

A pervasive pattern of passive resistance to demands for adequate social and occupational performance, beginning by early adulthood and present in a variety of contexts, as indicated by at least *five* of the following:

(1) procrastinates, i.e., puts off things that need to be done so that deadlines are not met
(2) becomes sulky, irritable, or argumentative when asked to do something he or she does not want to do
(3) seems to work deliberately slowly or do a bad job on tasks that he or she really does not want to do
(4) protests, without justification, that others make unreasonable demands on him or her
(5) avoids obligations by claiming to have "forgotten"
(6) believes that he or she is doing a much better job than others think he or she is doing
(7) resents useful suggestions of others concerning how he or she could be more productive
(8) obstructs the efforts of others by failing to do his or her share of the work
(9) unreasonably criticizes or scorns people in positions of authority

Note. From *Diagnostic and Statistical Manual of Mental Disorders* (3rd ed., rev., pp. 357–358) by the American Psychiatric Association, 1987, Washington, DC: Author. Copyright 1987 by the American Psychiatric Association. Reprinted by permission.

The passive-aggressive and aggressive types differed in how they responded to frustrations. As might be expected, the aggressive type (similar in some aspects to a current diagnosis of antisocial personality disorder) reacted with irritability and anger, temper tantrums, and destructive behavior. The passive-aggressive type manifested the aggression in passive ways—for example, pouting, stubbornness, procrastination, inefficiency, and obstructionism. In DSM-II (APA, 1968), the passive-aggressive subtype was made into a separate category, with the other two DSM-I passive-aggressive subtypes placed under the "other personality disorders" category.

In DSM-III (APA, 1980), not only did passive-aggressive remain a discrete personality disorder, but individuals characterized by the dependent features were placed in the current diagnosis of dependent personality disorder. Initially, however, passive-aggressive personality disorder was left out of the DSM-III draft, because Spitzer (1977) described the concept as "situational reactivity." As Malinow (1981) noted, the argument presented by Spitzer was that passive-aggressive behavior may represent a defense used by most individuals in positions of perceived helplessness (i.e., transient) rather than a personality disorder (i.e., a chronic maladaptive pattern).

Millon also noted that while other personality disorders were composed of a number of distinct traits, PAPD was defined almost solely by resistance to external demands. Because of this, he believed that PAPD was not represented by a range of diagnostic criteria necessary to define a personality disorder. He did, however, propose including in the description of this personality disorder such other characteristics as irritability, low frustration tolerance, discontented self-image, pessimism, and the use of unpredictable and sulking behaviors to provoke discomfort in others (Millon, 1981). Although these characteristics were not included in the DSM-III description, some of them have been incorporated in DSM-III-R (APA, 1987; see Table 15.1) and provide additional information with which to diagnose this disorder.

Early theorists of psychopathology described a personality type that seemed to have several characteristics of PAPD. For example, both Kraepelin (1913) and Bleuler (1924) described individuals who consistently responded to things in a negative fashion. Kraepelin described both extreme mood fluctuations and an overresponsiveness to negative experiences, while Bleuler further described a group who were quick to become frustrated and irritated after their typical negative interpretation of situations.

Some psychoanalytic theorists have also described a similar character type. Reich (1945), for example, described a masochistic personality type in which the person chronically complained and tended to passively aggress against others. These people had an inability to tolerate unpleasant feelings and autonomic arousal. Millon (1981) suggests that PAPD does not have a complex intrapsychic structure. Instead, feelings are experienced without the benefit of an intrapsychic modification. This explanation is consistent with the vacillating emotional state of the passive-aggressive personality.

A variation of this disorder was described in transactional analysis by Berne (1964). Berne describes a pattern in which someone is mildly destructive—for example, spilling a drink at a party—yet still obtains forgiveness. In this pattern or game, called the "schlemiel," the passive-aggressive person gets satisfaction both from being destructive and from being forgiven for it.

Research and Empirical Data

Although there has been very little research on PAPD, two studies have examined its characteristics. Specifically, Whitman, Trosman, and Koenig (1954) examined 400 outpatients and found that the most common personality diagnosis based on DSM-I nomenclature was the passive-aggressive type, with 23% meeting the diagnosis for dependent type, and 19% for the passive-aggressive type. They also noted that twice as many men as women met criteria for PAPD. The most frequently associated symptom picture with this personality disorder included anxiety (41%) and depression (25%). In both the passive-aggressive and passive-dependent subtypes, overt expression of aggression was inhibited by guilt or fear of retaliation. It was suggested that a key component of the treatment plan should be attacking the fear of aggression and dependency.

Small, Small, Alig, and Moore (1970) also conducted a 7- to 15-year follow-up on 100 patients who had been diagnosed as passive-aggressive (according to DSM-II) during a psychiatric hospitalization. They found that difficulty in interpersonal relationships and social behavior, along with affective and somatic complaints, were the primary forms of symptomatology. They also noted a high proportion of passive-aggressives who had been depressed and abused alcohol.

Cognitive Therapy Conceptualization

Automatic Thoughts and Attitudes

The automatic thoughts of individuals with PAPD reflect their negativism, autonomy, and desire to follow the path of least resistance. For example, they see any requests from others as intrusive and demanding.

Their response is to resist the request automatically rather than evaluate whether they want to do it. They vacillate between thinking that others have taken advantage of them and that they are unworthy. This negativism is pervasive in their thinking. Passive-aggressive patients look for a negative interpretation of most events. Even during neutral or positive events, they seek out and focus on the negative aspects. This differs from negative thoughts during depression: Depressed individuals focus on self-deprecating thoughts or negative thoughts about the environment or future, while passive-aggressive patients assume that others do not appreciate them or are trying to control them. When they receive negative feedback from someone, passive-aggressive patients assume that they have been misunderstood once again.

Negative automatic thoughts also indicate the anger felt by these patients. This group of patients is often insistent that things need to be a certain way, and these unreasonable "shoulds" result in the low frustration tolerance exhibited by this group. This rigidity is unlike the goal-directedness of the obsessive-compulsive personality, however, in that the emphasis of the passive-aggressive patient is not an achievement ("I should do this"), but on autonomy—that is, not being subject to others' rules ("I should not have to do this"). Some typical automatic thoughts are presented in Table 15.2

In addition, these patients hold an assumption that is typical with patients who have difficulty being assertive. That is, they believe that open conflict is terrible and will result in disapproval or even rejection. However, while passive-aggressive persons fail to assert themselves, they nevertheless deeply resent submitting to others' demands. They do not want to follow implicit or explicit directions, but they only passively try to thwart other persons—not wanting open conflict, yet also not wanting to comply. Rules are seen as ways others try to thwart them. It does not matter to passive-aggressives that others are also required to follow these rules. They see the situation only from their own frame of reference, which suggests that they are being treated unfairly. One patient, for example, was furious that she had not received a billing statement. This

TABLE 15.2
**Typical Automatic Thoughts in Passive-Aggressive
Personality Disorder**

How dare they tell me what to do!
I'll do what I want to do.
Nobody gives me credit for the work I do.
People take advantage of me.
Nothing ever works out for me.
People should treat me with more respect.

patient had refused to set up an appointment, had not responded to the therapist's calls or letters, and had never indicated that she needed the statement until she started making angry calls. Unlike a patient with a paranoid personality disorder, who might be wary of hidden motives, this patient thought that she was being treated unfairly. Another patient was angry that his car was towed when he parked in a no-parking zone on a weekend. Although the lot was clearly marked, he was furious that he had been towed.

Partly as a result of their poor occupational and social performance, passive-aggressive patients develop a pessimistic outlook. They believe that "life is miserable" and focus on the negative aspects of experience. It is as though these patients perceive everything through a filter of negativity. Unlike depressive patients, who might report a general negative attitude, passive-aggressive patients do not expect that hard work will produce life's rewards for them. This may result from their belief that they do work hard, and their inability to recognize the negative contribution of their cognitive and behavioral style, which does make it difficult for them to be successful. They see the attainment of goals as being determined capriciously. These patients also assume that they are victims of fate and do not perceive clearly how their own actions affect their lives. When things go well for them, they assume that something negative is bound to happen. Some of these typical attitudes and assumptions are listed in Table 15.3.

Behavior

Behaviors of PAPD clients reflect their cognitive patterns. Passive-oppositional behavior, such as procrastination and doing poorly on jobs, is related to cognitions that stem from being resentful of having to meet obligations ("I shouldn't have to do it"). The attitude associated with procrastination is one of taking the course of least resistance (e.g., "No need to do it now"). Since they do not want to risk any adverse con-

---

TABLE 15.3
Typical Attitudes and Assumptions in Passive-Aggressive Personality Disorder

People don't understand me.
Life is miserable—nothing works out for me.
People take advantage of you if you let them.
It doesn't matter what you do—nothing works out anyway.
Being direct with people could be dangerous.
Rules are arbitrary and stifle me.

sequences for facing such situations directly (and because they often do not have the skills to be effectively assertive), passive-aggressive individuals respond to demands by "getting back" through the passive means described. When faced with the negative consequences of not adequately meeting obligations, they become angry at those in authority, rather than seeing how their own pattern has contributed to these results. This anger may occasionally be expressed in an angry outburst, but is more likely to result in further passive means of retaliation, such as sabotage. In therapy, this might include not paying for sessions, not showing up on time, or refusing to collaborate in the treatment. In one instance, a passive-aggressive patient forgot her session. The therapist called to reschedule at the next available time, 2 days away. The patient, angry both that the first appointment had been missed and that the second was not immediate, responded before hanging up by saying, "I'll be there if I'm still alive." This response would either engage the therapist in more interaction prior to the session or cause the therapist to worry during that time.

Affect

The common negative affective states for PAPD patients are anger and irritability. This is not surprising, since they believe that they are being required to meet arbitrary standards and that they are misunderstood or unappreciated. For instance, one patient was angry that the street signs in a town were too small for her to read. Furthermore, they often fall short of meeting their own goals, both professionally and personally. Their failure to see how their behavior and attitudes have contributed to their problems results in further anger, as they think that the environment has thwarted them once again.

Also contributing to their anger and irritability are their vulnerability to external control and their interpretation of others' requests as interfering with their freedom. In interactions with others, they expect control by others and oppose this vehemently.

Reasons for Entering Therapy

Among the typical reasons for PAPD patients to enter therapy are complaints by others that they are resistant to meeting expectations. This can occur in marriages as well as in employee-supervisor relationships. The complaints by the spouse usually include the patient's not contributing to household responsibilities. One wife reported that her husband would be unresponsive to her until she became unresponsive in turn and threatened to leave the relationship. At that point, he would cooperate with her temporarily until she again became committed to the relationship. Then the pattern of his withdrawal and resistance to her demands would resume. Often these patients will enter treatment on the insistence of supervisors because of procrastination and evasion of rules at work.

Depression is another reason PAPD patients enter treatment. A contributing factor to depression with these patients is a chronic lack of rewards, both interpersonally and occupationally. For example, their following the path of least resistance, and their resistance to external demands, can result in the belief that nothing goes right for them. Also, their view of their environment as one in which they are vulnerable to control by others can result in a negative view of the world at large. This often results in a chronic level of dysthymia. However, when these patients are faced with failure or loss, they may experience depression that is more severe. Being autonomous, they are invested in preserving their freedom of action. If circumstances occur in which the patients do not believe they are directing their lives without outside interference, they may become severely depressed.

Assessment Strategies

In assessing PAPD in an interview situation, the interviewer may note that it is difficult to obtain complete information. These patients may give incomplete, terse answers, and may also appear irritated at having to answer a question, although patients with other diagnoses respond to the same question easily. Even when they appear active in responding to questions, these patients often fail to provide a direct answer, and will either avoid the question completely or give extraneous details. Cognitions may include "I shouldn't have to answer this," or "The interviewer is trying to control me."

Next, a negativistic attitude will usually be displayed as these patients describe how difficult their lives are and how things never work out for them. They will show no insight into how they might be contributing to their own difficulties, blaming others instead.

An attitude such as "I won't let people push me around," of course, is not sufficient to merit a diagnosis of PAPD. It is necessary to obtain relevant information about a person's achievement in academic, social, and occupational activities. The passive-aggressive patient will usually report a number of "false starts" and unsuccessful attempts at reaching goals. This pattern will be more chronic than with a depressed patient. On questioning, passive-aggressives may report that they lost a job because "the boss was unfair," or "I wasn't given any freedom on the job," or "I was a victim of discrimination." Although paranoid patients may also report discriminatory and abusive motives by others, they will be more wary than passive-aggressive patients. The latter will focus more on the perceived interference from others that prevents them from having things their own way.

Once a diagnosis has been made, an assessment of social skills is helpful in treatment planning. Some patients may have the skills to assert themselves appropriately, but may not use them due to dysfunctional attitudes. For example when faced with situations where they might actively discuss things with others, their strategy of following the path of least resistance may interfere with their doing so. In addition, the desire to do things their own way will make it less likely that they will approach others with a spirit of compromise. While most passive-aggressive patients will have attitudes that interfere with appropriate social behavior, some patients may lack the skills for appropriate social response. In such a case, this may be an important component of the treatment plan.

Broad Clinical Strategies

Frequently, when patients with a personality disorder enter treatment, they will not be interested in changing long-standing patterns of thought and behavior. Instead, they enter treatment because of an Axis I diagnosis, such as depression, or because of pressure from other people. This is particularly the case for people with PAPD, since they are likely to believe that their difficulties are a result of others rather than themselves. Initially, therefore, treatment will be focused on determining what goal brought the patients into treatment.

A first general approach with passive-aggressive patients is to focus on collaborative empiricism—that is, actively engaging them in the therapeutic process (Beck, 1976). Although this is a central component of cognitive therapy in general, it is especially important with passive-aggressive patients, since they defy authority figures. It is important, therefore, that they realize that they are actively making choices in treatment and are not being directed or manipulated by the therapist. The therapist may initially encourage them to chose from several homework assignments or issues for discussion in the session. Later, patients are encouraged to develop their own strategies in addressing problems. This is helpful in working within the patients' desire for autonomy while at the same time discouraging their typically passive approach. This collaboration can also be facilitated by using an experimental approach. For example, if a patient firmly believes his or her automatic thoughts or assumptions, it is best if the therapist does not try to debate their accuracy, but rather sets them up as hypotheses that may or may not be true. Then therapist and patient can jointly set up some "experiment" to test their validity.

A second strategy with passive-aggressive patients is helping them make contact with their automatic thoughts. Their lack of insight indicates that they rarely examine how their cognitions contribute to their affect and behavior. This very broad strategy will be central to the treatment program, and considerable time must be devoted early in treatment to explaining the rationale behind the cognitive model. By becoming more aware of their thoughts, the patients will learn to identify those automatic thoughts that contribute to negative affect and dysfunctional behavior. Finally, of course, they must learn to evaluate those thoughts more objectively.

Another important general strategy is for the therapist to maintain consistency in treatment. Rules that are set regarding time, payment, and so on, must be followed consistently. Since these patients blame others for their problems, this procedure will serve to illustrate that often the patients' attitudes and behaviors are what produce negative consequences. For example, if a patient is late for a session (as is often the case with this type of patient), the therapist will end the session at the usual time. When such behavior occurs, the therapist may want to elicit feedback from the patient to determine whether this is a typical passive-aggressive response to the therapy or therapist. The automatic thought might be "I don't have to get there on time—nobody's going to tell me what to do." By such discussion, the therapist can help the patient learn direct rather than indirect means of expression. For example, if the client does not want to schedule a session at a specific time, he or she can tell the therapist that this time is undesirable or inconvenient. It may take a while before these patients can examine how their attitudes and behaviors contribute to their difficulties, but the groundwork can be set with this approach.

The next important component of treatment is helping PAPD patients examine their methods of "getting back" at people. For example, if a patient feels angry at someone and responds by not doing his or her own work well, beliefs such as "People should be punished," or "I'll do whatever I want," should be examined. Advantages and disadvantages of such a strategy should be explored and alternative strategies generated. To reach this end, it will be necessary to examine the sequence of events that occurs in interactions with others. Despite the obvious disadvantages of being negative and unpredictable with others, there are some benefits of this behavior—or it would not be maintained. For example, with a history of poor performance and unpredictability, passive-aggressive patients may find that they are not asked to perform certain undesirable tasks as much. (This, paradoxically, often produces resentment, as the patients may think that others are thereby trying to control them.) The therapist and patient need to examine these "positive" outcomes in order that the patient may not only see the consequences of this behavior, but will be motivated to use alternative ways of responding.

A general strategy for inducing patients to exhibit appropriate social skills is also helpful. For those who lack social skills, the therapist will need to teach these skills in a step-by-step fashion. When cognitions are interfering with the execution of available appropriate social behavior, modification of specific cognitions will be necessary.

Specific Techniques

With these general strategies in mind, a number of specific techniques can be used to modify cognitions, affect, and behavior in passive-aggressive patients. In order to help them identify automatic thoughts, the same steps used with most patients may be tried initially. Specifically, automatic thoughts during affective shifts are identified in the session, and homework assignments are made to identify other automatic thoughts that occur between sessions. For example, one patient became irritated during the session and reported thinking, "I don't have to do anything. You are trying to dominate me." Since these patients are resistant to requests or demands, as well as interested in following the path of least resistance, it is expected that they will not readily identify automatic thoughts.

At this point, the therapist and patient must work together to identify what cognitions might be interfering with the patient's performing the task. There are usually two types of such cognitions: The first contributes to negative affect (e.g., depression and irritability), and the second consists of cognitions about responding to "demands" (e.g., "I need to do it my way," "Why are others always forcing me to do things?," "It's easiest if I just sit back and let the dust settle"). As these cognitions are identified, the therapist and patient can evaluate whether there is evidence to support the conclusions or interpretations as valid, and whether there are alternative and more valid explanations. If the interpretation is determined to be undistorted, therapist and patient should discuss the realistic consequences, as well as strategies to resolve the problem. For example, a patient might feel sad when he or she thinks, "Everyone hates me at work, and I'm not doing a good job." The idea that everyone hates the person is probably an overgeneralization; therefore, the therapist can help the patient dispute it by generating contradictory data. The thought about not doing well at work may, in fact, be accurate. Therefore, an assessment of how poorly the patient is doing, what cognitive and motivational factors are contributing to poor performance, and how the patient can modify those factors would be most helpful.

Passive-aggressive patients may answer a question regarding the available evidence to support their belief with "Because it feels that way." This "emotional reasoning" will crop up frequently with these patients, and it is helpful to confront it. It may be useful for the patients to carry a notecard stating, "Feelings are not facts," to remind themselves that their emotional state is based on their interpretation of the situation— not necessarily on reality. It may also be useful to generate examples from the past when the patients "felt" a certain thing to be true, based on little evidence, and later found that they were not correct.

When patients are given homework to collect automatic thoughts, they might be told that it is a "no-lose" assignment. If they do it, it is helpful in that the therapist and patients can see what automatic thoughts are contributing to anxiety and depression. If they do not do it, this is also useful, because cognitions that interfere with task completion can then be identified. For example, one patient did not complete the assignment of collecting automatic thoughts. She had remembered it several times during the week, but each time had this thought: "Why bother? Nobody's going to make me do something that I don't want to do. I just don't think it'll be helpful, so I'm not doing it."

The particular techniques in cognitive therapy that establish collaboration will be important with these patients. At the beginning of each session, an agenda must be set so that both therapist and patient are planning the structure and content of the session. Feedback should be requested at the end of each session and after specific interventions. This is done to be sure that the patient understands the rationale for procedures, and also to obtain any negative cognitions he or she might be having about the therapist or therapy. As noted earlier, "experiments" can be set up to test the validity of certain cognitions the patient is experiencing.

Frequently, doing a cost-benefit analysis of behavior can be helpful. For example, if a patient does not go to a meeting at work because "I shouldn't have to," or "It was scheduled at a bad time," the patient may believe that an advantage of not going is in indirectly expressing his or her unhappiness at the "unfairness" of the situation. A cost-benefit analysis, however, may make it clear that not going to the meeting has negative consequences. The therapist and patient can then discuss ways in which the patient can express dissatisfaction more directly, so that his or her supervisor does not incorrectly interpret the lack of attendance.

Once patients realize that their strategies often do not accurately communicate the message they want to send, it will be important to enhance their assertiveness skills. Passive-aggressive patients sometimes have the effective alternative response in their repertoire, but do not use it because of dysfunctional assumptions. Typically, however, there is a skills deficit in terms of how these patients respond. In such cases, possible alternative responses can be discussed and role-played in the sessions, and later practiced as homework assignments.

Case Study

Ms. X was a 28-year-old graduate student who entered treatment severely depressed, anxious, and hopeless. She refused to give detailed information at the intake assessment, claiming that she did not feel comfortable with the intake psychologist. Ms. X did report that she was a graduate student and that her grades had gone down during the past year. Although she had looked forward to graduate school, she felt that it was not what she had expected. The teachers appeared unfair and arbitrary to her, and she resented the amount of work required to obtain her degree. To complicate matters, Ms. X had ended a relationship about 6 months before the intake. She alternated between feeling hurt that her boyfriend had ended the relationship, and angry that she had not ended it first. (By her own admission, their relationship was not a good one, and she thought that if she had more self-confidence she might have ended it herself.)

She reported little about her childhood, except that she was distant from her sister and believed her parents "should never have had children." She later indicated that she never knew what to expect from them, as they would "fly off the handle at anything," and provided financial but no emotional support. Her current relationship with her sister and parents was strained, and she was ambivalent as to how she felt about them. At times she was consumed with rage toward them; at other times she desired a close relationship.

It was difficult to get Ms. X. to specify clear goals for treatment, although she did want to reduce her depression and anxiety. Throughout treatment, she was resistant to meeting suggestions. She refused to keep a daily record of dysfunctional thoughts, since she was sure it would not work. When she expressed discouragement about many aspects of her life, such as her dress, she would discount all suggestions made by the therapist. She did occasionally comply with these requests outside the session, despite her adamant refusal during the session.

One of the first aspects of treatment was helping Ms. X evaluate her romantic relationship. Although it had ended 6 months earlier, she dwelled on it frequently. In sessions, the therapist and Ms. X accumulated a great deal of evidence that this relationship had not been a satisfying one to her. One intervention she initiated and used was countering each positive image with a negative image, in order to recall the balance in the relationship. Although she believed that "only time" would heal these wounds, and that she could not facilitate this process, Ms. X gradually was able to focus less on the relationship. Although she had avoided her boyfriend for months, if she should happen to encounter him on the streets she would feel hurt that he did not acknowledge her. Alternative explanations for his behavior were generated. For instance, it was considered possible that he was responding to her ignoring him, rather than hating her as she automatically concluded.

Ms. X also experienced considerable distress over her coursework. She thought that she was putting in a great deal of time, yet she was still getting poor grades. She felt that this was largely because her professors were unfair. While trying to study, she would spend a great deal of time ruminating about the unfairness of her relationship ending, and of having to do so much work. The therapist suggested a thought-stopping technique, in which she would respond to such thoughts with a mental "Stop!" and then put her mind on her work again. Ms. X initially refused to attempt the technique. Later, when she became increasingly concerned about her grades, she was able to use it about 20% of the time that she found herself ruminating. The therapist used this example as an entry into her unwillingness to work on and difficulty in attaining goals. Specifically, here was a potential solution to one of her problems that she had refused to try. Given the cognitive model, the therapist assumed that intervening thoughts were preventing her from meeting her goals. Ms. X was given an assignment to gain awareness of these thoughts, so that they could be examined in the next session.

The first time, she did not complete the assignment. In the following session, the therapist and Ms. X were able to identify some automatic thoughts that were interfering with her work, such as "Why should I?," "This won't work," and "I don't have to do this." In session, the point was made that Ms. X certainly did not have to do it for the therapist, but that it might be to her own advantage for her to challenge these cognitions. With the therapist, Ms. X generated some responses and wrote them on flashcards so she would recall them outside the session. As might be expected, she said that she was not sure it was a good idea, or that she could do it. At the next session, she reported having used the flashcards and "Stop!" technique, and that this had helped her to concentrate when studying.

One of Ms. X's frequent responses to questions was "I have mixed feelings about that." The therapist tried to separate out what those feelings were and what kinds of thoughts were contributing to them. It was also important to establish that, once the distortions in thinking contributing to the strong negative emotion were addressed, it was nevertheless reasonable to have mixed feelings about many issues.

The early phase of treatment, then, was spent in reducing depression and anxiety. When Ms. X believed that some resolution of her preoccupation over the relationship had occurred, and that her concentration during studying was less impaired, she wanted to terminate treatment. At that point, the therapist and Ms. X looked at the advantages (primarily the possibility that she could examine and modify dysfunctional attitudes that had led to depression and interpersonal difficulties, and could enhance the techniques she was learning for coping with negative emotions) and the disadvantages (time, expenditures) of continuing.

Although the patient was reluctant, she agreed to continue working on chronic patterns. Her negativity and the belief that she was treated unfairly were addressed. When she assessed something as negative (or hopeless, worthless, etc.), she was advised to assess the impact of this negative consequence and also to note positive features. For example, Ms. X had complained for a number of sessions about not having enough time to do a research project. One day she found out that, because the professor was moving, she would not have an opportunity to continue the research. She was extremely irritated that now she wouldn't have the opportunity for a publication. In sessions, the therapist and Ms. X focused on both the advantages and disadvantages of this turn of events, rather than seeing it as a totally negative situation. In addition, they examined whether the professor's leaving had anything to do with Ms. X personally or had to do with other things. Evidence also emerged that she would have an opportunity to pursue other research projects both while in school and afterwards.

As Ms. X began to look more openly at her patterns of response, she and the therapist began a "workbook" of situations that caused her trouble. In this workbook, Ms. X would note her automatic patterns of both cognitive and behavioral responses, and assess them for accuracy and effectiveness. Then, together, the therapist and Ms. X would develop alternative patterns. They would note the advantages and disadvantages of each of the methods. By keeping track of such situations, they were able to cluster them into a few categories, such as "unfair treatment," "demands," and "negativity." For each, they were able to develop a strategy. For example, for "unfair treatment," Ms. X would automatically assume that she had been treated unfairly. She would often take it personally, and then label the other person, and sometimes behave in a passively provocative manner toward that person. A more rational strategy was to first assess if there was actual unfairness. If Ms. X concluded that she had been treated unfairly, she had to determine if it was a personal matter or if others were similarly treated (e.g., during class). She then had to determine what kind of action (if any) she would take about the treatment. She would also have to address her expectations about the way others should treat her or the way things should be.

Sometimes Ms. X's behavior during sessions was added to the workbook. For example, before the therapist went on vacation, Ms. X refused to schedule a session with a replacement, yet made comments about "not being around" when the therapist returned. The therapist explained that those comments made her uncomfortable and asked Ms. X to state her concerns directly. It emerged that Ms. X felt angry at the therapist for interrupting treatment and leaving her. Therapist and patient were able to address these issues, and even found some advantages of the short departure from therapy (e.g., giving Ms. X a chance to practice therapeutic techniques on her own).

Overall, Ms. X made significant gains in reducing negativity and passive-aggressive behavior. She still responded automatically with irritation to many situations, but the frequency and duration of such irritation diminished over time. She was able to take responsibility for her behavior in some situations and to respond in ways that were more likely to meet her goals.

Relapse Prevention

One of the best strategies for relapse prevention is to have booster sessions. As with other patients with personality disorders, the ingrained dysfunctional beliefs of PAPD patients can become dormant until the patients are placed in situations that trigger them. Prior to termination, situations to which patients are vulnerable can be identified. As noted above, they might develop a "workbook" of such situations that includes typical automatic dysfunctional patterns, as well as more rational and functional cognitions and behavior. Examples of such situations might include being treated unfairly, being ordered to do something, or assessing a negative situation. Booster sessions are a means to keep the patients from resuming dysfunctional patterns. During these sessions, successful strategies can be reviewed, problem areas discussed, and troubleshooting for potential problems completed. It should be explained throughout treatment that therapy is a way to learn to cope effectively with a variety of situations. It is reasonable that during times of additional stress, a patient will need to use therapy as a resource to help him or her cope.

Therapist Problems

It should not be surprising that patients with PAPD are difficult to work with, because of their negativistic attitude and because they are frequently unwilling to try alternative ways of approaching their problems. In addition, of course, a passive-aggressive patient will resist many of the steps of treatment—as well as proving to be a difficult patient in such practical matters as payment, punctuality, and reliability. As noted earlier, a collaborative approach with the patient may help alleviate some of these problems. For example, it may be important, after explaining the rationale of a therapeutic technique or homework assignment, to have the patient describe how he or she thinks it will be useful in reaching goals. Getting patients to develop their own "minigoals" is ideal, but should not be expected initially. In terms of therapist frustration, it might be helpful for the therapist to conceptualize PAPD patients' behavior as a learned maladaptive behavior pattern rather than as something to be taken personally. Although they are difficult to work with, progress can be made, and it is rewarding to see these patients respond more functionally.

Chapter 16
Synthesis and Prospects for the Future

The concept of personality disorders is in a state of constant change. In reviewing the development of the concept through successive editions of the American Psychiatric Association's *Diagnostic and Statistical Manual of Mental Disorders*, we see that the theoretical view, range of problems, definitions, and terminology continue to evolve (or, according to some, devolve). New disorders are identified as others are eliminated: For example, the inadequate personality (301.82) and the asthenic personality (301.7) in DSM-II disappeared in DSM-III, while narcissistic personality disorder (301.81), which did not exist in DSM-II, emerged in DSM-III. Other terms change: For example, the emotionally unstable personality (51.0) in DSM-I became the hysterical personality (301.5) in DSM-II and histrionic personality disorder (301.50) in DSM-III and DSM-III-R.

As we write this, the committees on diagnosis and nomenclature of the American Psychiatric Association are hard at work revising the present diagnostic scheme into DSM-IV. Blashfield and Breen (1989) suggest that the face validity of many of the current DSM-III-R personality disorder diagnoses is low, and that there are high levels of overlap in meaning for several of the disorders. The present confusion is compounded when we look at the differences between the DSM-III-R criteria and the *International Classification of Diseases*, ninth edition (ICD-9; World Health Organization, 1977) or the soon to be published ICD-10 (World Health Organization, in preparation) criteria for personality disorders. It is essential that ongoing research work toward delineating the overlapping categories on Axis II and identifying the specific diagnostic factors that indicate the existence of a particular disorder. Further, is essential that the criteria of the nosological categories have more than face or clinical validity; through statistical studies, they must demonstrate discriminant and factorial validity. The ultimate choice of categories depends on their offering the clinician a conceptual framework for diagnosis, leading to useful clinical strategies and interventions.

Assessment

Scales such as the Millon Clinical Multi-Axial Inventory–II (MCMI-II; Millon, 1987a), the Personality Disorder Examination (PDE; Lorenger, Sussman, Oldham, & Russakoff, 1988), or the Structured Clinical Interview for the DSM-III-R (SCID; Spitzer, Williams, & Gibbon, 1987) can all be useful in identifying personality disorders. For the cognitive therapist, the most useful evaluation instruments would include those that directly evaluate the patient's schemas and compare the patient's expressed (or inferred) schemas with the clinically acknowledged schematic structures seen in the various disorders. One such scale that lists the specific beliefs of each of the personality disorders is presented in the appendix.

Clinical Issues

While no empirically validated treatment protocols are available, a summary of treatment guidelines presented in this volume, based in part on a review of the available literature (Pretzer & Fleming, 1989) and in part on clinical experience, can be proposed:

1. *Interventions are most effective when based on an individualized conceptualization of the patient's problems.* Turkat and his colleagues (especially Turkat & Maisto, 1985) have clearly demonstrated the value of developing an individualized conceptualization of each patient's problems on the basis of a detailed evaluation, and of testing the validity of the conceptualization both through collecting additional data and through observing the effects of interventions. Formulation of a clear understanding of the patient's problems aids in the development of an effective treatment plan and minimizes the risk of the therapist's being confused by the sheer complexity of the patient's problems. In addition, the practice of testing the conceptualization against empirical data (Turkat & Maisto, 1985) or clinical observation (Freeman, Pretzer, Fleming, & Simon, 1990, Ch. 2) allows the therapist to identify and correct the errors in conceptualizations that are inevitable, given the complexity of patients with personality disorders.

Assessment of all five DSM-III-R axes (Clinical Syndromes and V Codes; Developmental Disorders and Personality Disorders; Physical Disorders and Conditions; Severity of Psychosocial Stressors; and Global

Assessment of Functioning) is important, so that the information collected is as complete as possible. Full historical data, including family history, developmental history, social history, educational and vocational information, medical and psychiatric history, and present level of function, should all be part of the conceptualization. We cannot place too much emphasis on the need continual revision of the conceptualization as new information is collected. The "litmus test" for any conceptualization is whether it explains past behaviors, accounts for present behaviors, and predicts future behaviors. Basic elements are summarized in Table 16.1.

TABLE 16.1
Cognitive Therapy of Personality Disorders

A. *Conceptualization of Case*
   1. Include past history, development
   2. Basic views of self, others
   3. Conditional and core beliefs
   4. Relation of beliefs to cognitions
   5. Dysfunctional strategies
   6. Adaptive beliefs and strategies
   7. Development of psychopathology
   8. Make diagram
B. *Collaboration and Guided Discovery*
C. *Therapeutic Relationship*
   1. Interest in goals, family, work
   2. Role model
   3. Personal experiences as examples
   4. Help with decisions, skills
   5. Empathy and understanding
   6. Use of "transference reactions"
D. *"Automatic Thoughts" and "Rational Responses"*
E. *Role Playing*
   1. Skill development, assertiveness training
   2. Reverse role playing
      a. Therapist modeling skills
      b. Increase empathy and understanding
   3. "Relive" early experiences
F. *Imagery*
   1. Images of key figures in present
   2. Childhood experiences
G. *Identify and Test "Basic Beliefs"*
   1. Downward arrow technique
   2. Behavioral experiments
H. *Build in New "Schemas"*
   1. Cubbyhole technique

(continued)

TABLE 16.1 *(continued)*

I. *Set/Change Goals and Priorities*
    1. "Balance sheet" technique
J. *Issues of "Homework"*
    1. Need for clear rationale
    2. Use of diary
    3. Practice skills in office
       a. Automatic thoughts
       b. Labeling "errors"
       c. Testing and responding to automatic thoughts
    4. Problems
       a. Skill development
       b. Relation to beliefs and strategies
          1) Noncompliance
          2) Obsessive note taking
          3) Histrionic display
K. *Booster Therapy*
L. *Relapse Prevention*

2. *Schemas may be reconstructed, modified, or reinterpreted. The exact nature of schematic change across all disorders can be thought of as existing on a continuum.* The most profound change would be the construction of new schemas or the reconstruction of maladaptive schemas. The next point on the continuum would represent a maintenance of the schemas with modification, either major or minor. The other anchor point on the continuum would be schematic reinterpretation, wherein the schematic structure is maintained, but the previously maladaptive schemas are reframed in a more functional way.

3. *It is important for therapist and patient to work collaboratively toward clearly identified, shared goals.* Clear, consistent goals for therapy are necessary to avoid skipping from problem to problem without making any lasting progress. However, it is important for these goals to be mutually agreed upon, in order to minimize the noncompliance and power struggles that often impede treatment of patients with personality disorders. It can be difficult to develop shared goals for treatment when these patients present many vague complaints and express an unwillingness to modify behaviors that the therapist sees as particularly problematic. However, the time and effort spent in developing mutually acceptable goals generally pay off.

Since cognitive therapy is a collaborative therapy, the therapist and patient work together as a team. By virtue of the nature of the personality disorder, the severity of the disorder, and the complications of multiple Axis I and Axis II problems, the collaboration is not always

50–50. With some patients it may be 30–70, or even 10–90, with the therapist providing most of the energy or work within the session or in the therapy more generally. Part of the therapeutic focus in the treatment of some personality-disordered patients would be to help the patients make maximum use of their resources, in order to cope with the relationship difficulties that hinder developing a strong working alliance. With other patients, particularly those with dependent personality disorder, the personality problems can often be used in the service of the therapeutic relationship. A dependent patient's need for a "helper" may be met, but also balanced by not allowing a total and absolute abdication by the patient of any and all independent thought or action.

4. *The therapist should be realistic regarding the length of therapy, goals for therapy, and standards for self-evaluation.* Many therapists learning behavioral and cognitive-behavioral approaches to therapy and looking at the outcome research begin to believe that they should be omnipotent, vanquishing psychopathology quickly and easily in 12 sessions or less. The result is frustration and anger at the "resistant" patient when therapy proceeds slowly, and guilt and self-condemnation when it goes badly. Obviously, complex, deeply ingrained problems require more than 15 or 20 sessions of therapy. Behavioral and cognitive-behavioral interventions can accomplish substantial, apparently lasting changes in some patients with personality disorders, but more modest results are achieved in other cases, and little is accomplished in still others (Freeman et al., 1990; Turkat & Maisto, 1985). When therapy proceeds slowly, it is important neither to give up prematurely nor to perseverate with an unsuccessful treatment approach. When treatment is unsuccessful, it is important to remember that therapist competence is not the only factor influencing the outcome of therapy.

5. *It is important to focus more than the usual amount of attention on the therapist-patient relationship.* The dysfunctional interpersonal behaviors that these patients manifest in relationships outside of therapy are likely to develop within the therapist-patient relationship as well. Not only are these behaviors likely to disrupt therapy if they are not addressed successfully, but their emergence provides an opportunity for more effective intervention since they provide the therapist with the opportunity to do *in vivo* observation and intervention (Freeman et al., 1990; Linehan, 1987a,c; Mays, 1985). With individuals who have interpersonal problems of the magnitude common among patients with personality disorders, the effectiveness and efficiency of intervention can be substantially increased if problems in the therapist-patient relationship are used as opportunities for intervention, rather than being viewed as problems to be eliminated as quickly as possible.

One type of problem in the therapist-patient relationship that is more common among patients with personality disorders than among other patients is extreme and/or persistent misperception of the therapist by the patient. This phenomenon can be understood in terms of the individual's inappropriately generalized beliefs and expectancies. Patients with personality disorders are often quite vigilant for any indications that their fears may be realized, and can react quite dramatically when the therapist's behavior appears to confirm their anticipations. When these strongly emotional responses occur, it is important for the therapist to recognize what is happening, quickly develop a clear understanding of what the patient is thinking, and directly but sensitively clear up the misconceptions and misunderstandings. Otherwise, these reactions can greatly complicate therapy.

6. *Interventions that increase a patient's sense of self-efficacy often reduce the intensity of the patient's symptomatology and facilitate other interventions.* Many individuals with personality disorders manifest extreme emotional and behavioral responses in part because they doubt their ability to cope effectively with particular problem situations. If it is possible to increase patients' confidence that they will be able to handle these problem situations if they arise, this often lowers the patients' level of anxiety, moderates their symptomatology, and makes it easier to implement other interventions. This can be done through interventions designed to correct any exaggeration of the demands of the situation or minimization of an individual's ability to handle the situation, through helping the patient to develop improved coping skills, or through a combination of the two (Freeman et al., 1990, Ch. 7; Pretzer, Beck, & Newman, in press).

7. *The therapist should not rely primarily on verbal interventions.* The more severe a patient's problems are, the more important it is to use behavioral interventions to accomplish cognitive as well as behavioral change (Freeman et al., 1990, Ch. 3). For example, many unassertive patients benefit substantially from discussing appropriate assertion and their fears regarding assertion, and proceed to try assertive behavior with only a little encouragement from the therapist. However, patients with dependent personality disorder or passive-aggressive personality disorder typically have such strong fears regarding assertion that it is difficult to induce them even to role-play assertive behavior, let alone to try assertion in real life. A gradual hierarchy of "behavioral experiments" not only provides an opportunity for the patient to master the skills involved in appropriate assertion, but also can be quite effective in challenging unrealistic expectations.

8. *The therapist should consider beginning with interventions that do not require extensive self-disclosure by the patient.* Many patients with personality disorders are quite uncomfortable with self-disclosure because of their lack of trust in the therapist, discomfort with even mild levels of in-

timacy, fear of rejection, and so on. When feasible, it can be useful to begin treatment by working on a problem that can be approached through behavioral interventions not requiring extensive self-disclosure (Freeman et al., 1990, Ch. 8). This allows time for the patient gradually to become more comfortable with therapy (and with the therapist), and for the therapist gradually to address the patient's discomfort with self-disclosure.

For some patients, the entire course of therapy may be limited by their difficulty in self-disclosing or, more generally, trusting. By taking the behavioral focus noted earlier, the therapist can help these patients to ameliorate certain symptoms, but they may continue to manifest the same personality style.

9. *The therapist should try to identify and address the patient's fears before implementing changes.* Patients with personality disorders often have strong but unexpressed fears about the changes they seek or are asked to make in the course of therapy, and attempts to induce the patients simply to go ahead without addressing these fears are often unsuccessful (Mays, 1985). If the therapist makes a practice of discussing a patient's expectations and concerns before each change is attempted, this is likely to reduce the patient's level of anxiety regarding therapy and improve compliance. The patient may have fears of changing (e.g., "What will it be like to be different?"), fears of the effect of changing on significant others (e.g., "Will they still love me if I'm different?"), or fears of failing to change (e.g., "What if I try to change, and after all of my work I still fail?").

10. *The therapist should anticipate problems with compliance.* Many factors contribute to a high rate of noncompliance among patients with personality disorders. In addition to the complexities in the therapist-patient relationship and the strong fears discussed above, the dysfunctional behaviors of patients with personality disorders are strongly ingrained and often are reinforced by aspects of the patients' environment. Also, each personality disorder produces its own problems with compliance. For example, the individual with avoidant personality disorder is likely to resist any assignments that involve social interaction, and the patient with borderline personality disorder is likely to feel compelled to prove his or her autonomy through noncompliance. Episodes of noncompliance can provide an opportunity to identify issues that are impeding progress in therapy, so that they can be addressed and become grist for the therapeutic mill.

11. *The therapist should not assume that the patient exists in a reasonable or functional environment.* Patients with personality disorders are often the product of seriously atypical or dysfunctional families and continue to live in atypical environments. The therapist may be misled by the apparent simplicity of some interventions. Some behaviors, such as assertive-

ness, are so generally adaptive that it is easy to assume that they are always a good idea and easily implemented. When implementing changes, it is important to assess the likely responses of significant others in the patient's environment, rather than presuming that the significant others will automatically respond in a reasonable way. Helping patients to deal with their internal schemas is complicated by the patients' needing to learn how to cope with the schemas of others or with more generally held family, religious, or cultural schemas.

12. *The therapist must attend to his or her own emotional reactions during the course of therapy.* Interactions with patients with personality disorders can elicit strong emotional reactions from the therapist, ranging from empathic feelings of sadness to strong anger, discouragement, fear, or sexual attraction. It is important for therapists to be aware of their responses for several reasons. First, it is important to be sure that these reactions do not impede therapeutic work and lead to responses that are not appropriate or therapeutic for a patient. Second, these emotional responses can be a useful source of data. Since emotional responses do not occur randomly, an unusually strong emotional response is likely to open windows on important dysfunctional beliefs of both patient and therapist, or to be a reaction to some aspect of the patient's behavior. Accurate recognition of the therapist's own responses can speed recognition of the patient's cognitive patterns. Third, it is important for the therapist to recognize his or her emotional responses so that he or she can think carefully about whether to disclose them or not. On the one hand, disclosure of emotional responses raises the level of intimacy in a relationship and may be threatening to patients who are uncomfortable with intimacy. On the other hand, if the therapist does not disclose an emotional response that is apparent to the patient from nonverbal cues, it can easily be misinterpreted or can lead the patient to distrust the therapist. Finally, recognition by therapists of their emotional responses to patients provides an opportunity for the therapists to use cognitive techniques such as the Dysfunctional Thought Record (Beck, Rush, Shaw, & Emery, 1979) to gain perspective on their reactions. If strong emotional reactions persist, it may be necessary to obtain consultation from an objective colleague.

13. *The therapist should help the patient to deal with unpleasant emotions that might interfere with therapy.* Change, explorations of the unknown, or voyages to feared areas can evoke emotional responses. The emotional reactions may be mild and easily managed, or severe and debilitating. When personality-disordered patients are asked to challenge the very essence of their being and to change who they perceive themselves to be, negative emotions are likely to result. These reactions may be powerful enough to drive patients from therapy in an attempt to "regroup" and strengthen their armor. If, however, the patients are informed about the

possibility of the anxiogenic or dysphoric reactions, and then helped to develop appropriate strategies, they are more likely to stay in therapy and work on the difficult process of schematic change.

14. *Limit setting is an essential part of the overall treatment program.* Theorists of diverse views, from the psychoanalytic (Gunderson, 1984; Kernberg, 1984) to the cognitive-behavioral (Freeman et al., 1990), share the idea that setting firm, reasonable limits serves several purposes in the therapy of Axis II patients. First, it helps the patients to organize their lives and protects them from their own excesses that may, in the past, have caused problems for self or others. Second, it serves to help the therapist model a structured, reasoned approach to problem solving. Third, it offers a structure that allows the therapist to maintain control of the long-term and possibly stormy therapeutic relationship.

We see this volume as providing an impetus to the application of our work to the treatment of personality disorders. It will, we hope, serve the same purpose as *Cognitive Therapy of Depression* (Beck et al., 1979)—that is, to offer a treatment guide in clinical outcome studies to assess the clinical efficacy of cognitive therapy for the treatment of this very complex and difficult group. Toward this end, research protocols must be developed to test the model, theoretical conceptualizations, and treatment strategies. At the time of this writing, plans are being formulated to test in a controlled study the efficacy of our approach in the treatment of three personality disorders: the avoidant, dependent, and obsessive-compulsive personality disorders. At a later date, we aim to conduct efficacy trials with other personality disorders, and thus to provide a strong working base for the cognitive therapy of this difficult group of patients. As we move into the 1990s, we see new hope that conditions that were once considered refractory to therapeutic interventions will be found to be modifiable in the same way as the affective and anxiety disorders are.

Content of Schemas
in Personality Disorders

Listed below are some of the typical beliefs associated with each specific personality disorder.[1] Although there is some inevitable and necessary item overlap between nosological categories, these lists are helpful in making a diagnosis. Further, they will aid the therapist in targeting key beliefs for therapeutic intervention.

I. *Avoidant Personality Disorder*
1. I am socially inept and socially undesirable in work or social situations.
2. Other people are potentially critical, indifferent, demeaning, or rejecting.
3. I cannot tolerate unpleasant feelings.
4. If people get close to me, they will discover the "real" me and reject me.
5. Being exposed as inferior or inadequate will be intolerable.
6. I should avoid unpleasant situations at all cost.
7. If I feel or think something unpleasant, I should try to wipe it out or distract myself—for example, think of something else, have a drink, take a drug, or watch television.
8. I should avoid situations in which I attract attention, or I should be as inconspicuous as possible.
9. Unpleasant feelings will escalate and get out of control.
10. If others criticize me, they must be right.
11. It is better not to do anything than to try something that might fail.
12. If I don't think about a problem, I don't have to do anything about it.

[1]Borderline personality disorder is not included in this list, as we see it as less specific in content than the other disorders.

13. Any signs of tension in a relationship indicate the relationship has gone bad; therefore, I should cut it off.
14. If I ignore a problem, it will go away.

II. *Dependent Personality Disorder*

1. I am needy and weak.
2. I need somebody around available at all times to help me to carry out what I need to do or in case something bad happens.
3. My helper can be nurturant, supportive, and confident—if he or she wants to be.
4. I am helpless when I'm left on my own.
5. I am basically alone—unless I can attach myself to a stronger person.
6. The worst possible thing would be to be abandoned.
7. If I am not loved, I will always be unhappy.
8. I must do nothing to offend my supporter or helper.
9. I must be subservient in order to maintain his or her good will.
10. I must maintain access to him or her at all times.
11. I should cultivate as intimate a relationship as possible.
12. I can't make decisions on my own.
13. I can't cope as other people can.
14. I need others to help me make decisions or tell me what to do.

III. *Passive-Aggressive Personality Disorder*

1. I am self-sufficient, but I do need others to help me reach my goals.
2. The only way I can preserve my self-respect is by asserting myself indirectly—for example, by not carrying out instructions exactly.
3. I like to be attached to people but I am unwilling to pay the price of being dominated.
4. Authority figures tend to be intrusive, demanding, interfering, and controlling.
5. I have to resist the domination of authorities but at the same time maintain their approval and acceptance.
6. Being controlled or dominated by others is intolerable.
7. I have to do things my own way.
8. Making deadlines, complying with demands, and conforming are direct blows to my pride and self-sufficiency.
9. If I follow the rules the way people expect, it will inhibit my freedom of action.
10. It is best not to express my anger directly but to show my displeasure by not conforming.
11. I know what's best for me and other people shouldn't tell me what to do.
12. Rules are arbitrary and stifle me.
13. Other people are often too demanding.
14. If I regard people as too bossy, I have a right to disregard their demands.

IV. *Obsessive-Compulsive Personality Disorder*
1. I am fully responsible for myself and others.
2. I have to depend on myself to see that things get done.
3. Others tend to be too casual, often irresponsible, self-indulgent, or incompetent.
4. It is important to do a perfect job on everything.
5. I need order, systems, and rules in order to get the job done properly.
6. If I don't have systems, everything will fall apart.
7. Any flaw or defect of performance may lead to a catastrophe.
8. It is necessary to stick to the highest standards at all times, or things will fall apart.
9. I need to be in complete control of my emotions.
10. People should do things my way.
11. If I don't perform at the highest level, I will fail.
12. Flaws, defects, or mistakes are intolerable.
13. Details are extremely important.
14. My way of doing things is generally the best way.

V. *Antisocial Personality Disorder*
1. I have to look out for myself.
2. Force or cunning is the best way to get things done.
3. We live in a jungle and the strong person is the one who survives.
4. People will get at me if I don't get them first.
5. It is not important to keep promises or honor debts.
6. Lying and cheating are OK as long as you don't get caught.
7. I have been unfairly treated and am entitled to get my fair share by whatever means I can.
8. Other people are weak and deserve to be taken.
9. If I don't push other people, I will get pushed around.
10. I should do whatever I can get away with.
11. What others think of me doesn't really matter.
12. If I want something, I should do whatever is necessary to get it.
13. I can get away with things so I don't need to worry about bad consequences.
14. If people can't take care of themselves, that's their problem.

VI. *Narcissistic Personality Disorder*
1. I am a very special person.
2. Since I am so superior, I am entitled to special treatment and privileges
3. I don't have to be bound by the rules that apply to other people.
4. It is very important to get recognition, praise, and admiration.
5. If others don't respect my status, they should be punished.
6. Other people should satisfy my needs.
7. Other people should recognize how special I am.

8. It's intolerable if I'm not accorded my due respect or don't get what I'm entitled to.

9. Other people don't deserve the admiration or riches that they get.

10. People have no right to criticize me.

11. No one's needs should interfere with my own.

12. Since I am so talented, people should go out of their way to promote my career.

13. Only people as brilliant as I am understand me.

14. I have every reason to expect grand things.

VII. *Histrionic Personality Disorder*

1. I am an interesting, exciting person.

2. In order to be happy I need other people to pay attention to me.

3. Unless I entertain or impress people, I am nothing.

4. If I don't keep others engaged with me, they won't like me.

5. The way to get what I want is to dazzle or amuse people.

6. If people don't respond very positively to me, they are rotten.

7. It is awful if people ignore me.

8. I should be the center of attention.

9. I don't have to bother to think things through—I can go by my "gut" feeling.

10. If I entertain people, they will not notice my weaknesses.

11. I cannot tolerate boredom.

12. If I feel like doing something, I should go ahead and do it.

13. People will pay attention only if I act in extreme ways.

14. Feelings and intuition are much more important than rational thinking and planning.

VIII. *Schizoid and Schizotypal Personality Disorders*

1. It doesn't matter what other people think of me.

2. It is important for me to be free and independent of others.

3. I enjoy doing things more by myself than with other people.

4. In many situations, I am better off to be left alone.

5. I am not influenced by others in what I decide to do.

6. Intimate relations with other people are not important to me.

7. I set my own standards and goals for myself.

8. My privacy is much more important to me than closeness to people.

9. What other people think doesn't matter to me.

10. I can manage things on my own without anybody's help.

11. It's better to be alone than to feel "stuck" with other people.

12. I shouldn't confide in others.

13. I can use other people for my own purposes as long as I don't get involved.

14. Relationships are messy and interfere with freedom.

IX. *Paranoid Personality Disorder*

1. I cannot trust other people.

2. Other people have hidden motives.
3. Others will try to use me or manipulate me if I don't watch out.
4. I have to be on guard at all times.
5. It isn't safe to confide in other people.
6. If people act friendly, they may be trying to use or exploit me.
7. People will take advantage of me if I give them the chance.
8. For the most part, other people are unfriendly.
9. Other people will deliberately try to demean me.
10. Often people deliberately want to annoy me.
11. I will be in serious trouble if I let other people think they can get away with mistreating me.
12. If other people find out things about me, they will use them against me.
13. People often say one thing and mean something else.
14. A person whom I am close to could be disloyal or unfaithful.

References

Abend, S. M., Porder, M. S., & Willick, M. S. (1983). *Borderline patients: Psychoanalytic perspectives*. New York: International Universities Press.

Abraham, K. (1921/1953). Contributions to the theory of the anal character. In *Selected papers of Karl Abraham* (D. Bryan & A. Strachey, Trans.). New York: Basic Books.

Abraham, K. (1924/1948). The influence of oral eroticism on character formation. In *Selected papers of Karl Abraham* (D. Bryan & A. Strachey, Trans.). London: Hogarth Press.

Abraham, K. (1927/1948). Manifestations of the female castration complex. In *Selected papers of Karl Abraham* (D. Bryan & A. Strachey, Trans.). London: Hogarth Press.

Adams, P. (1973). *Obsessive children: A sociopsychiatric study*. New York: Brunner/Mazel.

Akhtar, S., & Thomson, J. A. (1982). Overview: Narcissistic personality disorder. *American Journal of Psychiatry, 139*(1), 12–20.

Allen, D. W. (1977). Basic treatment issues. In M. Horowitz (Ed.), *Hysterical personality*. New York: Jason Aronson.

American Psychiatric Association (APA). (1952). *Diagnostic and statistical manual of mental disorders* (1st ed.). Washington, DC: Author.

American Psychiatric Association (APA). (1968). *Diagnostic and statistical manual of mental disorders* (2nd ed.). Washington, DC: Author.

American Psychiatric Association (APA). (1980). *Diagnostic and statistical manual of mental disorders* (3rd ed.). Washington, DC: Author.

American Psychiatric Association (APA). (1987). *Diagnostic and statistical manual of mental disorders* (3rd ed., rev.). Washington, DC: Author.

Anderson, R. (1966). *Neuropsychiatry in World War II* (Vol. 1). Washington, DC: Office of the Surgeon General, Department of the Army.

Angyal, A. (1965). *Neurosis and treatment: A holistic theory*. New York: Viking Press.

Arieti, S. (1955). *Interpretation of schizophrenia*. New York: Robert Brunner.

Bach, S. (1977). On the narcissistic state of consciousness. *International Journal of Psycho-Analysis, 58*, 209–233.

Bandura, A. (1977). *Social learning theory*. Englewood Cliffs, NJ: Prentice-Hall.

Barley, W. (1986). Behavioral and cognitive treatment of criminal and delinquent behavior. In W. Reid, D. Dorr, J. Walker, & J. Bonner (Eds.), *Unmasking the psychopath.* New York: Norton.

Baron, M. (1981). *Schedule for Interviewing Borderlines.* New York: New York State Psychiatric Institute.

Baron, M., Asnis, L., & Gruen, R. (1981). The Schedule of Schizotypal Personalities (SSP): A diagnostic interview for schizotypal features. *Psychiatry Research, 4,* 213–228.

Bartlett, F. C. (1932). *Remembering.* New York: Columbia University Press.

Bartlett, F. C. (1958). *Thinking: An experimental and social study.* New York: Basic Books.

Baumbacher, G., & Amini, F. (1980–1981). The hysterical personality disorder: A proposed clarification of a diagnostic dilemma. *International Journal of Psychoanalytic Psychotherapy, 8,* 501–532.

Beardslee, W. R., Bemporad, J., Keller, M. B., & Klerman, G. L. (1983). Children of parents with major affective disorder: A review. *American Journal of Psychiatry, 140*(7), 825–832.

Beck, A. T. (1963). Thinking and depression: I. Idiosyncratic content and cognitive distortions. *Archives of General Psychiatry, 9,* 324–444.

Beck, A. T. (1964). Thinking and depression: II. Theory and therapy. *Archives of General Psychiatry, 10,* 561–571.

Beck, A. T. (1967). *Depression: Clinical, experimental, and theoretical aspects.* New York: Harper & Row. (Republished as *Depression: Causes and treatment.* Philadelphia: University of Pennsylvania Press, 1972.)

Beck, A. T. (1976). *Cognitive therapy and the emotional disorders.* New York: International Universities Press.

Beck, A. T. (1983). Cognitive therapy of depression: New perspectives. In P. J. Clayton & J. E. Barrett (Eds.), *Treatment of depression: Old controversies and new approaches.* New York: Raven Press.

Beck, A. T. (1987). Cognitive therapy. In J. K. Zeig (Ed.), *The evolution of psychotherapy.* New York: Brunner/Mazel.

Beck, A. T. (1988). *Love is never enough.* New York: Harper & Row.

Beck, A. T., & Emery, G., with Greenberg, R. L. (1985). *Anxiety disorders and phobias: A cognitive perspective.* New York: Basic Books.

Beck, A. T., Rush, J., Shaw, B., & Emery, G. (1979). *Cognitive therapy of depression.* New York: Guilford Press.

Bell, M. (1981). *Bell Object-Relations Self-Report Scale.* West Haven, CT: Psychology Service, VA Medical Center.

Berne, E. (1964). *Games people play.* New York: Ballantine.

Bernstein, D. A., & Borkovec, T. D. (1976). *Progressive relaxation training: A manual for the helping professionals.* Champaign, IL: Research Press.

Bird, J. (1979). The behavioural treatment of hysteria. *British Journal of Psychiatry, 134,* 129–137.

Birtchnell, J. (1984). Dependence and its relationship to depression. *British Journal of Medical Psychology, 57,* 215–225.

Blackburn, R., & Lee-Evans, J. M. (1985). Reactions of primary and secondary psychopathos to anger-evoking situations. *British Journal of Clinical Psychology, 24,* 93–100.

Blashfield, R. K., & Breen, M. J. (1989). Face validity of the DSM-III-R personality disorders. *American Journal of Psychiatry, 146,* 1575–1579.

Bleuler, E. (1924). *Textbook of psychiatry* (A. Brill, Trans.). New York: Macmillan.

Bowlby, J. (1969). *Attachment and loss: Vol. 1. Attachment.* New York: Basic Books.

Bowlby, J. (1977). The making and breaking of affectional bonds. *British Journal of Psychiatry, 130,* 201–210.

Breuer, J., & Freud, S. (1893–1895/1955). Studies on hysteria. In J. Strachey (Ed. and Trans.), *Complete psychological works of Sigmund Freud* (Standard Ed., Vol. 2). London: Hogarth Press.

Burnham, D. L., Gladstone, A. I., & Gibson, R. W. (1969). *Schizophrenia and the need-fear dilemma.* New York: International Universities Press.

Burns, D. (1980). *Feeling good.* New York: Morrow.

Bursten, B. (1973). Some narcissistic personality types. *International Journal of Psycho-Analysis, 54,* 287–300.

Buss, A. H. (1987). Personality: Primitive heritage and human distinctiveness. In J. Aronoff, A. I. Robin, & R. A. Zucker (Eds.), *The emergence of personality.* New York: Springer.

Buss, D., & Craik, K. (1983). The act frequency approach to personality. *Psychological Review, 90,* 105–126.

Cameron, N. (1963). *Personality development and psychopathology: A dynamic approach.* Boston: Houghton Mifflin.

Cameron, N. (1974). Paranoid conditions and paranoia. In S. Arieti & E. Brody (Eds.), *American handbook of psychiatry.* New York: Basic Books.

Caplan, P., & Hall-McCorquodale, I. (1985). Mother-blaming in major clinical journals. *American Journal of Orthopsychiatry, 55*(3), 345–353.

Carr, A. T. (1974). Compulsive neurosis: A review of the literature. *Psychological Bulletin, 81,* 311–318.

Casey, P. R., Tryer, P. J., & Platt, S. (1985). The relationship between social functioning and psychiatric functioning in primary care. *Social Psychiatry, 20*(1), 5–9.

Chambless, D. L., & Renneberg, B. (1988, September). *Personality disorders of agoraphobics.* Paper presented at the World Congress on Behaviour Therapy, Edinburgh, Scotland.

Chatham, P. M. (1985). *Treatment of the borderline personality.* New York: Jason Aronson.

Chick, J., Waterhouse, L., & Wolff, S. (1980). Psychological construing in schizoid children grown-up. *Annual Progress in Child Psychiatry and Development,* 386–395.

Clarkin, J. F., Widiger, T. A., Frances, A., Hurt, S. W., & Gilmore, M. (1983). Prototypic typology and the borderline personality disorder. *Journal of Abnormal Psychology, 93,* 263–275.

Cleckley, H. (1976). *The mask of sanity* (5th ed.). St. Louis: Mosby.

Clifford, C. A., Murray, R. M., & Fulker, D. W. (1980). Genetic and environmental influences of obsessional trains and symptoms. *Psychological Medicine, 14,* 791–800.

Coché, E. (1987). Problem solving training: A group cognitive therapy modality. In A. Freeman & V. Greenwood (Eds.), *Cognitive therapy: Applications in psychiatric and medical settings.* New York: Human Sciences Press.

Colby, K. M. (1981). Modeling a paranoid mind. *The Behavioral and Brain Sciences, 4,* 515–560.

Colby, K. M., Faught, W. S., & Parkinson, R. C. (1979). Cognitive therapy of paranoid conditions: Heuristic suggestions based on a computer simulation model. *Cognitive Therapy and Research, 3,* 5–60.

Cupoldi, J., Hallock, J., & Barnes, L. (1980). Failure to thrive. *Current Problems in Pediatrics, 10,* 1–43.

Curran, J. P. (1977). Skills training as an approach to the treatment of heterosexual-social anxiety: A review. *Psychological Bulletin, 84,* 140–157.

Daltito, J. A., & Perugi, G. (1988). A case of social phobia with avoidant personality disorder treated with MAOI. *Comprehensive Psychiatry, 27*(3), 255–258.

Deffenbacher, J. L., Storey, D. A., Stark, R. S., Hogg, J. A., & Brandon, A. D. (1987). Cognitive-relaxation and social skills interventions in the treatment of general anger. *Journal of Counseling Psychology, 34*(2), 171–176.

Deutsch, H. (1942). Some forms of emotional disturbance and their relationship to schizophrenia. *Psychoanalytic Quarterly, 11,* 301–321.

DiGiuseppe, R. (1983). Rational emotive therapy and conduct disorders. In A. Ellis & M. E. Bernard (Eds.), *Rational-emotive approaches to the problems of childhood.* New York: Plenum.

DiGiuseppe, R. (1986). The implication of the philosophy of science for rational-emotive theory and therapy. *Psychotherapy, 23*(4), 634–639.

DiGiuseppe, R. (1989). Cognitive therapy with children. In A. Freeman, K. M. Simon, L. Beutler, & H. Arkowitz (Eds), *Comprehensive handbook of cognitive therapy.* New York: Plenum Press.

D'Zurilla, T. J., & Goldfried, M. R. (1971). Problem solving and behavior modification. *Journal of Abnormal Psychology, 78,* 107–126.

Easser, B. R., & Lesser, S. R. (1965). Hysterical personality: A reevaluation. *Psychoanalytic Quarterly, 34,* 390–415.

Edell, W. S. (1984). The borderline Syndrome Index: Clinical validity and utility. *Journal of Nervous and Mental Disease, 172,* 254–263.

Eisely, L. (1961). *Darwin's century.* Garden City, NY: Doubleday/Anchor.

Ellis, A. (1957a). Rational psychotherapy and individual psychology. *Journal of Individual Psychology, 13*(1), 38–44.

Ellis, A. (1957b). Outcome of employing three techniques of psychotherapy. *Journal of Clinical Psychology, 13*(4), 344–350.

Ellis, A. (1958). Rational psychotherapy. *Journal of General Psychology, 59,* 35–49.

Ellis, A. (1962). *Reason and emotion in psychotherapy.* New York: Lyle Stuart.

Ellis, A. (1985). *Overcoming resistance: Rational-emotive therapy with difficult clients.* New York: Springer.

Ellis, H. (1898). Auto-eroticism: A psychological study. *Alienist and Neurologist, 19,* 260–299.

Erikson, E. (1950). *Childhood and society.* New York: Norton.

Esman, A. H. (1986). Dependent and passive-aggressive personality disorders. In A. M. Cooper, A. J. Frances, & M. H. Sacks (Eds.), *The personality disorders and neuroses.* New York: Basic Books.

Fabrega, H., Mezzich, J. E., Mezzich, A. C., & Coffman, G. A. (1986). Descriptive

validity of DSM-III depressions. *Journal of Nervous and Mental Disease,*
174(10), 573–584.

Fagan, T., & Lira, F. (1980). The primary and secondary sociopathic personality:
Differences in frequency and severity of antisocial behaviors. *Journal of*
Abnormal Psychology, 89(3), 493–496.

Fairbairn, W. R. D. (1940). *Schizoid factors in the personality. Psychoanalytic studies of*
the personality. London: Tavistock.

Fenichel, O. (1945). *The psychoanalytic theory of neurosis.* New York: Norton.

Fleming, B. (1983, August). *Cognitive therapy with histrionic patients: Resolving a*
conflict in styles. Paper presented at the meeting of the American Psychological Association, Anaheim, CA.

Fleming, B. (1985, November). *Dependent personality disorder: Managing the transi-*
tion from dependence to autonomy. Paper presented at the meeting of the
Association for Advancement of Behavior Therapy, Houston, TX.

Fleming, B. (1988). Cognitive therapy with histrionic personality disorder:
Resolving a conflict of styles. *International Cognitive Therapy Newsletter, 4,*
4–12.

Fleming, B., & Pretzer, J. (in press). Cognitive-behavioral approaches to personality disorders. In M. Hersen (Ed.), *Advances in behavior therapy.* Newbury
Park, CA: Sage.

Foon, A. E. (1985). The effect of social class and cognitive orientation on clinical
expectations. *British Journal of Medical Psychology, 58*(4), 357–364.

Frances, A. (1985). *DSM-III personality disorders.* New York: BMA Audio Cassettes.

Frances, A. (1987). *DSM-III personality disorders: Diagnosis and treatment.* New
York: BMA Audio Cassettes.

Frances, A. (1988). Dependency and attachment. *Journal of Personality Disorders,*
2, 125.

Frances, A., Clarkin, J. F., Gilmore, M., Hurt, I., & Brown, I. (1984). Reliability
of criteria for borderline personality disorder: A comparison of DSM-II and
the Diagnostic Interview for Borderlines. *American Journal of Psychiatry, 141,*
1080–1084.

Frances, A., & Nemiah, J. C. (1983). Treatment planning: Which psychodynamic therapy for a painfully shy patient? *Hospital and Community Psychiatry,*
34(12), 1111–1112, 1117.

Frank, J. D. (1973). *Persuasion and healing* (2nd ed.). Baltimore: Johns Hopkins
University Press.

Frazee, H. E. (1953). Children who later become schizophrenic. *Smith College*
Studies in Social Work, 23, 125–149.

Freeman, A. (1986). Understanding personal, cultural, and family schema in
psychotherapy. In A. Freeman, N. Epstein, & K. Simon (Eds.), *Depression in*
the family. New York: Haworth Press.

Freeman, A. (1987a). Cognitive therapy: An overview. In A. Freeman &
V. Greenwood (Eds.), *Cognitive therapy: Applications in psychiatric and medical*
settings. New York: Human Sciences Press.

Freeman, A. (1987b). Understanding personal, cultural, and religious schema in
psychotherapy. In A. Freeman, N. Epstein, & K. Simon (Eds.), *Depression in*
the family. New York: Haworth Press.

Freeman, A. (1988a). Cognitive therapy of personality disorders. In C. Perris, I. Blackburn, & H. Perris (Eds.), *Cognitive psychotherapy: Theory and practice.* New York: Springer Verlag.

Freeman, A. (1988b). Cognitive therapy of personality disorders. In C. Perris & M. Eisemann (Eds.), *Cognitive psychotherapy: An update.* Umeå, Sweden: DOPUU Press.

Freeman, A., & Leaf, R. (1989). Cognitive therapy of personality disorders. In A. Freeman, K. Simon, L. Beutler, & H. Arkowitz (Eds.), *Comprehensive handbook of cognitive therapy.* New York: Plenum.

Freeman, A., Pretzer, J., Fleming, B., & Simon, K. (1990). *Clinical applications of cognitive therapy.* New York: Plenum Press.

Freeman, A., & Simon, K. M. (1989). Cognitive therapy of anxiety. In A. Freeman, K. Simon, L. Beutler, & H. Arkowitz (Eds.), *Comprehensive handbook of cognitive therapy.* New York: Plenum.

Freud, S. (1905/1953). Three essays on the theory of sexuality. In J. Strachey (Ed. and Trans.), *Complete psychological works of Sigmund Freud* (Standard Ed., Vol. 7). London: Hogarth Press.

Freud, S. (1908/1963). Character and anal eroticism. In P. Reiff (Ed.), *Collected papers of Sigmund Freud,* (Vol. 10). New York: Collier.

Freud, S. (1909/1955). Notes upon a case of obsessional neurosis. In J. Strachey (Ed. and Trans.), *Complete psychological works of Sigmund Freud* (Standard Ed., Vol. 10). London: Hogarth Press.

Freud, S. (1914/1957). On narcissism: An introduction. In J. Strachey (Ed. and Trans.), *Complete psychological works of Sigmund Freud* (Standard Ed., Vol. 14). London: Hogarth Press.

Gagan, R., Cupoldi, J., & Watkins, A. (1984). The families of children who fail to thrive: Preliminary investigations of parental deprivation among organic and nonorganic cases. *Child Abuse and Neglect, 8,* 93–103.

Gilbert, P. (1989). *Human nature and suffering.* Hillsdale, NJ: Erlbaum.

Giles, T. R., Young, R. R., & Young, D. E. (1985). Behavioral treatment of severe bulimia. *Behavior Therapy, 16,* 393–405.

Gilligan, C. (1982). *In a different voice.* Cambridge, MA: Harvard University Press.

Gilson, M. L. (1983). *Depression as measured by perceptual bias in binocular rivalry.* Ann Arbor: University Microfilms No. AAD83-27351.

Gittelman-Klein, R., & Klein, D. (1969). Premorbid asocial adjustment and prognosis in schizophrenia. *Journal of Psychiatric Research, 7,* 35–53.

Goldfried, M., & Newman, C. (1986). Psychotherapy integration: An historical perspective. In J. C. Norcross (Ed.), *Handbook of eclectic psychotherapy.* New York: Brunner/Mazel.

Goldstein, A. P., Martens, J., Hubben, J., Van Belle, H. A., Schaaf, W., Wirsma, H., & Goedhart, A. (1973). The use of modeling to increase independent behaviour. *Behaviour Research and Therapy, 11,* 31–42.

Goldstein, W. (1985). *An introduction to the borderline conditions.* Northvale, NJ: Jason Aronson.

Greenberg, D., & Stravynski, A. (1985). Patients who complain of social dysfunction: I. Clinical and demographic features. *Canadian Journal of Psychiatry, 30,* 206–211.

Greenberg, R. P., & Bornstein, R. F. (1988a). The dependent personality: I. Risk for physical disorders. *Journal of Personality Disorders, 2,* 126–135.

Greenberg, R. P., & Bornstein, R. F. (1988b). The dependent personality: II. Risk for psychological disorders. *Journal of Personality Disorders, 2,* 136–143.

Greenberg, R. P., & Dattore, P. J. (1981). The relationship between dependency and the development of cancer. *Psychosomatic Medicine, 43,* 35–43.

Guidano, V. F., & Liotti, G. (1983). *Cognitive processes and emotional disorders.* New York: Guilford Press.

Gunderson, J. G. (1984). *Borderline personality disorders.* Washington, DC: American Psychiatric Press.

Gunderson, J. G., & Singer, M. T. (1975). Defining borderline patients: An overview. *American Journal of Psychiatry, 132,* 1–9.

Guntrip, H. (1969). *Schizoid phenomena, object relations, and the self.* New York: International Universities Press.

Hales, R. E., Polly, S., Bridenbaugh, H., & Orman, D. (1986). Psychiatric consultations in a military general hosital. A report on 1,065 cases. *General Hospital Psychiatry, 8*(3), 173–182.

Hamilton, M. A. (1967). Development of a rating scale for primary depressive illness. *British Journal of Social and Clinical Psychology, 6,* 278–296.

Hare, R. (1985a). Comparison of procedures for the assessment of psychopathy. *Journal of Consulting and Clinical Psychology, 53,* 7–16.

Hare, R. (1985b). A checklist for the assessment of psychopathy. In M. H. Ben-Aron, S. J. Hucker, & C. Webster (Eds.), *Clinical criminology.* Toronto: M. & M. Graphics.

Hare, R. (1986). Twenty years of experience with the Cleckley psychopath. In W. Reid, D. Dorr, J. Walker, & J. Bonner (Eds.), *Unmasking the psychopath.* New York: Norton.

Harlow, H. (1959). Love in infant monkeys. *Scientific American, 200,* 68–86.

Harris, G. A., & Watkins, D. (1987). *Counseling the involuntary and resistant client.* College Park, MD: American Correctional Association.

Henn, F. A., Herjanic, M., & VanderPearl, R. H. (1976). Forensic psychiatry: Diagnosis and criminal responsibility. *Journal of Nervous and Mental Disease, 162*(6), 423–429.

Hill, A. B. (1976). Methodological problems in the use of factor analysis: A critical review of the experimental evidence for the anal character. *British Journal of Medical Psychology, 49,* 145–159.

Hill, D. C. (1970). Outpatient management of passive-dependent women. *Hospital and Community Psychiatry, 21,* 38–41.

Hinkle, L. E. (1961). Ecological observations on the relation of physical illness, mental illness, and the social environment. *Psychosomatic Medicine, 23,* 289–296.

Hoch, A. (1909). A study of the mental make-up in the functional psychoses. *Journal of Nervous and Mental Disease, 36,* 230–236.

Hoch, P., & Polatin, P. (1939). Pseudoneurotic forms of schizophrenia. *Psychiatric Quarterly, 23,* 248–276.

Hogan, R. (1987). Personality psychology: Back to basics. In J. Aronoff, A. I. Robin, & R. A. Zucker (Eds.), *The emergence of personality.* New York: Springer.

Hollon, S. D., Kendall, P. C., & Lumry, A. (1986). Specificity of depressogenic cognitions in clinical depression. *Journal of Abnormal Psychology, 95*(1), 52–59.

Horney, K. (1945). *Our inner conflicts.* New York: Norton.

Horney, K. (1950). *Neurosis and human growth.* New York: Norton.

Horowitz, M. (1975). Sliding meanings: A defense against threat in narcissistic personalities. *International Journal of Psychoanalytic Psychotherapy, 4,* 167–180.

Horowitz, M. (Ed.) (1977). *Hysterical personality.* New York: Jason Aronson.

Horowitz, M. (1979). *States of mind.* New York: Plenum.

Hurt, S. W., Hyler, S. E., Frances, A., Clarkin, J. F., & Brent, R. (1984). Assessing borderline personality disorder with self-report, clinical interview, or semi-structured interview. *American Journal of Psychiatry, 141,* 1228–1231.

Ingram, R. E., & Hollon, S. D. (1986). Cognitive therapy for depression from an information processing perspective. In R. E. Ingram (Ed.), *Information processing approaches to clinical psychology.* New York: Academic Press.

Jones, E. (1918/1961). Anal erotic character traits. In *Papers on psychoanalysis.* Boston: Beacon Press.

Jones, E. (1948/1967). *Papers on psychoanalysis.* Boston: Beacon Press.

Jones, R. A. (1977). *Self-fulfilling prophecies: Social, psychological, and physiological effects of expectancies.* Hillside, NJ: Erlbaum.

Juni, S., & Semel, S. R. (1982). Person perception as a function of orality and anality. *Journal of Social Psychology, 118,* 99–103.

Kagan, J. (1989). Temperamental contributions to social behavior. *American Psychologist, 44*(4), 668–674.

Kagan, R. (1986). The child behind the mask: Sociopathy as a developmental delay. In W. Reid, D. Dorr, J. Walker, & J. Bonner (Eds.), *Unmasking the psychopath.* New York: Norton.

Karno, M., Hough, R. L., Burnam, M. A., Escobar, J. I., Timbers, D. M., Santana, F., & Boyd, J. H. (1986). Lifetime prevalence of specific psychiatric disorders among Mexican Americans and non-Hispanic whites in Los Angeles. *Archives of General Psychiatry, 44*(8), 695–701.

Kass, D. J., Silvers, F. M., & Abrams, G. M. (1972). Behavioral group treatment of hysteria. *Archives of General Psychiatry, 26,* 42–50.

Kelly, G. (1955). *The psychology of personal constructs.* New York: Norton.

Kendler, K. S., & Gruenberg, A. M. (1982). Genetic relationship between paranoid personality disorder and the "schizophrenic spectrum disorders." *American Journal of Psychiatry, 139,* 1185–1186.

Kendler, K. S., Gruenberg, A. M., & Strauss, J. S. (1981). An independent analysis of the Copenhagen sample of the Danish adoption study of schizophrenics: II. The relationship between schizotypal personality disorder and schizophrenia. *Archives of General Psychiatry, 38,* 982–984.

Kernberg, O. F. (1967). Borderline personality organization. *Journal of the American Psychoanalytic Association, 15,* 641–685.

Kernberg, O. F. (1970). Factors in the treatment of narcissistic personality disorder. *Journal of the American Psychoanalytic Association, 18,* 51–58.

Kernberg, O. F. (1975). *Borderline conditions and pathological narcissism.* New York: Jason Aronson.

Kernberg, O. F. (1977). Structural change and its impediments. In P. Hartocollis (Ed.), *Borderline personality disorders: The concept, the syndrome, the patient.* New York: International Universities Press.

Kernberg, O. F. (1984). *Severe personality disorders: Psychotherapeutic strategies.* New Haven: Yale University Press.

Kety, S. S., Rosenthal, D., Wender, P. H., & Schulsinger, F. (1968). The types and prevalence of mental illness in the biological and adoptive families of adopted schizophrenics. In D. Rosenthal & S. S. Kety (Eds.), *The transmission of schizophrenia.* Oxford: Pergamon Press.

Kety, S. S., Rosenthal, D., Wender, P. H., & Schulsinger, F. (1971). Mental illness in the biological and adoptive families of adopted schizophrenics. *American Journal of Psychiatry, 128,* 302–306.

Klein, M. (1952). Notes on some schizoid mechanisms. In M. Klein, P. Heinmann, S. Isaacs, & J. Riviere (Eds.), *Developments in psychoanalysis.* London: Hogarth Press.

Knight, R. (1953). Borderline states. *Bulletin of the Menninger Clinic, 17,* 1–12.

Kochen, M. (1981). On the generality of PARRY, Colby's paranoia model. *The Behavioral and Brain Sciences, 4,* 540–541.

Koenigsberg, H., Kaplan, R., Gilmore, M., & Cooper, A. (1985). The relationship between syndrome and personality disorder in DSM-III: Experience with 2,462 patients. *American Journal of Psychiatry, 142,* 207–212.

Kohlberg, L. (1984). *The psychology of moral development.* New York: Harper & Row.

Kohut, H. (1966). Forms and transformations of narcissism. *Journal of the American Psychoanalytic Association, 14,* 243–272.

Kohut, H. (1971). *The analysis of the self.* New York: International Universities Press.

Kolb, J. E., & Gunderson, J. G. (1980). Diagnosing borderline patients with a semi-structured interview. *Archives of General Psychiatry, 37,* 37–41.

Kolb, L. C. (1968). *Modern clinical psychiatry* (7th ed.). Philadelphia: W. B. Saunders.

Kraepelin, E. (1913). *Psychiatrie: Ein lehrbuch* (8th ed., Vol. 3). Leipzig: Barth.

Kretschmer, E. (1925). *Physique and character.* New York: Harcourt, Brace.

Landau, R. J., & Goldfried, M. R. (1981). The assessment of schemata: A unifying framework for cognitive, behavioral, and traditional assessment. In P. C. Kendall & S. D. Hollon (Eds.), *Assessment strategies for cognitive-behavioral interventions.* New York: Academic Press.

Lange, A. J., & Jakubowski, P. (1976). *Responsible assertive behavior: Cognitive/behavioral procedures for trainers.* Champaign, IL: Research Press.

Lazare, A., Klerman, G. L., & Armor, D. J. (1966). Oral, obsessive, and hysterical personality patterns. *Archives of General Psychiatry, 14,* 624–630.

Lazare, A., Klerman, G. L., & Armor, D. J. (1970). Oral, obsessive, and hysterical personality patterns: Replication of factor analysis in an independent sample. *Journal of Psychiatric Research, 7,* 275–290.

Leibenhuft, E., Gardner, D. L., & Cowdry, R. W. (1987). The inner experience of the borderline self-mutilator. *Journal of Personality Disorders, 1,* 317–324.

Leitenberg, H., Yost, L. W., & Carroll-Wilson, M. (1986). Negative cognitive errors in children: Questionnaire development, normative data, and comparison between children with and without self-reported symptoms of depression, low self-esteem, and evaluation anxiety. *Journal of Consulting and Clinical Psychology, 54*(4), 528–536.

Levy, D. (1966). *Maternal overprotection.* New York: Norton.

Like, R., & Zyzanski, S. J. (1987). Patient satisfaction with the clinical encounter: Social psychological determinants. *Social Science in Medicine, 24*(4), 351–357.

Lilienfeld, S., VanValkenburg, C., Larntz, K., & Akiskal, H. (1986). The relationships of histrionic personality disorder to antisocial personality and somatization disorders. *American Journal of Psychiatry, 143*(6), 718–721.

Linehan, M. M. (1979). Structured cognitive-behavioral treatment of assertion problems. In P. C. Kendall & S. D. Hollon (Eds.), *Cognitive-behavioral interventions: Theory, research and procedures.* New York: Academic Press.

Linehan, M. M. (1981). A social-behavioral analysis of suicide and parasuicides: Implications for clinical assessment and treatment. In H. Glazer & J. Clarkin (Eds.), *Depression: Behavioral and directive intervention strategies.* New York: Brunner/Mazel.

Linehan, M. M. (1987a). Dialectical behavior therapy: A cognitive behavioral approach to parasuicide. *Journal of Personality Disorders, 1,* 328–333.

Linehan, M. M. (1987b). Dialectical behavior therapy for borderline personality disorder: Theory and method. *Bulletin of the Menninger Clinic, 51,* 261–276.

Linehan, M. M. (1987c). Dialectical behavior therapy in groups: Treating borderline personality disorders and suicidal behavior. In C. M. Brody (Ed.), *Women in groups.* New York: Springer.

Linehan, M. M., Armstrong, H. E., Allmon, D. J., Suarez, A., & Miller, M. L. (1988). *Comprehensive behavioral treatment for suicidal behaviors and borderline personality disorder: II. Treatment retention and one year follow-up of patient use of medical and psychological resources.* Unpublished manuscript, University of Washington, Department of Psychology, Seattle, WA.

Linehan, M. M., Armstrong, H. E., Suarez, A., & Allmon, D. J. (1988). *Comprehensive behavioral treatment for suicidal behaviors and borderline personality disorder: I. Outcome.* Unpublished manuscript, University of Washington, Department of Psychology, Seattle, WA.

Lion, J. R. (Ed.). (1981). *Personality disorders: Diagnosis and management.* Baltimore: Williams & Wilkins.

Livesley, W. J. (1986). Trait and behavioral prototypes of personality disorder. *American Journal of Psychiatry, 143*(6), 728–732.

Longabaugh, R., & Eldred, S. H. (1973). Premorbid adjustments, schizoid personality and onset of illness as predictors of post-hospitalization functioning. *Journal of Psychiatric Research, 10,* 19–29.

Lorenger, A., Sussman, V., Oldham, J., & Russakoff, L. M. (1988). *The Personality Disorder Examination.* Unpublished manuscript.

Luborsky, L., McLellan, A. T., Woody, G. E., O'Brien, C. P., & Auerbach, A. (1985). Therapist success and its determinants. *Archives of General Psychiatry, 42,* 602–611.

Lykken, D. (1957). A study of anxiety in the sociopathic personality. *Journal of Abnormal and Social Psychology, 55,* 6–10.

MacKinnon, R. A., & Michaels, R. (1971). *The psychiatric interview in clinical practice.* Philadelphia: W. B. Saunders.

MacLeod, C., Mathews, A., & Tata, P. (1986). Attention bias in emotional disorders. *Journal of Abnormal Psychology, 95*(1), 15–20.

Mahoney, M. (1980). Behaviorism, cognitivism, and human change processes. In

M. A. Reda & M. Mahoney (Eds.), *Cognitive psychotherapies: Recent developments in theory, research, and practice.* Cambridge, MA: Ballinger.

Malinow, K. L. (1981). Passive-aggressive personality. In J. R. Lion (Ed.), *Personality disorders: Diagnosis and management.* Baltimore: Williams & Wilkins.

Malmquist, C. P. (1971). Hysteria in childhood. *Postgraduate Medicine, 50,* 112–117.

Marmor, J. (1953). Orality in the hysterical personality. *Journal of the American Psychoanalytic Association, 1,* 656–671.

Marshall, W. L., & Barbaree, H. E. (1984). Disorders of personality, impulse, and adjustment. In S. M. Turner & M. Hersen (Eds.), *Adult psychopathology and diagnosis.* New York: Wiley.

Martin, J., Martin, W., & Slemon, A. G. (1987). Cognitive mediation in person-centered and rational-emotive therapy. *Journal of Counseling Psychology, 34*(3), 251–260.

Masterson, J. F. (1978). *New perspectives on psychotherapy of the borderline adult.* New York: Brunner/Mazel.

Masterson, J. F. (1980). *From borderline adolescent to functioning adult: The test of time.* New York: Brunner/Mazel.

Masterson, J. F. (1982, April 17). *Borderline and narcissistic disorders: An integrated developmental approach.* Workshop presented at Adelphi University, Garden City, NY.

Masterson, J. F. (1985). *Treatment of the borderline adolescent: A developmental approach.* New York: Brunner/Mazel.

Mathews, A., & MacLeod, C. (1986). Discrimination of threat cues without awareness in anxiety states. *Journal of Abnormal Psychology, 95*(2), 131–138.

Mavissakalian, M., & Hamman, M. S. (1987). DSM-III personality disorder in agoraphobia: II. Changes with treatment. *Comprehensive Psychiatry, 28,* 356–361.

Mays, D. T. (1985). Behavior therapy with borderline personality disorder: One clinician's perspective. In D. T. Mays & C. M. Franks (Eds.), *Negative outcome in psychopathology and what to do about it.* New York: Springer.

McCord, W., & McCord, J. (1964). *The psychopath: An essay on the criminal mind.* Princeton, NJ: Van Nostrand.

McDougall, W. (1921). *An introduction to social psychology* (14th ed.). Boston: John W. Luce.

McFall, M. E., & Wollersheim, J. P. (1979). Obsessive-compulsive neurosis: A cognitive-behavioral formulation and approach to treatment. *Cognitive Therapy and Research, 3,* 333–348.

McGlashan, T. (1985). *The borderline: Current empirical research.* Washington, DC: American Psychiatric Press.

Meehl, P. E. (1962). Schizotaxia, schizotypy, schizophrenia. *American Psychologist, 17,* 827–838.

Meichenbaum, D. (1977). *Cognitive-behavior modification: An integrative approach.* New York: Plenum.

Mellsop, G. W. (1972). Psychiatric patients seen as children and adults: Childhood predictors of adult illness. *Journal of Child Psychological Psychiatry, 13,* 91–101.

Mellsop, G. W. (1973). Adult psychiatric patients on whom information during childhood is missing. *British Journal of Psychiatry, 123,* 703–710.

Mellsop, G. W., Varghese, F., Joshua, A., & Hicks, A. (1982). The reliability of Axis II of DSM-III. *American Journal of Psychiatry, 139*(10), 1360–1361.

Millon, T. (1969). *Modern psychopathology: A biosocial approach to maladaptive learning and functioning.* Philadelphia: W.B. Saunders.

Millon, T. (1981). *Disorders of personality: DSM-III, Axis II.* New York: Wiley.

Millon, T. (1983). *Millon Clinical Multi-Axial Inventory.* Minneapolis: National Computer Systems.

Millon, T. (1987a). *Millon Clinical Multi-Axial Inventory—II.* Minneapolis: National Computer Systems.

Millon, T. (1987b). On the genesis and prevalence of the borderline personality disorder: A social learning thesis. *Journal of Personality Disorders, 1,* 354–372.

Millon, T., & Everly, G. (1985). *Personality and its disorders.* New York: Wiley.

Modell, A. (1976). The holding environment and the therapeutic action of psychoanalysis. *Journal of the American Psychoanalytic Association, 24,* 255–307.

Moore, H. A., Zusman, J., & Root, G. C. (1984). Noninstitutional treatment for sex offenders in Florida. *American Journal of Psychiatry, 142*(8), 964–967.

Morris, D. P., Soroker, E., & Burrus, G. (1954). Follow-up studies of shy, withdrawn children: I. Evaluation of later adjustment. *American Journal of Orthopsychiatry, 24,* 743–754.

Morrison, L. A., & Shapiro, D. A. (1987). Expectancy and outcome in prescriptive vs. exploratory psychotherapy. *British Journal of Clinical Psychology, 26*(1), 59–60.

Nannarello, J. J. (1953). Schizoid. *Journal of Nervous and Mental Disease, 118,* 237–249.

Neisser, U. (1976). *Cognition and reality.* San Francisco: W. H. Freeman & Co.

Nezu, A. M., & Nezu, C. M. (Eds.). (1989). *Clinical decision making in behavior therapy: A problem-solving perspective.* Champaign, IL: Research Press.

Norcross, J. C., Prochaska, J. O., & Gallagher, K. M. (1989). Clinical psychologists in the 1980's: II Theory, research, and practice. *The Clinical Psychologist, 42*(3), 45–53.

Nurnburg, H. G., Hurt, S. W., Feldman, A., & Suh, R. (1987). Efficient diagnosis of borderline personality disorder. *Journal of Personality Disorders, 1,* 307–315.

Oakley, M. E., & Padesky, C. A. (in press). Cognitive therapy for anxiety disorders. In R. M. Eisler & M. Hersen (Eds.), *Progress in behavior modification.* Newbury Park, CA: Sage.

Oates, R., Peacock, A., & Forest, D. (1985). Long-term effects of nonorganic failure to thrive. *Pediatrics, 75*(1), 36–40.

Overholser, J. C. (1987). Facilitating autonomy in passive-dependent persons: An integrative model. *Journal of Contemporary Psychotherapy, 17,* 250–269.

Overholser, J. C., Kabakoff, R., & Norman, W. H. (1989). Personality characteristics in depressed and dependent psychiatric inpatients. *Journal of Personality Assessment, 53,* 40–50.

Padesky, C. A., & Beck, J. S. (1988). Cognitive threapy treatment for avoidant personality disorders. In C. Perris & M. Eisemann (Eds.), *Cognitive psychotherapy: An update.* Umeå, Sweden: DOPUU Press.

Perry, J., & Klerman, G. (1980). Clinical features of borderline personality disorder. *American Journal of Psychiatry, 137,* 165–173.

Perry, J. C., & Flannery, R. B. (1982). Passive-aggressive personality disorder: Treatment implications of a clinical typology. *Journal of Nervous and Mental Disease, 170,* 164–173.

Person, E. (1986). Manipulativeness in entrepreneurs and psychopaths. In W. Reid, D. Dorr, J. Walker, & J. Bonner (Eds.), *Unmasking the psychopath.* New York: Norton.

Piaget, J. (1926). *The language and thought of the child.* New York: Harcourt, Brace.

Piaget, J. (1936/1952). *The origin of intelligence in children.* New York: International Universities Press.

Piaget, J. (1970). *The child's conception of time.* New York: Basic Books.

Piaget, J. (1974). *Experiments in contradiction.* Chicago: University of Chicago Press.

Piaget, J. (1976). *The grasp of consciousness.* Cambridge, MA: Harvard University Press.

Piaget, J. (1978). *Success and understanding.* Cambridge, MA: Harvard University Press.

Pilkonis, P. A. (1984). Avoidant and schizoid personality disorders. In H. E. Adams & P. B. Sutker (Eds.), *Comprehensive handbook of psychopathology.* New York: Plenum Press.

Pilkonis, P. (1988). Personality prototypes among depressives: Themes of dependency and autonomy. *Journal of Personality Disorders, 2,* 144–152.

Pollack, J. M. (1979). Obsessive-compulsive personality: A review. *Psychological Bulletin, 86,* 225–241.

Pretzer, J. L. (1983, August). *Borderline personality disorder: Too complex for cognitive-behavioral approaches?* Paper presented at the meeting of the American Psychological Association, Anaheim, CA. (ERIC Document Reproduction Service No. ED 243 007)

Pretzer, J. L. (1985, November). *Paranoid personality disorder: A cognitive view.* Paper presented at the meeting of the Association for Advancement of Behavior Therapy, Houston, TX.

Pretzer, J. L. (1988). Paranoid personality disorder: A cognitive view. *International Cognitive Therapy Newsletter, 4*(4), 10–12.

Pretzer, J. L., Beck, A. T., & Newman, C. F. (in press). Stress and stress management: A cognitive view. *Journal of Cognitive Psychotherapy: An International Quarterly.*

Pretzer, J. L., & Fleming, B. (1989). Cognitive-behavioral treatment of personality disorders. *the Behavior Therapist, 12,* 105–109.

Provence, S., & Lipton, R. (1962). *Infants in institutions.* New York: International Universities Press.

Quay, H. C. (1965). Psychopathic personality as pathological stimulation seeking. *American Journal of Psychiatry, 122,* 180–183.

Quay, H. C., Routh, D. K., & Shapiro, S. K. (1987). Psychopathology of childhood: From description to validation. *Annual Review of Psychology, 38,* 491–532.

Rabins, P. V., & Slavney, P. R. (1979). Hysterical traits and variability of mood in normal men. *Psychological Medicine, 9,* 301–304.

Rado, S. (1953). Dynamics and classification of disordered behavior. In *Psychoanalysis of behavior*. New York: Grune & Stratton.

Raskin, R., & Novacek, J. (1989). An MMPI description of the narcissistic personality. *Journal of Personality Assessment, 53*, 66–80.

Rasmussen, S., & Tsuang, M. (1986). Clinical characteristics and family history in DSM-III obsessive-compulsive disorder. *American Journal of Psychiatry, 143*, 317–322.

Rehm, L. (1977). A self-control model of depression. *Behavior Therapy, 8*, 787–804.

Reich, J. H. (1987). Instruments measuring DSM-III and DSM-III-R personality disorders. *Journal of Personality Disorders, 1*, 220–240.

Reich, J. H., & Noyes, R. (1987). A comparison of DSM-III personality disorders in acutely ill panic and depressed patients. *Journal of Anxiety Disorders, 1*, 123–131.

Reich, J. H., Noyes, R., & Troughton, E. (1987). Dependent personality disorder associated with phobic avoidance in patients with panic disorder. *American Journal of Psychiatry, 144*, 323–326.

Reich, W. (1945). *Character analysis* (3rd, enlarged ed.). New York: Simon & Schuster.

Reid, W. H. (Ed.) (1981). *The treatment of the antisocial syndromes*. New York: Van Nostrand.

Reider, R. O. (1979). Borderline schizophrenia: Evidence of its validity. *Schizophrenia Bulletin, 5*, 39–46.

Robins, L. (1966). *Deviant children grown up*. Baltimore: Williams & Wilkins.

Robins, L., Helzer, J., Weissman, M., Orvaschel, H., Gruenberg, E., Burke, J., & Regier, D. (1984). Lifetime prevalence of specific psychiatric disorders in three sites. *Archives of General Psychiatry, 41*, 949–958.

Roff, J. D., Knight, R., & Wertheim, E. (1976). A factor analytic study of childhood symptoms antecedent to schizophrenia. *Journal of Abnormal Psychology, 85*, 543–549.

Rosenthal, D., Wender, P. H., Kety, S. S., Welner, J., & Schulsinger, F. (1971). The adopted away offspring of schizophenics. *American Journal of Psychiatry, 128*, 307–311.

Rush, A. J., & Shaw, B. F. (1983). Failure in treating depression by cognitive therapy. In E. B. Foa & P. G. M. Emmelkamp (Eds.), *Failures in behavior therapy*. New York: Wiley.

Salzman, L. (1973). *The obsessive personality*. New York: Jason Aronson.

Saul, L. J., & Warner, S. L. (1982). *The psychotic personality*. New York: Van Nostrand.

Scarr, S. (1987). Personality and experience: Individual encounters with the world. In J. Aronoff, A. I. Robin, & R. A. Zucker (Eds.), *The emergence of personality*. New York: Springer.

Schank, R. C., & Abelson, R. P. (1977). *Scripts, plans, goals, and understanding*. Hillsdale, NJ: Erlbaum.

Shapiro, D. (1965). *Neurotic styles*. New York: Basic Books.

Shapiro, D. (1981). *Autonomy and rigid character*. New York: Basic Books.

Shelton, J. L., & Levy, R. L. (1981). *Behavioral assignments and treatment compliance: A handbook of clinical strategies*. Champaign, IL: Research Press.

Siever, L. J. (1981). Schizoid and schizotypal personality disorders. In J. R. Lion (Ed.), *Personality disorders: Diagnosis and management*. Baltimore: Williams & Wilkins.

Siever, L. J., & Gunderson, J. G. (1983). The search for a schizotypal personality: Historical origins and current status. *Comprehensive Psychiatry, 24*, 199–212.

Simon, K. M. (1983, August). *Cognitive therapy with compulsive patients: Replacing rigidity with structure*. Paper presented at the meeting of the American Psychological Association, Anaheim, CA.

Simon, K. M. (1985, November). *Cognitive therapy of the passive-aggressive personality*. Paper presented at the meeting of the Association for Advancement of Behavior Therapy, Houston, TX.

Slavney, P. R. (1978). The diagnosis of hysterical personality disorder: A study of attitudes. *Comprehensive Psychiatry, 19*, 501–507.

Slavney, P. R. (1984). Histrionic personality and antisocial personality: Caricatures of stereotypes? *Comprehensive Psychiatry, 25*, 129–141.

Slavney, P. R., Breitner, J. C. S., & Rabins, P. V. (1977). Variability of mood and hysterical traits in normal women. *Journal of Psychiatric Research, 13*, 155–160.

Slavney, P. R., & McHugh, P. R. (1974). The hysterical personality. *Archives of General Psychiatry, 30*, 325–332.

Slavney, P. R., & Rich, G. (1980). Variability of mood and the diagnosis of hysterical personality disorder. *British Journal of Psychiatry, 136*, 402–404.

Small, I. F., Small, J. G., Alig, V. B., & Moore, D. F. (1970). Passive-aggressive personality disorder: A search for a syndrome. *American Journal of Psychiatry, 126*, 973–983.

Smith, D. (1982). Trends in counseling and psychotherapy. *American Psychologist, 37*(7), 802–809.

Smokler, I. A., & Shevrin, H. (1979). Cerebral lateralization and personality style. *Archives of General Psychiatry, 36*, 949–954.

Spitzer, R. L. (1977, September 20). *Memorandum to members of the advisory committee on personality disorders, American Psychiatric Association*.

Spitzer, R. L., Endicott, J., & Gibbon, M. (1979). Crossing the border into borderline personality and borderline schizophrenia: The development of criteria. *Archives of General Psychiatry, 36*, 17–24.

Spitzer, R., Forman, J., & Nee, J. (1979). DSM-III field trials: 1. Initial interrater diagnostic reliability. *American Journal of Psychiatry, 136*, 815–817.

Spitzer, R. L., Williams, J. B. W., & Gibbon, M. (1987). *Instruction manual for the Structured Clinical Interview for the DSM-III-R (SCID)*. New York: Biometrics Research Department, New York State Psychiatric Institute.

Spivack, G., & Shure, M. B. (1974). *Social adjustment of young children: A cognitive approach to solving real-life problems*. San Francisco: Jossey-Bass.

Standage, K., Bilsbury, C., Jain, S., & Smith, D. (1984). An investigation of role-taking in histrionic personalities. *Canadian Journal of Psychiatry, 29*, 407–411.

Stangl, D., Pfohl, B., Zimmerman, M., Bowers, W., & Corenthal, C. (1985). A structured interview for the DSM-III personality disorders: A preliminary report. *Archives of General Psychiatry, 42*, 591–596.

Stephens, D. A., Atkinson, M. W., Kay, E. W., Roth, M., & Garside, R. F. (1975). Psychiatric morbidity in parents and sibs of schizophrenics and non-schizophrenics. *British Journal of Psychiatry, 127,* 97–108.

Stephens, J. H., & Parks, S. L. (1981). Behavior therapy of personality disorders. In J. R. Lion (Ed.), *Personality disorders: Diagnosis and management* (2nd ed.). Baltimore: Williams & Wilkins.

Stone, M. H. (1985). Negative outcome in borderline states. In D. T. Mays & C. M. Franks (Eds.), *Negative outcome in psychotherapy and what to do about it.* New York: Springer.

Stravynski, A., Marks, I., & Yule, W. (1982). Social skills problems in neurotic outpatients: Social skills training with and without cognitive modification. *Archives of General Psychiatry, 39,* 1378–1385.

Sullivan, H. S. (1956). *Clinical studies in psychiatry.* New York: Norton.

Svrakic, D. (1985). Emotional features of narcissistic personality disorder. *American Journal of Psychiatry, 142*(6), 720–724.

Temoshok, L., & Heller, B. (1983). Hysteria. In R. J. Daitzman (Ed.), *Diagnosis and intervention in behavior therapy and behavioral medicine.* New York: Springer.

Templeton, T., & Wollersheim, J. (1979). A cognitive-behavioral approach to the treatment of psychopathy. *Psychotherapy: Theory, Research, and Practice, 16*(2), 132–139.

Thompson-Pope, S. K., & Turkat, I. D. (in press). Reactions to ambiguous stimuli among paranoid personalities. *Journal of Psychopathology and Behavioral Assessment.*

Torgersen, S. (1980). The oral, obsessive and hysterical personality syndromes. *Archives of General Psychiatry, 37,* 1272–1277.

Turkat, I. D. (1985). Formulation of paranoid personality disorder. In I. D. Turkat (Ed.), *Behavioral case formulation.* New York: Plenum.

Turkat, I. D. (1986). The behavioral interview. In A. R. Ciminero, K. S. Calhoun, & H. E. Adams (Eds.), *Handbook of behavioral assessment* (2nd ed.). New York: Wiley.

Turkat, I. D. (1987). The initial clinical hypothesis. *Journal of Behavior Therapy and Experimental Psychiatry, 18,* 349–356.

Turkat, I. D., & Banks, D. S. (1987). Paranoid personality and its disorder. *Journal of Psychopathology and Behavioral Assessment, 9,* 295–304.

Turkat, I. D., & Carlson, C. R. (1984). Data-based versus symptomatic formulation of treatment: The case of a dependent personality. *Journal of Behavior Therapy and Experimental Psychiatry, 15,* 153–160.

Turkat, I. D., & Levin, R. A. (1984). Formulation of personality disorders. In H. E. Adams & P. B. Sutker (Eds.), *Comprehensive handbook of psychopathology.* New York: Plenum Press.

Turkat, I. D., & Maisto, S. A. (1985). Personality disorders: Application of the experimental method to the formulation and modification of personality disorders. In D. H. Barlow (Ed.), *Clinical handbook of psychological disorders.* New York: Guilford Press.

Turner, S. M. (1987). The effects of personality disorder diagnosis on the outcome of social anxiety symptom reduction. *Journal of Personality Disorders, 1,* 136–143.

Turner, S. M., Beidel, D. C., Dancu, C. V., & Keys, D. J. (1986). Psychopathology of social phobia and comparison. *Journal of Abnormal Psychology, 95*(4), 389–394.

United States Joint Armed Services. (1949). *Nomenclature and methods of recording mental conditions.* Washington, DC: Author.

Vaillant, G. (1978). Natural history of male psychological health: IV. What kinds of men do not get psychosomatic illness? *Psychosomatic Medicine, 40,* 420–431.

Vaillant, G., & Drake, R. (1985). Maturity of ego defenses in relation to DSM-III Axis II personality disorder. *Archives of General Psychiatry, 42,* 597–601.

Vieth, I. (1977). Four thousand years of hysteria. In M. Horowitz (Ed.), *Hysterical personality.* New York: Jason Aronson.

Volkan, V. (1981). *Linking objects and linking phenomena: A study of the forms, symptoms, metapsychology, and therapy of complicated mourning.* New York: International Universities Press.

Wachtel, P. L. (Ed.). (1982). *Resistance: Psychodynamic and behavioral approaches.* New York: Plenum Press.

Waelder, R. (1925). The psychoses, their mechanisms, and accessibility to influence. *International Journal of Psycho-Analysis, 6,* 259–281.

Waldinger, R. J., & Gunderson, J. G. (1987). *Effective psychotherapy with borderline patients: Case studies.* New York: Macmillan.

Walker, L. (1979). *The battered woman.* New York: Harper & Row.

Walker, L. (1980). Battered women. In A. M. Brodsky & R. T. Hare-Mustin (Eds.), *Women and psychotherapy.* New York: Guilford Press.

War Department. (1945). *Nomenclature and recording diagnoses* (Technical Bulletin No. 203). Washington, DC: Author.

Ward, L. G., Freidlander, M. L., & Silverman, W. K. (1987). Children's depressive symptoms, negative self-statements, and causal attributions for success and failure. *Cognitive Therapy and Research, 11*(2), 215–227.

Watt, N. F. (1978). Patterns of childhood social development in adult schizophrenics. *Archives of General Psychiatry, 35,* 160–165.

Weintraub, W. (1981). Compulsive and paranoid personalities. In J. R. Lion (Ed.), *Personality disorders: Diagnosis and management.* Baltimore: Williams & Wilkins.

West, M., & Sheldon, A. E. R. (1988). Classification of pathological attachment patterns in adults. *Journal of Personality Disorders, 2,* 153–159.

Whitman, R. M., Trosman, H., & Koenig, R. (1954). Clinical assessment of passive-aggressive personality. *Archives of Neurology and Psychiatry, 72,* 540–549.

Widiger, T. A., & Frances, A. (1985). The DSM-III personality disorders: Perspectives from psychology. *Archives of General Psychiatry, 42,* 615–623.

Widiger, T. A., & Sanderson, C. (1987). The convergent and discriminant validity of the MCMI as a measure of DSM-III personality disorders. *Journal of Personality Assessment, 51*(2), 228–242.

Widiger, T. A., Sanderson, C., & Warner, L. (1986). The MMPI, prototypal typology, and borderline personality disorder. *Journal of Personality Assessment, 50,* 540–553.

Woerner, M. G., Pollack, M., Rogalski, C., Pollack, Y., & Klein, D. F. (1972). A comparison of personality disorders, schizophrenics, and their sibs. In M. Roff, L. N. Robins, & M. Pollack (Eds.), *Life history research in psychopathology* (Vol. 2). Minneapolis: University of Minnesota Press.

Wolff, S., & Barlow, A. (1979). Schizoid personality in childhood: A comparative study of schizoid, autistic and normal children. *Journal of Child Psychology and Psychiatry, 20,* 29–46.

Woody, G. E., McLellan, A. T., Luborsky, L., & O'Brien, C. P. (1985). Sociopathy and psychotherapy outcome. *Archives of General Psychiatry, 42,* 1081–1086.

Woolson, A. M., & Swanson, M. G. (1972). The second time around: Psychotherapy with the "hysterical woman." *Psychotherapy: Theory, Research, and Practice, 9,* 168–175.

World Health Organization. (1977). *International classification of diseases* (9th ed.). Geneva: Author.

World Health Organization. (in preparation). *International classification of diseases* (10th ed.). Geneva: Author.

Yarrow, L. (1961). Maternal deprivation. *Psychological Bulletin, 58,* 459–490.

Young, J. (1983, August). *Borderline personality: Cognitive theory and treatment.* Paper presented at the meeting of the American Psychological Association, Anaheim, CA.

Young, J. (1984, November). *Cognitive therapy with difficult patients.* Workshop presented at the meeting of the Association for Advancement of Behavior Therapy, Philadelphia, PA.

Young, J. (1987). *Schema-focused cognitive therapy for personality disorders.* Unpublished manuscript, Center for Cognitive Therapy, New York.

Young, J., & Swift, W. (1988). Schema-focused cognitive therapy for personality disorders: Part I. *International Cognitive Therapy Newsletter, 4*(5), 13–14.

Zetzel, E. (1968). The so-called good hysteric. *International Journal of Psycho-Analysis, 49,* 256–260.

Zimmerman, M., Pfohl, B., Stangl, D., & Coryell, W. (1985). The validity of DSM-III Axis IV. *American Journal of Psychiatry, 142*(12), 1437–1441.

Zuroff, D., & Mongrain, M. (1987). Dependency and self-criticism: Vulnerability factors for depressive affective states. *Journal of Abnormal Psychology, 96,* 14–22.

Zwemer, W. A., & Deffenbacher, J. L. (1984). Irrational beliefs, anger, and anxiety. *Journal of Counseling Psychology, 31*(3), 391–393.

Index